Biographical Directory of the Council of Economic Advisers

Biographical Directory of the Council of Economic Advisers

EDITED BY

Robert Sobel AND
Bernard S. Katz

Greenwood Press

NEW YORK
WESTPORT, CONNECTICUT
LONDON

Library of Congress Cataloging-in-Publication Data

Council of Economic Advisers (U.S.)
Biographical directory of the Council of Economic Advisers.

Bibliography: p.
Includes index.
1. Council of Economic Advisers (U.S.)—Directories.
2. Economists—United States—Directories. I. Sobel, Robert, 1931 Feb. 19– . II. Katz, Bernard, 1932– . III. Title.
HC102.5.A2C68 1988 338.973′0025 86–14984
ISBN 0–313–22554–0 (lib. bdg. : alk. paper)

British Library Cataloguing in Publication Data is available.

Library of Congress Catalog Card Number: 86–14984
ISBN: 0–313–22554–0

First published in 1988

Greenwood Press, Inc.
88 Post Road West, Westport, Connecticut 06881

Printed in the United States of America

The paper used in this book complies with the Permanent Paper Standard issued by the National Information Standards Organization (Z39.48–1984).

10 9 8 7 6 5 4 3 2 1

Dedicated to the lovely ladies,
Linda and Meryl

CONTENTS

PREFACE

Presidents have never lacked for economic advisers. The first chief magistrate, George Washington, had one in Secretary of the Treasury Alexander Hamilton, whose four financial reports provided him with the framework for much of his domestic program. But Hamilton was a soldier-statesman-lawyer, not a professional economist. How could he be? The profession did not exist at the end of the eighteenth century.

Washington's successors in the next century relied upon cabinet members, bankers, and cronies for economic advice, but not much of this was needed, since government's role in the economy was far more limited than it was to become later on. The three great and lasting economic issues of the time—internal improvements, the tariff, and money—were dealt with by politicians and businessmen. Few of them felt the need to consult with professional economists, who usually found places in universities.

When financial panic struck, presidents looked to Wall Street bankers for assistance. When candidates sought expertise in framing economic issues, they consulted businessmen and journalists and did not send emissaries to Harvard, Yale, or other places when covens of economists were gathering, some fairly itching to be called upon for advice.

This would change in the twentieth century. Woodrow Wilson utilized the services of economists during World War I, but only sporadically and sparingly. Then, after the war, Secretary of Commerce Herbert Hoover consulted them on a regular basis. Several leading academics, among them Wesley Clair Mitchell, Frank Taussig, and William Z. Ripley, helped develop policy and influence legislation. Harvard's Julius Klein was plucked to serve as Assistant Secretary of Commerce under Hoover and played a role in devising programs to deal with the Great Depression.

The movement of economists into government accelerated under Franklin D. Roosevelt, as the economics departments of Ivy League and Big Ten schools were decimated. Economists flowed into executive departments and helped staff New Deal agencies. This continued during World War II, and economists helped plan the conversion from a war to a peace economy throughout the conflict.

Clearly, plans for this transition would be needed, and they would have to be drawn up by economists. So they were, presented to Roosevelt and his successor Harry Truman. Several of their framers, along with administration and legislative leaders, pressed for an overarching program, and Leon Keyserling,* a prominent government economist, wrote what was called by some the "Full Employment Act," but eventually came to be known as the Employment Act of 1946, which mandated government action to help provide what the original title promised. And as part of the act—to make it operational—the Council of Economic Advisers was established.

No one was quite sure exactly what the Council was supposed to do, though the legislation did state that it would assist and advise the president in preparing an annual economic report. The *Wall Street Journal* called it a "Magna Carta for Economists," and so it was. From that time to the present, all chief executives have recognized the value of having expert economists on call, and for a while it seemed that these would be on the Council. This was Keyserling's hope. An original member who became chairman in 1949, he was one of the most powerful figures the Council would ever know.

Not all of his successors were so influential, and in fact there were times when it appeared that the body might be disbanded. But the possibility of this happening was remote. Rather, the influence of its members, the chairmen in particular, had waxed and waned according to the proclivities of the president and the political abilities of the members.

Having said this, it would be foolhardy for any student of the profession and the political process to ignore these figures. Economists certainly do not. To have served on the Council is deemed a badge of honor, a certificate of sorts that can lead to desirable academic and consulting appointments. Of course, not all of America's leading economists have served, and some have turned down appointments—Samuelson, John K. Galbraith, and Milton Friedman come to mind, and there are many others. Yet the call to influence decision making, to sit at the right hand of the president, or even to walk a few steps behind him, can be irresistible.

Who were and are these people, what were their ideas, and how did they influence economic thought and government behavior? These are the questions addressed in the following essays. The authors, practicing scholars in the field, have gone through the relevant literature to present answers and offer their interpretations of concepts and actions.

For the sake of easy reference the members have been presented in alphabetical order. Cross-references are indicated by an asterisk appearing after a person's name. Also included, at the end of the book, is an appendix listing councils by presidential administration, so that readers and researchers who wish to obtain a clear concept of the kind of advice and action that was taken chronologically can utilize the entries in that fashion.

ROBERT SOBEL

INTRODUCTION

By the winter of 1944–45, it was obvious that the Allied powers would win World War II, and a number of individuals in the victorious countries began to think of the shape of the postwar world. World War II had required the greatest mobilization effort of any war in history, and the economic dislocations due to this effort were huge. The reconversion to a peacetime economy would likewise necessitate much work and sacrifice. The so-called transition problems would be many and varied, as munitions contracts had to be cancelled, soldiers reintegrated into the labor force, war bureaucracies dismantled and the pattern of peaceful life restored. Most economists believed that there would be some sort of recession as there was after World War I and that the country had to avoid the unemployment of the 1930s. A smaller number of economists felt that the major problem of the immediate postwar years would be inflation as deprived consumers drew down their stock of war forced savings. However, the experience with joblessness in the 1930s, coupled with the aftermath of World War II, made unemployment a major concern, especially since rising prices had not been a problem for nearly twenty-five years. Public opinion focused on the predicted recession, which was estimated to range from mild to severe, and how best to ameliorate it. This was not without good reason, as no one knew exactly the best way to keep employment high.

As early as January 1942 the National Resources Planning Board called for a positive governmental program of postwar expansion and full employment. In late 1944, President Roosevelt created the Office of War Mobilization and Reconstruction (OWMR) and asked it to deal explicitly with many readjustment problems. However, in his remarks during the signing ceremony, FDR indicated that the OWMR alone could not adequately deal with unemployment problems. In part, this attitude reflected FDR's dissatisfaction with the absence of the Kilgore Amendment to the OWMR bill. This amendment would have provided a form of unemployment compensation, as well as a Bureau of Programs, to deal with the unemployed.

On January 22, 1945, Senator James E. Murray introduced S. 380, a bill entitled the Employment Act of 1945. Some thirteen months later President Truman signed Public Law 304, thus ratifying the Employment Act of 1946. These two bills were so different that Senator Murray considered disowning the final version. What happened in the course of Congressional hearings to alter the shape of this bill is instructive for what it teaches us about concern for unemployment and the government's responsibility to the unemployed. However, S. 380 was not created entirely out of the throes of postwar concern for a stable economy. It has a rich and engaging history.

Any law has a history and is the product of crosscurrents in public opinion, political compromises, and various interest groups' influence. The legislative history of P.L. 304 goes back at least six months before its original introduction, but the transformation of conventional wisdom on economic affairs, which provided the intellectual foundations for the law, began much earlier. The influence of John Maynard Keynes cannot be underestimated, nor can public opinion regarding the economic dislocations of the Depression and World War II.

The unique economic events of the 1930s and early 1940s and our reaction to them forever changed the way in which Americans were to think of macroeconomic stabilization policy. The old neoclassical logic, with its self-adjusting mechanism to achieve full employment, was declared bankrupt. No longer could one seriously propose a program which would turn economic policy back to the days of Harding and Hoover. The federal government, epitomized by Roosevelt's New Deal programs and war agencies, had stepped in as the final arbitrator of economic policy. The public learned to look to Washington for cures to the worst economic problems and to ensure a brighter future. People came to expect positive governmental policies to avert the worst of cyclical swings in unemployment and prices.

The specific form and content of the Employment Act of 1946 can be interpreted as part of the debate over a reconversion policy and the role of economic planning to prevent unemployment. In early 1943, the Senate created a Special Committee to study postwar economic problems and to present potential solutions. The House followed with a similar committee of its own in 1944. Such committees were necessary because business, labor, consumers, and farm groups had been clamoring for special treatment in the postwar economy. Roosevelt's creation of the OWM was, in part, a response to this interest group pressure. By November 1943, Senator Harley Kilgore had begun work on a reconversion bill designed to aid in the settlement of industrial and labor problems. This proposed legislation, coupled with the Baruch-Hancock Report on Reconversion in February 1944, stressed the need for intelligent and comprehensive economic planning and an enlargement of the OWM. The Kilgore bill also proposed a National Production-Employment Board to provide specific plans.

Senator James E. Murray, a longstanding liberal on economic and social matters, controlled the Senate's War Contracts Subcommittee and succeeded in having Kilgore's bill placed before the subcommittee. But despite his co-sponsorship along with Harry Truman, Kilgore's bill was emasculated. The legislation which emerged provided for little more than war contracts and surplus property disposal, and the restructuring of the OWM to include reconversion. This was not the overarching reconversion-unemployment bill the sponsors had sought.

During the debates over the 1944 Kilgore bill, James Patton of the Farmers Union proposed that full employment became a permanent federal obligation. After the defeat of a true reconversion bill in 1944, Murray placed Patton's suggestions in a full employment bill. Berton Gross, a War Contracts Subcommittee staffer, was asked by Murray to prepare a draft of the full employment bill along the general lines suggested by Patton. Murray then attached this as an appendix to his committee's year-end report issued in December 1944. Gross and his staff had consulted leading liberal economists such as Alvin Hansen and Leon Keyserling* in drafting the bill, developed a definition of full employment, and placed the responsibility for the execution of this program with the Bureau of the Budget. Furthermore, because any full employment programs would have to be passed by Congress, the bill called for the creation of a Joint Committee on the Budget to be the receptacle for any such programs.

The appendix became the point of departure for discussion of a full employment bill, and Senator Murray started to organize co-sponsors. Murray and Gross were able to introduce a final draft of the Full Employment Act on January 22, 1945. It was placed on the docket as S. 380. In retrospect, this represented the high-water mark of liberal thought on reconversion unemployment policy, for all subsequent debate and compromises amounted to an unrelenting erosion of the ideals and programs proposed by the Murray bill.

This original bill, S. 380, provided for the following key points: (1) it would be the responsibility of the federal government to ensure that anyone wishing to work would be able to locate a job; (2) the president was to prepare each year a National Production and Employment Budget which would include estimates of the size and composition of the labor force, investment plans for all levels of government, plus those of the private sector; (3) if insufficient investment existed to provide full employment, then the president would develop programs to achieve this level of employment. He was to have similar responsibility for, and powers over, the control of inflation; (4) this budget was to be prepared in the Executive Office of the President; and (5) the bill would establish a Joint Congressional Committee on the National Budget to study the president's document and either recommend or change any legislation implied in it.

The Murray bill mandated that the government define full employment and then establish and maintain programs to ensure an inflation-free, fully employed economy. The Senate passed this bill on to the House substantially unchanged. Only two amendments, other than editorial ones, were attached to the original bill, and both of these were acceptable to the bill's sponsors. However, conservative sentiment mounted against the bill, and it became clear that the more conservative House would severely alter the language and substance of the version passed by the Senate.

A large number of major business and agriculture groups threw the weight of their opinion against the Senate bill. The prime movers against S. 380 were the U.S. Chamber of Congress, National Association of Manufacturers, state and local Chambers of Commerce, the Farm Bureau, and a number of the top executives of leading corporations, especially those of General Motors.

These groups focused their arguments on relatively few issues and were successful in generating a large newspaper and educational campaign against the bill. Their arguments amounted to the following: (1) that full employment in a democratic society cannot be guaranteed and that freedom was not necessarily compatible with low rates of unemployment; (2) a fear that larger government expenditures would erode business confidence and that the tax and expenditure program to ensure full employment would kill incentives and induce inflation; and (3) that the economic planning apparatus was going to move the economy in the direction of the economy of the USSR. The greatest attention and derision are directed at the sections in the bill calling for sophisticated economic forecasts and employment planning. The case of the Soviet Union was constantly held up as the end result of such efforts.

H.R. 2202, the Full Employment Bill, was introduced on February 15, 1945, and was immediately referred to the House Committee on Expenditures in the Executive Department. This standing committee was quite conservative, and in late September, after much posturing, alliance making and media attention, the committee sat to consider not only the Senate bill but also two substitute bills. The hearings reflected the conservative bent of the House, and with little or no assistance from the administration, liberals were unable to prevent major alterations in the original bill. The House version which emerged had, in effect, negated most of S. 380.

Specifically, the House bill accomplished three major objectives: (1) it eliminated the statement regarding the right to job opportunity and on federal responsibility for full employment. Instead, the House substituted a policy of aiming for a high level of employment and gross national product (GNP), trying to eliminate or prevent large economic fluctuations, and keeping the government out of competition with private business; (2) the national budget was excised along with its appraisal of economic trends, full employment programs, and investigation of monopoly and income distribution. The House replaced this with an economic report on the health of the economy; (3) also created was a three-member Council of Economic Advisers (CEA) whose function was to provide expert advice and policy recommendations to the president.

In fact, the House committee had severely reduced the Senate's bill. The specific policy guidelines and recommendations of the Senate were replaced with language that was much more vague and ambiguous, and no specific programs were developed. The full House considered this version in mid-December, and after some acrimonious debate, passed it by an overwhelming majority. It was left to a conference committee to work out an agreeable compromise between the widely differing Senate and House versions to the full Employment Bill. The primary reason the House so severely revised the bill was the representatives' unquestioned conservative outlook, which made them receptive to pressures applied by conservative interest groups. President Truman, although he was associated with efforts to protect postwar employment while still a senator in 1944, provided little help. Furthermore, the bleak economic predictions for the postwar economy had not materialized, causing many to question the necessity for such a piece of legislation.

The conference committee began its deliberation in late January 1946, and at first it appeared that the bill would die there. The members of the House and Senate, each reflecting his own views, were unable to agree. A major problem was the statement of policy on full employment. After much argument and the striking of the phrase "full employment," the conferees were able to agree on wording to promote "useful employment, productive and purchasing power" consistent with other "needs, obligations and essential conditions of national policy." Most of the rest of the compromise bill reflected the House's bias, for no specific programs, policies, definitions, goals, studies, or objectives were mentioned. The language was vague enough to be open to several interpretations, and the bill amounted to a statement favoring full employment (but not defining it) unless other economic considerations were judged to be more important.

Besides the Declaration of Policy, the bill had three other sections. The first called for an economic report of the president to be delivered each year to the Congress. This report was to compare current economic trends with the aforementioned policy statement and to recommend programs to obtain these goals. The second section established the Council and the means of appointment, terms, pay, and duties. Last, the bill created a joint committee on the economic report which was to study the president's report and attempt to evaluate the feasibility of his programs for achieving the goals of the Employment Act of 1946. This version of the conference committee bill passed the House and Senate readily and was signed into law by President Truman on February 20, 1946.

As seen from the perspective of thirty-five years of economic experience, can we argue that the act has been instrumental in guiding postwar policy? In all probability no one would want to place responsibility for the (mostly) rosy performance of the economy on such a flimsy foundation. The reasons for the unparalleled expansion and health of the economy, at least up to 1975, are rooted in the economic history of the world economy and the unique U.S. role in this history. Certainly the situation of our economy would not have been much different with or without the advice of the CEA or the passage of the Employment Act of 1946. If this is true, what, then, can be learned from more than three decades of experience with the policy, objectives, and economic advice provided for in the 1946 act?

The debate over S. 380 and H.R. 2202 throws into sharp relief the complex, almost Byzantine, motives for economic policy making. Economic political ideology being what it was, Congress probably could never pass an act with more teeth in it. The range of public opinion was too wide on economic matters for legislators to place such powers in the executive branch. Second, presidents have a tendency to ignore the advice of their economic advisers whenever the political winds dictate. As a result, economic policy does not reside with the CEA, and, furthermore, it is unclear precisely what role the Council's members play in policy making. Third, the Employment Act of 1946 has made government at least partially responsible for the state of the economy. No longer is it possible for public officials to avoid responsibility for economic conditions. However, in all honesty, this would have occurred without this piece of legislation. Keynesian economics, the Depression, and the New Deal had already conspired to ensure continued governmental involvement with the macreconomy. This seems unlikely to change, and, if anything, governments are having to accept ever great responsibility, at least in a political sense, for the economics of their administrations.

BIBLIOGRAPHY

Bailey, Stephen K. *Congress Makes a Law*. New York: Columbia University Press, 1950.

Catton, Bruce. *The War Lords of Washington*. New York: Harcourt Brace, 1948.

Flash, Edward G. *Economic Advice and Presidential Leadership*. New York: Columbia University Press, 1965.

Janeway, Eliott. *The Struggle for Survival*. New Haven: Yale University Press, 1948.

GEOFREY T. MILLS

ACKLEY, GARDNER
(b. January 30, 1915), CEA August 3, 1962-February 15, 1968

Presidential adviser, professor, ambassador, and economist can all be used to describe Gardner Ackley. A man of medium size, thinning brown hair, and pleasant demeanor, Ackley, a naturally reticent man, is precise in his choice of words. Born in Indianapolis, Indiana, Hugh Gardner Ackley has always been called Gardner as his father's name was also Hugh. His family then lived in Detroit for a brief period before moving to Kalamazoo, where he attended public schools. In 1936 he received his B.A. degree from what was then Western State Teachers College in Kalamazoo, with majors in both English and history.

Unable to find suitable employment, Ackley decided to pursue an advanced degree and chose to study economics, although he had only taken principles of economics as an undergraduate. This was because his interest was stirred by the condition of the times—the Great Depression. He resented the Depression and felt there had to be some way to make things better, and that economics must be it. Furthermore, Ackley chose economics rather than English or history because he discovered there were fewer applicants for the available graduate teaching fellowship positions in the economics department at the University of Michigan. He received the M.A. degree in 1937 and the Ph.D. three years later.

In 1937 Ackley married Bonnie A. Lowrey, whom he had met when they were both students at Western State. They have two sons who are married and currently have one child each. David, the older son, is a businessman in Michigan, and Donald, who lives in Virginia, is also a businessman.

Following in the footsteps of both of his parents (his father was a mathematics professor at Western State, and his mother had been a Latin teacher), Ackley began his career in academia in 1939 as an instructor in the economics department at Ohio State University. The next year he was invited to join the economics faculty at the University of Michigan. He served there as an instructor in 1940–41, an assistant professor in 1946–47, an associate professor in 1947–52, a professor in 1952–68, and as the Henry Carter Adams Distinguished University Professor of Political Economy from 1969 until his retirement in 1984. In addition, he served as chairman of the economics department from 1954 to 1961.

Ackley's association with the University of Michigan has been interrupted a number of times to serve the government. While he had no real plan to combine his academic career with government service, in retrospect, he has appeared content with the mixture and has clearly found government service to be strenuous, exciting, and rewarding. He has held the following government positions, a few concurrent with his responsibilities at Michigan:

Consultant, National Resource Planning Board, 1940–41

Economist, Office of Price Administration (OPA), 1941–43 and 1944–46 (Executive, Textiles Branch in 1945 and Assistant Director, Consumer Goods Division in 1946)

Economist, Office of Strategic Services, 1943–44

Consultant, Economic Stabilization Agency, 1950–51

Economic Adviser and Assistant Director, Office of Price Stabilization, 1951–52

Consultant, Secretary of the Army, 1961

Member, Council of Economic Advisers, 1962–68 (Chairman 1964–68)

Ambassador to Italy, 1968–69

Occasional Consultant to Federal Reserve Board of Governors, Council of Economic Advisers, Secretary of the Treasury, etc., 1970 to present

Member, National Advisory Council on Social Security, 1978–80

While at the Office of Price Administration, Ackley worked on controlling prices of secondary nonferrous metals, including scrap metals. It has been remarked that Ackley may have been the first Ph.D. dealing in junk and making it respectable.

Actually, Ackley was in charge of writing price regulations for brass and copper scrap and secondary nonferrous metal ingots. This was part of a larger price control scheme in response to the drastic shortage of nonferrous metals related to World War II. Initially, there had been price controls only on virgin metals, but the wartime shortage soon created an expanded market for scrap, and for ingots made from scrap, which also needed to be controlled. Because of the industrial structures of the two industries, price and allocation controls for the secondary metals were far more complex than for the primary metals.

Ackley was appointed to the Council of Economic Advisers on August 3, 1962, to fill the vacancy caused by James Tobin's* return to Yale. Another Council member at that time was Kermit Gordon*, who was a close friend of Ackley's from their OPA days. When notified of his nomination, Ackley could not say no. Like Heller, Ackley was a so-called new economist or Keynesian. Both believed that the government, especially in its roles as spender, taxer, borrower, and creator of money, could and should use its power to deal with the problems of unemployment, inflation, economic growth, and instability. At his confirmation hearings before the Senate Committee on Banking and Currency, he said that "fiscal policy is one of the instruments which no modern government can afford not to use in pursuit of its objectives of stability and growth." This philosophy was readily translated into action, as a review of Ackley's years on the CEA shows.

When Heller resigned from the CEA, he recommended that he be succeeded by Ackley. In a telephone interview with the author Heller recalls Ackley's clear thinking and clear writing as his most dominant characteristic. He had praise for Ackley's "razor sharp mind" and the fact that he had no wasted motion—he gets right down to the core of whatever he is doing. Having worked with him on the

CEA, Heller was well aware of Ackley's enormous capacity for hard work. According to him, it was not unusual for them to work eighty hours a week on a regular basis. President Johnson agreed with Heller's recommendation, and on November 16, 1964, Ackley assumed the chairmanship of the Council.

Ackley's term on the CEA occurred during the longest continuous period of economic expansion in United States history. Many felt that this was made possible through the use of fiscal, monetary, price stabilization, and growth policies recommended by the CEA, the policy makers faced challenges in order to keep the economy expanding and inflation in check in order to break the postwar string of short-lived and incomplete expansions.

The CEA took seriously the mandate of the Employment Act to "promote maximum employment, production, and purchasing power" during the Kennedy and Johnson administrations. Even during the early years of the recovery from the 1960–61 downturn the Council had a "we can do it all" attitude. In their 1963 report they indicated that the nation was making important progress to full employment, low inflation and faster growth, and economic opportunity.

Although GNP had risen 7 percent, inflation was nearly nonexistent (the Consumer Price Index [CPI] had risen only 1.2 percent), and unemployment was down to 5.6 percent, there were fears that the twenty-two-month-long recovery might end prematurely. Accordingly, the Council recommended fiscal policies that would support, but not spur, the expansion. In anticipation of a slowdown, the Council talked of the use of tax cuts *during* an expansion to act as a fiscal stimulus providing promise for future prosperity and growth.

In 1963 the economy expanded at a more rapid pace than even the optimistic predictions of the CEA. However, there were disappointment and concern that the unemployment rate had not declined further. The Council again recommended the use of fiscal policy for the maintenance and acceleration of expansion, this to be accomplished by means of a tax cut. When one was finally passed by Congress and signed into law in 1964, the Council expressed some concern about issues of poverty and technological change.

Both the economy and the attitude of the CEA continued to be upbeat in 1964, playing an integral part of the formulation of the Great Society. The Council proposed to broaden human goals, and while recognizing that economic policy cannot make men wise it could provide finances for public cultural endeavors. The CEA believed that the improvement of the economy was proof that activist policies could triumph over sluggish economies. In its opinion, this was a bold break from the past and a wide consensus of responsible opinion recognized that federal policy must be formulated to form an engine for growth.

By the end of 1964, unemployment was down to 5 percent. Although the Council was still dissatisfied with the unemployment level, prosperity had been attained. The challenge now was to see that it was sustained.

And sustained it was. The economy in 1965 was vigorous and the strength of the advance was so exceptional that it surpassed the CEA's own optimistic forecasts. As the economy approached full employment (the unemployment rate was down to 4.1 percent in December) prices remained remarkably stable, with the CPI increasing by only 1.8 percent. In spite of this, in order to ensure continued price stability, the CEA reaffirmed its strong commitment to the wage-price guideposts of 1962.

However, amid all this optimism and success there was yet a new challenge. With the increasing involvement in the Vietnam War came increasing defense expenditures. While the expansionary impact of the 1964 tax cut was still rippling through the economy, the CEA called for fiscal restraint. The private sector demand would be forced to slow down its rate of growth in order to accommodate the increased defense spending.

The greatest challenge, however, was not the mere implementation of fiscal restraint; it was the uncertainty of the future course of defense spending. At that time, the U.S. involvement in Vietnam could have gone either way. President Johnson and others continued to reassure the public that the end of U.S. involvement was in sight, bringing with it a massive decline in defense spending. If the private sector was restrained and then government spending also slowed down, the expansion would be threatened.

As it turned out, defense spending increased even more rapidly than had been anticipated. This, along with a 3.9 percent unemployment rate (a thirteen-year low), caused upward pressure on prices. Attention and resources were diverted from some of the more noble causes, and once again the Council focused on keeping the economy moving upward at a steady pace. This required the use of both fiscal and monetary restraint to keep the economy from overheating. In addition to the tight monetary policy instituted early in 1966, there were restrictive tax policies and reductions in nondefense spending. Later in the year, monetary policy was tightened even further.

In a sense, the Council was using the economy as a laboratory to test the validity of Keynesian economics. First there was the tax cut in 1964 to stimulate the economy; then other policies were implemented to slow the economy down. The CEA's activist policies were vindicated by their success in continuing the upward progression of the economy. In addition to large-scale changes, such as the 1964 tax cut, they became advocates of frequent, but small, tax changes and the judicious use of a mix of fiscal and monetary policies.

As might be expected, the CEA did not have complete control of the economy. In 1966 the economy recorded its first significant price increase in seven years when the CPI went up by 3.3 percent. Ackley played an activist role in attempting to curb inflation. He openly skirmished with business and labor when they tried to raise prices or wages above the CEA's guideposts. The government was successful in forcing a rollback of inflationary price increases of aluminum (1965), steel (1966), molybdenum (1966), and automobiles (1967).

The year 1968, Ackley's last on the CEA, saw the continued use of activist policies. When private demand was sluggish during the first half of the year, expansionary fiscal and monetary policies were implemented in order to try to sustain prosperity. Once again the policies seemed to work, as unemployment remained below 4 percent for the second straight year and inflation remained at around 3 percent.

A milestone was reached in that year when the expansion reached its eighty-first month and surpassed the eighty-month expansion which had accompanied World War II. This becomes even more significant in comparison to the thirty-month average length of the twenty-six previous expansions between 1854 and 1960.

According to his nomination hearings before the Senate Committee on Banking and Currency, Ackley intended to serve on the Council for only two years. However, nearly five and a half years passed before Ackley left the Council on February 15, 1968. This is second only to the record five years, nine months held by Raymond J. Saulnier*. Looking back on those years, Ackley has said to the author in conversation that he would like most to be remembered for the continuation of the period of prosperity. He added that he is also proud of the low unemployment that was achieved during that time.

Although the CEA had many successes during Ackley's tenure, there are some things that he would have done differently had he had the opportunity. Primarily, he says that he should have "fought harder to raise taxes in the last year and a half" that he served.

President Johnson rewarded Ackley for his services by appointing him ambassador to Italy. In comments to the author Walter Heller has said that Johnson had the "highest regard for Gardner Ackley." The president even commented to Heller that Ackley's CEA, with its forty-person staff, put out as much useful stuff as the entire Pentagon.

It was due to a longtime interest in that country that Ackley was appointed ambassador to Italy. As a Fulbright Research Scholar he had been at the University of Rome in 1955–56. With funding from the Ford Foundation, he returned to Italy for the academic year 1960–61. He was there again in 1976–77 while on a sabbatical leave from Michigan. Ackley has authored a number of papers and books on the Italian economy. He was designated a Cavaliere ("Knight") del Gran Croce, Ordine della Merita, Repubblica d'Italia, Italy's highest civilian decoration, in 1969. When Richard Nixon became president, he replaced Ackley with a new ambassador. Ackley returned to the University of Michigan in 1969 as the Adams Professor.

In addition to serving the government, Ackley has also served the economics profession. He has been a member or chairman of a number of American Economic Association committees, was on the board of editors of the *American Economic Review* from 1953 to 1956, and held the office of vice president in 1962. Twenty years later, he was elected president of the association.

Many honors have been bestowed upon Ackley for his achievements. He was awarded honorary LL.D. degrees from Western Michigan University, his alma mater, in 1964, and from Kalamazoo College in 1967. He received the Distinguished Alumnus Award from WMU in 1970 and the Distinguished Faculty Achievement Award from the University of Michigan in 1977. He has also been elected to membership in the American Academy of Arts and Sciences and the American Philosophical Society.

Ackley has been a prolific writer throughout his career, having authored well over one hundred articles, books, monographs, pamphlets, government reports, and book reviews. Many of these works have been translated into foreign languages. Included in this list is his textbook, *Macroeconomic Theory* (1961), which was used around the world for many years, and was replaced in 1978 by *Macroeconomics: Theory and Policy*. He has also written extensively on inflation, including *Stemming World Inflation* (1971), "Administered Prices and the Inflationary Process" (1959), "Two-Stage Recession and Inflation, 1973–75" (1975), and "The Costs of Inflation" (1978). In addition, Ackley has written "The Economy," a column of opinion which has been a regular feature in *Dun's Review* since 1971. His final column appeared in the November 1984 issue.

Gardner Ackley retired from the University of Michigan and was granted emeritus status in June 1984. He continues to write and speak and to work on some major assignments for the American Economic Association.

BIBLIOGRAPHY

Ackley, Gardner. "Commodities and Capital: Prices and Quantities." *American Economic Review* 33, no. 1 (March 1983): 1–34.

———. *Macroeconomic Theory*. New York: Macmillan, 1961.

———. *Macroeconomics: Theory and Practice*. New York: Macmillan, 1968.

———. *Stemming World Inflation*. Paris: Atlantic Institute, 1971.

EUGENE B. GENDEL

BLOUGH, ROY

(b. August 21, 1901), CEA June 29, 1950-August 20, 1952

Roy Blough was one of the long line of economists to come from the institutional/humanist school started at the University of Wisconsin by John R. Commons. The son of a midwestern minister in the Church of the Brethren, Blough was able to couple this training with his natural human concern for the downtrodden of society, becoming one of the earliest to be educated in Keynesian fiscal policy. Although Blough's primary area of interest was tax policy, banking and international finance were a close second. But even this characterization is a bit misleading as economics was not nearly as fragmented and specialized around World War II as it was later to become, and a list of Blough's professional papers reveals expertise in almost every area of economic inquiry. His interest in the use of the tax system for countercyclical fiscal policies, coupled with a fundamental belief in the ability of the American economy to care for all of its citizens, earned him the reputation of being a leftist economist. In fact, upon learning of Blough's appointment to the CEA, Senator Robert Taft (R-Ohio) remarked that "the President now has three left fields on the team to advise him on economic affairs" (the others being Leon Keyserling* and John D. Clark*).

In actuality, this is unfair to Blough. While he certainly was a Democrat, he was not a leftist in economic matters. He was opposed to deficit spending, on anything other than a temporary basis, as an inherently inflationary policy. Furthermore, he feared that a large and growing national debt would curb production and reduce GNP. Blough earned his reputation as a leftist because he was unwilling to sacrifice all economic considerations to an immediate balancing of the budget, a fast reduction of the national debt, and an extreme fear of inflation. By training, philosophy, and upbringing, Blough occupied a middle ground between traditional Republican conservative economists and the then emerging liberal Keynesians who believed large and continuous deficits to be of no importance. In the history of economic thought he is a transitional figure straddling the older neoclassical economics and the new macroeconomics of Keynes.

Roy Blough followed a well-worn path to the Council. He moved in and out of government service and the academic life, always maintaining a university base to work from. He built a solid reputation at major universities, in tandem with advisory and/or consulting positions at various state and federal agencies. His publication record is enviable, and he was able to maintain a stream of high-quality research even while at the Treasury Department in World War II.

Blough's interest in tax and fiscal matters began at an early age. While working on his doctorate at Wisconsin, he helped to finance his education by a stint as the statistician for the Wisconsin Tax Commission. This, probably more than anything, influenced his liberal inclinations about the ability of tax policy to help manage the economy. Wisconsin, in those days, was a hotbed of liberal economic schemes, and the Tax Commission was to leave a permanent stamp on his thinking. After the completion of his degree in 1922, he was promoted to chief statistician and was given responsibility for the entire research division of the commission. Blough stayed at this post until 1932, and it was here that he refined his ideas about the curative powers of fiscal and tax policies. The stock market collapse of 1929 and the emerging Depression must have convinced him that the government could, or should, play a positive role in restoring economic health. This experience also made him more receptive to the economics and policy measures proposed by Keynes in the late 1930s, and forever convinced him of the need for flexibility in economic policy making.

In the mid–1930s, Blough moved to the Graduate School of Public Administration of the University of Cincinnati, and then later to the economics department at Columbia. He would maintain at least an informal connection with Columbia and New York City for the rest of his life. It was during these years that he completed a great deal of work for the New Deal's relief agencies. He was the director of research and statistics on state and city finances for the Federal Emergency Relief Administration and a consultant to the Social Security Board. In 1935 and 1936, the Twentieth Century Fund sponsored a study on taxation entitled *Facing the Tax Problem*. This became a taxonomy of the fiscal problems of the 1930s and offered a liberal plan of taxation for the immediate future. Blough served as associate director of the taxation committee, and in the summer of 1937 he found the time to serve with the Treasury Department on tax policy and other matters.

The years from 1930 to 1938 saw Blough build and consolidate his reputation as an expert in fiscal and tax affairs. During this time he published some twenty articles on taxes and the fiscal position and policies of governments, and edited a number of books. All of this was in addition to his many assignments as consultant and expert adviser to various agencies. By 1938 this activity had solidly established his reputation as a tax expert of slightly liberal, yet prudent, inclinations. Blough had staked out his territory on the moderate edge of the New Deal, and he felt quite comfortable there. It was probably about this time, and certainly by 1940, that he was exposed to Keynes' ideas. The exact impact that the British economist had on Blough is problematic, and one could argue that the economic devastation of the Depression had a greater impact on him. Whatever the influence, he had evolved into a practical liberal in the sense that he was willing to break new ground rather than stand firm on the old, dusty landscape that was economics in the early 1930s.

In June 1938, Blough began the first of two protracted assignments of federal government service. In that year, he joined the Treasury Department as director of tax research. He stayed in this post until December 1944, when he was promoted to assistant to the Secretary of the Treasury. He remained with the Treasury through reconversion and into the autumn of 1946.

Blough maintained his scholarly output while at the Treasury, authoring some thirty-five articles, reports, and essays, most of them on taxes. His principal duties at the Treasury were to help preside over the fiscal conduct of the war. In general, he favored financing as much of the war as possible on a ''pay as you go'' basis, which meant, of course, raising taxes. This increase in taxes would also have the beneficial effect of soaking up excess spending power and thereby reducing inflation. The most common notion was that with the war effort taking such a high percentage of GNP there was little left in the way of consumer goods production. The domestic population, if left to their own devices, would then use their war-generated income to bid up the prices of what consumer goods were available. As a result, the Treasury Department felt that it had to tax as much as possible in order to avoid an inflation which could injure war output. Blough was an enthusiastic supporter of these policies, and so fearful did he become of a postwar inflation that he was one of a handful of individuals who did not advocate an immediate decrease in taxes after the cessation of hostilities. This is hardly the advice of a dyed in the wool Keynesian.

Beginning with the autumn term in 1946, Blough joined the faculty of the University of Chicago as a professor of economics and political science. He spent, for him, a relatively quiet three and a half years at Chicago. It seems that he could never really shake the policy-making action of Washington, and he spent a fair amount of time there and in New York City on various assignments. Blough may have missed the intense environment of the East, or he may have found his views increasingly in the minority at Chicago; in any case, when Truman asked him to join the Council in May 1950, he eagerly accepted.

Blough's years at the CEA were marked by some controversy, but not enough to make big news. Besides the rather ordinary Republican flak about his economic views, Blough, and the entire Council for that matter, came under little fire. The Korean War dominated the headlines, along with the Communist hunting of those years, and there evolved a consensus of sorts on economic policy. Taxes were increased to help finance the war, and wage and price controls were set in place along the World War II model. However, Korea, unlike the earlier war, was not a strong drain on the economy, and inflation never became a problem. Wage and price controls were a nuisance to some, but many prices never reached their ceilings. A strong monetary policy is generally credited for this latter result. The Federal Reserve Board and the Treasury did not reach their famous accord until March 1952, and as a result, inflation was kept in check. Except for the usual assortment of complaints, there was little controversy during this period. Leon Keyserling, the chairman of the Council, became a controversial figure, but more for his opinions and personality than for his economics. In point of fact, Truman's fiscal policy during Blough's tenure was entirely moderate, and there is nothing in the record to suggest that the president received other than sound, middle of the road advice.

Blough stayed at the CEA through the end of Truman's presidency, and then settled into the life of a senior research professor at Columbia University. At that time, Columbia had one of the strongest economics departments in the nation, and Blough stayed until his retirement in 1970. Retirement is a misnomer in this instance, for after this date he held several visiting appointments and was a member of the Council on Foreign Relations and the Commission to Study the Organization of Peace. He was named a trustee and deacon of the Riverside Church and was an active member of the Department of Church and Economic Life of the National Council of Churches, a post he held for a quarter of a century. He supported Adlai Stevenson in the presidential elections of the 1950s, and advised the candidate on economic affairs and wrote a few position papers for him. He generally supported moderate liberals instead of conservatives.

It was during his years at Columbia that he expanded his interests in international economics and finance, as well as economic development. All of these interests touch, at least tangentially, on tax policy, and they were a natural extension of his previous work. In the mid and late 1950s, he served in the United Nations as principal director of the Department of Economic Affairs and participated in several technical assistance missions to Latin and South America. Blough was an adviser to the Committee for Economic Development off and on until 1972. That was the heyday of growth economics when the United States and the U.N. were happily attempting to ignite self-sustained growth all over the world. That most of their efforts ended in failure was not due to lack of commitment.

We see, beginning about 1952, a gradual shift in his focus to the international arena in general, and to the economics of development in particular. Much of his time, after his stint with the Council, became occupied with worldwide economic affairs. This was so much the case that in 1966 he was named to the prestigious S. Sloan Colt Chair of Banking and International Finance at Columbia.

Blough also served admirably as a steward to the economics profession. A vice president of the American Economics Association (AEA), and president of the Midwestern Economics Association (MEA), he was also the editor of a number of journals in both economics and finance. He was an encouraging and sympathetic colleague and an inspiration to those graduate students who worked under his tutelage.

These lists of accomplishments give an indication of the sort of man and economist Roy Blough was. Today, economists are known for their extreme expertise in a narrow, even arcane, area of the discipline. Economic knowledge is fragmented and very specialized. Graduate education, with its highly technical bent, reinforces this tendency. Educated in the 1920s, and gaining his political awareness in the Depression, Roy Blough was able to operate with a much different world view than other economists. He was one of the last of the institutional/economists before the mathematical/scientific revolution shook the profession.

Blough's upbringing as the son of a minister attuned him to the human side of economics, and all his life he sought out opportunities to put his beliefs into practice. Although he was most well known for his expertise on tax policy, it would be more correct to label him a humanistic economist, so great was his concern for people and their problems. Blough always sought out the impact of economic policy on individual humans. He had little tolerance for such abstract groups as "consumers," "producers," or "the disadvantaged." No doubt this is why Robert Taft felt Blough to be left of center and why Blough favored Stevenson over Eisenhower. Much of his work for church and international peace groups was done gratis, reflecting his belief that these organizations needed all the support and encouragement they could get. At the end of his career, Roy Blough had embraced his intellectual roots with a passion. Economics with a human face had always been his strong suit.

BIBLIOGRAPHY

Blough, Roy. *Economic Policy for the Farm Sector*. Washington, D.C.: The American Enterprise Institute, 1967.

———. *International Business*. New York: McGraw-Hill, 1966.

———. *Regional Integration and the Trade of Latin America*. New York: Committee for Economic Development, 1968.

———. *The World Price of Oil: A Medium-Term Analysis*. Washington, D.C.: The American Enterprise Institute, 1976.

———, and Newcomer, Mable. *Facing the Tax Problem*. New York: Twentieth Century Fund, 1937.

———, and Prais, S. J. *The Analysis of Family Budgets*. Cambridge, England: Cambridge University Press, 1955.

———, and Taylor, Lester D. *Consumer Demand in the United States: Analysis and Projections*. Cambridge, Mass.: Harvard University Press.

GEOFREY T. MILLS

BRANDT, KARL

(b. January 9, 1899, d. February 8, 1975), CEA November 1, 1958-January 20, 1961

Karl Brandt, agricultural economist, expert on German affairs, and conservative Republican, served on the Council of Economic Advisers from 1958 to 1961. In this capacity, as well as in earlier consulting positions for the federal government, Brandt saw his role as that of analyst and provider of information. Yet, in his private work, he was a forceful and articulate spokesman for specific policy actions.

Brandt was born in Essen, Germany, to Maximilian and Wilhelmina Troschwitz Brandt. A 1921 graduate of Wurttenberg College of Agriculture, he received his Doctor of Agriculture degree from the University of Berlin in 1926. After serving as director of the German Farm Tenants Bank, he returned, in 1929, to the University of Berlin, where he held several posts. He began as a farm manager and later became a professor in the College of Agriculture and director of the Institute of Agricultural Market Research. Brandt also served as a consultant on agricultural policy for the Weimar Republic until 1933.

A member of the anti-Nazi movement, Brandt, an Episcopalian, left Germany in 1933 with his wife, the former Anitta Hewel-von Lindenfels. They immigrated to the United States, where they had four sons, Klaus, Jobst, Groetz, and Ralph. In this country, Brandt first served as professor of agricultural economics at the New School for Social Research in New York. In 1938 he began his primary career at the Stanford University Food Research Institute. He served as professor of economics, associate director, and director, retiring from the institute in 1964.

In the course of his career, Karl Brandt held several guest professorships. He was at Louisiana State University in 1937–38, the universities of Heidelberg and Goettingen in 1948–49, and the Free University of Berlin in 1954–55. Having served as economic adviser to the Secretary of Agriculture in 1942, Brandt became a consultant to the War Food Administration in 1944. After the war, he served as an economic adviser on food and agricultural issues for the U.S. military government in Berlin, under General Lucius Clay. His service on the Council of Economic Advisers was under the Eisenhower administration.

Much of Brandt's work at Stanford's Food Research Institute involved writing reports on specific agricultural issues. His pamphlets on topics such as whaling and whale oil and fats and oils were factual expositions of the commodity markets of the time. Elsewhere, Brandt made specific suggestions for ameliorating the postwar farm income problem. He recommended a program which supplemented market forces rather than replacing them, as existing price parity and acreage restriction programs attempted to do. In 1945 Brandt proposed a farm income insurance scheme. This plan would guarantee farmers a minimum annual income and provide some guidance in product planning. He designed the program so as to avoid high prices which would encourage excess production volume.

Brandt's opposition to excessive interference with the market was moderated by a recognition that individuals do not always have control over their own economic circumstances. He believed that long-term mass unemployment, such as occurred during the Depression, contributed to the erosion of the ethical and moral foundations of society. The responsibility for preventing a recurrence of the economic conditions of the 1930s lay with the government. While the government's primary function was to provide an appropriate setting for the efforts of private enterprise, direct public action against unavoidable economic disasters was imperative.

This perception of the role of government was rooted in an ideology focused on the superiority of the free market system. To Brandt the issue of statecraft is the minimization of central control consistant with freedom and economic progress. Basic social security was necessary for the equal opportunity Brandt considered a prerequisite for the effective working of the market system. In the context of the farm problem, this philosophy implied the necessity of supporting farm incomes, but led Brandt to oppose the parity and acreage restriction programs then in effect.

Parity formulas, by setting rigid price supports, causes surpluses to accumulate. These surpluses eventually led either to low prices or to production controls and "regimented scarcity." The interference with relative prices and the restriction of consumption resulting from artificially high prices were among the most serious effects of the parity program. The price supports also destroyed the competitiveness of American farm products in world markets.

Brandt's general concept of a sound agricultural policy involved government protection against extreme farm income fluctuations. Policy should be designed to maximize consumption, allow gradual change in prices, and facilitate adjustment to technological change. Brandt saw the real key to a healthy agricultural sector as a strong general economy which could absorb marginal farmers. The condition of the competitive farm sector would be greatly improved by an increase in competition in the industrial sector. Monopoly wages and prices in industry and fixed margins in wholesaling and retailing prevented farmers from maintaining their relative income position.

More specifically, Brandt supported the development of markets for agricultural products. In addition to the maintenance of consumer purchasing power, he advocated school lunch and food stamp programs as ways to increase outlets for farm products while relieving poverty. Research to develop new outlets for agricultural commodities should, however, be left primarily to private industry. Such attempts at market augmentation were far superior to production restrictions that cut into constitutional and private property rights.

Brandt's general philosophy on agricultural policy can be characterized as cautiously interventionist. The price system had to be allowed to allocate re sources, and high-cost farmers had to stop producing. The government should, however, ease the discomfort involved in transition and cushion the blows to farmers from events out of their control.

At the end of his term on the Council of Economic Advisers in 1961, Brandt was still arguing against rigid price support programs, which he perceived as providing an undesirable subsidy to producers of substitutes for agricultural products and to foreign competitors. Government policies increased barriers to the mobility of resources and failed to ameliorate the problems of particularly depressed farm regions such as Appalachia and the Ozarks. Subsidies in the form of rapid depreciation of farm equipment and tax-free gasoline for farm use were more compatible with Brandt's philosophy, which he viewed as a forceful government promulgating competition in the market place promoting growth and stability. In this framework, Brandt's concern with appropriate farm policy was moderated by a conviction that the Malthusian specter was a remote one and that in spite of serious localized problems, the general plight of farmers was less extreme than popularly imagined.

Brandt's free market orientation was strengthened by his political abhorrence of noncapitalist and nondemocratic institutions. He criticized agricultural production controls as potentially leading to total control of agriculture and then to "cartelization" of industries and trade. He evoked the image of the Weimar Republic and the rise of Nazi Germany as a historical example of a similar developmental path.

Much of Brandt's commentary on the postwar reconstruction of Germany was in a similar political vein. He considered the revival of the German economy imperative in order to keep Western Europe free and democratic. He perceived Roosevelt's idea of building world peace on the basis of friendship with the Soviet Union as a serious blunder. Brandt's anti-Communist feelings emerged repeatedly in his arguments for German reindustrialization. He saw the goal of the Soviets as being the establishment of a Soviet-style world government.

The philosophy evidenced in these attitudes led to Brandt's active support of conservative political forces in the United States. Together with Milton Friedman, Gottfried Haberler, and others, Brandt worked as an adviser to Barry Goldwater's 1964 presidential campaign. Other Republican economists, including Arthur Burns*, Paul McCracken*, and Henry Wallich*, all of whom had also served on the CEA under Eisenhower, remained neutral in this election. They disagreed with what they considered Goldwater's extreme views on deficit spending for stabilization purposes, poverty programs, and civil rights legislation. After Goldwater's defeat, Brandt's strong conservative convictions led him to collaborate with the former candidate in the founding of the Free Society Association. This organization intended to educate the public through the provision of literature, speakers, and possible subsidies to journalists and writers of conservative articles. While Ku Klux Klan members were not welcome, John Birch Society members were encouraged to join this political forum.

In addition to his political activities, Karl Brandt was a prolific writer on foreign affairs, particularly in relation to Germany. His first-hand knowledge of that country before World War II was supplemented through continual contact, including two terms as visiting professor in German universities in 1948–49 and 1954–55. During the war Brandt argued that the Nazis could not be starved out, and that the Allies had no choice but to pursue a clear military victory. One vulnerable spot in the German armor was likely to be the transportation system, and Brandt recommended using this area to disrupt the Nazi economic system.

Even before the end of the war, Brandt was urging the development of reconstruction plans for Germany. He considered the prevailing anti-German attitude destructive and saw the need for recreating a sovereign, economically independent, democratic German state as quickly as possible. The idea of forcing the Germans to suffer for their sins could only damage the other Western economies. Brandt wanted to convince the American public and the government that their self-interest would, in general and specifically in this case, be best served by concern for the general welfare and would be harmed by an isolationist policy. This perspective was in line with Brandt's view that the U.S. refusal to lend the Europeans sufficient funds to pay for our exports was a significant factor leading to the agricultural crisis of 1928. International cooperation was vital to any economic success. His concern over the rehabilitation of the European economy even led Brandt to advocate international management of the German coal mines to alleviate the postwar fuel crisis.

Brandt's involvement with U.S. policy relating to Germany continued throughout his career. He wrote journal articles and letters to the editor of the *New York Times* urging diplomatic moves toward the solution of the Berlin crisis. Brandt also addressed international economic issues, particularly in relation to agrarian reform in the less developed countries. In 1966 he advocated the use of American foreign aid as a tool to create pressure for agrarian reforms. Brandt's concept of agrarian reform was not, however, the standard one. He was concerned with encouraging technological advance in the agricultural sectors of the nonindustrialized countries. Breaking up large plantations into smaller holdings to allow property to be more widely distributed was a dangerous step in the direction of a Stalinist plan. Typical agrarian reform could cause the West to lose out to tyranny.

Brandt's alternative was to promote multinational investment in less developed nations, foster the coexistence of family farming with large-scale, technologically advanced farms, and ensure a higher standard of living for tenant farmers.

Brandt's conservative political philosophy was motivated partly by his experience with the decline of democracy accompanying social planning in prewar Germany. His support of some degree of government intervention in the market emerged from his awareness of conflict of interest inherent in the capitalist system. He wrote repeatedly of the need for the government to diminish political friction and unify the goals of conflicting groups. This perception of the complexities of maintaining a viable economy influenced his policy recommendations in agriculture and in foreign affairs. It also contributed to his concern over the future of the economics profession. Brandt expressed reservations about the methodological developments which he perceived as leading economics away from meaningful social science and toward the "deceptive mirror-effects" of mathematics and statistics. He questioned the advisability of training too many economists as mathematicians for the sake of prestige. He urged a focus on theory to explain facts and on the human motivations and political assumptions integral to economic analysis.

Brandt was honored in 1950 with the conferral of an honorary doctorate from the University of Heidelberg. He was also elected president of the Farm Economics Association for the 1955–56 term. In addition to his books, Brandt published in *Foreign Affairs*, *Journal of Farm Economics*, *Annals of the American Academy of Political and Social Science*, and other journals.

Karl Brandt died in Menlo Park, California, in 1975, at the age of seventy-six. He is remembered as a strong-willed, rather authoritarian man for whom economics was only a small part of life. In addition to his concern with scientific and political issues, Brandt enjoyed working in his large garden, preparing fish in his smokehouse, and collecting diverse gadgets.

A man with little patience for the dissent involved in democratic institutions, Brandt was an ardently conservative supporter of capitalism. He had an active curiosity about the world and was able to perceive weaknesses in the system he cherished and to articulate policies he felt would strengthen it.

BIBLIOGRAPHY

Brandt, Karl. "Discussion: Farm Fundamentalism, Past and Future." *Journal of Farm Economics* 44 (1962): 1231–37.

———. *Germany: Key to Peace in Europe*. Claremont, Calif.: Claremont College Press, 1949.

———. "Germany's Vulnerable Spot: Transportation." *Foreign Affairs* 21 (January 1945): 221–38.

———. "The Orientation of Agricultural Policy in the Coming Decade." *Journal of Farm Economics* 37 (1955): 793–806.

———. "A Price Policy for Agriculture, Consistent with Economic Progress, That Will Promote Adequate and More Stable Income for Farming." *Journal of Farm Economics* 27 (1945): 807–12.

———. "Problems of Invasion and Occupation." *Foreign Affairs* 22 (1943): 699–710.

———. *The Reconstruction of World Agriculture*. New York: W. W. Norton, 1945.

———. "The Underdeveloped Nations." In Melvyn Laird, ed., *The Conservative Papers*. Chicago: Quadrangle Books, 1974.

SANDRA R. BAUM

BURNS, ARTHUR F.

(b. April 27, 1904, d. June 26, 1987), CEA March 19, 1953-December 1, 1956

Arthur F. Burns was born in Stanislau, Austria. His family immigrated to the United States and settled in Bayonne, New Jersey, in 1910, where his father worked as a housepainter. Burns attended the local schools, where he earned excellent grades. He was awarded a scholarship to Columbia University. His original career objective was in architecture, but his studies in economics soon led him in another direction.

Burns received his bachelor's and master's degrees from Columbia in 1925 and his doctorate in 1934. While there, he met and studied under Wesley C. Mitchell. Mitchell was responsible for hiring him to work at the National Bureau of Economic Research in 1930 while he was still a graduate student. That same year, he married Helen Bernstein. Earlier, in 1927, Burns had joined the economics faculty at Rutgers University; he remained there until 1944, at which time he was hired at Columbia. In the stimulating environments of the National Bureau, Rutgers, and Columbia, Burns matured as an economist.

Mitchell and Burns enjoyed a close personal and professional relationship which lasted until Mitchell's death in 1948. In his introduction to Burns' *Production Trends in the United States Since 1870*, published by the National Bureau, Mitchell described the work as "the most important contribution to our knowledge of increase in production . . . since [John Stuart] Mill wrote." This is high praise indeed for what had started as a doctoral dissertation. In this work, Burns showed that the retardation of growth in individual industries did not imply a slowdown in the growth of total output of the nation. The rapid development of new industries produced the retardation in the growth of the old, and this was necessary for the continued rapid growth of total output. Therefore, retardation might be found in every industry but not in the aggregate output of the economy. In other words, what might characterize each of the parts might not be characteristic of the whole.

In 1938 Mitchell and Burns collaborated on a paper dealing with statistical indicators requested by Secretary of the Treasury Henry Morgenthau, this being one of the early works in which the authors probed leading, coinciding, and lagging indicators widely used by economists today. After the war, in 1947, they co-authored a treatise on cyclical fluctuations called *Measuring Business Cycles*. This work is still considered one of the major studies on the subject. At the time of publication, however, the book excited considerable controversy. Tjalling Koopmans, a major critic of the work, referred to it as "measurement without theory." He argued that Burns and Mitchell had developed a tool kit for measuring cyclical changes without first setting forth the theory of business cycles they expected the measurements to test. This was in his view an inefficient way to proceed in science.

Koopmans favored another approach to an understanding of economic change. The correct approach, he contended, was to take a provisional theory, create a mathematical model to express the theory, obtain the statistics on the variables called for in the model, and see how the model fit the facts. The preferred, provisional theory at that time was that advanced by John Maynard Keynes. Koopmans' approach was widely adopted in the following decades, particularly in academic circles, but the controversy remains alive, in large part because no one theory has been able to prove its superiority in predicting economic change.

When they wrote *Measuring Business Cycles*, Burns and Mitchell believed that the science of economic fluctuations was only beginning to pass into an inductive stage. They asserted that business cycle theorists ''have not infrequently been handicapped by a sadly incomplete, sometimes by a badly twisted, knowledge of the facts. . . . When this order of inquiry is followed—explanation preceding a thorough knowledge of what is to be explained—the results are likely to be unhappy.''

When Mitchell stepped down as director of research at the bureau in 1945 he turned the post over to his former student. During his tenure as research director, Burns wrote a series of reports on the theme that theorizing on the basis of an incomplete set of facts posed a serious danger to the development of an economic science. In these articles and papers, he also expressed skepticism about the determinacy of the then dominant Keynesian theory of income and employment based on its tacit assumption of consumption function and intended investment independence of the free market adjustment processes. He suggested that the widespread opinion that Keynes had explained the determinants of the volume of employment at any given time and that this knowledge would enable government to maintain a stable and high level of national income and employment reflected a pleasant but dangerous illusion.

Burns continued at his post as director of research until 1953, when he went to Washington to the Council of Economic Advisers under President Eisenhower. In the early 1950s, the Council had fallen into disfavor with many members of the Congress of both parties. In fact, only a very limited amount of funding had been appropriated for the operation of the Council by a Democratic controlled Congress when Burns arrived. After a period of uncertainty about the status of the Council early in 1953, a reorganization plan devised by Burns was adopted, the main feature of which was to concentrate authority in a chairman and make him directly responsible to the president. Burns was appointed chairman, and the president was able to secure additional funding for the work of the Council.

Shortly after his arrival in Washington, Burns was confronted with another problem, the prospect of a business cycle recession. In fact, the National Bureau of Economics subsequently dated July 1953 a business cycle peak. This was the same month that Burns was nominated and confirmed as chairman of the reconstituted Council. Even before then, Burns had diagnosed the occurrence of an imbalance between changes in production and sales. He reported to the president that business firms were faced with a condition where their output was rising rapidly while their sales remained sluggish. They were therefore making efforts to adjust their inventories. On top of that, the cessation of hostilities in Korea in the summer of 1953 was providing an opportunity to cut back on defense spending. The efforts of businessmen to adjust inventories to an appropriate balance with current sales led to some reduction in output, and so too did a decline in defense outlays. As a result, employment dropped appreciably in manufacturing industries, and to a lesser degree in other parts of the economy.

During the course of the recession, the cabinet discussed every week, at the president's request, economic developments and prospects, and the governmental actions needed to strengthen the economy. Every week Burns reported to the president and then again to the cabinet, and nearly every week some action was taken to check the recession. Burns' account of the 1953–54 recession appears in the 1954 and 1955 *Economic Reports of the President* and in an essay, "Dealing with Recession and Inflation." These reports and other memoranda disclose the wide range of actions he recommended to offset recession, promote growth, and prevent inflation.

Some prominent observers at the time contended that the decline was picking up momentum and that unless the federal government sharply reduced taxes and kept expenditures rising, the recession would degenerate into a depression. In contrast, Burns' professional opinion was that the nation was experiencing an inventory decline, and that significant increases in federal outlays were not necessary. On the contrary, when asked for his judgment about the wisdom of cutting back on defense outlays during the slide, he counseled that a prudent cutback would not endanger the prospects for recovery. His assessment proved to be accurate.

The last chapter of the 1954 *Economic Report* summarized the administration's four principles for dealing with recession. The first and foremost principle was to take preventive action. The second was to avoid a doctrinaire position, to work simultaneously on many fronts, and to make sure that the actions harmonized and reinforced one another. The third was to pursue measures that would foster the expansion of private activity by stimulating consumers to spend more money and businessmen to create more jobs. The fourth principle was to act promptly and vigorously if economic conditions required it.

In 1957 Burns returned to his teaching duties at Columbia University, and he also became president of the National Bureau. Shortly after his return from Washington, in a talk to graduate economics students at Columbia, he discussed the role of an economist in government. He suggested that economists must realize that they are not the sole custodians of economic knowledge and that they must recognize that others in public life also possess knowledge of economic and business affairs. Still, he suggested, there is some quality that sets the economist apart and enables him to help public officials in reaching sound decisions. This consists of approaching the factors of economic life scientifically. Once again, Burns stresses the importance of facts, of the relationship of the parts to the whole, and of the importance of the indirect or unseen as well as the seen.

In late 1957 Burns delivered four lectures at Fordham University which were published in 1958 under the title *Prosperity Without Inflation*. The third of these, ''The New Environment of Monetary Policy,'' excited the most attention. Burns suggested there that various financial developments—the growth of governmental expenditures, steep tax rates, the decreased dependence of corporations on external financing, the great flexibility of loan instruments, the relative decline of commercial bankers among financial intermediaries, and the large holdings of Treasury securities by financial institutions—have all tended to reduce the effectiveness of traditional monetary restraints.

In 1959 Burns was elected president of the American Economic Association. The theme of his presidential address, ''Progress Towards Economic Stability,'' was that a conjuncture of structural changes in the economy had served to modify the business cycle of our times. The net result was that the intensity of cyclical swings in output had become smaller and the links that previously tied together the cyclical movements of production, employment, personal income, and consumption had become looser. He also warned his audience that the parallelism of the short-term movements in physical production and prices was breaking down.

During the long expansion of the 1960s, it became fashionable in academic circles to talk of the death or obsolescence of the business cycle. The new economics of that era stressed that closing the gap between actual and potential output was the crucial goal of economic policy. Burns voiced his skepticism about the new approach on many occasions. He emphasized that the fashionable growth model could not ignore business cycle theory—the imbalances that develop between investment and consumption, as an example.

In 1969 he was appointed Counselor to the President, a cabinet-level rank. The following year, 1970, he was appointed chairman of the Federal Reserve System, a post he held until 1978. His tour of duty began during a recession and ended in an expansion; it covered the sharp downturn from 1973 to 1975, and was a period when price and wage inflation was persistent.

The lack of systematic progress in curbing inflation during the 1970s was doubtless a source of much anguish for Burns, who had for so long stressed that price stability was a necessary condition for long-run prosperity in a free society. Some students of monetary policy laid the blame for this chronic inflation on the Federal Reserve. Burns offered a different interpretation of these events. He expressed his thoughts on the worldwide inflation a year after leaving the Federal Reserve in the 1979 Per Jacobsson Lecture in Belgrade. He suggested that although the central banks had doubtless made errors, what was unique about the inflation was its stubborn persistence, and this persistence was a reflection of changing social and political values since the 1960s. He concluded that although central banks are capable of some stabilizing action, their practical capacity for curbing an inflation that is continually driven by political forces is very limited. In 1981 Burns was appointed U.S. ambassador to the Federal Republic of Germany, and at age 77 he began a new career as a diplomat.

Burns had two sons. David is a lawyer, and Joseph is an economist. The family spent many summers at their farm in Vermont, where Burns built a separate cabin for use as a study. Geoffrey Moore and Milton Friedman were among the professional colleagues and friends who lived nearby.

We live too close to the critical period during which Burns had great responsibility for the conduct of U.S. monetary policy to assess objectively his stewardship of these matters. We can, however, record that his lifetime reputation as outstanding scholar and teacher, wise counselor, firm administrator, and person of unquestioned integrity remains intact. Burns died in Baltimore, Maryland, at age eighty-three from complications following heart surgery.

BIBLIOGRAPHY

Burns, Arthur. ''An Economist in Government.'' *Columbia University Forum* 1, no. 1 (Winter 1957): 1–6.

———. *The Business Cycle in a Changing World*. New York: Columbia University Press, 1969.

———. *Frontiers of Economic Knowledge*. Princeton: Princeton University Press, 1954.

———. *Production Trends in the United States Since 1870*. New York: National Bureau of Economic Research, 1934.

———. *Prosperity Without Inflation*. New York: Fordham University Press, 1958.

———. *Reflections of an Economic Policymaker*. Washington, D.C.: American Enterprise Institute, 1978.

———, and Samuelson, Paul. *Full Employment: Guideposts and Stability*. Washington, D.C.: American Enterprise Institute, 1967.

Mitchell, Wesley Clair, and Burns, Arthur. *Measuring Business Cycles*. New York: National Bureau of Economic Research, 1947.

———. ''Statistical Indicators of Cyclical Revivals.'' Bulletin 69. New York: National Bureau of Economic Research, 1938.

JOHN P. CULLITY

CLARK, JOHN D.

(b. September 26, 1884, d. November 6, 1961), CEA August 9, 1946-February 11, 1953

John Davidson Clark was a man of many talents and interests. He was not only an economist who served on the Council of Economic Advisers but also a successful lawyer, oil executive, politician, teacher, and academic administrator. In examining the various stages of Clark's life, one has the impression that his mind was energetic and diverse. Above all, he was acutely aware of the social and political interplay underlying much economic debate.

Born in Fort Collins, Colorado, Clark was the son of Gibson and Frances Amanda (Johnson) Clark. After graduation in 1902 from the Cheyenne High School in Wyoming, he attended the University of Nebraska and completed the A.B. in three years. Besides academic pursuits, he played on the basketball team, edited both his senior yearbook and the *Daily Nebraska*, and entered the legal fraternity Phi Delta Phi and a social fraternity later known as Chi Phi. In 1905 Clark went to New York to study at Columbia University and was awarded the LL.B. two years later. Upon his return to Cheyenne he established a legal practice specializing in irrigation problems and later in petroleum affairs. On June 24, 1908, Clark married Joyce Broady, and eventually had two sons.

During his twelve years as a lawyer in Cheyenne, the young Clark was drawn into Democratic politics. He was chairman of the Democratic County Convention in 1908. When he was twenty-seven years old, he was a delegate to the 1912 National Convention and a member of the Resolutions Committee in Baltimore when Woodrow Wilson, the governor of New Jersey, was nominated. By the time of the next presidential campaign, Clark had already spent a year as the city attorney of Cheyenne, and was appointed chairman of the Democratic State Convention. In 1917, after his term as city attorney had ended, he became president of the chamber of commerce and served on the school board from 1911 to 1917. Other work from 1907 to 1919 included a position as the chairman of the committee that drafted the act for the commission form of city government (1911) and the act organizing the state highway department (1917). Being appointed in 1911 special assistant to the Attorney General of the United States, he served as counsel from 1911 to 1917 for Wyoming in interstate litigation over Laramie River rights in the Supreme Court of the United States.

After World War I, Clark's interests turned away from law and politics in favor of the business world. Such changes in career and intellectual pursuits were not uncommon in his life. Indeed, as an interview in *Harper's Magazine* puts it, "Mr. Clark says depreciatingly that he has never found it satisfactory to stick to one line for long." From 1919 to 1928 Clark worked for the petroleum industry in several capacities. Starting as general counsel of the Midwest Refining Company in Denver, he sat on the board of directors and in 1921 became a vice president. Three years later, the company was bought by the Standard Oil Company of Indiana as part of its drive to become a completely vertically integrated oil company. In 1926, when Clark was appointed president of the Midwest Refining Company, the consolidated parent was the world's largest manufacturer of gasoline. While still a director of Standard Oil, Clark sat on other boards of related companies and also participated in several federal and state investigations of the petroleum industry. In addition to business activities, he was appointed a delegate of the Rotary Club of Chicago to an international convention in Ostend in 1927 and, in the following year, was elected vice president of the Denver Chamber of Commerce.

In 1928 the corporate executive decided to change his professional path yet again. At the age of forty-four, he returned to academe to prepare for a career as a teacher and thus fulfill a lifelong ambition. Johns Hopkins University admitted Clark to the doctoral program which he completed in 1931 by successfully defending his Ph.D. dissertation, *The Federal Trust Policy*.

By examining the goals and accomplishments of the antitrust laws, Clark strives to prove that the policy is indeed a satisfactory compromise. The historical focus starts with the Sherman Act and continues through the era of Theodore Roosevelt, the Clayton and Federal Trade Commission acts to 1931. In Clark's nomenclature, there are four ways of dealing with the price mechanism:

1. The government owns all the means of production. Such a program would severely limit individual incentive and industry.
2. Complete laissez-faire. Historically, this classical liberalism has been open to abuses and endangered the public. (The Standard Oil Trust is mentioned in this regard.)
3. Let ''combinations'' continue as long as economies of scale prove economically advantageous.
4. The Sherman Act. This legislation does not prohibit all and any economic combinations; it addresses itself to trusts which eliminate competition.

Clearly, the extremes of socialism and laissez-faire do not appeal to Clark, who wanted to preserve the economic efficiency of capitalism while checking its abuses of power. As he expressed it, ''The problem is to protect the public from price exploitation while maintaining that economic system which best insures economic progress.''

The Sherman Act is hailed as a ''successful statute'' since it does not prohibit all mergers and consolidations, yet simultaneously discourages monolithic price fixers. Indeed, Clark claims that competition is a direct result of the act and attacks businessmen who complain that the Sherman Act is too successful (that is, competition is excessive). Furthermore, Clark remarks that the depressions of 1907, 1921, and 1929 cannot be imputed exclusively to the Sherman Act, as depressions occurred before the act. Moreover, the economy had seen periods of both prosperity and depression. Clark views the Sherman Act as the perfect law that straddles the extremes of the right and the left.

Clark's dissertation, published in 1931, is not a rigorous microeconomic study of how trusts affect prices and markets; in truth, little quantitative analysis is performed, and some sweeping generalizations are made without detailed supporting proof, as in his assertion that the act has actually fostered competition. However, in the context of his life and thought as a whole, what is striking in the dissertation is his moderation and search for a balance between extremes of policy. In praising the efficiency of the free market, he does not hesitate to single out its abuses, and ultimately endeavors to preserve the better aspects of the system while correcting its excesses. Such a spirit of compromise was typical of Clark.

In a discussion in the *American Economic Review* of March 1933, Clark's remarks on stabilizing oil output concede that the Sherman Act was being ignored by the Department of Justice. The objective appeared to be one of limiting output to ensure the maintenance of existing producers. Although he admits that the approach was extralegal, it was still a flexible and temporary expedient. Moreover, the producers will argue for repeal as soon as the oil glut diminishes. Plainly Clark was not rigidly interpreting the Sherman Act and was willing to tolerate short-term deviations if economically desirable.

Having been elected to Phi Beta Kappa in 1931, Clark taught as a professor at the University of Denver. In November 1934 the American Bar Association asked him to sit on a committee investigating New Deal agencies. After a professorship at the University of Nebraska, Clark was named in March 1936 to a five-member team advising a Senate committee on how to reorganize the executive department for efficiency and economy. In 1939 Clark left Washington, D.C., not to return as an active participant until 1946, when Truman appointed him to the Council of Economic Advisers.

Meanwhile, the extraordinary policies of the Roosevelt era did not turn Clark into a doctrinaire New Dealer. While enthusiastic about his Columbia Law School classmate, Clark assailed Roosevelt's NRA program. Supporting other New Deal policies, he rejected monetary manipulation and the public works schemes.

From 1937 to 1945, Clark took part in local academic, political, and business affairs. He lectured at the University of Denver during 1937–41 and eventually was elected to the Wyoming legislature, serving in 1941 under the Republican Governor N. H. Smith. Clark also sat on the Wyoming Council of National Defense. Concurrently, he was made dean of the College of Business Administration at the University of Nebraska while maintaining a post in the economics department. Clark also found time to be a director of the American National Bank of Cheyenne, which he helped to organize, and of the Omaha branch Federal Reserve Bank. Moreover, he was president of the American Finance Association in 1943 and sat on the Nebraska State Development Committee over the next two years.

Finally, Clark was recalled to the nation's capital in 1946 at the apogee of his career as one of the three original members of the President's Council of Economic Advisers. In the wake of the Employment Act of 1946, which called for full employment, output, and income, President Truman appointed Edwin G. Nourse*, Leon H. Keyserling*, and Clark to the Council.

The news of Clark's elevation drew various comments and reactions. Some considered him the most conservative of the trio; others regarded him as a foe of monopoly since he was recommended by antitrust Senator Joseph O'Mahoney. John J. Corson, a journalist, conceded that Clark was solidly based but unextraordinary. The *Nation's Business* viewed him as a nonextremist of high quality. Clark as a person was perhaps best sketched in an interview with *Harper's* magazine in 1949:

> Slight of build, moderate of stature, he has a mobile face which you feel you have seen in many English-speaking lands . . . more like a businessman, or lawyer, than an academician; he is definitely relaxed, not tense. . . . Mr. Clark, at least on casual encounter, strikes one as fascinated by the "game", whether of politics or life in general, rather than troubled by visions of ultimate purpose. Yet Mr. Clark is definitely not frivolous. He simply isn't solemn.

The reporter quite correctly discerned Clark's interest in "the game" and the political ramifications of economics.

Clark's interpretation of the purpose of the Council of Economic Advisers and the Employment Act was more activist than Nourse's, yet probably not as much as Keyserling would have liked to see. Again, Clark emerges as the moderate seeking a balance. In his writings he has argued that the Employment Act of 1946 is by no means a commitment to state planning of the economy. In his eyes, the job of the Council of Economic Advisers was to examine economic policies, their effectiveness, and to what extent the various branches and bureaus contributed to achieving economic policy goals.

Meanwhile, the problems of macroeconomic policy were addressed in the first *Economic Report of the President*, prepared and signed by all three Council members. Emerging from the Great Depression, policy makers were anxious to avoid a new slump while the Council was warning about the dangers of inflation. Clark in particular was disturbed during the postwar years by the higher cost of living and escalating profits and wages, which, in his view, would ultimately lead to a collapse and rapid deflation.

His concerns were strongly voiced in his testimony on February 9, 1949, before Congress in which he depicted the dangers of an unstable boom-bust economy. Clark advocated two firm measures to stabilize the economy: provide a floor to support agricultural prices, and dampen the rise of industrial prices via demand management. Specifically, Clark favored imposing corporate taxes; allowing the Federal Reserve System to increase reserve requirements and control installment credit; encouraging individuals to invest more in savings bonds; and controlling commodity exchanges, and even prices and wages.

Such a summary of Clark's position sounds quite interventionist and unlikely to agree with the usual laissez-faire view of an oil executive and bank director. However, if one reads Clark's testimony carefully, it is clear that he is attempting to placate the business sector and even criticizes some aspects of more liberal policy. For example, he takes pains to point out that the latest tax proposal would still leave corporate after-tax profits higher than in 1946 and 1947, two years of tremendous capital investment. The Federal Reserve's policy of debt management (maintaining Treasury bonds at par) is admittedly "inflationary" (but indispensable to economic stability), and the wage and price controls are in reality limited to certain applications such as delaying increases in vital industrial prices like steel for a certain period of time pending government investigation. Likewise, labor contracts in the steel industry should be subject to arbitration if wages escalate too rapidly.

By the middle of 1949, Clark felt that inflation was moderating and that a recession could be avoided. In his summary of the president's midyear economic report, Clark enumerates the government's stabilizers to cushion the effects of economic cycles. The Federal Reserve System provides liquidity to forestall credit collapses, the Federal Deposit Insurance Corporation (FDIC) prevents runs on banks, farm prices are supported and farmers need not fear farm foreclosures, the jobless are protected to some degree by unemployment insurance, and so forth. Significantly, the subject of price controls does not loom as large as in the February report. Ostensibly, the easing of economic vigor in 1949 relieved the Council of the obligation to pursue further the politically unpleasant matter of strict price controls. Clark's version of such controls was less than fully interventionist, as the February report showed, and Nourse was quite opposed to the idea. Hence, in his July summary, Clark, in shifting emphasis from fighting inflation—already beginning to abate—to avoiding a sharp decline in industrial output.

Although the Council was established to advise the president on economic matters, Clark and Keyserling had broadened their scope to include testifying on Capitol Hill (Nourse, in contrast, refused to appear before committees).

Clark, who was appointed vice chairman of the Council on May 10, 1950, left the Council on February 11, 1953, and published two articles shortly thereafter. The articles are interesting in so far as Clark, now free from his official responsibilities and their inevitable politics, reveals more of his opinions and feelings.

After leaving his post Clark argued for the continuation of the Council of Economic Advisers in its present form and not replace it, as proposed, by one economist who would be a member of the president's confidential staff. In the context of stabilizing farm prices, Clark points out that the other committees and organizations dealing with the agricultural sectors assuage the farmers' economic problems only after a crisis has built up; the advantage of the CEA is its broad macroeconomic outlook, allowing it to foresee and correct economic problems before they distress the farmers directly. Moreover, Clark says that the

CEA has been open to Congressional and public demands for expert opinion and communication on economic issues; presumably one economist directly reporting to the president would not be as accessible.

Finally, in the May 1953 issue of the *Journal of Finance*, in "Gaps in the Patman Committee Report," Clark made some caustic remarks on the uselessness of monetary policy as a weapon against inflation, which had reemerged by late 1950 as the crucial concern of the Council. Clark ascribes much of the success in slowing down wholesale prices in early 1951 not to the Federal Reserve's new monetary policy of reducing reserves and forcing up interest rates but to the price freeze instituted on January 20 of that year. To fight inflation by open market operations and higher rates is to take a dangerous economic road. Only through higher industrial output can the cost of living ultimately be controlled. Indeed, if monetary growth is to be manipulated at all, then Clark favors only a policy of rationing bank loans and allocating credit. Interest rates should not be allowed to rise, and open market operations are useless.

Of greater interest is Clark's description of the internal politics surrounding the famous accord between the Treasury and the Federal Reserve in 1951. Previously, the central bank's policy goals had been subject to those of the Treasury. Since government bond prices were maintained at par, and interest rates were suposed to be relatively stable, the Federal Reserve had no scope to pursue an active monetarist policy to influence macroeconomic trends. Even by raising reserve requirements in 1948 to slow down the overheating economy, the central bank had to supply reserves at the discount window by purchasing government bonds at par from the commercial banks. Thus rates were hardly affected.

On February 19, 1951, the Federal Reserve issued an "ultimatum" to the Treasury stating that it would no longer maintain the par value of government bonds. Clearly, this ultimatum was also a declaration of independence and the expression of a power struggle between the Treasury and the Fed.

Certainly the debate behind closed doors was not entirely dispassionate, and Clark implies that the Council of Economic Advisers took sides with the Treasury. The president then reiterated the need to support government debt prices at par and even quoted an older statute, exhumed by the Treasury, giving him the executive power to restrain the expansion of bank loans. The latter point was surely a warning to the Federal Reserve that its limited power would be curtailed even more.

Despite the combined forces of the president, the Treasury, and the Council of Economic Advisers, the Federal Reserve renounced the par value program and emerged with far greater independence after the accord was announced on March 6. Clark's retelling of the background suggested that the Council was not simply standing on the sidelines during this historically important decision. On reading this article, one again is aware not only of Clark the economist but also of Clark the politician.

Another striking aspect of the article is the absence of Clark's usual moderation. Moreover, his strongly stated dislike of monetary policy adds a very sharp tone to the prose. Doubtless he was both intellectually opposed to the accord and pleased that he could express himself freely after leaving the Council.

In 1951 Clark retired from public life in Washington, D.C., and returned to Cheyenne, Wyoming, where he took up his law practice and was reelected a director of American National Bank of Cheyenne. Eventually he became chairman of the board. Occasionally he lectured out of state on economic affairs.

His first wife, Joyce Broady, passed away in 1957, and Clark was remarried to Mrs. Robert N. (Alice) Mattson, a judge's widow. In turn, she passed away on September 12, 1961. Clark himself died at his home on November 6, 1961, apparently of massive heart failure. He and Joyce Broady had two sons, Robert G. Clark, a lawyer, and John Broady Clark, who died in 1951. John Clark was survived by his son Robert and five grandchildren.

BIBLIOGRAPHY

Clark, John D. ''Gaps in the Patman Committee Report.'' *Journal of Finance* 9 (May 1953): 206–11.

———. ''Stabilization of the Oil Industry.'' *American Economic Review* (March 1933): 81–84.

Grattan, C. Harley. ''Truman's Three Wise Men.'' *Harper's* 198 (June 1949): 54–60.

MASON J. KLINCK

DAVIS, JOSEPH STANCLIFFE

(b. November 5, 1885, d. January 3, 1975), CEA May 2, 1955-October 31, 1958

Joseph Stancliffe Davis was an agricultural economist and an advocate of modified free market policies. His prolific writings on agricultural matters are pervaded by a consistent philosophy of limited government planning as a necessary supplement to economic forces.

Davis was born on a small farm in Chester County, Pennsylvania. His parents, William Harmar Davis and Mary [Charles Siddall] Davis, were of Welsh descent. Joseph became self-supporting at the age of fourteen, when his father died leaving virtually no estate. After graduating from West Chester State Normal School, he taught for two years in rural Pennsylvania schools. In 1904 Davis went to Harvard University, where he received his B.A. in economics and history, summa cum laude, in 1908, and his Ph.D. in economics in 1913. At Harvard, he was an active debater and, as a practicing Congregationalist, a member of the Harvard University Christian Association.

Davis continued at Harvard as a member of the faculty and a contributing editor of the *Review of Economic Statistics* until 1921. Because of inadequate eyesight, he did not serve in the armed forces during World War I. He did, however, interrupt his Harvard career in 1918 to spend a year in London as a statistician for the Allied Maritime Transport Council. This assignment followed the publication, in 1917, of his first book. An extension of his dissertation, *Essays in the Earlier History of American Corporations* was a two-volume work on the colonial history of American corporations.

Davis moved to Stanford University, where he was one of three original directors of the Food Research Institute, in 1921. He was chosen for the post by his co-directors, who were scientists, because they saw the need for his economic expertise in analyzing world food problems. At the time, Davis knew little about food, agriculture, and marketing. After his move, he continued to write occasional articles on European economic and financial developments for several years.

Most of the writings which emerged from Davis' thirty-year career at the institute, however, focused on the economic and political aspects of agricultural policy. Among the best known is the twenty-volume *Wheat Studies*, published from 1925 to 1944, which he edited. Davis also wrote numerous essays analyzing the problems and policies associated with the agricultural crisis of the Depression and World War II eras. He consistently opposed excessive government interference with market mechanisms and maintained a faith in the benevolent workings of the invisible hand. Still, he recognized the need for some public planning in the agricultural sector.

Early in his career, Davis began to argue that the prevalent fear of a food shortage was a "bogey." His faith in the development of technology and his reading of history convinced him that resource constraints would not limit American food production for the foreseeable future. By 1949, however, the unforeseen postwar baby boom led him to write *The Population Upsurge in the United States*, where he predicted that the surprising growth in population would lead to food shortages. His view on the subject is further expressed by his 1954 article, "Adam Smith and the Human Stomach," in which he criticizes the alarmist view of impending food shortage while conceding that the entire world is not and will not in the foreseeable future be well fed.

This moderate position was characteristic of Davis' overall philosophy. He was always conscious of the variable nature of economic conditions and was careful to advocate policies that would be flexible enough to accommodate changing conditions. While he served as chief economist for the Federal Farm Board from 1929 to 1931, Davis worked for the development of farmers' cooperatives. He considered efforts of this nature to ameliorate agricultural surpluses to be superior to the development of specific price and production controls. He was concerned throughout his professional life about the danger of specific income support policies implemented in times of emegency becoming permanent programs which hampered the workings of the market.

Davis saw a particular danger of overplanning in the agricultural sector resulting from the prevailing faith in "agricultural fundamentalism." Davis used this term to describe the belief that agriculture was unique in its role as the primary industry in the economy. Agricultural fundamentalists held that support of farm prices and farm incomes was justified by the special role played by food and food production in the maintenance of the entire society. While granting the essential nature of agricultural produce, Davis argued that the farm sector constituted only a small fraction of the entire food industry. As society advanced, manufacturing industries became more and more important, while the agricultural sector of the economy carried less and less weight. He had little patience with the argument that maintenance of a large farm sector was necessary to the moral fiber of society.

In his 1934 essay, "Agricultural Fundamentalism," Davis took the position that despite the overall importance of food, the low incomes of farmers were a sign of the low marginal value of agricultural production. While measures were necessary to protect nonreproducible resources and to mitigate fluctuations in farm incomes, farm prices should not be raised to artificially high levels. Such price supports would encourage too many resources to be devoted to this sector of the economy. Low incomes and the resulting exodus of marginal farmers into other occupations were necessary and healthy developments.

Davis did recognize the weaknesses of the market system in agriculture. Thus, a focus on optimal planning for the agricultural sector accompanied his ceaseless warnings about the dangers of too much planning and of allowing emergency measures to develop into permanent market interference. In 1934 Davis argued, in "On Economic Planning," that while comprehensive planning had glaring deficiencies, gradual implementation of planning for the coordination of efforts and for the rational achievement of stated goals was a necessary step for American agriculture. Davis favored the formation of a federal farm board to coordinate policy and of an international body to further the stability of the agricultural sector.

In his work on international commodity agreements, undertaken less out of personal interest than from the desire for Rockefeller Foundation funding, Davis made his characteristic argument that many commodity problems could be attributed to erroneous policy. He expressed support for international agreements that would allow flexible policy, while promoting international harmony and moderating agricultural cycles. He was also concerned with protecting the interests of weak nations and groups within nations and with improving the levels of consumption, employment, productivity, and trade throughout the world economy. His philosophy in the international arena, as well as on the domestic front, supported government attempts to moderate market outcomes, without imposing rigid price supports and production quotas which would hurt consumers and misallocate resources.

Davis' comments tended, in general, to be more critical of current attempts to strengthen farm income than those of his colleagues. In a joint report, written with Edwin Nourse* and John Black in 1937, Davis amended the committee statements on the success of the Depression policies by reiterating his hesitation with regard to overregulation of the markets. One of his recurring concerns was the possibility of political maneuvering by special interest groups which would detract from the ability of policies to achieve their stated goals.

Davis was convinced that the longer necessary emergency provisions remained in place, the less effective they would be. People would learn to manipulate the rules to avoid complying with their intent, and the special circumstances for which the policies were designed would change. This was an argument in favor of flexible policy design, a requirement for which Davis frequently expressed support. In line with this perspective, Davis was always critical of parity formulas for price and income maintenance. He considered such a reference point too rigid and probably too high to be realistic.

In spite of his warnings against the extent of market control existing in Depression and post-Depression agricultural policy, Davis was careful not to argue that the outcome of market forces was optimal or should be left alone. To Davis, market place forces were always moving the economy to an equilibrium. However, the process would be accelerated given the increase of understanding of the processes at work, and at less cost.

While production controls and price supports were policies which should be reserved for emergency situations, laissez-faire was not the optimal policy, even in normal times. The doubts Davis expressed in the last years of his life about the ability of the economy to avoid another serious depression were a further indication of his belief in the necessity of government intervention.

In line with Davis' criticism of the federal agricultural policies of the 1930s and 1940s as overly restrictive was his disagreement with the prevailing notion of the miserable plight of the farmers. While Davis recognized that farmers had suffered serious income declines, he considered the notion of farmers as an underprivileged class unfounded. Agricultural prices had to be allowed to fall at times, and marginal farmers had to shift into more profitable enterprises. His answer to wheat surpluses was not a network of restrictions, which would be inconsistent in a free and democratic world. Instead, he proposed efforts to expand consumption, facilitate the dispersion of stocks, and accept temporarily low prices. Davis thought that the agricultural market should be perceived from the consumer's perspective as well as from the point of view of the farmer. Artificially high prices were not a viable solution. The government's intrusion in the marketplace should take the form of encouragement with assistance.

In the late 1940s, Davis' interests turned away from agricultural economics, in the direction of consumption economics and standards and levels of living. He continued to work in these areas intermittently for the remainder of his career.

Davis had extensive nonacademic professional involvement before serving on the Council of Economic Advisers. In 1924 he was a member of the staff of the Dawes Commission on Reparations, and in 1928 he participated in a study of the fiscal and economic position of Mexico. Davis was chief economist at the Federal Farm Board from 1929 to 1931. He accepted this position only because he felt that he could not decently refuse, and found it a difficult and unrewarding assignment. He was also a member of the Food and Nutrition Board of the National Research Council from 1940 to 1945 and a member of the Institute of Pacific Relations from 1941 to 1947.

In the course of his career, Davis was president of the American Statistical Association and the American Farm Economic Association, both in 1936. He achieved the honor of being elected president of the American Economic Association for the 1944 term.

Joseph Davis came out of retirement in 1955 to become a member of Eisenhower's Council of Economic Advisers, under Arthur Burns*. He attributed his selection largely to his 1953–54 service as economic adviser to the President's Commission on Foreign Economic Policy and to a 1954 paper entitled "The Economic Potentials of the United States." As with previous government appointments, he accepted this position on the Council reluctantly.

Davis' three-and-a-half-year service occurred during an era of national concern over declining farm incomes. Although farmers' relative incomes were higher in the 1950s than in the prewar period, their real incomes had declined considerably since their wartime highs. The result was increasing pressure from farm groups for government support. Even an economically conservative Republican administration was forced, during this period, to institute extensive farm support programs.

Davis' philosophy of restraint held that the necessary subsidies of the 1930s had been kept in place too long and should have been withdrawn as farm incomes rose. These ideas were welcome to more disinterested observers. In an editorial comment on the day after Davis' nomination, the *New York Times* praised him for his opposition to "unsound, politically motivated panaceas." It also noted the persistent awareness in Davis' work of the hazards of allowing the special interests of farmers to obscure national interests.

During Davis' tenure on the CEA, the Eisenhower administration actively addressed the problem of mounting agricultural surpluses with policies for which Davis could have only guarded support. Eisenhower's politically motivated concern with the preservation of family farming as a way of life necessary to the preservation of the social order was in direct conflict with Davis' opposition to agricultural fundamentalism. Davis did, however, feel that the federal government had a responsibility to maintain conditions favorable to more stable farm incomes. Moreover, he was concerned with the details of specific programs which he perceived as temporarily necessary.

Davis resigned from the Council in 1958 at the age of seventy-two and returned to retirement. He perceived his term there as a rewarding but tiring experience. In the following years, his main concern was with the care of his wife, Florence, who had been seriously crippled by a stroke. Friends saw him mellowing into a warmer personality during this period. When Davis died in 1975 in Los Altos, California, at the age of eighty-nine, he left a daughter, Christine and two sons, Robert and Joseph, Jr., as well as four grandchildren.

Joseph Davis considered himself more talented as a researcher than as a teacher, and always considered his research of the highest priority. He claimed to have no desire for government jobs, feeling that he could render better public service in a private capacity. Nonetheless, he spent over seven years working for the federal government because of his strong sense of civic duty. While he is remembered primarily as an agricultural economist, he preferred to think of himself as more of a general economist. Davis perceived his standing in the profession to be damaged by his failure to concentrate more narrowly and by his lack of interest in modern technical developments. However, the honors and appointments bestowed upon him during his career, the respect with which he is remembered by colleagues, and his prolific and insightful writings all testify to his outstanding ability and performance as an economist and public servant.

BIBLIOGRAPHY

Davis, Joseph. *Essays in the Earlier History of American Corporations*. Cambridge, Mass.: Harvard University Press, 1917.

———. *International Commodity Agreements: Hope, Illusion or Menace?* New York: Committee on International Economic Policy, 1947.

———. *On Agricultural Policy, 1926–1938*. Stanford: Food Research Institute, 1939.

———. *The Population Upsurge in the United States*. War-Peace Pamphlets, No. 12. Stanford: Food Research Institute, 1949.

SANDRA R. BAUM

DUESENBERRY, JAMES STEMBLE
(b. July 18, 1918), CEA February 2, 1966-June 30, 1968

In retrospect, the last half-decade of the 1960s can be clearly seen as the period when the seeds of the inflationary instability of the seventies were sown. For those who took part in the policy-making process at the time, however, the view was quite different. For them, the optimism and enthusiasm of the Kennedy years had scarcely begun to fade. The battle against the excessive unemployment associated with the ''GNP gap'' had been decisively won. They were confident that the weapons at their disposal were adequate to defeat the two remainng villains, poverty and the business cycle, in equally decisive fashion.

On December 27, 1965, President Johnson nominated James Stemble Duesenberry to the Council of Economic Advisers to replace Otto Eckstein*, who was leaving the Council to return to his teaching duties at Harvard. Professor Duesenberry's appointment was confirmed by the Senate on January 24, 1966, and he was sworn in as a member of the Council on February 2, 1966. He served for a period of almost two and one-half years, and on June 30, 1968, he resigned his position on the Council to return to teaching. His colleagues on the Council during most of this period were Gardner Ackley*, who served as chairman, and Arthur Okun*, who replaced Ackley as chairman when the latter was appointed ambassador to Italy on February 15, 1968. While publicly Duesenberry often seemed overshadowed by these two dominant personalities, the imprint of his presence is clearly visible in the economic policy record.

As a young teenager, Duesenberry undoubtedly observed the economic hardship brought on by the Great Depression in his native state of West Virginia. As was characteristic of so many economists of his generation, his motivation in studying economics was to gain sufficient knowledge of the functioning of the economic system to be able to prevent such a disaster from ever recurring.

He entered the University of Michigan as a freshman in 1935. As an undergraduate he roomed with Robert Roosa, who would also ultimately play an important role in economic policy making, serving as an Undersecretary of the Treasury Department in the Kennedy administration. Duesenberry graduated from Michigan with an A.B. degree in economics in June 1939 and stayed on to enter the Ph.D. program there in the fall of that year. By the time of the U.S. entry into World War II, he had earned his master's degree (1941) and was well on his way to the completion of his doctorate. Pearl Harbor interrupted his studies, however, and he joined the Army Air Corps as a private in 1942. He was not destined to see action overseas however. In light of his technical training, he was put to work as a statistician. In that capacity he was soon promoted to officer status and left the Air Corps as a captain when the war ended in 1945.

Having completed his coursework at Michigan before the war, he took a temporary position as an instructor at Massachusetts Institute of Technology for the spring semester of 1946 and set to work on his doctoral dissertation. In the fall of that year he accepted a position as a teaching fellow at Harvard University, where he was destined to stay for the remainder of his professional career.

Duesenberry completed his dissertation and was awarded the Ph.D. from Michigan in 1948 (it should not go unnoted that Gardner Ackley sat on his thesis committee). His work brought him immediate national attention and was published as *Income, Saving and the Theory of Consumer Behavior* by the Harvard University Press in 1949. The importance of this contribution can be readily appreciated if it is noted that statistical studies of consumer saving done up to the end of the war showed a significant positive correlation between household disposable income and the savings rate. Because of this finding it was widely feared that, with the inevitable decline in government outlays at the end of the war, private investment expenditures would be insufficient to absorb the predicted huge flow of private savings. The result would be a deficiency of demand that would plunge the economy back into a state of general depression.

In his dissertation Duesenberry argued that the apparent positive correlation between the savings rate and income was a statistical artifact of the Great Depression caused by a phenomenon he called the "ratchet effect." During business cycle peaks (such as occurred in 1929) households become accustomed to high levels of consumption. They attempt to maintain this standard when their incomes fall in the subsequent contraction. As they do so their savings rate will fall, but will rise again when incomes rise during the recovery phase of the cycle. This phenomenon was responsible for the strong correlation between income and the savings rate found in data covering the period of the Depression. (The National Income Accounts data, on which many of these studies were based, began in 1929.) But, argued Duesenberry, this correlation could not be used to predict consumer behavior after the war. The large household incomes generated by the economic expansion during the war would raise the living standards aspired to by households so that levels of economic expenditure more consistent with historical savings rates could be anticipated.

Duesenberry's prediction was, of course, almost immediately vindicated. After a brief lull in 1946, the economy took off on a post-war boom fueled by the strength of consumer spending. Since he had predicted this outcome entirely on the basis of prewar data, he became an instant celebrity, at least among economists. This brilliant initial accomplishment launched him on a long and successful career as a member of Harvard's star-studded economics faculty.

Although alternative theories of consumer behavior have arisen that have largely supplanted Duesenberry's "relative income hypothesis" as the generally accepted explanation of the cyclical behavior of the savings rate, his theory contains a uniqueness that would continue to distinguish his work from that of the majority of subsequent theorists. Rather than basing his theory solely on purely economic principles, he made explicit use of the psychological concept of habit formation. This willingness to step outside the narrow confines of traditional economic theory to find commonsense solutions to practical economic problems was to be a hallmark of his work throughout the remainder of his career.

During the 1950s he made important contributions over a wide range of fields from economic development to business cycles and the theory of economic growth in mature economies. As the decade drew to a close, however, his attention began to focus on the many practical problems associated with the conduct of monetary policy. In his characteristic commonsense fashion he began to realize that the important issues in this area could not be resolved without systematically taking into account the institutional structure of the monetary system. This approach led him to a pioneering role in the development of the now widely used system of ''flow of funds'' accounting. This system allows the explicit tracking of the flow of credit from the initial act of saving through the labyrinth of the financial system to the ultimate borrower. This development led to a greatly increased understanding of the way in which monetary policy exerted its influence on the level of economic activity.

The prevailing view at the time was that a policy of tight money worked by forcing up the general level of interest rates. This had the effect of increasing the cost of borrowing in a fairly uniform way across all borrowers and thus had a general dampening effect on all interest-sensitive categories of spending. The then prevalent view that such spending was only mildly responsive to interest rate changes thus buttressed the Keynesian argument that monetary policy had a relatively weak effect on the economy. Analysis of the flow of funds revealed, however, that there was an additional and potentially much more powerful mechanism at work. Since banks and other depository institutions operated in a strictly regulated environment, their interest rates were not free to respond quickly to market forces. As a result, a tight money policy that tended to increase the general level of interest rates would have the effect of drying up the flow of funds into these institutions as savers sought the higher yields now available in freer markets. When this occurred, those borrowers who traditionally rely on depository institutions as their primary source of funds (typically home buyers and small businesses) found themselves ''frozen out'' of the market.

Because of this ''credit rationing'' effect, Duesenberry argued that restrictive monetary policy could have a strong restraining effect on the economy but that the brunt of this restraint would be borne by the construction industry and small business. His findings thus buttressed the prevalent Keynesian view that monetary policy was like a string. It could be used to restrain an overheated economy (by pulling on the string), but it was not very useful for stimulating a sluggish economy (pushing on the string will accomplish little). Nonetheless, even when economic restraint was desirable, Duesenberry felt that a broad-based fiscal policy such as a general tax increase would be preferable to a restrictive monetary policy because of its more equitable impact on the economy.

It has been reported that, while he was deeply involved in this research,

Duesenberry was approached by the Kennedy administration with an offer of an appointment to the Council in 1963. He turned down the offer with the plea that he was too busy with his research. This choice of priorities seems, in retrospect, to have been precisely correct. When he was again called upon to serve by President Johnson he would find his study of financial markets particularly valuable. He nonetheless continued to serve as a consultant to the Council as he had done regularly since 1961.

When President Kennedy took office in the first quarter of 1961, the economy was mired in the recession that had begun early in the previous year. Of particular concern to Kennedy's economic advisers was the fact that the recession had come so quickly on the heels of the relatively severe recession of 1957–58. After peaking at 7.5 percent in mid–1958, the unemployment rate had barely fallen below 5 percent before it began to rise again in 1960. It was therefore felt that policies should be devised not only to reverse the current recession but to encourage sustained economic growth over the longer term. In order to focus the public's attention on this broad objective, the Council of Economic Advisers began to publish an estimate of "potential GNP." The difference between this estimate and actual GNP was dubbed the "GNP gap," and policies were prescribed that would close this gap at a prudent and deliberate pace.

In keeping with the predominantly Keynesian complexion of the Kennedy/Johnson advising team, the favored policy tool to be employed was fiscal policy as exemplified by the now famous tax cut of 1964. The Federal Reserve Board was encouraged to play an important but passive role—monetary policy was to be "accommodative." The monetary authority was to avoid pulling on the string in opposition to the expansionary goals of the administration's fiscal policies. While it took a little time to get all the pieces in place, the program was a huge success. By the time James Duesenberry took his seat on the Council, the GNP gap had been officially closed. The *Economic Report of the President* for 1966 showed first quarter GNP to be slightly above potential GNP, an event heralded by the report as "a major economic accomplishment."

As he settled into his new job, then, Duesenberry was joining a group that was flushed with victory. They could be justly proud of their past accomplishments. It was not a time, however, for them to rest on their laurels. They seem to have recognized that the task of *maintaining* prosperity and encouraging the continued growth of economic potential could well be more difficult than attaining it.

This concern was heightened by the fact that the closing of the GNP gap had not been accomplished entirely according to plan. While the Council would like to have seen the growth rate of GNP taper off gradually as that goal was approached so that the growth path of GNP "eased onto" a path roughly coincident with that of potential GNP, the investment boom that had been building since the early sixties accelerated dramatically in 1965, transforming the final assault on potential GNP into a mad dash that was bound to overshoot its target. In response to this, the Council had already begun recommending the dismantling of the stimulative fiscal policies that had been put in place. In January 1966 President Johnson sent to Congress, along with Duesenberry's nomination, a recommendation that certain excise taxes that had recently been repealed be reinstated. This recommendation was enacted by Congress as the Tax Adjustment Act of 1966 in March.

Despite these worries, the mood of the Council and, indeed, of the majority of economists, can only be described as confident and optimistic. It was widely believed that Keynesian economics had conquered the business cycle. After five full years of uninterrupted economic expansion, few expected a recession to occur in the foreseeable future. It would not be too much of an exaggeration to say that the Council was absolutely convinced that the tools of fiscal and monetary policy were adequate to prevent such an event from ever occurring again. The problems they faced were those of "fine tuning." They recognized a trade off between inflation and unemployment—the goal was to choose the lowest unemployment rate (about 4 percent, in their judgment) consistent with a politically acceptable rate of inflation and to devise policy measures that would maintain the unemployment rate at that level. At the same time they were optimistic that additional policy measures could be devised that would allow the unemployment rate goal to be reduced.

The Federal Reserve board did not seem at the time to be quite as strongly wedded to the goal of "full employment." In the spring of 1966 the Fed abandoned the "accommodating" role it had played throughout the 1960s expansion and slammed on the monetary brakes. The result was the infamous "credit crunch" of 1966.

Duesenberry and his colleagues at the CEA were, of course, strongly opposed to this action by the Fed. The consequences were precisely what Duesenberry's research had predicted. Interest rates rose dramatically by historical standards, but the effect on business investment was quite mild. The impact of the crunch was felt primarily by home buyers and small businesses as the flow of funds through the depository institutions serving these groups virtually dried up. The CEA immediately set to work to lobby the Fed to softening its policy stance and to work out changes in the regulatory rules that would serve to reduce the distortion in the flow of funds. They were successful on both counts. Before the end of 1966 the Fed abandoned its tight money policy, and the credit crunch was over—interest rates began to fall.

Having successfully limited the consequences of the credit crunch to a mere "growth recession" or "mini-recession" (that an episode in which the unemployment rate failed to exceed 4 percent could be referred to in these terms serves to illustrate the extreme economic optimism of the times), the Council turned its attention to devising policies to minimize the adverse economic impact of the war in Vietnam. In this effort they faced three major obstacles. The first was the inability (or perhaps the political reluctance) of the Johnson administration to provide the Council with reliable prior estimates of the scope or duration of the war. The second, political opposition to the Council's recommendations by the Congress. The third, and perhaps the most important, was the limited nature of the economic theories upon which their policy recommendations were based. Included among these theories was Duesenberry's own relative income hypothesis.

While the Council was certainly aware of the potentially inflationary impact of the high level of expenditures associated with the war, the problem of devising appropriate offsetting policy actions was considerably complicated by assurances from the administration that the war could end at any time. Thus, as early as 1966 the Council was busy devising demobilization plans to counter the economically depressing consequences of a sudden decrease in military spending. Given the Council's overriding concern to maintain "full employment," they were reluctant to put in place any restrictive fiscal measure that could not be quickly dismantled in case of a cessation of hostilities. Their solution to this problem was an explicitly temporary income tax surcharge. This measure was expected to have the same restrictive effect on consumer spending as a permanent tax increase but would have the advantage that no additional legislation was required to rescind it at the end of the war, but it could be renewed as necessary if the war continued. The recommendation for a 6 percent income tax surcharge applicable for only one year (1968) was sent to Congress in January 1967.

The difficulties this measure encountered in the Congress have come to exemplify the political obstacles that make fiscal policy an unwieldy countercycle tool. While some resistance was anticipated from conservative legislators who would have preferred cutting some of the Great Society programs as a means to fiscal restraint, what was not fully anticipated was the reluctance of a large group of Democrats who balked at imposing a tax aimed at financing a war which they opposed. The combined strength of these two groups was sufficient to delay passage of the measure for almost a full year and a half, even though the vast majority in the Congress clearly recognized the need for some form of fiscal restraint. By the time it was finally enacted into law in June 1968, economic realities required that the 6 percent be increased to 10 percent, and James Duesenberry was cleaning out his desk in preparation for his return to academia.

The income tax surcharge turned out to be too little and too late. When Duesenberry left his post on the Council the inflation rate was running at 5 percent per year and increasing. But it seems doubtful that earlier enactment of the income tax surcharge would have changed this outcome sufficiently. The inadequacy of the policy measure was twofold. First, it was too weak a measure to have a significant impact on aggregate demand. In its deliberations, the Council failed to consider adequately the possibility that a *temporary* tax measure might have a much smaller impact on consumer spending than a permanent one. A popular explanation for this failure is that Duesenberry's theory of consumer behavior failed to distinguish between temporary and permanent changes in disposable income. More recently developed competing theories, most notably Milton Friedman's "permanent income hypothesis," did make such a distinction and predicted a much smaller impact for temporary changes. The mild response of consumer spending to the income tax surcharge when it was finally enacted was generally received by the economics profession as a piece of evidence supporting Friedman's theory over Duesenberry's.

Second, and perhaps more important, was the absence of any strong economic rationale for the Council's ultimate policy objective. The presumption that an unemployment rate target below 4 percent could be maintained indefinitely without accelerating inflation was just that—a presumption. Such a policy had never been tried before, so there was no reliable way of knowing whether or not it would work. The result was a grand and ultimately quite costly experiment that demonstrated that it would not work. Selecting an optimistically low unemployment rate target and asking the Fed to "accommodate" monetary policy to achieve that target required the Fed to subordinate its traditional responsibility for maintaining the purchasing power of the currency to this new goal. The result was a loss of control over the price level.

James Duesenberry returned to Harvard in the summer of 1968 with unemployment safely below 4 percent. While he seems to have been much more comfortable in his customary professional role, he did not shun further involvement in the public arena. In 1969 he accepted an appointment as chairman of the board of the Federal Reserve Bank of Boston, a position he held until 1974. In 1972 he was made chairman of the department of economics at Harvard. In this position he skillfully guided the department through some particularly difficult times, including a period of considerable dissention following the denial of tenure to some of the department's radical members. When he stepped down from the chairmanship in 1977, the department had firmly reestablished its traditional role of leadership in the field. James Duesenberry returned to the department to serve as professor of money and banking.

BIBLIOGRAPHY

Duesenberry, James. *Business Cycles and Economic Growth.* New York: McGraw-Hill, 1957.

———. *Income, Saving and the Theory of Consumer Behavior.* Cambridge, Mass.: Harvard University Press, 1949.

———. *Money and Credit: Impact and Control.* New York: Prentice-Hall, 1964.

———; Bostwick, Barry; and Carron, Andrew S. *Capital Needs in the Seventies.* Washington, D.C.: Brookings Institution, 1975.

———; Mayer, Thomas; and Aliber, Robert E. *Money, Banking and the Economy.* New York: Norton, 1981.

JAMES M. HVIDDING

EADS, GEORGE C.
(b. March 3, 1942), CEA June 6, 1979-January 20, 1981

George Eads was born in Clarksville, Texas, where his father worked as a machinist in a World War II production plant. After being transferred to Houston and Galveston, his father settled in Yuma, Arizona. When a back injury forced him to quit work as a machinist, he began his career in cotton and lettuce farming. Yuma, a small town on the Colorado River, is surrounded by a desert bigger than the combined states of Rhode Island, Connecticut, and Massachusetts. This isolated area is best known in the daily weather reports as the hottest place in the United States. In school George's interest in music outweighed his interest in sports, and he played trombone in school bands from the time he was in junior high school until he completed his graduate education. His and his younger brother's fascination for music was encouraged by their mother, an elementary school teacher.

After graduating from Yuma High School, Eads began his undergraduate studies at Wesleyan University, where he studied for one year before transferring to the University of Colorado in the fall of 1961. A Phi Beta Kappa scholar, he graduated summa cum laude in 1964 with a major in economics. After getting married, he began graduate school at Yale University. He was awarded two Woodrow Wilson Fellowships and a Ford Foundation Fellowship in Business and Economics on his path to the completion of the Doctor of Philosophy degree in 1968.

Upon finishing his graduate studies at Yale, Eads' first faculty appointment was at Harvard, where he stayed for two years. After another two-year faculty position in the economics department at Princeton University, he began his first term in government service as special assistant to the Attorney General in the Antitrust Division of the Justice Department. During his stay in Washington, D.C., he was offered a position at George Washington University and returned to academe as an associate professor. In 1974 he left the university to join the newly formed Executive Office's Council on Wage and Price Stability, which was headed by Albert Rees. After service as assistant director of government operations and research, he was made executive director for another government organization, the National Commission on Supplies and Shortages. This temporary commission studied ways the government contributes to and can help alleviate materials supply problems. Its report, *Government and the Nation's Resources*, was presented to the president and Congress in December 1976.

Eads resigned his government position in 1977 to join the Rand Corporation (a nonprofit research organization) as a senior economist. He continued to do work for various government agencies through government research contracts with Rand. As principal investigator for the Environmental Protection Agency study on nonaerosol fluorocarbon emissions, he directed research to determine the most cost-effective way to regulate such industrial uses of fluorocarbons as refrigeration equipment, solvents, and quick freezing of food. He also continued a National Science Foundation grant originally obtained by Lee Johnson, a former employee of Rand's California office in Santa Monica, to study cross-subsidization in federal regulation of business.

In Santa Monica, Eads organized and directed Rand's Regulatory Policies and Institutions Program. The program was designed to aid government decision making on regulatory processes in the areas of energy, health, urban policy, and housing. Eads remained at Rand until 1979, when he returned to Washington to begin his two-year term with the Council of Economic Advisers.

In addition to his full-time appointments, Eads served as a consultant to the Department of Justice, Department of Transportation, Civil Aeronautics Board (CAB), National Science Foundation, Office of Technology Assessment, and the Council of Economic Advisers (prior to his own appointment), as well as Frontier Airlines.

He admits to a certain lack of organization in his working habits, which he has jokingly referred to as the reason for his inability to hold a job for more than two years. An early riser, he works quickly on a variety of small projects on the government's relationship to business rather than concentrating all his time on one project. This preference no doubt contributes to his organizational problems, but made him well suited to the demands of the Council.

In the early part of his career, before he joined Rand Corporation, most of Eads' professional papers concerned the regulated transportation industries. The first of these involved statistical estimation of long-run airline cost and demand equations for air travel. Next, appealing to a wider audience, were his papers on the government's role in promoting technological advances in civilian aviation and the effect of airline regulation on capacity utilization, cost performance, growth strategy, and fare levels. His book, *The Local Service Airline Experiment*, focused on the inefficiency created by the CAB regulations and subsidization policies concerning local airlines. In his conclusion he recommended a change in the subsidy program to selecting the least-cost airline operator through a bid system rather than the old system, which excluded cost considerations (this has since been done), and an end to CAB's control over entry into the national airline industry. This book, and his 1975 Brookings Institution article on promoting competition in the trunk airline industry, expressed the economic arguments that influenced the congressmen that wrote and voted for the airline deregulation legislation in 1978. Other regulation papers covered telecommunications. George Eads also wrote reviews for economic journals on books concerned with the transportation industry and other regulatory issues.

Beginning in 1977 his published works took a broader perspective on the relationship between government and business. No doubt his 1975–77 term on the National Commission on Supplies and Shortages and his new affiliation with

Rand as a senior economist and program director gave him the experience and interest to expand his scope. His first Rand staff report, *Achieving "Appropriate" Levels of Investment on Technological Change: What Have We Learned?*, transcended the traditional regulated industries area in which he was so well known. Later came papers on mineral supplies and shortages, regulation and technical change, and a unique view of the chemical industry as a "regulated" industry. The role of government to which he directed his attention concerned the safety, quality, and environmental regulations that applied to all industries. This new "social" regulation differed from the traditional regulation of the transportation industry and posed new problems, such as the increased sensitivity to the balancing of costs and benefits. George Eads' writings continued to broaden in this new direction, and his most recent publications have dealt with the issues of product safety regulation and the measurement of the costs and benefits of regulation. His vision of the government's relationship to business reached a pinnacle when he began his research on the broad, all-encompassing industrial policy of the United States. This study area includes all topics that relate government to business, including regulation, antitrust, environmental regulation, product and workplace safety, international trade restrictions, tax laws, and so on. These last few publications (written after he left the CEA) were influenced by his term on the CEA when he was faced with the same issues in advising President Carter on regulation reform.

The pattern of his publications is clear. Starting with an emphasis on a particular regulated industry—the airlines—he expanded his work to include other regulated transport industries. His view then broadened to the issues of social regulation, investment, and technology, and finally he encompassed all previous topics by writing about national policies toward business.

The nomination of Eads to the Council was made in the Senate on April 25, 1979. At this time Eads endorsed deregulation in some areas but not in others, expressed doubt that the cost of regulation was a primary cause of inflation, and pleaded for more flexibility in complying with regulations in a cost-effective manner. His views reflect a pragmatic approach to the role of government, consistent with the Carter campaign platform, although they are, for the most part, politically neutral.

The major microeconomic issues facing the Carter administration in 1979 and 1980 and Eads during his term on the Council were the challenge of meeting the nation's energy needs and improving the business sector performance of the economy. Eads, as a Council member, and Charles Schultze*, as the chairman of the Council of Economic Advisers, advised the president on the various proposals to reduce the nation's dependence on foreign oil and its vulnerability to domestic supply disruptions. Eads was thrown directly into a hot and important national issue. Quick judgments on the appropriate responses to the energy challenge were often required, and the application of economic principles was evident in the following evaluations. For the immediate period, the administration was trying to avoid large, sudden increases in the price of oil. By reducing demand for oil when faced with reductions in supply (such as that caused by the 1979 Iranian crisis), the United States and other oil importing nations hoped to soften the pressure on price increases. In the event of a severe supply disruption, the administration was ready to intervene in the marketplace with a standby motor fuel rationing plan. A fully operational Strategic Petroleum Reserve would also cushion an imported oil shortfall and buy time while other conservation measures were put in place.

For the longer view the administration was relying on the market system, permitting high oil prices to redirect energy use and encourage production. One such proposal was the gradual decontrol of natural gas and crude oil prices, which began in 1978. By January 1980 prices for domestically produced oil began to approach world prices. However, the administration was concerned about the secondary effects of crude oil decontrol: windfall profits for domestic oil producers and a reduction in real income for consumers. Once again, government intervention in the marketplace was rationalized with the resulting windfall profits tax, which redirected a significant portion of the private gains to public use, including aid to low-income households.

Conservation measures were also proposed by the Carter administration for residential space heating and cooling. Lower thermostat settings in households and increased insulation would reduce both energy use and cost. The administration's program required utilities to provide home ''energy audits'' for customers, financial assistance to households for energy use improvements, and special incentives to encourage solar energy use. It was hoped that these programs, together with previously enacted conservation legislation (such as the 1975 Energy Policy and Conservation Act, which mandated improvements in automobile fuel efficiency), would result in a substantial drop in the U.S. consumption of oil. The CEA, however, was skeptical of the effectiveness of income redistribution and home conservation plans, and considered these efforts as primarily window dressing.

With administration proposals to reduce demand and increase oil supplies, it was feared that not enough investment would be generated to provide new sources of energy. It was difficult to determine if the cost of synthetic fuel would be greater than the price of oil because future oil prices were hard to predict and, because of OPEC's control, not completely determined by market forces. Investors would be less likely to consider synthetic fuel projects unless oil prices were near the estimated cost to produce their alternative fuels. Given that the costs and technology were also uncertain, the administration established the Energy Security Coroporation to provide loans and other assistance to help private enterprises and reduce the risks that they would incur in developing synthetic fuel projects.

Government deregulation was part of President Carter's campaign pledge to limit the role of government as well as a prominent feature of his anti-inflation program. George Eads' background in this area was without equal, and he picked up where his CEA predecessor, William Nordhaus*, left off on such issues as the relationship between regulation and productivity, removing obsolete regulatory structures, and new approaches to regulatory reform.

The role of the CEA in these areas, which were also the domain of Congress and various administration agencies, is perhaps best illustrated by the work done by the interagency Regulatory Analysis Review Group (RARG). RARG was established by President Carter and was comprised of representatives from all executive branch economic and regulatory agencies. The agency was chaired by the CEA. It reviewed and commented on selected regulatory analyses and independently examined the impact of regulatory rules. Thus the CEA provided the administration with an independent and primarily economic view of regulatory reform issues, unfettered by attachment to longstanding agencies with their own special interests and constituents.

The Council was concerned whether there was an inverse relationship between regulation and productivity. A loss of measured productivity can occur when regulations divert capital and labor from the production of measurable goods to goods whose value is difficult to measure (for example, environmental cleanliness, workplace and product safety). When regulation yields benefits less than the cost of capital and labor, both measured and unmeasured productivity suffers. Finally, productivity is directly reduced by many government regulations such as trucking regulations that reduce competition and building codes that discourage innovation.

Removing obsolete regulatory structures takes the form of deregulating previously regulated industries because society's need for regulation no longer exists or never did. The Airline Deregulation Act of 1978 exemplifies the gradual phase-out of obsolete regulatory activities, and the CEA provided advice for similar action in the trucking, railroad, telecommunications, and finance industries.

Eads promoted the increased use of balancing costs and benefits in designing regulations, especially in the areas of the environment, health, and safety. With Executive Order 12044, the administration attempted to encourage balanced and cost-effective regulation by requiring regulatory analysis for executive branch agencies and departments. An analysis examining costs, burdens, and other possible alternatives must be prepared by agencies for each major regulation. The purpose of this analysis is to identify costs and burdens and to quantitatively analyze them, if possible. It is devised to help in the decision-making process and can also be used by the public to evaluate the objectives of the agencies. The president established the Regulatory Council, composed of thirty-six federal departments and agencies, to improve the coordination among various regulatory programs. In 1979, for example, the Regulatory Council began a comprehensive analysis of how regulation affects the automobile, coal, and nonferrous metal industries.

New approaches to social regulation are intended to modify the present "command-and-control" approach that uses detailed regulations to force compliance. The CEA favorably responded to the Environmental Protection Agency's (1) ''offset'' policy, under which new firm activities resulting in emissions will only be permitted if they can purchase reductions in the emissions from existing sources; and (2) ''bubble'' policy, which permits a company to trade reductions in pollution from one source for increases in pollution from another. These alternatives to the ''command-and-control'' approach increased the flexibility of traditional regulation and allowed firms to choose the lowest cost combinations of activities for a given level of pollution.

Another major area in which George Eads offered his expertise was international trade. The CEA addressed various trade policy issues (automobile import quotas, trigger price mechanism for steel imports, grain embargo, and so on) by holding a seat on the cabinet and sub-cabinet executive committees, including the Economic Policy Committee and the Trade Policy Committee. The chairman of the CEA, Charles Schultze, wanted to lead the way with CEA involvement on trade policy issues. However, with the Reagan administration the CEA has let these trade matters go to other agencies.

Eads was in a strong position to contribute in the international trade area, having served as a consultant to Special Group on Positive Adjustment Policies, the Economic Policy Committee, and the Organization for Economic Cooperation and Development (OECD). As a member of the CEA, he was U.S. representative on the OECD's Transparency Group. This group asked its members to look at their country's microeconomic policies (trade, regulation, agriculture, and so on), pull them together to constitute the nation's ''industrial policy,'' and see how they affect economic growth and development. The CEA has urged OECD nations to consider the fact that trade protection for home industries is costly since increased foreign competition for some domestic industries is beneficial to consumers (by offering lower-priced items) and to the nation by lowering the inflation rate. In the long run international trade benefits a nation through positive adjustment, by matching growth in imports with growth in exports.

After leaving the Council, George Eads rejoined the Rand Corporation for one year at its Washington office. His work there on industrial policy, product safety, and regulatory issues has led to several recent publications. In December 1981 Eads returned to academe as full professor in the School of Public Affairs at the University of Maryland, teaching courses such as policy analysis seminar on the Clean Air Act.

Although Eads no longer has to contend with the hectic pace of a Council member, he nevertheless has surrounded himself with a variety of projects concerning the instruments, techniques, and policies that government imposes on business. His broad experience in these areas makes his contributions particularly relevant and insightful, and his reputation in articulating the government's industrial policy is growing.

BIBLIOGRAPHY

Eads, George. *The Local Service Airline Experiment*. Washington, D.C.: Brookings Institution, 1972.

White, Lawrence. *Reforming Regulation: Processes and Problems*. Englewood Cliffs, N.J.: Prentice-Hall, 1981.

THOMAS H. BRUGGINK

ECKSTEIN, OTTO

(b. August 1, 1927, d. April 23, 1984), CEA September 2, 1964-February 1, 1966

Otto Eckstein came to the Council of Economic Advisers from Harvard University, where he was both a professor and editor of the prestigious *Review of Economics and Statistics*. When Walter Heller* suggested to President Johnson that he choose Eckstein as a replacement for John P. Lewis*, who left the Council to direct the U.S. Trade Mission to India, the president was positively gleeful. His reason: the diminutive (5 feet, 6 1/2 inch) Eckstein had received degrees from both Princeton (1951) and Harvard (1955); by contrast, none of President Kennedy's noted economic experts had such Ivy League credentials. At the September swearing-in ceremony, the president remarked with a grin, "Walter Heller and Gardner Ackley[*] may have the height on you, Dr. Eckstein, but we do expect you to add depth worthy of both Harvard and Princeton." Eckstein was expected to be the CEA's troubleshooter, probing new ways to bring economic policy to bear on such old problems as inflation, unemployment, and the balance of payments deficit.

At his August 1964 appearance before the Senate Eckstein received rave reviews from Senator Edward Kennedy and Senator William Proxmire. Both senators recognized Eckstein's qualifications and experience would be a highly regarded addition to the functioning of the Council. His expertise on water resource development was highlighted. Eckstein was, by that time, also a renowned expert on wage and price setting mechanisms, growth, and employment.

His appearance before the Senate was one of the shortest on record—about two pages of transcript—and Eckstein was asked only one question: "What are you going to advise the President on?" His answer was a confident "I will advise him on those things he wants advice on."

With the dynamic Eckstein on board, the CEA was touted as having "youth, class, brains, and drive."

Known as much for his prowess at collecting and interpreting data as for his theoretical insights, Eckstein had poured the ideological foundations for President Kennedy's "Let's get the country moving again" campaign in 1960 with his research publications on employment and economic growth. His thesis was that U.S. growth was too slow. He viewed the economic problem as how to keep things going and to simultaneously reduce the unemployment rate. Otto Eckstein had a fervent belief that growth and high employment would help the nation and the average citizen. More to the point, a healthy economy would benefit minorities and the poor even more. He was never convinced by the "natural rate of unemployment" hypothesis. The prospect of helping the disadvantaged was always in the forefront of Eckstein's thinking, given his keen social conscience and liberal ideology.

Under President Johnson, whom Eckstein admired greatly, the economic recovery continued. By September 1964, when Eckstein joined the CEA, the country had experienced an almost record peacetime recovery of forty months; the expansion appeared likely to continue into 1965. Johnson was proud of his achievements and his new Council; the fruits of the Great Society were being harvested. By early 1964, the U.S. economy showed record profits, above average gains in real GNP, relative price stability, the reduction of the balance of payments deficit to an annualized $500 million, and a reassuring decline of unemployment to 5.1 percent. Johnson, furthermore, was the first Democratic president since Grover Cleveland to have won the full confidence of business—something Kennedy had never achieved. And his CEA was applauded in the business and financial press.

These were halcyon years for the CEA. The increasing confidence of the public in the competence and judgment of the Council created an environment in which Johnson became increasingly dependent on his CEA. The willingness and ability of the Kennedy-Johnson CEA chairs to make modern Keynesian macrostabilization policy meaningful and understandable to members of Congress and to the public had significantly speeded up the acceptance of that policy and increased the public's support for existing fiscal policy. Indeed, the 1960s witnessed a coherent, dominant set of Keynesian voices in macroeconomic policy discussions; this included an awesome holy fraternity of Heller, James Tobin*, Ackley, Paul Samuelson, Eckstein, and Arthur Okun*.

Eckstein was born in Ulm, Germany, the son of a businessman, Hugo Eckstein. As a boy, he fled with his family to England in 1938 to escape the anti-Semitic policies of Hitler and eventually immigrated to the United States in 1939. He remembered from his childhood the misery that the Great Depression had brought to his family and others. He once claimed that his passion for economics dated to that period in his life. While many school boys yearned for a chemistry set, young Otto might have preferred an input-output matrix of the economy. In his yearbook at Stuyvesant High School in New York, he declared his goal of studying economics. This was, indeed, his calling and first love. Even later in life, when colleagues were involved in hobbies such as boating and skiing, Eckstein preferred his policy-oriented, applied economic research as "leisure" activity.

Eckstein became a U.S. citizen in 1945, and after serving in the U.S. Army Signal Corps as a private (in Japan) in 1946 and 1947, he majored in economics at Princeton University and graduated summa cum laude in 1951. He went on to Harvard, where he earned a master's degree in 1952 and a doctorate in 1955.

Several economists were influential in Eckstein's formative years. At Princeton his mentor had been the premier American economist, Jacob Viner, who recognized his talents and encouraged him to hone his analytical powers. When Eckstein arrived at Harvard in the fall of 1951, he already possessed skills beyond his peers. He had a unique graduate career: because of his exceptional Princeton training, he took an unprecedented action and opted not to take any formal courses or seminars. Instead, he spent his time reading and studying on his own. Arthur Smithies, then chair, allowed this option and became his Harvard mentor.

When Eckstein became an instructor in 1955, it was widely remarked that it was a rare, if not unique, step for Harvard to hire one of its own Ph.Ds—to ''devour its own young.'' Harvard was on a tutorial system, and he met his future wife, Hariett Mirkin, an economics major, when she was his tutee. Soon it dawned on them that a romantic attachment was forming; they descended on Smithies' office with their dilemma. Arthur lent a sympathetic ear and resolved the matter by reassigning Hariett to another tutor.

Eckstein became an assistant professor in 1957. In his early teaching career, he displayed a charming brashness. Harvard seemed slow to grant him tenure, and in 1959 he went to the University of Michigan for a job interview. He was then the ranking young man in macroeconomics and public finance. Although he would have preferred to remain at Harvard, after his seminar was over, he confidently told the faculty search committee, ''If Harvard doesn't appoint me this year, I'm going to quit.'' Even the great Harvard was not going to string him along. Early the next year he was appointed associate professor and granted tenure. He became a full professor in 1963 at thirty-six years of age. At the time of his death, he was the Paul M. Warburg Professor of Economics in the university.

Eckstein had completed his dissertation in 1955, later published in the Harvard Economic Studies series as *Water Resource Development: The Economics of Project Evaluation* (1958). His timing was perfect—this was the first comprehensive study of the federal government and the economy. The core of the theoretical model was published in the *Quarterly Journal of Economics* (1957). His lasting contributions included investment criteria relevant to benefit-cost analysis, as well as applications to flood control, navigation, irrigation, and electric power generation.

Eckstein's text, *Public Finance* (1967), led to his ''Four Rules'' to ensure an institutionalized process in the public sector which provides that basic economic principles are actually applied and receive a hearing in political decision making:

1. The organizational structure should be arranged in such a way that one decision unit is responsible for a given objective.
2. Costs must be viewed over a number of years covering the lifetime of the entire program.
3. Decision making is improved by creating an institutional setup under which pressures on the decision makers lead them in the direction of economic choice.
4. Procurement must leave incentives for efficiency.

Eckstein's papers on public finance remain classics in the professional literature. In discussing the economic benefits of public programs, he has insisted that distinctions be made between equity effect and efficiency effects. Efficiency alters the size of the pie, while equity involves the purely normative division of the pie among individuals in the economy.

Just a few months following his assignment in September 1964 to the Council Eckstein was entrusted with the task of studying steel price increases and their effect on the inflation rate. President Johnson needed a definitive and objective research study of the economic situation and the problems of the steel industry. From the president's policy perspective, the impending steel industry battle would prove the year's most important collective bargaining negotiation, the first general contract renewal in that industry since the memorable 1962 Kennedy confrontation over prices.

The president was shrewdly aware that his proposed new study, regardless of its empirical results and policy advice, was destined to be "zero sum": it would offend either business or labor. Thus he decided to pawn it off on the CEA rather than entrust it to his own White House staff. The president's strategy was to distance himself from its findings, relying on what would be publicly perceived as a more objective, dispassionate analysis, then basing decisions about the uses of the study's results on considerations of political expediency.

The study, done under the primary supervision and guidance of Eckstein, took some four months to complete and was released on May 1, 1965. Johnson's statement on the "Steel Study" became front page headlines in the May 4 *New York Times*. The two other CEA members, Ackley and Okun, specifically stated that they stood "firmly behind the conclusions."

Three days after the steel report made headlines, the Business Council met in Hot Springs, Virginia. Only a small minority of those business leaders present questioned the propriety of the government's intrusion into what steel prices ought to be. This congenial attitude was in marked contrast to the reaction of this same group and other business leaders in 1962 when President Kennedy publicly denounced as unjustified the price increase the industry attempted to put into effect. President Johnson's tactful approach, and Eckstein's scholarship, accounted for the reception by business of the new steel report.

At Johnson's request, Harvard granted Eckstein an additional year leave of absence to continue at the Council until early 1966. During that second year, a series of more intractable problems emerged with the Vietnam War buildup. In December 1965 Eckstein saw that with the anticipated increases in expenditures for Vietnam, government expenditures would rise appreciably. Since the U.S. economy was already operating at or near full employment, the CEA told Johnson that, to maintain budget flexibility and avoid inflationary pressure, he should ask for a significant increase in taxes. Unfortunately, an early tax increase proved for Johnson to be politically unfeasible in a Congressional election year. The president decided to avoid a certain defeat in Congress—to minimize his possible losses—and turned to a number of weaker tools to fight emerging inflation.

Eckstein loved Washington because of his influence as an inside person and because Washington was a tough place. Through the late 1960s, Otto Eckstein desperately tried to persuade Johnson that failure to raise taxes to cover the costs of the war would come back to haunt the country. The decade of the sixties closed with decided disillusionment. The year 1966 was a disaster for the guideposts—the tides of excess demand could not be talked down.

Four years after he left the CEA, Eckstein pondered whether a policy of benign neglect of the domestic economy would have done better than discretionary intervention in 1961–69. Eckstein believed that, if one considered the entire period, the record of the 1960s seems to repeat the verdict of the 1950s. Discretionary policy did harm as well as good. The automatic policy developed by the Committee for Economic Development in 1947, Eckstein believed, would have done better. But as Eckstein realized, the failures of fiscal policy in the 1960s had not been primarily failures in diagnosis and prescription, nor even in forecasting, although the forecasts were occasionally far off the mark. The failures were largely political, the most notable example being the absence of a tax increase in face of the inflationary pressure that accompanied the Vietnam experience.

Otto Eckstein accomplished many goals and gained many deeper economic insights during his two years in Washington. These were happy and exciting years for him and his family. While in the executive offices, he never forgot he was serving the president. He was outspoken and provided his insights candidly, even when they were at odds with what the president wanted to hear. But once the president made a decision, Eckstein became a team player in implementing the policies. Although he put in sixty-five hours a week, and perhaps more at budget time, he nevertheless found time to make numerous public speaking appearances, an assignment for which there was always excess demand. One of his favorite topics was the need for better information, more reliable and timely statistics, and more accurate forecasting models. He had a natural gift of humor. Always on the edge of their seats, audiences were highly entertained, even when Eckstein reviewed the ''boring'' statistical troops. He took economic analysis and revealed its mysteries to the ordinary citizen.

Before and after his Washington service, Eckstein was involved with many professional organizations. He was a fellow of the National Association of Business Economists and a member of the American Statistical Association and the Econometric Society. He served as vice president of the American Economic Association and as president of the Eastern Economic Association. Another important contribution to the Harvard department of economics was Eckstein's editorship of the *Review of Economics and Statistics*. He had become editor in 1964 after assisting his predecessor, Seymour Harris, for a number of years. When Eckstein returned to Harvard he reassumed his duties as editor and served in that capacity until 1971. As editor, Eckstein consolidated the transformation, initiated by Harris, of that journal into one of the foremost professional publications with a special focus on empirical research.

Two factors heightened Eckstein's interest in applied economics, econometric forecasting techniques, and policy analysis. First, his years at the CEA made him appreciate the need for better forecasts of the economy to improve fiscal policy timing and effectiveness. The "troika" was responsible for producing accurate GNP forecasts. These sectorial forecasts, in which a qualitative estimate of actual demand (GNP) was derived for estimates of major components of national income and product, were also policy forecasts which assumed enactment of the president's programs. The procedure was a blend of formal statistical and mathematical techniques and informed judgment, the weighing of each a function of the problem facing the troika, the adequacy of existing equations, and who was making the judgment. The equations themselves were kept a top-level secret. The model Eckstein developed at the Council consisted of between twenty and thirty equations which captured all important relationships in the national income accounts. It resembled an econometric model. One of the exogenous variables, government purchases, was introduced into the model, and the resulting output forecast was internally consistent.

Second, Eckstein was not enamored of the direction the economic profession was taking at Harvard and other leading universities. He knew theory and applied it pragmatically; he spoke rather harshly of the sophisticated mathematical models and abstract theories which were becoming fashionable, and seemed disillusioned with economic theory for its own sake, at levels of abstraction unrelated to the actual world.

Data Resources, Inc. (DRI), which he founded with Donald Marron in 1968, provided a perfect opportunity to explore a new dimension, allowing him to withdraw from the abstract theorizing that he saw as a dead end. He had already worked out his fundamental insights as to how the economy worked from his early input-output research under Wassily Leontief, even before his extensive studies of the American economy for Congress and his micro-macro economic analysis and modeling while at the CEA. Eckstein also relished the challenge of adding yet another facet to his portfolio of achievements.

Otto Eckstein's life was certainly not measured out with coffee spoons: he was blessed with a high metabolic rate. He is remembered as "the most caring of people." Always busy, Eckstein could bring order to any problem regardless of the original chaos. His four loves were teaching, public service, enterprise or company-building, and his family, including his three children, Warren Mathew, Felicia Ann, and June Beth.

As an economist's economist, Eckstein made many seminal contributions to the literature of public finance, benefit-cost analysis, macroeconomic modeling, wage-price models and core inflation theory. From his first publication in the *Quarterly Journal of Economics* (*QJE*) (1957) until his final article in the *Review of Economics and Statistics*, published shortly before his death, Eckstein published eight books, edited two others, and wrote six public reports and thirty professional journal articles and contributions to books. Many unpublished speeches and working papers are circulating, as well as additional comments on the research of others. A compendium volume of his works, edited by Roger Brinner (one of his former students), will soon be available as a fitting memorial.

In teaching and public service, Otto Eckstein basically wanted to use what he enjoyed most: exercising his economics skills to promote the greatest good for the greatest number. One story, recounted by a colleague, is illustrative of his dedication to teaching. Early in the Kennedy administration, there was an important meeting in Washington on fiscal policy. The meeting at the Treasury Department started promptly at 9 A.M., but Eckstein arrived late, at perhaps 11:00 or 11:30. As he sat down at the conference table, a colleague made the semi-reproachful remark, "You missed the most important part of the meeting." To which Eckstein, who had just arrived on the commuter flight from Harvard, replied, "I just couldn't miss my Ec 10 lecture—you never know, one of those students might someday be President of the United States."

While at Harvard, he made an indelible, permanent contribution to strengthening the introductory courses and rebuilding the undergraduate economics program. It has been observed that more Harvard undergraduates have heard Otto Eckstein than any other single lecturer in the 350-year history of Harvard.

In the late 1960s, a more radical wing tried to form a "counter-department," with its own Marxist courses, at Harvard. On the other side, the younger generation of economists seemed to be saying, "Anything other than rigorous mathematical models or Walrasian general equilibrium is junk." Eckstein had an interesting reaction to all this, although he did not participate actively in the ensuing policy battle, and professionally eschewed controversial welfare state or distribution problems. He was always interested in a just, fair society, but he was not a utopian or a Social Darwinist. He saw a role for government and social policy, but also believed strongly in markets, and that policy recommendations must pass muster in terms of efficiency.

BIBLIOGRAPHY

Eckstein, Otto. *Core Inflation*. Englewood Cliffs, N.J.: Prentice-Hall, 1981.
———. *The Great Recession*. New York: North-Holland, 1978.
———. *Public Finance*. Englewood Cliffs, N.J.: Prentice-Hall, 1967.
———. *Tax Policy and Core Inflation*. Washington, D.C.: Government Printing Office, 1980.

C. DANIEL VENCILL

FELDSTEIN, MARTIN
(b. November 25, 1939), CEA October 14, 1982-July 10, 1984

Martin Feldstein was born in 1939 to parents living in New York City. When Martin was ten years old, his father, an attorney then practicing in New York City, and his mother, a housewife, moved to Long Island, where Martin continued his education in the public schools. In 1957, the year that Martin entered Harvard, his father died. Shortly thereafter his mother began working as an executive secretary in the phonograph record industry.

His first inclination, upon entering Harvard, was to become a lawyer or a physician. However, after taking economics as a freshman, he selected economics as his major while completing the requirements for a premedical or prelegal course of study. His undergraduate dissertation, written under Thomas Schelling, a Harvard economist, reveals this combination of interests: it dealt with financing biomedical research.

After graduating from Harvard in 1961, Feldstein won a Fulbright Fellowship to study the British health service while attending graduate school at Oxford University in England. There, under the tutelage of Terrance W.M. Gorman, he studied and did econometric research on the British health system. It was at this time that Feldstein made a commitment to the economics profession.

He became a lecturer—in the British sense—in public finance at Oxford before returning to Harvard in 1965. By the time he completed his Ph.D. in 1967, he already had fifteen publications to his credit, including works in the *Oxford Economic Papers*, the *Review of Economic Studies*, *Economics*, *Kyklos*, the *Journal of the Royal Statistical Society*, and the *Economic Journal*.

Feldstein attained the rank of associate professor by 1969 and became a full professor at Harvard by 1977. From 1969 to 1977 he published no less than one hundred papers in every leading English language journal of economics including the *American Economic Review*, the *Journal of Political Economy*, the *National Tax Journal*, and in various volumes published by the National Bureau of Economic Research, as well as in numerous symposia and conferences. As of the date of his appointment to the CEA, his prolificacy since becoming a full professor at Harvard showed no sign of decline. His publication record from 1977 to the middle of 1982 numbered sixty-five papers, most of which are in academic journals.

Feldstein's family life is quite traditional. Although his wife Margaret has a Ph.D. in economics from M.I.T., she has been primarily responsible for raising their two daughters and taking care of their home. Their private life is simple. In addition to a home in Belmont, ten minutes from Harvard Square, they have a home in Vermont, providing a retreat where Feldstein, although neither a hunting nor fishing enthusiast, enjoys the outdoors. His major form of recreation, however, is economics.

Feldstein has been described as neither charmer nor wit, slow in speech and patient in explanations. To Feldstein content is more important than style. While switching from sweaters to pinstripes, his suits are always slightly rumpled as a touch of the professor comes through. He is known among his colleagues as a first class lecturer. When asked about his prominence in the profession, however, he says with a smile, "I'm just a humble scholar trying to do a few regressions."

Feldstein came to the Reagan administration at a time when the so-called supply-side experiment of tax and expenditure cuts seemed to be producing few of the predicted results. The unemployment rate had risen to more than 10 percent, and the economy was yielding signs of a very sluggish recovery. Moreover, the federal deficit was expected to fall between $150 and $200 billion, threatening to crowd out employment and expanding investment. Feldstein's research, at least during the last ten years, had stressed macroeconomic problems. He was the right person to replace Murray Weidenbaum*, an economist whose research and knowledge were largely confined to microeconomic issues.

Perhaps the best statement of the intellectual framework within which Feldstein operated as chairman of the Council of Economic Advisers is contained in a speech he gave a few months prior to his appointment.

> The new economic philosophy can be understood best as a retreat from the Keynesian ideas that have dominated economic policy for the past thirty-five years. A central feature of this revolution in economic thinking is the rejection of the Keynesian view that the way to raise income and reduce unemployment is to expand demand. Instead of Keynesian demand management, the new view focuses on capacity creation through capital formation and research.
>
> The new thinking also rejects the Keynesian fear of saving—the belief that a higher savings rate only creates unemployment, that Keynes developed in response to his British experience of the 1920's and 1930's. In its place we recognize that more saving is a prerequisite of the increased capital formation that can raise productivity and the standard of living. (Feldstein, "Conceptual Foundation")

He continues:

> There is of course nothing new in these ideas. They are in reality a return to the basic notion that Adam Smith expounded when he wrote *The Wealth of Nations* and that economists have believed and developed in the two centuries since the publication of that great work. We have known all along that a nation's wealth and prosperity depend ultimately on its capacity to produce and therefore on its stock of physical capital and the skills and efforts of its labor force, its entrepreneurs, and its investors. The economic rewards provided by our capitalist system are the key to obtaining the accumulation of capital, the willingness to take risks, the supply of entrepreneurship and the work effort of the general labor force. Moreover, the working of the free market without government

interference, will in general see that these resources and efforts are allocated to their most productive uses.

Feldstein came to the Reagan administration with a reputation for being a "conservative" economist. His brand of conservatism, however, is the product of evolution rather than predisposition, in much the same way that, according to George Stigler, most economists, as they mature, have moved to more free market oriented ideologies. This is a result of comparing the successes of market solutions (often labeled "conservative") with the failures of nonmarket (government interventionist or "liberal") solutions to important economic issues.

For Feldstein, researching the area of health economics had proved fruitful. A large proportion of British government expenditures went to its health system. Many raw data existed that had not yet been analyzed. Upon returning to the United States, he extended his investigation into the U.S. health system and the practice of third party payments used to finance its service. He discovered that health insurance distorted decisions and caused relative prices of health care to increase. His research led him to the conclusion that the market ought to play a larger role in the allocation process, and that the role played by the third party payment system ought to be trimmed.

Feldstein feels that his current "conservative" (he doesn't like the word) attitude is the inevitable view of an economist who has examined the evidence about the way the system was actually working, and has drawn the conclusion that a return to a more market oriented system would increase efficiency.

Thus it was in the microeconomic area that Feldstein first began to identify the distorting effects of government involvement in the economy. His interest in health economics and health insurance led him into the whole field of social insurance, including the areas of Social Security and unemployment compensation. He created a little industry for himself, identifying the impact of these programs on capital formation, a topic which has continued to sustain his interest since his graduate school days at Oxford.

The seeds of Feldstein's emphasis on the study of savings and capital formation were probably sown in his undergraduate days at Harvard, and later at Oxford. The political hue and cry that he heard was to "get the country moving again." Economic growth models—centered around the Harrod-Domar version—provided the intellectual framework within which economists would try to implement that political mandate.

The essence of these models identified an economy's long-term rate of growth as being dependent upon the productivity of capital and the savings rate—the productivity of capital being viewed as a technological variable, the savings rate as a variable reflecting the availability of resources for capital formation. Since these growth models were developed and promoted by ardent Keynesians, the importance of maintaining the savings rate through policy actions was downplayed. The primary concern was capital formation and technological progress, and governments were expected to develop policies which promoted both. In their attempt to do so, however, they also developed policies which discouraged savings, thus violating one of the principal policy implications of the growth models. They created a combination of anti-saving policies and pronouncements, which has nurtured an anti-saving attitude among the U.S. population. This is augmented with tax rules that penalize savings, a social security program that discourages savings, credit markets that foster mortgages and limit returns to the small saver. Add to this government deficits that absorb savings and resources for investment. It is little wonder why capital formation had fallen to the point where net investments for plant and equipment at the end of the 1970s dropped to 2.5 percent of GNP.

Feldstein prefers to distinguish between well-founded programs that the administration has implemented, and the extremes of supply side theory originally used to sell the program. He feels that the new economic policy implemented by the Reagan administration is based upon a real evolution in Congressional thinking—thinking which produced a program that, in fact, went further than the administration would have gone, that is, to the use of indexing to adjust tax rates for inflation and the various tax adjustments for corporations and investors. He sees the new fiscal program, in combination with a slower growth in the money supply, as the prescription for undoing the damage inflicted upon the economy by Washington during the 1960s and 1970s. It was during this period that high inflation, a low rate of capital formation, and a decline in productivity growth resulted from too rapid a growth in the money supply and excessive growth in government spending and taxation. All of this combined to crowd out private investment and reduce private incentives to work and save.

Furthermore, he sees as a crucial feature of the new approach to economic policy the complete rejection of the Keynesian fear of saving and a recognition that a higher savings rate—produced by such things as the expanded Individual Retirement Account provisions, tax reductions for investment and business income, the slowing of inflation, and a removal of interest rate ceilings for small savers—would benefit the economy by freeing resources for capital formation.

As for all the arguments—both pro and con—associated with the "supply-side" tax cuts, Feldstein has observed that what was actually achieved was much closer to real spending cuts (in fact, a reduction in the growth of government spending) without any real personal tax cut. This result was due, he observed, to "bracket creep" (the effects of inflation on the average personal tax rate) and the increase in Social Security taxes. Moreover, to reduce the swelling federal deficit, which he sees as a major threat to capital formation, Feldstein favors further reductions in federal expenditures—especially in revenue sharing, Medicare, and Medicaid, and various welfare programs, as well as slowing the growth of Social Security benefits—and, if necessary, an increase in government tax revenues.

This, according to Feldstein, was the game plan when he was chairman. He considered the 1981–82 recession as indispensable and inevitable in the process of reducing inflation, the continued success of which depends on a continued

Fed policy of slow money supply growth *and* on the continuation of slowing the growth of government spending.

Toward the end of 1983, however, as projections of future budget deficits grew larger and larger, Feldstein, contrary to Reagan administration policy and strategy, publicly began calling for increasing tax revenues. Such a view was anathema to other members of the president's staff, to strict supply siders, and to some editorial writers. Nevertheless, in spite of the disfavor of administration officials, Feldstein, in speech after speech and interview after interview, continued his public appeal for higher tax revenues to reduce future deficits.

In spite of the media flap and the apparent policy conflict within the administration—there were others calling for tax increases, including David Stockman, the director of the Office of Management and Budget—Feldstein completed his anticipated two-year tenure as chairman of the CEA and returned to Harvard on schedule in August 1984, the time set by the university if he was to continue his tenure there. In fact, by April 1984, *Newsweek* reasoned that Feldstein evolved into a team player. There was expressed relief by some in the administration that Feldstein would no longer command headlines.

With all the speculation in late 1983 as to when he would resign, very little attention was given to the motive or meaning behind Feldstein's actions, and to the reason why he was not fired from his post as chairman of the CEA. One possible explanation, and a favorite of the media-minded, is the "flagpole theory." Feldstein was to test the winds for using a tax increase to reduce the deficit. Whatever the truth of this, the winds responded with a loud "no" when, after Feldstein's departure, the president was reelected in 1984, running on a no tax increase platform and carrying forty-nine states.

An alternative, and more plausible, view is that Feldstein's call for an increase in tax revenues was not inconsistent with another Reagan administration objective, a reduction in government spending. Indeed, in all of his speeches the two were always coupled. This probably reflects Feldstein's training as an economist and his interest in viewing the economy from a "real," rather than "nominal," point of view.

The basic principles of economics teach that real taxes are best measured by government expenditures rather than government revenues. Real taxes are those actual goods and services, or resources, which the government takes from the private sector for its purposes. Nominal taxes are simply the government's total dollar tax receipts from all sources other than borrowing. The difference between real taxes, that is, government expenditures, and nominal taxes, is the deficit. In pushing for a combination of higher tax revenues to reduce the deficit *and* significant reductions in government spending, Feldstein was not only arguing for higher nominal taxes, but also for lower real taxes. He was arguing for less "crowding out," a return of the economy's resources to private use where they are employed more efficiently to promote the growth of output and employment.

It is difficult at this time to assess Feldstein's impact. His early ideas and research findings seem to have been more influential in shaping economic policy than his chairmanship of the CEA. For instance, he has argued that taxing unemployment benefits would serve to increase incentives for recipients to get back to work. Although it is difficult to establish causality, his research in this area could only have contributed to the consequent imposition—in 1978 and 1982—of limitations on the tax-free status of those benefits. Moreover, the press credited him for the idea when it reemerged shortly after he became chairman of the CEA.

Within the administration, his thinking during the first half of his tenure is known to have been highly regarded. It has been reported that Feldstein was always on hand when other economic advisers and confidants were speaking to the president. Indeed, while Treasury Secretary Donald Regan was arguing for accelerating the final installment of the tax cut—due July 1983—Feldstein is known to have opposed such a move. The idea was never formally proposed to Congress.

In late January 1983, it was reported that the president would be asking Congress to consider taxing medical insurance premiums as income, something that was part of the tax reform plan offered by the Reagan administration. This was undoubtedly a Feldstein idea designed to reduce the excessive use of third party payments for health care, a major factor in the rising cost of medical care and a concern Feldstein had demonstrated years before when he was studying the health care industry.

Martin Feldstein has returned to his role as an ''academic scribbler'' and continues to speak as frankly as he did when he was chairman of the CEA.

BIBLIOGRAPHY

Feldstein, Martin. *The American Economy in Transition*. Chicago: University of Chicago Press, 1980.

———. *Capital Taxation*. Cambridge, Mass.: Harvard University Press, 1983.

———. ''The Conceptual Foundation of Supply Side Economics.'' Paper delivered at a conference held at Atlanta Federal Reserve Bank in conjunction with Emory University, March 1, 1982.

———. *Inflation, Tax Rules, and Capital Formation*. Chicago: University of Chicago Press, 1983.

———. *New Directions in Public Health Care*. San Francisco: Institute for Contemporary Studies, 1976.

ANDREW WEINTRAUB

FELLNER, WILLIAM J.
(b. May 31, 1905, d. September 15, 1983), CEA October 31, 1973-February 25, 1975

Since the inception of the Council of Economic Advisers in 1946, successive administrations have had to contend with the question of the Council's proper political role. A natural tension exists between economists on the Council, drawn mainly from the academic world, and the presidents who appoint them. Sound economic advice is not always politically palatable. President Johnson insisted that Walter Heller* not go public with his belief in the need for a tax increase in the 1960s. Martin Feldstein's* public warnings about budget deficits led the Reagan administration to openly consider the abolition of the Council or harnessing it under the control of the Treasury or Commerce departments.

In the fall of 1973 the proper political role of the Council was at issue. Critics felt that the Council had taken too active a role in the 1972 presidential campaign and was prone to serving the political needs of the Nixon administration in its official pronouncements on economic performance. These complaints eased when the Watergate-beleaguered Nixon nominated William J. Fellner to fill the Council vacancy created by the departure of Marina von Neumann Whitman.* This careful choice helped assure the continued independence and integrity of the Council in the public mind and stands as a tribute to Fellner's stature. He was little known outside of his profession, but his nomination was widely praised by academic economists aware of his scholarly achievements and independence of mind. Though he was generally conservative on most issues, Fellner's selection was supported by leading economists from all schools of thought.

William John Fellner was born in Budapest, Hungary, the youngest of four brothers. The Fellner family ran several manufacturing enterprises founded by William's grandfather in the 1860s. William's early education included attendance at a Lutheran gymnasium which stressed Latin and other classical studies. This background no doubt added to the scholarly tone of his later work. The year following his graduation was spent working in a family-owned factory. He then enrolled at the University of Budapest to study law, but remained there only one year. Because the family business included the manufacture of sugar, alcohol, and paper, Fellner was encouraged by his father to undertake technical study at the Federal Institute of Technology in Zurich, where he earned a diploma in chemical engineering in 1927.

While in Zurich, he formed important friendships with two fellow Hungarians. He met John von Neumann, who was to become a famed mathematician and economic thinker, and began a long friendship that many years later led to much travel between Princeton and Yale for both. (Almost a half century later Fellner was appointed to the Council to replace Marina von Neumann Whitman, the daughter of his great friend.) Fellner's other close companion in Zurich was Emery Reves, who lured him to his first economics class. Fellner was immediately drawn to economics and was able to gain family permission to pursue advanced study in economics at the University of Berlin. He was accompanied to Berlin by his two friends. Von Neumann was to study mathematics at the same university, and Reves became a journalist with a Berlin newspaper and gained some prominence with his interviews and profiles of leading European political figures.

Fellner completed his Ph.D. in 1929 with high honors. His doctoral dissertation, reflecting an early interest in the United States, examined the economic effects of Prohibition. He left Berlin to rejoin his three brothers in Budapest as a partner in the family manufacturing business. William was much younger than his brothers and was especially close to the oldest, Paul, who emerged as leader within the family and eventually became a member of the Hungarian Parliament. (Following World War II, Fellner was instrumental in resettling all of his brothers to California.) Responsibilities within the family business increased for the brothers when their father died in 1934. In January 1936 William Fellner and Valerie Korek were married in Budapest. His wife recalls his days in 1930s Budapest as fully occupied with business matters while his continuing interest in economics was nourished by night. Fellner read economics into the late hours, and weekly meetings with two business associates who shared his fascination were devoted to discussion and debate. On occasion he would attend a professional economics conference. His hopes for an academic career steadily grew.

Fellner had come to the belief that the future direction of the economics discipline would be dominated by British and, especially, American economists. His visits to the United States in 1928 and 1934 left him favorably impressed with the country. In 1938 he and his wife left Budapest to settle in California. (They did not return to their native Hungary until 1971. Their return had its triumphant side; a lecture given by this conservative economist from the West had to be moved to the largest auditorium at the University of Budapest to accommodate an overflow audience.)

In 1939 Fellner joined the faculty of the University of California at Berkeley as a lecturer in economics. By 1944 he had become a U.S. citizen and was rising rapidly through the academic ranks, reaching full professor in 1947. His scholarly activity began in earnest at Berkeley with the publication of three major books between 1942 and 1949.

A Treatise on War Inflation (1942) was written while he was an assistant professor and was the first publication of the University of California's newly formed Bureau of Business and Economic Research, of which Fellner was a member. In his book Fellner attempted to devise an equitable and noninflationary approach to war finance. He recommended a program of monetary restraint, taxation of redundant income by use of the progressive individual income tax, and compulsory saving. Increased corporate taxation was to be avoided so that incentives and efficiency in the postwar period would not be hindered.

Monetary Policies and Full Employment (1946), also published under the auspices of the Bureau of Business and Economic Research, takes issue with the notion that mature economies tend toward mass stagnation, blaming the Great Depression on inept government policy. Fellner goes on to oppose an unconditional full employment guarantee, which he believes would be used by monopoly elements to raise wages and prices. A noninflationary guarantee would necessitate direct controls. His alternative would avoid both mass stagnation and direct controls, and the radical institutional changes that would accompany either. His policy prescription has a very Keynesian ring, calling for expansionary fiscal and monetary policies at the first sign of a recession, with the stimulus to be eliminated when business investment revives or inflationary pressures appear. An acceptable level of employment would be assured without the dangers inherent in a rigid full employment guarantee. Fellner's distaste for the inflationary potential of an employment guarantee foreshadows a position he adopted years later as a Council member when he argued that the target unemployment rate was set too low.

Fellner showed his scholarly versatility with a book on microeconomics entitled *Competition Among the Few* (1949). A thorough and largely nonmathematical exposition of the various oligopoly theories and bilateral monopoly is presented along with some extensions of the standard treatment. Coverage includes the Stackelberg solution, institutional considerations, social welfare effects, and public policy issues. One notable feature of Fellner's analysis is the replacement of the restrictive Cournot-Edgeworth assumptions with mathematical reaction functions to model the mutual interdependencies of oligopolistic rivals. Though not well received by all reviewers at its publication, the book has stood the test of time and has continued to be commonly cited as a standard reference on oligopoly theory in advanced textbooks. While at Berkeley, Fellner contributed numerous articles to the leading journals on topics such as bilateral monopoly and the effect of uncertainty on the firm's price decision.

As McCarthyism rose to the forefront of the American political scene in the late 1940s and early 1950s, controversy raged throughout the California state university system over the question of faculty loyalty oaths. About this time Fellner began to contemplate a move to the East Coast to be closer to the more influential academic institutions of the day and the center of policy making in Washington. The inhospitable atmosphere in California may have added some urgency to his thinking. He was visiting professor at Harvard University for the 1950–51 academic year. Lloyd G. Reynolds, then chairman of the Yale economics department, was recruiting several prominent European-born economists. In 1952, following Henry Wallich* and Robert Triffin by one year, Fellner became professor of economics at Yale.

Honorary membership in Phi Beta Kappa in 1952 and continued service as a

Treasury Department consultant gave Fellner recognition beyond the immediate circle of academic economists. He was the Alfred Marshall Lecturer at Cambridge University in England for 1957–58 and became Sterling Professor of Economics at Yale in 1959. From 1959 to 1960 he served as a member of the Paris-based Office of European Econonic Cooperation Committee of International Experts on Rising Prices. When some of his Yale colleagues, most notably James Tobin*, accepted posts in the Kennedy administration, Fellner gave them his encouragement, accepting an increased teaching burden and serving as economics department chairman from 1962 to 1964 to ease the staff shortage. In 1964 a regular series of conferences between academic economists and Central Bank–Treasury officials from Western governments began for the purpose of discussing the problem of international payments imbalances. The participants became known as the Bellagio group (its first meeting was in Bellagio, Italy); Fellner was an active member, serving on its organizing committee. In 1969 he was elected president of the American Economic Association, the professional achievement said to have given him the greatest personal satisfaction.

During his many years at Yale, Fellner continued to be a prolific author. The thesis of his *Trends and Cycles in Economic Activity* (1956) is that sustained economic growth depends on three factors. The first is an economy's capacity to offset diminishing returns with technological and organizational improvements (the inclusion of organization is reminiscent of Alfred Marshall's idea that invention augmented by organizational improvement lends added credence to a law of increasing returns). The other two factors are resource mobility and a flexible monetary mechanism to provide price stability. One chapter of the book furnishes an exceptionally readable narrative on major world economic downturns since 1825.

To fill a gap in the Yale curriculum, Fellner offered a course on economic thought; his lectures from this course formed the basis of *The Emergence and Content of Modern Economic Analysis* (1960). This book focuses on contemporary economic analysis and benefits from Fellner's strong historical orientation.

Fellner's longstanding interest in the effect of uncertainty on economic behavior culminated in the publication of *Probability and Profit* (1965). The book is an outgrowth of his contribution to a symposium of articles on decision making under uncertainty published in the *Quarterly Journal of Economics* in November 1961. Observed behavior held to be irrational by the standard axioms of decision theory is rationalized by Fellner's concept of semiprobability. When subjective probabilities are precarious, they can be "slanted" (revised downward) to form semiprobabilities. These decision weights can be used to calculate the expected change in utility from a given course of action. Several applications are presented. In one suggestive of an earlier journal article, Fellner concludes that average cost pricing may be a rational tendency in the face of uncertainty. This book was written when hopes were high that expected utility concepts could be applied to a host of real world problems. In later years such hopes faded.

As a result of Fellner's continued participation in the Bellagio group, he edited

Maintaining and Restoring Balance in International Payments (1966) with Fritz Machlup and Robert Triffin, and contributed two essays to the volume. One essay elaborated on the payments problems of concern at the time, and the other urged the adoption of proposals to allow greater exchange rate flexibility.

By 1970 Fellner had begun his long association with the American Enterprise Institute for Public Policy Research (AEI) in Washington, D.C., and was having more frequent contacts with top administration policy advisers. In the summer of 1970 he was one of a group of economists who held consultations with Paul McCracken*, then Nixon's chairman of the Council of Economic Advisers, to identify policy areas in which AEI study would be helpful. The outcome was *Economic Policy and Inflation in the Sixties* (1972), a volume of essays published by the AEI which reviewed past policy mistakes and made suggestions for the conduct of future policy. Fellner provided the volume's introduction and one essay in which he outlined a policy position that he was later to strongly advocate as a Council member. His view was that demand-side management to achieve full employment targets inevitably produces chronic and accelerating inflation. This would then require policy restraint. The cycle of stop-go would continue. He ruled out direct controls because they would lead to shortages and were incompatible with the American political system. His "second-best solution" called for a noninflationary monetary-fiscal policy mix coupled with a public sector jobs program to provide work for those who would otherwise be unemployed due to the adoption of his noninflationary target unemployment rate. Like most other conservative economists, he regarded inflation as the major economic menace. However, he was not doctrinaire in his conservatism, and there was nothing to prevent his advocacy of a jobs program to improve the political feasibility of his other proposals. Fellner believed that the policy mix in place at the time wage and price controls were instituted in August 1971 was appropriate and hoped that the control authorities would not be needlessly intrusive. His recommendations were consistent with the position he expressed in a 1971 Brookings paper in which he concluded that the conventional Phillips Curve does not offer policy makers a menu of inflation-unemployment combinations. His accelerationist view, perhaps more widely associated with Milton Friedman and Edmund Phelps, regards attempts to push unemployment below its natural rate as futile and perverse, leading to accelerating inflation.

During much of Nixon's time in office, economic policy was unevenly applied. Restrictive monetary policy led to the 1969–70 recession with little relief from inflation. Wage and price controls were imposed in 1971, and policy was expansionary in the election year of 1972. Policy seemed increasingly in the hands of those with little pretension to economic expertise, such as John Connally and Melvin Laird. Chastened by its experience with controls, the administration shifted its thinking toward views much like those expressed by Fellner. Against this backdrop and amid some criticism of the political role of the Council of Economic Advisers came the announcement of Marina von Neumann Whitman's intention to leave the Council in the summer of 1973. She suggested to Council chairman Herbert Stein* that William Fellner, longtime von Neumann family friend, would be a very capable replacement.

Fellner formally retired from Yale in July 1973 with the title of Sterling Professor of Economics Emeritus. The academic year preceding his retirement was spent on leave, and, encouraged by colleague Gottfried Haberler, he became a resident scholar at the AEI. While vacationing in Switzerland with his wife late in the summer of 1973, Fellner was offered the Council vacancy in a phone conversation with Stein. He accepted with a sense of duty and a desire to experience the public arena. Wide praise greeted the announcement of his nomination on September 24, 1973, with the press enthusiastically speculating that Fellner would follow Stein as the next Council chairman.

Fellner's distinction was thought to assure easy Senate confirmation. Some fears were raised following his uncharacteristically blunt remarks at an AEI sponsored press conference held on September 27, 1973, in connection with the publication of a paper by Fellner critical of some administration policies. Such public appearances are highly unusual for nominees prior to confirmation. His comments were in large part an amplification of the views he expressed in the 1972 AEI policy study. He said that the current policy mix seemed about right following the overstimulation of the preceding election year, and that the wage-price freeze was bad economics and bad politics and should be quickly ended. Melvin Laird's recent suggestion of a refundable tax increase was called inadvisable by Fellner since the refund might come at a time of economic strength. Fellner's most controversial statement was a call for substituting a 5 percent target rate of unemployment for the administration's 4 percent goal, which he regarded as unrealistic and inflationary. Fellner cited an important demographic change of the early 1970s, one generally recognized by economists in later years. A large influx of women and younger people into the labor force, with their lack of skills and more frequent job searches, had made the 4 percent unemployment target a questionable one. Pursuit of the 4 percent goal would require excessive stimulation leading to chronic shortages in certain segments of the labor market and to inflation. Fellner endorsed a federally subsidized employment program to offset some of the hardships that his 5 percent unemployment target would entail. President Nixon said at his next press conference on October 6, 1973: "I have found that economists are the most independent breed of the human species, except for members of the press." Nixon disavowed his nominee's call for an end to all price controls by year's end and commented that Fellner was a man of "rather, shall we say, outspoken" views.

Fellner's call for a 5 percent unemployment target was expected to be the major point of contention with the Democratic controlled Senate. His hearing before the Senate Committee on Banking, Housing and Urban Affairs on October 11, 1973, lasted less than one hour and was conducted in a cordial atmosphere. Senator William Proxmire (D-Wis) dominated the questioning, quizzing Fellner on a wide variety of issues but invariably returning to the rationale for Fellner's

5 percent target and the consequences of its adoption. Proxmire regarded Fellner as ''highly competent'' but had ''very strong policy differences with him and reservations as to his position.'' Nevertheless, Proxmire moved that the nomination be reported favorably, assuring confirmation by the full Senate. Fellner took his oath of office on October 31, 1973.

During his tenure on the Council, Fellner's primary responsibilities were in the macroeconomic, international finance, and housing policy areas. Herbert Stein believes that Fellner gained wider acceptance among policy makers for the idea that inflationary demand-side management cannot solve macroeconomic problems and that this is the enduring legacy of his Council service.

One of Nixon's last nominations was the selection of Alan Greenspan* to succeed Stein as Council chairman, due at least in part to Fellner's favorable impressions of Greenspan. The new chairman took his oath of office on September 4, 1974, after the Nixon resignation. On September 24, 1974, Fellner announced his resignation from the Council effective the following February after completion of the Council's annual report to the president. Fellner stated that his departure did not result from policy differences or disenchantment with government work. He had taken on the burden of Council work at a comparatively advanced age and was understandably anxious to resume his scholarly research at the AEI.

Upon his return to the AEI, Fellner became project director of the institute's annual volume, *Contemporary Economic Problems*, to which he was also a regular contributor. His last book, *Towards a Reconstruction of Macroeconomics: Problems of Theory and Policy* (1976), appeared shortly thereafter and provided a full exegesis of his macroeconomic views. One major theme, also expressed in subsequent journal articles, is the credibility hypothesis. Government policy to combat inflation can be effective only if businesses and workers are convinced that the rising unemployment and declining real output brought on by demand restraint will not be followed by a reversal of policy. Without this policy credibility, wages and prices will not ease. The less credible the policy the greater is the decline in real output required to control inflation and the slower is the adjustment process. Skeptics of rational expectations find Fellner's assertions about the credibility effect unconvincing. They point to the difficulty of maintaining a credible policy in a democratic society with its frequent changes of government and turnover of advisers. They also cite historical episodes when wages and prices behaved poorly in spite of apparently credible policy.

After his Council service, Fellner was a consultant to the Congressional Budget Office. His research and advice on inflation and tax bracket creep are credited with leading to Congressional passage of tax indexation legislation in 1981 to become effective in 1985. He continued his association with prestigious organizations as a fellow of the American Academy of Arts and Sciences and a corresponding member of the Bavarian Academy of Sciences. His seventieth birthday was celebrated by his colleagues and former students with the publication of a Festschrift entitled *Essays in Honor of William Fellner: Economic Progress, Private Values and Public Policy*, edited by Bela Balassa and Richard Nelson.

Fellner's work has long been admired in Western Europe, especially in West Germany. He maintained close ties with the West German diplomatic corps in Washington and was a friend of Herbert Giersch, a former member of the West German Council of Economic Advisers. The esteem of the West Germans brought Fellner two major awards. In 1979 he received the Commander's Cross of the Order of Merit of the German Federal Republic. In 1982 he was awarded the Bernhard-Harms Prize of the Institute of World Economics at the University of Kiel, West Germany. Following the award ceremony held on June 26, 1982, Fellner presented a lecture entitled ''Economic Theory Amidst Political Currents: The Spreading Interest in Monetarism and in the Theory of Market Expectations,'' later published in a slightly abridged version in *Weltwirtschaftliches Archiv*. He regarded the recent attention given to monetarism and rational expectations by policy makers in the Western democracies as countercurrents to Joseph Schumpeter's ''March into Socialism.'' In Fellner's view, policy makers have been interested in finding alternatives to increased political and bureaucratic control of economic decisions. Although he had reservations about some of the propositions of monetarism and rational expectations, he felt that they offered policy guidance superior to neo-Keynesian fine tuning. The monetarist framework, simplified though it may be, focuses on a policy variable (the money supply) clearly under political control and permits the conduct of efficacious policy with limited infringement on the operation of market economies. Though many aspects of Keynesian and neo-Keynesian thought have been incorporated into his own work, Fellner believed that postwar neo-Keynesian policy had become too reliant on comprehensive structural models. In his view, these models were empirically undependable and required estimates of many variables outside of the control of political authorities. Fellner saw the credibility hypothesis as the ''valid core'' of rational expectations. Under this analytical construct, the public's ability to learn to anticipate the effects of inflationary demand-side management is explicitly recognized. Labor and producers will respond with increased wage and price demands, vitiating the intended benefits of a neo-Keynesian demand stimulus. According to Fellner, some neo-Keynesians have acknowledged the inadequacy of assuming the public's learning ability to be either nonexistent or at best very limited. But rather than discard their models, they add a new and more intrusive ingredient to their policy prescription, an incomes policy to control steepening inflation. Such market intervention was, as always, anathema to Fellner. He concluded his address on an optimistic note, saying that the increasing interest in monetarism and rational expectations was a hopeful sign that the economic and political freedoms fostered by unfettered markets may yet be preserved. The ''March into Socialism'' is not inevitable.

Fellner's lecture at the University of Kiel was to be one of his last opportunities to air his views in a large public forum. On September 15, 1983, he died suddenly of a heart attack in his Washington, D.C., home at the age of seventy-eight. On October 1, 1983, a memorial service was held at American University in Washington to eulogize Fellner. Tributes were made by Gottfried Haberler, Herbert Stein, James Tobin, Henry Wallich, and Bela Balassa. Referring to Fellner affectionately as "Willy," they praised him as a kind man of Old World courtliness and manners. The testimonials recalled him as a rare individual, fluent in several languages and blessed with a wry sense of humor. He was remembered as a person of high culture with an appreciation for art, music, and literature. The quality and importance of his life's work were cited, with special praise for the historical perspective he brought to that work. Fellner's appreciation for the tentative nature of our understanding of economic behavior was well known. His beliefs were undogmatic and his policy positions tempered with humanity. James Tobin, who often differed with Fellner, admired his "focus on essential issues, respect for evidence, and intellectual integrity." Fellner's passing reminds us that those European economists cast in the mold of the nineteenth-century classical liberal tradition, who came to America to enrich their discipline, are a vanishing breed.

BIBLIOGRAPHY

Fellner, William J. *Competition Among the Few*. New York: Knopf, 1949.

———. *The Emergence and Content of Modern Economic Analysis*. New York: McGraw-Hill, 1960.

———. *Monetary Policies and Full Employment*. Berkeley: University of California Press, 1946.

———. *Probability and Profit*. Homewood, Ill.: Irwin, 1965.

———. *Towards a Reconstruction of Macroeconomics: Problems of Theory and Policy*. Washington, D.C.: American Enterprise Institute, 1976.

———. *A Treatise on War Inflation*. Berkeley: University of California Press, 1942.

———. *Trends and Cycles in Economic Activity*. New York: Holt, 1956.

JAMES N. MARSHALL

GOLDFELD, STEPHEN MICHAEL
(b. August 9, 1940), CEA August 20, 1980-January 20, 1981

Stephen Michael Goldfeld, a member of the President's Council of Economic Advisers from 1980 to 1981, is a native New Yorker, having been born in the Bronx. He received a Bachelor of Arts degree from Harvard in 1960, majoring in mathematics, and a Doctor of Philosophy degree from Massachusetts Institute of Technology in 1963 in economics. He has held a Ford Doctoral Dissertation Fellowship, has been a Procter and Gamble Faculty Fellow, and has held a National Science Foundation Senior Postdoctoral Fellowship.

Goldfeld has held many professional positions. He was appointed assistant professor of economics at Princeton University in 1963 and was promoted to associate professor in 1966 and to professor in 1969. In 1971 he was named the Class of 1920 Professor of Economics and Banking at Princeton University. Concurrently, he was a visiting research professor at Catholic University in Louvain 1970–71, a Ford Visiting Professor at the University of California, Berkeley, 1975–76, and a Mendes-France Professor at Technion (Israel Institute of Technology), Haifa, in 1980. He was named chairman of the department of economics at Princeton University in 1981.

Goldfeld has held and holds a number of consultant and advisory positions. Prior to becoming a member of the Council of Economic Advisers, he served that group as senior economist (1966–67) and as consultant (1967–69). Other consulting positions show his areas of special interest. He was a member of the National Science Foundation Panel on Economics (1969–70) and a consultant for the Federal Home Loan Bank Board (1971–73). He was a guest scholar with Brookings Institution (1981) and a research associate with the National Bureau of Economic Research (1981). In addition, he has been a consultant for the state of Maryland, the American Telephone and Telegraph Company, and other corporations.

Goldfeld has made numerous contributions to the discipline of economics through the positions he has held, through his publications, and through testimony before Congressional committees. He began service with the Council of Economic Advisers while in his mid-twenties as senior economist and as a consultant and was nominated for membership on June 10, 1980. The Senate confirmed his appointment in August after a brief delay as it considered the likelihood of change after the presidential election. Goldfeld became a member on August 20, 1980, replacing Lyle Gramley*, who had resigned to become a governor of the Federal Reserve Board. He was replaced by Jerry Jordan* on July 14, 1981.

Goldfeld assumed chief responsibility for the economic forecasts of the Council, and it is interesting to compare forecasts presented in the January 1981 report of the Council with the results of the economic system as reported in the January 1982 report. It was predicted that unemployment during 1981 would be in the 7.5 to 7.75 percent range. In fact, the average was 7.6 percent. The forecast for 1981 indicated the rate of growth of real gross national product would be in the range of 1.5 to 2 percent. Actually, real GNP increased 1.95 percent. The forecast for the increase in the consumer price index was somewhat less accurate. It was predicted that consumer prices would increase by 12.5 percent. In fact, the rate of increase was 10.4 percent.

Goldfeld's impact on the economic system as a member of the Council of Economic Advisers was limited because he served on the CEA for only five months, Ronald Reagan having been elected president less than three months after Goldfeld's appointment. President Reagan assumed office in January 1981, the same month the Council of Economic Advisers issued the first annual report for which Goldfeld shared responsibility.

Goldfeld has had more influence on the discipline in his position as consultant, editor, and author. He is or has been an associate editor of the *International Economic Review*, the *Journal of Econometrics*, the *Review of Economics and Statistics*, and the *American Economic Review*. He was advisory editor for advanced textbooks in economics for the North-Holland Publishing Company and is on the board of editors of the *Pakistan Development Review*. His publications reflect his interests within the field of economics. He is the author or editor of five books, several of which have a co-author or co-editor, and of approximately sixty articles in professional journals. Three of the five books concern econometrics and mathematical economics, and one deals with monetary policy. He is co-author, with Lester Chandler, of an influential and widely used textbook, *Economics of Money and Banking*. His articles, many of which are co-authored, deal with both mathematical and monetary economics.

BIBLIOGRAPHY

Chandler, Lester, and Goldfeld, Stephen. *Economics of Money and Banking*, 7th ed. New York: Wiley, 1977.

Goldfeld, Stephen. *Commercial Bank Behavior and Economic Activity*. Amsterdam: North-Holland, 1966.

GEORGE G. SAUSE

GORDON, KERMIT

(b. July 3, 1916, d. June 21, 1976), CEA January 29, 1961-December 27, 1962

Kermit Gordon, a member of President John F. Kennedy's Council of Economic Advisers from January 1961 through December 1962, exemplified the Kennedy-Johnson era's commitment to the ideal of economic expertise in the service of activist government. His career in both public and not-for-profit organizations can serve as a case study of the achievements and limitations of the economist's role as public servant.

Gordon was the son of H. B. and Ida E. (Robinson) Gordon. He was raised in the Philadelphia area and attended public schools. Gordon studied at Swarthmore College, where he received a Bachelor of Arts degree with highest honors in 1938, majoring in economics. Perhaps due to the college's Quaker background, the Swarthmore economics department was distinctly oriented toward public policy issues, although it had no unified ideological or theoretical viewpoint. Gordon's career may reflect that early environment.

Gordon was named a Rhodes Scholar and attended University College, Oxford, where he read economics in 1938–39. He then spent a year as a research associate in the Swarthmore economics department before being named an administration fellow at Harvard University. Unlike almost all other prominent economic advisers on the New Frontier, Gordon never earned a doctoral degree. This lack, however, in no way detracted from his professional stature.

While in his early twenties, Gordon began his practice of shuttling between academia and government. He served briefly with the staff of the Temporary National Economic Committee. This group's hearings and studies generally represented the last gasp of antitrust sentiment during the New Deal era. However, in Gordon's later career, government measures to destroy monopoly power did not assume a major role in his thinking. For example, testifying before the Joint Economic Committee of Congress in 1966, Gordon maintained that wage-price guideposts were a better way to handle inflation than were measures to remove the firm's market power by fragmenting both business and labor. Like other New Frontier economists, Gordon did not wish to tamper drastically with the nation's industrial structure.

In 1941 Kermit Gordon joined the staff of the Office of Price Administration (OPA), where, along with a growing corps of economists and lawyers, he labored to keep wartime inflation under control. Gordon later characterized his two years with the OPA as "highly educational," but noted that it left him with "a deep-seated aversion to expansion of direct control over prices where there was any sensible way to avoid it." Thus he hoped to find alternatives to trust-busting and wage-price controls as means of combatting inflation.

Gordon enlisted in the United States Army as a private in 1943. He served as an economist with the Office of Strategic Services (OSS), the wartime forerunner of the Central Intelligence Agency. The OSS was a breeding ground for many of the postwar era's leading policy-oriented professionals. There Gordon met such future New Frontiersmen as Arthur Schlesinger, Jr. When he was discharged in 1945 with the rank of second lieutenant, he moved to the State Department as a special assistant to the Assistant Secretary for Economic Affairs.

Gordon in 1946 accepted an appointment as assistant professor of economics at Williams College in Williamstown, Massachusetts. He rose to the rank of full professor and in 1956 became the holder of the William Bough chair of economics. Five years later, on the eve of his taking leave to sit on the Council of Economic Advisers, Gordon became the David A. Wells Professor of Political Economy at Williams. During his Williams years, he continued his pattern of active involvement in government policy making. Most of the off-campus positions Gordon assumed related to the international economy and economic development. He remained a consultant with the State Department until 1953 and with the Office of Price Stabilization through 1951. He was also involved in drafting the influential *Report on Foreign Economic Policies*, the so-called Gray Report. For a year, in 1956–57, Gordon took leave from Williams to hold the post of executive assistant at the Ford Foundation; in 1960 he again joined the foundation and directed its economic development programs.

Gordon's first contact with John F. Kennedy's political advisers hardly pointed to the influence he would later wield in the Kennedy and Johnson administrations. In 1959, looking to widen his circle of economic experts, then Senator Kennedy approached Arthur Schlesinger, Jr., to ask for potential consultants. Schlesinger called Gordon, only to be told that Gordon planned to support Adlai Stevenson for the 1960 Democratic nomination. Gordon allowed Schlesinger to mention his name to Kennedy, but only on the condition that Kennedy be told of his presidential preference. Though Kennedy was willing to accept this caveat, Gordon did not at that point join the Kennedy camp.

With this inauspicious start, it is not surprising that President-elect Kennedy was cool to the idea of naming Kermit Gordon to his initial Council of Economic Advisers. Walter Heller*, however, insisted that Gordon was the man best suited for the job. He persuaded Kennedy to accept Gordon; and, as later observed, Gordon rapidly became very highly regarded by the White House.

Along with Chairman Heller and Yale University professor James Tobin*, Gordon served on a Council generally considered unsurpassed in its combination of intellectual sophistication and political savvy. The three shared an outlook which prevailed in the economics profession at the time and were able to move the president and his policies significantly toward their position. The viewpoint of the Council can broadly be described as neo-Keynesian. The members believed that fiscal policy was the preferred tool not only for combatting recessions but also for increasing the pace of economic growth during expansionary phases of the business cycle. They accepted the existence of a tradeoff between high employment and price stability, the so-called Phillips Curve, but felt that joblessness and sluggish growth were the more serious social ills and that inflation could be kept in check despite stimulative fiscal measures. The Council also considered the nation's balance of payments problems to be curable by measures compatible with a generally expansionary policy. Thus, for example, tax code changes could stimulate domestic rather than overseas investment. So, too, could the Treasury Department's "Operation Twist." This was designed to shift government debt toward short-term obligations, raising their interest rates to encourage inflows of mobile "hot money" from abroad; at the same time, lower interest rates for long-term borrowers would encourage private domestic investment.

During the 1960 presidential campaign, Kennedy had decried the slow economic growth and unemployment rates of the Eisenhower years. Nevertheless, upon assuming office, several constraints limited Kennedy's willingness to pursue the growth-oriented policies his CEA supported. Congressional leaders continued to oppose budget deficits, especially during cyclical upturns. Within the administration, other advisers and policy makers also doubted the wisdom of the CEA's orientation. Secretary of the Treasury C. Douglas Dillon and Federal Reserve Board Chairman William McChesney Martin feared accelerated inflation if fiscal policy were made more stimulative. Finally, Kennedy himself entered the White House with both intellectual and political qualms about deficits that were not aimed at ending recessions.

For most of the nearly two years that Gordon served on the Council of Economic Advisers, he, along with Heller and Tobin, undertook a quiet campaign to convert the Kennedy administration to a fiscal policy designed to enhance growth rates. In their January 1962 *Economic Report*, the Council members presented their intellectual rationale. While the Council expressed concern for price stability and international payments equilibrium, it put "maximum employment" at the top of its priorities. The report also emphasized the gap between actual and potential employment and output levels. Even though 1961 had been a year of renewed expansion, the gap represented both a troubling waste of human and material resources and an opportunity for remedial action; fiscal policy to raise effective demand was likely to result in real output and job increases, not price rises.

Within the Council, no strict division of labor occurred. However, Gordon had primary responsibilities in the areas of manpower, foreign aid and trade, natural resources, and wage-price relationships. It is in this last field that Gordon played an important role in formulating the wage-price guideposts that the Kennedy and Johnson administrations upheld from 1962 through 1966. In the spring of 1961, the economy had bottomed out and recovery had begun. As early as June 1961, the CEA had initiated a series of studies of wage-price behavior; at that point, Gordon described the Council as "groping for a strategy." In a working paper presented the next month, the Council's committee, under Gordon's chairmanship, took a position of ''studied neutrality'' on anti-inflation policies.

Yet in private communications among CEA members and in advice for the White House, the Council took a more activist line. They suggested that price increases should be confined to industries with slower than normal productivity growth and that sectors where productivity increased faster that the national average ought to cut prices. The Council also wanted wage increases not to imperil price stability. By the fall of 1961, it was agreed that the 1962 Council report would contain a section delineating guidelines for noninflationary wage and price behavior. Gordon took the main responsibility for drafting this section of the document. When the report was published in January 1962, it advised that wage rates rise no faster than the ''trend rate of overall productivity increase.'' If industries granting such raises had productivity advances greater than the national trend, price decreases were indicated. For industries where productivity increases lagged behind the trend, some degree of price increase was expected.

As enunciated by Gordon and his colleagues, the guideposts were far from rigid directives. Rather than present a single measurement of the trend line of productivity, the 1962 report showed an array of alternative indices. The report also hastened to point out that guideposts had to be modified to fit the needs of particular industries. Yet, at the same time, the Council offered no quantitative advice on how far the modifications should stray from the norm. Finally, the tone of the guideposts section of the report can only be described as diffident. There was no intention to supplant private sector decision making, to override market forces, or to serve as a definitive statement of what constituted appropriate behavior.

When Gordon testified on price-cost behavior before the Joint Economic Committee of Congress in 1966, his defense of the wage-price guideposts was almost equally circumspect. Guideposts had been predominantly educational, a salutary reminder to business that rising productivity justified rising real incomes for labor, and to workers that their wages were costs that businesses had to cover in the prices they charged. Though not perfect, the guideposts were less objectionable than other policy approaches.

Despite these qualms and qualifications, the wage-price guideposts were more than verbal fluff. The steel price controversy of April 1962 indicated that an activist president could make them a standard for action. The outline of the steel episode has often been presented and does not need to be recounted here. Kermit Gordon, along with Walter Heller, joined the president's efforts to get U.S. Steel and other manufacturers to roll back their $6 per ton increase. As an economist, however, Gordon was less inclined toward administrative sanctions against the offending steel firms than some other White House strategists. Within the administration, he pressed the position that, if a few companies were dissuaded from joining the price rise bandwagon, the offending firms would not be able to make the higher prices stick. When Inland, Armco, and Kaiser Steel announced that they would not raise prices, Bethlehem and U.S. Steel soon rescinded their increases. Thus the argument that market pressures were the real barrier to the steel price increases rings true; however, it is impossible to ascertain the contribution of governmental intervention to stimulating competitive forces.

The wage-price guideposts also played a significant defensive role in the political economy of the Kennedy years. As we have seen, the Council was growth-oriented and favored stimulative fiscal policies. By promulgating the guideposts, the Council (and by extension the White House) could contend that they had guarded against the inflationary dangers that others saw in expansionary fiscal policy. In his 1966 commentary, Gordon stated that the Council believed that the guidelines were designed to work within a band of unemployment rates. With unemployment above that band, the guideposts would be superfluous; with joblessness below that range, they would be ineffectual. While they were formulating the guidelines, Gordon and his colleagues had a belief they already exceeded the limits of the band. In other words, the guideposts anticipated a future of more rapid growth and lower unemployment. They were one of the Council's methods of paving the way for policies to stimulate that growth.

Gordon continued his service on the Council of Economic Advisers during 1962, as the economy continued its climb out of recession and as the Council pressed for a major, permanent tax cut in order to stimulate economic growth. Although Walter Heller appears to have been the prime mover in convincing President Kennedy that he should send a tax reduction proposal to the new Congress that convened in January 1963, Gordon too became a White House favorite. In October 1962 he announced his intention to resign and return to Williams College. When asked why, he recited the 4-Fs of family, finance, fatigue, and frustration. However, on November 28, 1962, President Kennedy nominated him to succeed David Bell as Director of the Bureau of the Budget. Kennedy noted that Gordon was an important member of the Council and would sustain the fine tradition of his predecessors.

The position of Budget Director carried a different set of responsibilities and opportunities from membership on the Council of Economic Advisers. The Council had focused on macroeconomics; as Budget Director, Gordon had to study a myriad of federal spending programs and appraise their effectiveness relative to alternative expenditures. In later reflections on the role of Budget Director, Gordon insisted that increasing the effectiveness of governmental outlays was a more important task than ascertaining precisely how much ought to be spent in the aggregate. Whereas the Council was advisory, the Bureau of the Budget had clear operating responsibilities in one of the presidency's most vital policy areas.

Despite the changed environment, Gordon handled the Budget Director's task with aplomb. He was capable of a blunt rejoinder. When Harry Byrd, the conservative senator from Virginia, asked him what a balanced budget would do for the country, he replied that it would add about 2.5 million people to the unemployment rolls, hold off recovery about four years, and diminish output by

10 percent. Byrd was neither convinced nor amused; he called, unsuccessfully, for Gordon's dismissal. Gordon was also called upon to explain minute details of the federal budget. When stories circulated that the government was paying to maintain a colony of baboons, he reported in a speech that the animals were an important part of a research program of the National Heart Institute.

In the aftermath of President Kennedy's assassination, Gordon quietly won the respect of Lyndon B. Johnson. The day after the assassination, Gordon prepared a one-page memorandum for the new president, indicating that Johnson could, by prompt effort, make the fiscal 1965 budget one that bore his imprint and reflected his priorities. The next month, Gordon, donning a Western-style khaki shirt borrowed from the president, joined Johnson at the LBJ Ranch for intensive work on the budget document. Gordon and Heller had already been at work on a federal poverty program proposal. They brought the president a plan for a limited number of demonstration projects to initiate the effort, but Johnson, aware of the upsurge of public support for antipoverty efforts and eager to spread appropriations among many Congressional districts, expanded their plan into his War on Poverty program. Gordon and Heller did endorse the principle of community action funding, the most innovative and controversial aspect of the poverty program. They also agreed that the antipoverty efforts should be waged in a new, independent government agency. This, too, was to become policy in the 1964 Economic Opportunity Act.

Gordon's influence in working with Lyndon Johnson on the 1965 budget won him recognition as one of the most powerful members of Johnson's executive team. Observers noted both his capacity for detailed analysis of specific programs and his skill in advocating stimulative fiscal policies. The president cajoled his Budget Director into staying at his post until June 1, 1965, but Gordon at that point left the administration to become vice president of the Brookings Institution, the well-known Washington public policy research organization. Gordon's resignation came at the onset of the American troop buildup in Vietnam. His highly regarded performance as Budget Director no doubt owes something to the fact that he did not have to contend with the fiscal distortions that Johnson's attempts to fight the war and achieve the Great Society produced.

Gordon's service at Brookings did not remove him from government roles entirely. He served as chair of Johnson's Health Insurance Benefits Advisory Council on the Administration of the Medicare Program for two years. He also continued to advise informally. For example, when Johnson and his adviser Joseph Califano were considering price controls in early 1966, Gordon contributed to the discussion with a memo on "Why Economists Dread Mandatory Price Controls." His government service continued under Richard Nixon's Republican presidency. Drawing upon his expertise in wage and price relations, Nixon named Gordon to the Pay Board established under the president's New Economic Program. Gordon remained as a public member of the board from October 1971 to December 1972. From 1969 to 1973, he was a member of the General Advisory Committee on Arms Control and Disarmament.

At the Brookings Institution, Gordon succeeded Robert D. Calkins as president in 1967. Gordon's leadership helped to reinvigorate what had been perceived as a rather stodgy organization. Gordon assembled prominent economists and other social scientists and coordinated their research on issues of public policy. He also stressed efforts to publicize their findings and disseminate their work as widely as possible.

Although Brookings was generally well regarded for the quality of its studies, it also gained a reputation during Gordon's presidency as a center for politically liberal scholars oriented toward the Democratic party. When Nixon became president in 1969, several well-known economists from the Johnson administration, notably Arthur Okun*, chairman of LBJ's Council of Economic Advisers, and Charles Schultze*, Gordon's successor at the Bureau of the Budget, joined Brookings. During the Nixon years, too, the institution published a yearly analysis of the federal budget, *Setting National Priorities*. While these were presented as nonpartisan documents, volumes which presented alternative federal policies for consideration could also be viewed as critiques of G.O.P. programs.

By 1971 members of Nixon's White House staff such as speechwriter Patrick Buchanan had concluded that Brookings served as a shadow government for out-of-office Democrats. Administration operative John Caulfield obtained the institution's tax returns, which revealed that it had received several federal contracts. It was then suggested that the relationship be severed. According to Caulfield, Charles Colson later suggested that Caulfield start a fire at Brookings to provide an opportunity to burglarize some files there belonging to government staffers who were thought to be hostile to Nixon administration policies. John Dean reported that he had interceded directly with John Ehrlichman to halt the scheme. Colson has insisted that no such plot existed, and that any reference to firebombing the building was facetious.

The Nixon administration's hostility to Gordon's Brookings Institution was somewhat ironic, despite the Democratic party loyalties of Gordon and many of the institution's scholars. Gordon was no radical, and Brookings had been condemned from the left for excessive caution and for serving the establishment. While Gordon favored activist government fiscal policy, he shared the economic mainstream's aversion to government regulation of private markets. As we have seen, he justified the 1962 wage-price guideposts as an alternative to direct intervention and continued to oppose controls through the Johnson era. While on the CEA, Gordon had persuaded Kennedy not to propose tighter federal regulation of trucking and water transportation. Similarly, he insisted to then Vice President Johnson that the federal government should let the private marketplace decide whether a supersonic transport plane was economically desirable.

Gordon's leadership at Brookings was cut short by a heart attack in February 1976. He died, at the age of fifty-nine, on June 21, 1976. He was eulogized at a memorial service later that month by Charles Schultze as a man who "made a difference." Surely Gordon's effectiveness as a public servant was enhanced by the era in which he served. The discretionary neo-Keynesian fiscal policies he and his CEA colleagues promoted were becoming the prevailing economic wisdom of the 1960s. Washington was also receptive to proposals for the kinds of meliorist social programs which he tended to favor. Gordon's moderate liberalism and policy-oriented economics were in tune with the times. With the mainstream of economic thinking now flowing further to the right, and without a political consensus behind extending federal domestic programs, one might wonder where Gordon might find himself in economic policy making today. Yet the many tributes that Kermit Gordon received during his life and at his death indicate that he was an exceptionally judicious and insightful spokesman for the programs he advocated and a talented administrator during his years of public service.

BIBLIOGRAPHY

Goodwin, Crawford. *Exhortation and Controls: The Search for a Wage-Price Policy, 1945–1971*. Washington, D.C.: Brookings Institution, 1975.

Gordon, Kermit. "How Much Should Government Do?" In V. W. Ruttan et al., eds., *Agricultural Policy in an Affluent Society*. Washington, D.C.: Government Printing Office, 1967.

———. "Price-Cost Behavior and Employment Act Objectives." United States Congress. Joint Economic Committee. *Twentieth Anniversary of the Employment Act of 1946: An Economic Symposium*. Washington, D.C.: Government Printing Office, 1966. Pp. 59–66.

———. "Reflections on Spending." In John Montgomery and Arthur Smithies, eds., *Public Policy*. Cambridge, Mass.: Harvard University Press, 1966.

DANIEL POPE

GRAMLEY, LYLE E.

(b. January 14, 1927), CEA March 18, 1977-May 27, 1980

Lyle E. Gramley was no stranger to Washington, D.C., when he was nominated by Jimmy Carter to join the Council of Economic Advisers in 1977. Since 1964 he had worked in Washington serving as an economist with the Federal Reserve System. During this period Gramley had earned a reputation as an eclectic economist, one who combined theory and reality to produce a practical, commonsense approach to formulating economic policy. As an economist Gramley has never believed in a doctrinaire approach to policy. He cautions against relying on simple rules—especially where monetary policy is concerned—but he has not allowed popular sentiment to force him to abandon the basic tenets of economic theory as a guide to action.

Although he has spent much of his working career in the nation's capital, Gramley lived in the Midwest in his early years. He was born in Aurora, Illinois, a small city about forty miles southwest of Chicago. Illinois ranks among the leading agricultural states, and during his high school days Gramley worked on a farm where he cared for horses and learned to shuck and thrash oats. He can still milk a cow by hand or machine—no mean set of accomplishments for a professional economist.

Gramley's educational roots are also in the Midwest. In 1951 he received a B.A. from Beloit College, where he was Phi Beta Kappa. He traces his interest in economics as a profession back to his undergraduate days, when he was enrolled in an economic principles course taught by a woman that truly impressed Gramley to the extent that he changed his intended major from engineering to economics. He pursued his interest in economics at the graduate level at Indiana University, where he received his Ph.D. in economics. At Indiana his major fields of concentration were business cycles and monetary economics.

Gramley's interest in business cycles and monetary theory led him to the Federal Reserve System, where he has spent most of his career as a professional economist. In 1955 Gramley joined the staff at the Federal Reserve Bank of Kansas City as a financial economist, thus beginning his commitment to public service. At the bank he was introduced to economic forecasting and devoted his research and writing to commercial banking, capital markets, and monetary policy. In 1962 he was appointed to the faculty of the University of Maryland, where he taught monetary theory to graduates and undergraduates. At Maryland he became acquainted with Charles Schultze*, who was later to become chairman of the Council of Economic Advisers under Jimmy Carter.

After leaving the University of Maryland, Gramley rejoined the Fed, this time on the staff of the Board of Governors in Washington, D.C. In 1977, at the time of his appointment to the CEA, he was serving as director of the Division of Research and Statistics. In this position he was responsible for economic forecasting, analysis of financial markets, and advising on monetary policy—solid preparation for his work with the Council of Economic Advisers. Gramley served on the Council until 1980, when he was appointed a governor of the Federal Reserve System.

In the position of governor he has a major influence on the direction of monetary policy. Gramley feels that he brings not only the training of an economist into this responsibility but, because of his roots in the Midwest, a strong empathy with broad sectors of the U.S. economy. He has expressed special concern over the plight of those sectors which are hit hardest by restrictive monetary policy, such as agriculture, small business, and residential housing.

Gramley has published many articles in the fields of banking and monetary policy and has stressed the importance of money as a tool of economic policy but cautions against the use of simple growth targets for monetary aggregates. His other publications include many that were written while he was with the Federal Reserve Banks. In his capacity as representative of the Federal Reserve System, Gramley has also made many speeches to professional business and banking organizations.

Gramley describes the three and a half years he spent as a member of the CEA as the most exciting of his professional career. On March 18, 1977, he joined Charles Schultze and William Nordhaus* as a member of Jimmy Carter's Council of Economic Advisers, with Schultze as chairman. Nordhaus, a professor at Yale University, assumed the role of chief theoretician. Gramley undertook the responsibility for economic forecasting and macro policy. Later, labor policy was also placed under his direction.

Although the Carter years are remembered for the monumental battle against inflation and unemployment (stagflation), the administration began its tenure in an atmosphere of mild optimism. In 1977 the economy was entering its third year of recovery and, although still a threat, the rate of inflation had receded significantly from its high level earlier in the decade. The economic priorities of the early Carter days were to stimulate economic growth, to increase employment, and to extend the benefits of a productive society to its less fortunate members. Although the energy problem surfaced early in the Carter administration, the full extent of its economic consequences was not realized until much later.

The Council may have been categorized as neo-Keynesian, but its implementation of this philosophy was moderate to conservative in nature. For example, the administration is noted for its sponsorship of the Full Employment and Balanced Growth Act (also known as the Humphrey-Hawkins bill). The original intention of the bill was to provide public jobs for all those unable to find employment in the private sector. The Carter version of the bill was distinctly more moderate. As suggested in the *Economic Report of the President* (1978), the bill does not speak to large federal programs nor seek governmental intrusions.

Rather, it reaffirms the importance of the private sector in realizing agreed upon goals. The Council's description of the Humphrey-Hawkins bill stresses its inflation-fighting provisions, its restraint in authorizing new programs to carry out the act, and the need for cooperation between Congress, the Federal Reserve, and the executive branch to produce a more coherent set of macroeconomic policies. The Council minimized the job creation section of the bill by indicating that the creation of work projects would only be a last resort.

For 1979 the Council predicted continued moderate expansion with real GNP growing at an annual rate of 4–5 percent and unemployment declining slowly. The only caution relative to this favorable outlook was the need for sustained fiscal stimulus to maintain the steady, though unspectacular, recovery.

Tax reduction was the cornerstone of the Carter program to maintain aggregate demand at a favorable level while reducing the relative size of the federal sector from 22 percent to 18 percent. The major fiscal initiatives of the Council centered on personal and corporate income tax reductions.

By mid-administration, however, the country was hit with a number of unanticipated economic shocks—many of them growing out of the earlier energy crisis. They included falling productivity, rising unit labor costs, and a declining exchange rate. These shocks translated into rampant inflation, which subsequently has been used to characterize the Carter years. The administration's priorities switched from encouragement of economic growth to controlling inflation. The battle against inflation was more difficult because the philosophy of the administration was to avoid hurting the less fortunate. It was reluctant to adopt measures which would fight inflation while eroding the position of low-income groups. The administration promised not to wring inflation out of the system by pursuing policies to bring about a recession as this would place the burden of adjustment on the weak. Instead the administration turned to deregulation and wage and price standards to reduce inflation. Although some maintain that Chairman Schultze favored the guidelines from the early days of the administration, Gramley himself cautioned against optimism regarding their success.

As previously noted, the character of the group assigned to formulate economic policy during this period has been described as neo-Keynesian by some observers. This term is generally used to describe those followers of John Hicks and Paul Samuelson who believe that full employment and economic growth can be managed through the proper use of fiscal and monetary policy. As economists they were brought up in the tradition that government had a positive role to play in the economy: the level of economic activity can and should be influenced through adjustments in aggregate demand. In addition, most neo-Keynesians believe that national income can be redistributed through a system of transfer payments and that the less fortunate members of society can be sheltered from economic hardship without disrupting the overall efficiency of the economy.

During the Carter administration beliefs about the role of government were severely tested and the validity of the Keynesian approach to economic policy was brought into question. There have always been economists like Milton Friedman who have questioned the ability of demand management policies to influence the level of economic activity. Now problems appeared that caused Keynesians to examine the limits of the ability of their policies to "fine tune" the economy. Underlying the growing skepticism were several fundamental weaknesses in their approach: the need for accurate information to choose the right fiscal policy and pursuit of fiscal policy without unwanted side effects, and the willingness to pursue unpopular policy measures when necessary.

First, adroit implementation of fiscal policy requires a clear picture of how the economy is operating as well as accurate forecasts for the future values of critical economic variables under a variety of policy alternatives. This level of precision and accuracy is only possible when the economy is relatively stable and the behavior of economic agents is consistent with past behavior. Economists are not fortune tellers. Some events cannot be foreseen; the significance of other events is overshadowed by more immediate concerns. Carter's CEA was surprised by a host of inflation-producing economic shocks including a sharp rise in food and energy prices, low productivity gains, and the declining exchange value of the dollar. The existence of these unpredictable and destabilizing elements meant that policies based on previous forecasts were unlikely to have the desired results.

Second, the government found that it could influence the course of economic events but that it could not legislate all the results. The rising prices which resulted from supply shocks also brought with them rising levels of unemployment. These circumstances presented a dilemma. Expansionary fiscal policies needed to cope with unemployment only reinforced the inflationary pressure in the economy. Reducing government spending or raising taxes to curb inflation would only lead to higher unemployment. Economists were forced to conclude that fiscal policy by itself was insufficient to produce steady economic growth with a tolerable level of inflation.

Finally, because the Carter administration wanted to avoid the hardship of a recession, they did not use sufficiently restrictive monetary and fiscal policies to combat rising price levels. Instead they chose to rely primarily on wage and price guidelines. Even at the time, Gramley was aware that fighting inflation required more than the suggestion to labor and industry that they restrain their demand for wage and price increases. Gramley's position on wage and price controls illustrates his belief that public policy, no matter how well intentioned, cannot overcome basic economic forces. At the same time that Gramley and the Council of Economic Advisers advocated the use of wage and price guidelines to combat inflation, Gramley warned that such measures would have only limited effectiveness. He conceded that the guidelines would perhaps have a short-term impact on reducing inflationary expectations. Gramley stressed, however, that the guidelines would have little permanent impact on the root causes for rising prices in a market economy—in this case, shortages, changes in the exchange value of the dollar, and demand pressures in an overheated economy. Furthermore, he cautioned that any suppressed inflation would be likely to surface when the controls were removed.

The Carter administration ended during troubled economic times. Inflation, interest rates, and unemployment—the so-called misery index—were well above traditional levels. The failure to resolve these problems brought the Keynesian approach to policy into question. Gramley, in reflection, has recognized the limitations of demand management in a complex economy and the limits that it can achieve.

When Gramley left the Council in 1980 to rejoin the Federal Reserve System as a governor, he brought with him a healthy respect for the destructive potential of inflation and a commitment to avoid policies which would lead to increased inflationary pressure.

Of the current issues which absorb Gramley's attention in his role as governor of the Federal Reserve System, the need to combat inflation continues to have a high priority. He brings up the subject frequently when speaking to professional financial associations. His concern also extends to the other issues which influence the implementation of monetary policy. These include the impact of federal deficits on interest rates and the effect of high interest rates on the American economy. He is also concerned with the effect of high interest rates on the exchange value of the dollar and its relationship to the trade deficit and to domestic industries which face increased import competition. Finally, he is concerned with the changes in the financial sector that followed deregulation.

All these issues are, of course, related. It was inflation and inflationary expectations which led originally to higher interest rates. High real interest rates have been sustained, in part, by the need to finance the federal deficit. Never has the need for coordination of fiscal and monetary policy been greater, yet mounting federal deficits keep interest rates high. The high interest rates have forced some sectors of the economy out of the credit markets. High interest rates also mean that the United States is less competitive in the field of international trade as well as threatening the economic stability of developing countries that sell to the United States.

Deregulation and the restructuring of the financial sector have created further problems in implementing monetary policy by reducing the control of monetary authorities over the financial sector. Deregulation was necessary to permit banks to compete for deposits on an equal footing with other financial institutions. But by reducing the distinction between savings and transactions balances and banking and nonbanking institutions pursuit of monetary policy has been made more difficult. Finally, the Federal Reserve Board itself has switched its operational target from control of interest rates to control of monetary aggregates.

The new, freer environment creates new challenges and responsibilities for central bankers. Although the positions he presents are usually his own and not necessarily those of the Fed, as a governor of the Federal Reserve System Gramley has an excellent forum to bring these issues before a concerned public.

He has always been concerned with the impact of restrictive monetary policy on vulnerable sectors of the economy. He has reason to believe that these sectors are subject to increasing vulnerability. Because the Fed targets monetary aggregates and not interest rates, interest rates have become more volatile, reaching higher levels when heavy demand pressure is put on credit markets by the government or the private sector or when monetary policy grows restrictive.

Because interest rates are allowed to float, interest rates and not credit availability serve as the transmission mechanism for monetary policy. The shift means that it has now grown more difficult to protect interest-sensitive sectors of the economy, such as residential housing and small business, from credit shortages. In the past Gramley was more optimistic regarding the ability of the banking authorities to allocate credit to these sectors. Now they are priced out of the credit market when interest rates rise.

Providing a wholly acceptable monetary policy for the 1980s has proved to be as controversial as providing fiscal policy during the Carter administration. In each case Lyle Gramley has encountered a new generation of problems, problems which were unanticipated just a few years ago. He has examined those problems with great care, and his pragmatic solutions contain equal amounts of economic theory, practical good sense, and concern for the individuals and institutions affected by policy. He recognizes the complexity of the problems and has never suggested popular but simple solutions. Before offering a solution he examines all its ramifications, immediate and long-term, desirable and disagreeable.

Looking back on his years as a member of the Council, Gramley suggests that we take an alternative perspective on the role of the CEA. The CEA is important not only for the policies it adopts but also for the policy mistakes it avoids. To Gramley the CEA's function is to prevent misguided economic policies. To him, the CEA analyzes recommended policies of other agencies to detailed and careful analysis resulting in recommendations to the president that are in the best interests of the nation.

BIBLIOGRAPHY

Gramley, Lyle. "Statement to Congress." *Federal Reserve Bulletin* (July 1982): 547–50.

Stein, Herbert. *Presidential Economics*. New York: Simon & Schuster, 1984.

MARIA M. McKINNEY

GREENSPAN, ALAN

(b. March 6, 1926), CEA September 4, 1974-January 20, 1977

From September 4, 1974, to January 20, 1977, Alan Greenspan served as the chairman of the President's Council of Economic Advisers. Nominated by President Richard Nixon during the politically disquieting month of July 1974, Greenspan was appointed and served for the full term under President Gerald Ford.

One of the significant aspects of Greenspan's appointment was that, while he was only the second Council member lacking a Ph.D. at the time of his appointment, he was the first business economist to serve as chairman of the Council. Reflecting that of President Ford, Greenspan's economic philosophy represented the respected doctrine of economic conservatism. He is, in his own words, a free enterpriser.

To Alan Greenspan conservative fiscal and monetary management is philosophy, and not simply policy. Free enterprise and the marketplace should be left untouched by any form of well-meaning government interference. This attitude is emphatic and basic, as seen in Congressional testimony on August 8, 1974. At this time he expressed strong feelings about the working of the mixed economy, of the partnership of government and private interest. To Greenspan, this mixing has resulted in an unbalanced, inflationary, economic structure.

All of Greenspan's predecessors on the Council were academics, and therefore their economic beliefs and theoretical frameworks of analysis were established in either academic journals or long treatises. With Greenspan, this written record was lacking. However, a profile of Greenspan's economic foundations can be established through the cohesive series of statements given in his Congressional testimony. To Greenspan, at the time of these hearings, inflation was the number one American problem. He feared that it would eventually weaken the economic system's viability. While control of inflation was to be sought through a stronger control of money and credit growth, the key to the inflation of the 1970s, according to Greenspan, was fiscal policy. Excessive government spending and its resulting deficits brought the government into private capital markets, thereby preempting private savings. Governmental fiscal actions force private borrowers to pressure the banking system to meet their money and credit demands. This, in its turn, requires the Federal Reserve to accommodate its constituency, private banks, resulting in an expansion of the money supply—a crowding out problem that is met by an accommodating monetary aggregate increase. In Greenspan's view, a first step in the fight against inflation is a reduction of federal spending. Any decrease in expenditures results in a lowered pressure on the price level through a decline in the money supply.

With respect to taxes, Greenspan is equally consistent in philosophy. Within a free society, Greenspan has maintained that the claim of government on a person's income is not unqualified. Moreover, the principal form of taxation, the progressive income tax, defies the rules of equity and also threatens the total amount of taxes collected through its disincentive effects. The pragmatic Greenspan did perceive the inconsistency in lowering taxes with an economy in an inflationary and deficit state. Whereas, in his view, taxes were generally a burden on the economy and were best reduced, the government's fiscal predicament in 1974 required a maintenance of tax levels as they were then constituted. Any tax reduction would have increased the size of the already too large fiscal deficit.

With respect to incomes policies, Greenspan abhorred the strangulation of the marketplace that wage and price controls represented. Introduced during the Nixon years, these controls, as viewed by Greenspan, were more hurtful than helpful to long-term price stability. His reference was, of course, to the surge in prices after controls were removed.

When questioned about his position on antitrust legislation, Greenspan replied that the interpretation of the laws was best left to the courts. When prodded further, Greenspan offered the view that the law's position toward monopolies was too inflexible, if not wrong, particularly to those monopolies that gained their status through efficient production. Greenspan argued that the structure of antitrust statutes was economically irrational. He maintained that the laws were both a misconstruction of history and economic theory. He did, however, recognize the negative effects associated with "coercive" monopoly, a monopoly that misallocated resources through its ability to restrict market entry of competitors.

The views enunciated by Greenspan were, to some, extreme—the economic beliefs of a man referred to as a "fundamental mystic," a believer in "the old time religion," a "radical." Indeed, a more pointed statement of this view was found in a letter by Senator William Proxmire of the Senate Banking Committee to his colleagues in Congress questioning the appointment of one who "has the almost incredible posture for an economic realist in these days—of opposing the progressive income tax."

The depictions of Greenspan by his detractors might appear extreme. Nevertheless, Greenspan's early economic training at New York University undoubtedly convinced him of the powerful forces at work in free markets. Just as important as his academic studies was Greenspan's early association with the philosopher and novelist Ayn Rand, whose persuasive belief in objectivism, or rational selfishness, has clearly influenced Greenspan's thoughts.

Rand's objectivism extols the virtues of total laissez-faire capitalism. This market approach to human behavior is exemplified by Rand's heroes in her novels, *The Fountainhead* and *Atlas Shrugged*. Her discussions with Greenspan solidified his belief that capitalism is moral as well as efficient and practical. Once the marriage of morality and the free market is accepted, it is hardly surprising that Greenspan would argue against a mixed economy. In issues of the *Objectivist*, an Ayn Randian periodical, Greenspan pursued his arguments against the confiscation of wealth by a welfare state through deficit financing. He has railed against consumer protectionism as but a way to shield the ineffective and inefficient producer. His points of view are representative of a strong ideologue. While his beliefs appear extreme, they belie a more conciliatory, if not softer, personality.

One of the admirable assets of Greenspan has been his capacity to move quietly and effectively among his colleagues of both the conservative and liberal banner. It is his nonaggressive ego that wins him friends and disarms enemies. Former Democratic CEA chairman Arthur Okun*, a natural opponent, has been won over by Greenspan's openness and amiability.

Born in 1926 in New York City, Alan Greenspan was the only child of broker Herbert and Rose (Goldsmith) Greenspan. His parents were divorced in 1931, and Greenspan was raised by his mother's sister in the Washington Heights section of Manhattan. Greenspan has admitted a certain shyness as a boy, and he was said to have strong commitments to all of his interests, a trait still evident today. One of these was music, an early and lasting love. (He ranks listening to Mozart and Corelli high on his leisure time priorities.)

Greenspan graduated from George Washington High School in New York with no particular distinction. He then attended the Juilliard School to study music for a short time, leaving in 1944 to join a dance band for which he played clarinet and saxophone. After a year of touring the country his attachment to books and ideas brought him back to the discipline of a formal education. Attending New York University, he majored in economics, graduating summa cum laude with a Bachelor of Science degree in 1948. Before graduating from NYU in 1950 with an M.A. in economics he married Joan Mitchell. The marriage was annulled after one year, but not before his wife introduced him to Ayn Rand.

After obtaining his master's degree Greenspan enrolled for the doctorate program at Columbia University. His studies were initiated under Arthur Burns* (who was to be the chairman of the Federal Reserve Board when Greenspan became chairman of the Council of Economic Advisers). Greenspan left Columbia before finishing his studies, which held his interest less and less. (However, after his tenure at the Council, Greenspan earned his doctorate, which was granted by NYU in 1977. His thesis was a series of analytical works based on earlier published writings.)

Greenspan's professional career has been primarily that of an economic consultant and forecaster. Except for a short stint as an instructor of economics at NYU from 1953 to 1955 and as a part-time lecturer at the Nathaniel Branden Institute in New York City, a forum for Ayn Rand followers, and his present association as adjunct professor of economics at NYU, Greenspan's activities have been oriented toward the business sector.

Greenspan's first position was with the National Industrial Conference Board, a nonprofit research organization supported primarily by business subscriptions and donations. His work, in part, at the board was to estimate the demand for the steel, aluminum, and copper industries. Greenspan stayed with the Conference Board until 1953, at which time he joined with William Townsend to form the consulting firm Townsend-Greenspan and Company. Greenspan moved from vice president to president of the company upon the death of Townsend in 1958.

At the time of his appointment as CEA chairman, the Townsend-Greenspan Company staff had grown from six employees to some twenty-five economists and other personnel; its expansion was slow and controlled. Greenspan explained the company's purposeful growth philosophy as deliberate to maintain quality. Expansion could also have been slowed by Greenspan's need to control. *Business Week* (April 28, 1975) indicated that Greenspan ran ''a one-man band,'' using his staff primarily for research. Despite this system Greenspan orchestrated the right tunes as his firm represented over 100 major industrial and financial institutions embracing the nation's top banks. Personal rewards also accrued as Greenspan's income, primarily from his consulting firm, amounted to $300,000 in the year of his Council appointment. The success of his firm can be attributed to Greenspan's ability to take fragmented numbers and develop them into a coherent totality. Greenspan has indicated that his company's function was to provide his clients general macro- and microeconomic information.

At the time of his CEA appointment Greenspan resigned and severed all connections with his firm. His stock was placed in a blind trust, and he did not receive profits from his firm until his return to the company. At the time of his departure the management of the company was turned over to an executive committee comprised of three women, all experienced and seasoned professionals of the firm.

By the time he was appointed as chairman of the Council, Greenspan had already come to know Washington. Despite his 1974 statement that he would not come to Washington until he could ''make things better,'' Greenspan did join the Nixon forces in 1967 and had risen to become one of Nixon's strong aides for the 1968 election. Prior to the election Greenspan was Nixon's director of domestic policy research. He was also the president-elect's transition representative to the Bureau of the Budget as well as his chairman of the Task Force on Foreign Trade Policy. Even after his return to New York after Nixon took office, Greenspan was called upon as an informal adviser as well as being appointed to the Task Force on Economic Growth (1969), the Commission on an All-Volunteer Armed Force (1969–79), and the Commission on Financial Structure and Regulation (1970–71).

Greenspan came to the Council with an unassailable reputation as an economic forecaster. He also came with his free enterprise philosophy. Having taken office in September 1974, Greenspan inherited an economy that was faced with what was considered an agonizing rate of inflation. In his role as chairman, forecaster, and policy strategist, Greenspan ran into some early difficult times. In September 1974, in his first public pronouncement as chairman, and as noted economists gathered for an economic summit on the inflation problem, Greenspan forecasted a steady economy. Greenspan misread the nation's economic position. In October he counseled Ford to ask Congress for a tax surcharge. His proposal was to be a budget offset to increased Social Security benefits offered by Ford. Both forecast and recommendation were in face of an economy that by the end of 1974 experienced one of its worst declines in output in the post–World War II period. Early in April 1975 Greenspan said that the worst was yet to come on the economic front; in fact, by then the economic decline had actually flattened out. However, from that point on his forecasting performances improved impressively.

The 1975 *Economics Report of the President* forecasted recovery. By the end of the year Greenspan's forecasted GNP target was on the mark despite his detractors' earlier voices to the contrary. The 1976 report reiterated a continuation of substantial economic gains. Accordingly, the 1976 first quarter GNP grew at an annual 7 percent rate. While the rate of growth slowed during the rest of the year, the performance of the economy fell within Greenspan's expectations.

For 1977 Greenspan was again skillful in his prediction. He forecasted a real GNP increase of between 5.5 and 6 percent, and the actual growth rate was again right on target. The 1977 report is notable not only for its forecasting accuracy but also for the delineation of four general principles of fiscal policy that Greenspan believed would assure sustained expansion.

In Greenspan's opinion, demand stimulus should be provided by tax reduction rather than increased government expenditures. As he viewed fiscal policy, its inefficiencies entered through the timing of the expenditures themselves. He argued that the impact of new programs would come at a time when it would not be needed. He also focused on the private sector misallocation costs of changes in government programs.

Greenspan also set out as a principle that tax reductions be permanent rather than of a temporary rebate form. This requirement used the permanent income hypothesis as its conceptual base. That is, Greenspan argued, consumers will increase their spending if they expect their real income increase from tax reductions to be "permanent." He further maintained that temporary tax rebates would not stimulate business investment, viewed on the same logic applicable to consumers. A surge in spending from nonpermanent tax reductions would not create further capital spending, as businesses would look beyond short-run incentives and determine their investment needs on consumer behavior over the longer run.

The third tenet he offered centered on the need to balance fiscal incentives between both consumption and investment. Here Greenspan focused on the necessity that investment outpace GNP in order to achieve sustained employment and income growth. He argued that once the past year's business investment had slowed, it required a financial stimulus over and beyond that simply provided by cuts in personal taxes. To Greenspan, the slowing of investment experienced in the economy during his tenure was also fostered by the lagged behavior of labor productivity. To counter both falling investment and productivity, he looked back to the early 1960s, when similar problems were eliminated by a reduction in corporate tax rates.

His last prescription to assure a steady economic expansion was a required balance among the components of aggregate demand. What Greenspan sought was a reduction of the imbalances that might accrue, such as overaccumulation of inventories or an insufficient accumulation of fixed capital. A rise in demand, if met with rising prices, could degenerate into a capital accumulation restraint over the long run due to an inflationary risk premium necessary for new investment projects.

In accord with his principles, Greenspan recommended a 1977 tax plan providing a permanent tax cut for individuals and corporations. The tax cut was comprised of a 10 percent reduction for individuals in the form of higher personal exemptions, and an increase in the low-income allowance and lower tax rates. A reduction in taxes would also accrue to corporations through a 2 percent reduction in the corporate tax rate.

The learning process for Greenspan in acting as policy maker can be seen through the Ford administration's tax policies. The fiscal program for 1977, a permanent reduction in taxes, compares to the temporary tax rebate proposal in 1975. In this earlier proposal the administration sought a similar $12 billion tax relief. However, that program was aimed solely at consumers and was a one-time tax reduction. For the business community only a one-year increase in the investment tax credit was offered. These tax reductions were designed not for long-term growth, but for a quick fix.

When Greenspan assumed office in September 1974, the unemployment rate for the month was 5.5 percent and inflation stood at 12.1 percent for the year. By December 1977 the unemployment rate had fallen from its high of 8.5 percent in 1975 to 6.3 percent. Inflation, as measured by the Consumer Price Index, had fallen to a 6.1 percent rate for the 1977 calendar year. Whereas Greenspan had misread the strength of the recession in place when he became chairman, by the end of his tenure both inflation and unemployment had fallen considerably from their previous highs.

Greenspan's devotion to his work has been noted often. His habits of being at his desk from 7:30 in the morning to the late evening hours carried through from New York to Washington. Joseph Kraft (*New York Times Magazine*, April 1976) suggests that he has little interest in either money or that which it can buy. Socially, Greenspan still exhibits the diffidence he had in his youth. Henry Mitchell of the *Washington Post* has labeled Greenspan a "social creeper," a term derived from viewing him at Washington parties where he would pass through the room saying, "Pardon."

It may well be that Greenspan's soft ways contributed to his success among his colleagues. Greenspan speaks candidly in a quiet baritone. His renowned command of the numbers of his profession is accompanied by wit and reason. Reportedly ill at ease with small talk or gossip, Greenspan is more at home in the discourse of economic analysis. His complex, sometimes special language has been dubbed "Greenspanese" by insiders.

What Greenspan earned at the Council was credibility, not only with numbers but with the president. While his early statements that inflation was "a political, not an economic problem" and his politically maladroit comment that inflation hit the wealthy harder than the poor may not have won him cheering crowds, they did reassert his characteristic bluntness. He did not seek to play the Washington political game. His function was to advise the president as to the state of the economy. It was general knowledge in Washington that Greenspan was the economist Gerald Ford listened to most often. He accomplished this by the force of probity, charm, and pragmatism. Where it had been argued that the Nixon Council was weakened by its political maneuvers, Greenspan's Council won respect for its reasoned ideology and its firm attitude to reporting and analyzing the numbers.

With the end of the Ford administration Greenspan returned to private life and reassumed the headship of Townsend-Greenspan and Company. His return to Washington in mid–1987 as Federal Reserve Board Chairman is a continuation of his role as economic policy maker.

Greenspan has served on two national commissions since he left the Council: the National Commission on Supplies and Shortages (1974–77) and the notable National Commission on Social Security Reform, of which he was appointed chairman. He has been a member of President Reagan's Economic Policy Advisory Board and the President's Foreign Intelligence Advisory Board; a member of *Time* magazine's board of economists; a senior adviser to the Brookings Panel on Economic Activity; a member of the board of overseers of the Hoover Institution at Stanford University; and a consultant for the Congressional Budget Office and the Federal Reserve Board.

He has held directorships in the following companies: Aluminum Company of America (ALCOA); American Broadcasting Company (ABC); Automatic Data Processing Inc.; General Foods Corporation; J. P. Morgan & Co., Inc.; Morgan Guaranty Trust Company of New York; and Mobil Corporation. He is currently on the board of the Council on Foreign Relations and holds memberships in the Conference of Business Economists (past chairman), National Association of Business Economists (past president [1970] and fellow), National Economists Club (Washington, D.C., past director), and is on the Executive Committee of the Trilateral Commission. A partial listing of his distinguished awards are: joint recipient, with Arthur Burns and William Simon, of the Thomas Jefferson Award for the Greatest Public Service Performed by an Elected or Appointed Official, presented by the American Institute for Public Service (1976); recipient of the Public Service Award, presented by Claremont Men's College (1977); recipient of the Distinguished Alumni Award, Graduate School of Business Administration, New York University (1978); and honorary degree, Doctor of Commercial Science, Pace University (1981).

BIBLIOGRAPHY

Greenspan, Alan. "Business Investment Decisions and Full Employment Models." *Proceedings of the Business and Economic Statistics Section*, American Statistical Association. Washington, D.C.: 1959, pp. 2–16.

———. "Investment Risk: The New Dimension of Policy." *The Economist* 264, no. 6988 (August 6 1977): 31–35.

———. "A Model of Capital Expenditures and Internal Rates of Return in the U.S. Economy." *Business Economics* 6, no. 3 (May 1981).

———. "The Quiet Revolution." *Across the Board*, The Conference Board Magazine 14, no. 5 (May 1977): 38–41.

———. "Stock Prices and Capital Evaluation." *Proceedings of the Business and Economic Statistics Section*, American Statistical Association. Washington, D.C.: 1961, pp. 102–17.

BERNARD S. KATZ

HELLER, WALTER

(b. August 27, 1915, d. June 15, 1987), CEA January 29, 1961-November 15, 1964)

On the wall behind Walter Heller's desk in his unassuming office at the University of Minnesota hung pictures of him with John F. Kennedy and Lyndon B. Johnson. On the floor in a corner near windows that face the rising skyline of Minneapolis were stacked scores of recently published economic principles textbooks. A long table extending beyond his desk held current periodicals, the latest books on business and economic policy, and transcripts of Heller's upcoming articles and speeches.

These three images represent the economic work of Walter Wolfgang Heller, chairman of the Council of Economic Advisers under two presidents. Heller was the consummate economic educator; his students have been and still are American presidents and governmental leaders, undergraduates, and the public in general. From his office he undertook the continuing challenge of educating the public about economics. He fit interviews for national newspapers and television networks and trips to appear before Congress and for speeches around the country into a schedule that included teaching hundreds of students in the economic principles course. It was not much different during the four years when he chaired the Council of Economic Advisers. His role had always been to raise the public's economic awareness and to push for a greater use of the tools of economics to advance the public interest. Many, including presidents, students, and journalists, claim that no one was better at this than Heller. In one of Heller's many appearances before Congress, Senator William Proxmire not only praised Heller as an economist but also as someone who could take the dismal science and make it interesting.

Born in Buffalo, New York, in 1915, Heller was raised in Milwaukee. He graduated from high school at age sixteen. He was clearly a product of the Depression era. Early in his undergraduate days at Oberlin College he decided on a career in economics. He often indicated that those who grew up during the Depression saw the economy flat on its back; he wanted to understand why and to try to do something about it. While at Oberlin Heller was influenced by economics professor Benjamin Wilson, who shuttled between Oberlin and Washington, where he served as an adviser to the National Recovery Administration. Heller was intrigued by the combination of academics and public service and committed himself to the pursuit of a career as an applied economist.

After graduating Phi Beta Kappa from Oberlin in 1935, Heller entered the graduate program in economics at the University of Wisconsin. He concentrated his graduate work in the areas of finance and taxation. Also during this period he met, courted, and married Emily Johnson, daughter of a University of Wisconsin professor. Walter and Emily Johnson Heller received their Ph.D.'s (hers was in physiology) during the same graduation ceremony in 1941.

Upon graduation Heller moved to Washington as an economist in the Treasury Department. While at the Treasury he worked to develop a withholding plan for the federal income tax system. This experience undoubtedly influenced his thinking about the role of taxes in the economy.

In 1946 Heller was offered a position as associate professor in the department of economics at the University of Minnesota. He grabbed it—it was his calling.

Throughout his early years at Minnesota, Heller would interrupt his academic career for stints in public service. During 1947–48 he was a financial adviser for Lucius Clay, the U.S. military governor in occupied Germany. He later served as financial adviser at the United Nations, worked on the Treasury team that devised a tax increase during the Korean War, advised King Hussein of Jordan, and acted as unpaid fiscal adviser for Minnesota governor Orville Freeman.

Before joining the Kennedy administration Heller devoted much time to issues of economic growth and how the policies of the federal government could influence economic performance. In an appearance before the National Conference on Social Welfare in Washington on August 10, 1960 he outlined his thoughts on economic policy goals: (1) a less restrictive and more flexible set of fiscal and monetary policies; (2) a thoroughgoing reform of the federal income tax structure; and (3) increased investment in human beings. Within six months of his talk he was in a position to implement his policies.

By 1960 Heller was not unknown in Washington, but he certainly was not well known. His advisory work for Orville Freeman, who was to become Kennedy's Secretary of Agriculture, and his friendship with Hubert Humphrey brought Heller to then-candidate Kennedy's attention in October 1960. During a Kennedy campaign stop in Minneapolis, Humphrey brought Heller to meet Kennedy as he hurried to prepare for an evening appearance. Humphrey pushed Heller past the candidate's entourage and into Kennedy's suite, where he introduced Heller as the "finest economist west of the Mississippi" (Heller quipped that he did not know what Humphrey would have said if they had been in St. Paul, on the other side of the river). Kennedy, although late for his next campaign appearance, proceeded to question Heller about various economic issues. Heller was impressed by Kennedy and composed a lengthy memo to him in which he elaborated on some of the issues they had discussed. He did not see or hear from Kennedy again during the campaign. After the election Heller met with the president-elect at his Georgetown home and accepted Kennedy's offer to chair the Council of Economic Advisers. There were more prominent economists in 1960 than Heller but Kennedy recognized in Heller qualities that he could well live with.

Heller went to Washington as an outsider and, as he said, as a mid-western populist. Enthusiastic, dedicated, and hard-working, Heller threw himself into the work of the Council. Just after the inauguration *Time* wrote about ''the present-minded professor who tempers earnestness with cordiality and intellect with a touch of ambitious worldliness.'' Heller would need all his intellect, cordiality, and ambition to survive in Washington.

In accepting President Kennedy's offer to chair the Council, Heller had only two conditions—first, that he serve not only as chairman of the Council but as the president's chief economic adviser, and second, that he be able to select the other members of the Council. He was certainly Kennedy's chief economic adviser, although he did not always have his way. Heller did have free rein in selecting his co-workers. He chose James Tobin* of Yale University and Kermit Gordon* of Williams College. All three were in their forties and had begun their careers in the midst of the Depression. This surely influenced their views and their work.

The Council had not been used extensively by either Truman or Eisenhower. Kennedy made it clear to Heller that he wanted to restore both the spirit and the letter of the Employment Act of 1946. The new president wanted solid information from his economic advisers which would help in the formulation of economic policy. This view and the president's challenge that Heller should use the White House as a pulpit for the public's education in economics certainly suited Heller. He not only took up the challenge of educating the public in economics, he also took on the economic education of the president.

Heller's major goal as chairman of the Council was to eliminate the gap between the economy's actual production and its potential output. He had very definite ideas about achieving this goal, but as a pragmatist he realized that he had to work within the administrative structure of the federal government. Heller perceived Douglas Dillon, Secretary of the Treasury, as primarily responsible for financial matters and taxes; David Bell, Director of the Bureau of the Budget, was responsible for budgetary matters. Heller saw the Council as providing economic forecasting for the president. These three individuals met as the ''troika.'' William McChesney Martin, chairman of the Federal Reserve System, was brought in to form the ''quadriad.''

These individuals met often, but not regularly, with the president. Heller used memos to communicate with Kennedy and would ask for a meeting of the troika or quadriad when issues warranted. Heller's staff generated forecasts about economic performance; he would then translate this information into a package which was usable by the president. Heller's goal was to give economic analysis a larger role in policy making.

Heller thought it imperative to change the federal tax system so as to stimulate the economy. He pushed for a more aggressive fiscal policy and an overthrow of Eisenhower's tight money policy. In Heller's view one way to move the economy out of the doldrums was to cut taxes. He mentioned the idea of a tax cut when he first met Kennedy in October 1960 and reintroduced it after the president assumed office. Kennedy was cautious, even negative, about the suggestion of cutting taxes. He had stressed the need for sacrifice during the campaign, and he did not see how a tax cut fit with this theme. At the same time, his innate conservatism during a time when there was a large budget deficit and the political opposition in Congress combined to convince Kennedy that the time was not right for a tax cut.

Heller persisted in the theme that a tax cut would get the economy going again and help reduce the deficit. The balanced budget at full employment concept became part of the White House vocabulary, and Kennedy even hinted that deficit financing, under certain circumstances, was acceptable. But Kennedy was not prepared to publically endorse a tax cut. Heller felt that he was making progress in educating the president by the end of 1961. Unfortunately, the mobilization of resources surrounding the Berlin crisis undermined any progress Heller had made. With the military buildup which accompanied the crisis, all that Heller was able to do was convince the president not to increase taxes.

Heller continued to gain the confidence of the president while at the same time elaborating on his idea of fiscal drag. In numerous public appearances Heller discussed fiscal drag and the need to provide a fiscal or tax stimulus even as the economy began to recover. By mid–1962 Kennedy was convinced that he needed to support a major tax cut during 1963.

Throughout the Kennedy years Heller, the other members of the CEA, and the economic consultants they brought to Washington moved the ''new economics'' of fiscal stimulus into the forefront of policy discussions. Heller worked to educate the president and the other policy heads. Perhaps Heller's greatest accomplishment during the Kennedy years was that he moved economics up on the policy agenda. He did this by convincing people that the new economics worked, that a tax cut amid a deficit and even in an expanding economy was a reasonable way to maintain and advance the economic expansion.

During the Kennedy years Heller brought a small army of economists to Washington to serve as members of the CEA staff or as special consultants. Economists such as Kenneth Arrow, Richard Cooper, Arthur Okun*, George Perry, Robert Solow, Nancy Teeters, Otto Eckstein*, Joseph Pechman, Paul Samuelson, and Charles Schultze* all added their expertise to policy matters. Although Heller was unable to thoroughly translate his ideas for a new economic approach into policy actions, his efficient style won the president's confidence, and his eloquent expression of his ideas won Congressional and public support. His economic reports, especially the *Economic Report of the President*, laid out an understandable and convincing argument for fiscal activism. The foundation was laid for the emergence of Heller's program over the next few years.

Heller was on his way to Japan when Kennedy was assassinated. The trade delegation of which he was a part returned to Washington, and Heller immediately set to work preparing materials for the new president. Heller had maintained a good working relationship with Lyndon Johnson while he was vice president. That relationship now blossomed.

Heller prepared a detailed memo for Johnson which provided an overview of the functioning of the Council and an update on all activities under way. He also outlined the agenda of key economic issues that the president would have to face in the next few months. The major topic of Heller's first conversation with President Johnson was the need for a tax cut. Heller felt that Kennedy's public education approach to the need for a tax cut coupled with Johnson's political skill would be sufficient to carry the day. He was right. Despite continuing opposition by the Treasury, Johnson would move to implement a tax cut in 1964.

Heller's relationship with Kennedy had been close, but he was even closer to Johnson. He often referred to this relationship as an unlikely alliance between the egghead and the political leader. The relationship may have been unlikely, but it was productive. Kennedy had bucked the tide in even discussing some of Heller's ideas for a more aggressive fiscal policy. Those discussions laid the groundwork, and Johnson used Heller's well-reasoned approach and his own political savvy to formulate a well-rounded economic program.

During the second portion of his four years as CEA chairman, Heller's two colleagues were Gardner Ackley* from the University of Michigan and John P. Lewis* from Indiana University. These three continued to provide the president with solid economic forecasts and with justification for Johnson's economic recommendations. For example, Johnson realized that he would have to make tradeoffs to get the tax cut through Congress. Heller formulated an economic plan that would keep expenditures in line so that the president could present a balanced budget plan to Congress.

Heller's impact on Johnson was not limited to a successful economic game plan for the 1964 tax cut. Much of the credit for the War on Poverty must go to Heller. The CEA chairman felt that investment in human capital was of vital importance and that the federal government needed to take an active role in eliminating the slack in the economy. Heller had pushed the idea with Kennedy; in fact, the subject of their last conversation was a program to "attack poverty." But Kennedy had not had time to act. Johnson's reaction to the idea was extremely positive.

Heller also had a major impact on the formulation of wage-price guideposts. The idea for such guideposts dates to early 1961. Heller felt that with so much slack in the economy only cost-push factors could raise prices. The January 1962 CEA report talks about noninflationary wage-price behavior. Johnson was more comfortable with the guideposts than was Kennedy. They were implemented as part of an overall economic plan but fell apart by mid-1966 as increasing expenditures for Vietnam rekindled demand-pull inflation.

Heller pushed hard for tax reform which would include a revenue sharing plan. His support for this program is revealing in part because it brought him into direct conflict with a longtime ally, organized labor. Heller had initially proposed a revenue sharing idea in a 1957 article in the *Canadian Tax Journal*. After the 1964 tax cut began to work Heller felt that the time was ripe for a reintroduction of the revenue sharing idea. He appointed Joseph Pechman to chair a task force which recommended the revenue sharing proposal. Heller pushed for the plan, but the idea was dropped in the late summer of 1964 due to opposition, especially from organized labor.

Heller had been prepared to leave Washington after the January 1964 economic report was completed. He had a strong commitment to academic life and, although he loved his work in Washington, felt that he needed to return to his professorial role before losing touch. So sure was he of an imminent departure that his family had returned to Minnesota in late 1963. Kennedy's assassination delayed Heller's plans to join them, but in the spring of 1964 he approached Johnson to resign.

Heller explained to the president the ''4-F syndrome''—family (his wife had been suffering from Lupus disease), finances (he estimated he was losing about $5,000 a year due to expenses in D.C.), fatigue (the sixteen-hour days with limited staff were too much), and frustration (not being able to accomplish all that he wanted). Johnson did not want Heller to leave, and few men could say no to Johnson. In the end Heller agreed to remain through the November election. He arranged for Ackley to replace him as CEA chairman and, after Johnson's election victory in November 1964, returned to Minnesota, leaving Washington amid high praise.

Walter Heller never claimed ownership of the ideas he proposed while chairman of the CEA. He told the Detroit Economic Club shortly after leaving Washington that today's economics was hardly new. Rather, it was a blending of Keynes, the classicists, and modern use of mathematics. Although the ideas were not new, Heller was able to formulate the ''blend of Keynes and the classics'' into the ''new economics'' of macroeconomic policy.

Heller worked tirelessly to educate his presidents, Congress, and the public about specific programs to achieve stated goals. He did this by changing the CEA from a low-key, almost invisible, little-used agency into a forceful unit preparing, presenting, and promoting economic forecasts and policy recommendations.

Heller's rejection of the view that the American economy was saturated with output and his promotion of the alternative view of stimulating the system through fiscal policies helped close the gap between actual and potential output. He could take full credit for the new economic approach even though none of the theory behind this approach was actually new.

Heller himself had indicated that the War on Poverty program and the 1964 tax cut gave him the most satisfaction. His greatest contribution may well have been the increased importance he brought to economists in public policy through the contributions of the Council of Economic Advisers. Heller argued that the CEA was an important and vital component of policy formulation. He was an outspoken critic of suggestions to eliminate the CEA. To Heller, the Council had no axe to grind, making it imperative to the president.

After leaving Washington Heller continued in his role as economic educator. His views changed somewhat, but he was still an economist well grounded in Keynesian economic theory. In his articles for the *Wall Street Journal* (he was a regular contributor) and *Time* (he was a member of its board of economists) and in his newsletter for National City Bank, Heller promoted programs to move the economy closer to its potential output and criticized programs that overlooked the importance of human capital in that growth process.

Heller remained active as a classroom teacher and as an adviser to corporations in the upper Midwest. He was a member of the boards of directors for numerous national and international firms. He continued to promote the advance of economic knowledge—as a member and past president of the American Economic Association, as a director and past chairman of the National Bureau of Economic Research, as adviser to political leaders, and as a consultant to various government agencies.

Walter Heller was often criticized for promoting programs that were no longer appropriate. The goals he espoused will never be inappropriate. His ability to advance those goals through well-reasoned and articulate arguments made him the consummate economic educator.

BIBLIOGRAPHY

Heller, Walter. *The Economy: Old Myths and New Realities*. New York: Norton, 1976.
———. *New Dimensions of Political Economy*. Cambridge, Mass.: Harvard University Press, 1966.
———. *Perspectives on Economic Growth*. New York: Norton, 1968.
———. Pechman, Joseph, and Simler, N. J. *Economics in the Public Service*. New York: Norton, 1982.
Rowan, Hobart. *The Free Enterprisers*. New York: Putnam's, 1964.
Sobel, Robert. *The Worldy Economists*. New York: Free Press, 1980.

BRUCE R. DALGAARD

HOUTHAKKER, HENDRIK SAMUEL
(b. November 22, 1924), CEA February 4, 1969-July 15, 1971

With more than a hundred publications which span from the highly theoretical to the most applied, Hendrik Samuel Houthakker has been an active contributor to the field of economics for more than thirty years. Born in 1924 in the Netherlands, he completed his graduate work there in 1949. During the 1950s he taught at Stanford University, the University of Tokyo, and Massachusetts Institute of Technology, and held research positions at Cambridge University and at the Cowles Commission for Economic Research at the University of Chicago. Since 1960 he has been on the faculty of Harvard University. Among his many honors, he received the American Economic Association's John Bates Clark Medal in 1963 and was vice president of the association in 1972. He has received honorary doctorates from the University of Amsterdam and the University of Fribourg and is an adjunct scholar of the American Enterprise Institute.

From 1969 to 1971, Houthakker served on President Nixon's Council of Economic Advisers. Upon his resignation from the Council, he returned to Harvard and is currently the Henry Lee Professor of Economics. In addition, since 1971 he has been the editor of Harvard's prestigious journal, the *Review of Economics and Statistics*. He is married to the former Anna-Teresa Tymieniecka and has three children.

Over the years, Houthakker has been involved in a number of studies of consumer demand. His concern with the application of economic theory is seen very clearly in this area. In reference to two comprehensive studies of consumer demand in which he participated, one examining consumption patterns in Britain and the other consumption patterns in the United States, he has pointed out that the two approaches were suggested by economic theory but were not constrained by the theory. Additionally, while utilizing novel statistical techniques neither study is primarily methodological. The results of the studies are substantive and not merely examples of methods. A more recent effort is an extensive study of eighty-two categories of expenditures for the period 1929–64 in the United States with expenditure projections for 1970 and 1975. The model is a dynamic one in which demand is assumed to depend not only on prices and income but also on preexisting stocks. Thus, Houthakker and his colleagues are able to test whether each category of consumption expenditure in the United States is based on what they call "habit formation" or "inventory adjustment." This variable turned out to be important in explaining consumer choice, and, for most of the expenditure categories, consumption was found to be characterized by habit formation rather than by inventory adjustment. In addition, income, as opposed to price, was found to be of greater importance in explaining general expenditure patterns. The authors speculate that the importance of habit formation and the minor role of prices in explaining consumer expenditure may reflect the relatively high income level of the United States. In support of this view, they refer to consumption studies done on other countries with lower per capita income levels where inventory adjustment and prices seem to play a more important role.

In another comprehensive study of household expenditure, Houthakker tested Engel's Law, which states that as income rises, the proportion of income spent on food tends to decline. Based on econometric analysis of forty surveys from thirty countries, Houthakker found that in each case Engel's Law was confirmed.

Houthakker also recognized that price and income elasticities of a country's imports and exports, relative to the elasticities of the imports and exports of its trading partners, could have an impact on a country's trade balance. In a study with Stephen P. Magee, the authors empirically estimated that the income elasticity of demand for total imports in the United States is about the same as that of other countries, while the income elasticity of other countries' demands for United States exports is quite low. Thus, even if other factors such as growth or inflation were the same in the United States as in the countries with which it trades, one would still expect the United States trade balance to deteriorate over time.

Even in what might be considered more theoretically oriented endeavors, many of which dealt with consumer theory, Houthakker was concerned with how the new extension of the theory could be incorporated into empirical work. As he argued in an article on the notion of direct and indirect utility functions and the assumption of additivity, which simplifies the application of consumer theory, consumer choice theory requires further integration with empirical research. It requires generalization and specialization. These special theories, in turn, may provide new directions for empirical analysis. Thus the reader is continuously reminded of how pure theory can be tested and applied.

A second theme which runs through much of Houthakker's writing is the need to encourage economic efficiency through the use of the market mechanism. He has often argued that so long as the supply and demand curves in a particular market are normal, then the role for the government is to promote the functioning of that market. This belief is forcefully elaborated in his analysis of the agricultural sector of the United States, as well as in writings on other commodity markets.

In the case of agriculture, his own empirical work and that of others has led him to conclude that farmers and consumers do respond normally to price changes. That is, farmers tend to vary supplies directly with price changes, while consumers vary quantities demanded inversely with price changes. Thus, he argues that the root of the so-called farm problem is not market failure; rather, it is, ironically, the result of growth. With growth, the demand for agricultural products has not risen proportionately with the growth of the economy, in accordance with Engel's Law, while supply has increased dramatically. Therefore, there will necessarily be adjustment problems for this sector. So he notes that a sector of the economy that experiences technological advances in a nongrowing market should not make claim to a constant or greater proportion of a nation's income. However, the only way that farmers will actually make the appropriate output response is if prices are market determined. Thus, he has consistently argued against agriculture price supports or federal marketing orders, the latter of which have led to the actual destruction of farm output and which, he says, amount to nothing more than government sponsored cartels, operated through farm cooperatives, that are exempt from antitrust laws.

To the extent that price fluctuations may be undesirable from an income distributional or political point of view, he has called for programs that are less likely to interrupt the functioning of the market than those which have been in practice in the United States. In this light, he has suggested that transitional and declining acreage payments be used to ease the shock of returning to a free market situation, and that the government increase the ability of private traders in agricultural markets to bear risk, by intervening in futures markets if prices move outside set ranges. This type of intervention would reduce the problem of price fluctuations to the individual farmer without destroying the allocative function of the market.

Similarly, he has tested empirically the functioning of various energy markets. Finding them also to be responsive to price changes, he has advocated the use of the price mechanism, over other strategies, for limiting energy consumption and encouraging producers to find new sources. In what may have amounted to an overly enthusiastic response to the energy problem of the early 1970s in terms of the timing of its prediction, he has argued that in some markets supply and demand conditions may have not changed. However, he argues that is certainly not the truth for the petroleum industry. He further notes that in the petroleum market the potential for increased output exists; at current OPEC prices surpluses will develop both through supply increases and declining demand.

Even as head of a committee concerned with curbing inflation in 1970, he was willing to accept the consequences of high prices in the copper market in order to allow the market mechanism to function. His reasoning was that most copper production was in the hands of large producers who possibly had previously been keeping the price below the free market level in order to discourage new suppliers from entering the market. In that case, a temporary rise in price would eventually lead to an increase in supply and lower prices. Thus, as an interviewer for *Forbes* commented, he found himself in the rather odd position of fostering price increases rather than decreases.

Similarly, Houthakker is consistent in arguing against the use of wage and price controls and for the devaluation of the dollar when faced with a balance of payments deficit.

Houthakker's belief that economic science can and should play an important role in addressing a wide range of politico-economic issues has shaped his research. He has argued that politicians move in when economists falter.

Thus, in the case of agriculture, we find Houthakker arguing that the farm problem should be analyzed from an economy-wide perspective and not as a power struggle between the agricultural and nonagricultural sectors. He recognized the root of the problem to be economic growth and the inherent adjustments which must be made by the sector which, in the absence of forces to the contrary, will naturally claim an ever smaller percentage of national output. Most politically motivated solutions, which seem to be based on the idea that the purpose of farming is not to provide consumers with food and fiber but rather to provide the farmer an income, have led to market inefficiencies and unnecessarily costly burdens on the rest of the society. To the extent that overpopulation of farms can be justified on political grounds, it can be achieved at less cost. Thus, he has suggested programs, such as those cited earlier, which would take into account all sectors of the economy—farmers, taxpayers, and consumers. He has stated that although the movement toward direct payments to farmers and away from price supports in the early seventies was advantageous from an economic point of view, since they resulted in less of a distortion of resources allocation, price supports tend to be preferred because "they make the benefits harder to identify."

Consistent with his free market philosophy, Houthakker denounced the Nixon administration's freeze on prices and wages. He stated that such measures are but an evasion of the short run political costs inherent in a more forward looking policy, and argued instead for measures to restore the forces of competition in the economy.

On numerous occasions Houthakker has argued against barriers to trade, based essentially on the principle of comparative advantage, and for flexibility in exchange rates. For example, in a 1964 article on the merits of devaluing the dollar, he maintained that while fixed exchange rate regimes are favored by bankers the costs to the economy are high in terms of employment and income.

Houthakker was also clearly concerned that political exigencies would take precedence over economic reasoning after the 1973 OPEC oil embargo. He recognized calls for energy self-sufficiency following the oil embargo to be costly and disruptive and expressed the hope that the policy was rather after "a *potential* for self-sufficiency to forestall extortion by OPEC, rather than actual autarchy." As exemplified above, Houthakker has been keen in bringing in economic analysis and quantitative measurement as tools for addressing many pressing national and international issues.

During his tenure on the Council of Economic Advisers from 1969 to 1971, Houthakker's areas of specialization were international finance and trade policy, foreign aid and economic development, agriculture, transportation, telecommunications, industrial organization and antitrust, labor relations, long-term growth, consumer affairs, natural resources, technology, and environmental problems. His ongoing concern for economic efficiency and the use of nondistorting mechanisms to handle problems of income distribution or other adjustments came through clearly in the publications of the Council in those years.

In fact, the *1970 Economic Report of the President* devoted an entire chapter to the role of the government in assuring competitive free markets and supplementing them when necessary to achieve efficiency and progress. In discussions of various markets in both the 1970 and 1971 reports, more specific policy recommendations are given. For example, recommendations for the improvement of agricultural markets by allowing greater price flexibility and direct income payments are reminiscent of Houthakker's earlier studies of the farming sector. In the area of foreign trade, statements are made against the imposition of import restrictions and for programs to aid firms and workers in adjusting to foreign competition. While we cannot be certain who wrote these and similar sections of the reports, we can at least rest assured that Houthakker must have felt quite comfortable with them.

The Nixon administration's wage and price control program began on August 15, 1971. Houthakker's disagreement with this policy has already been noted. However, these arguments were aired publicly by him as an outsider, as he had left the Council exactly one month prior to their imposition.

BIBLIOGRAPHY

Houthakker, Hendrik S. "Are Controls the Answer?" *Review of Economics and Statistics* 54 (August 1972): 231–34.

———. "Do We Need a National Food Policy?" *American Journal of Agricultural Economics* 58 (May 1976): 259–69.

———. "An International Comparison of Household Expenditure Patterns." *Econometrics* 25 (October 1957): 532–51.

———. "The Permanent Income Hypothesis." *American Economic Review* 48 (June 1958): 400–421.

———, and Magee, Stephen. "Elasticities in World Trade." *Review of Economics and Statistics* 51 (May 1969): 111–25.

———, and Taylor, Lester. *Consumer Demand in the United States: Analysis and Projections*. Cambridge, Mass.: Harvard University Press, 1970.

Prais, S. J., and Houthakker, Hendrik. *The Analysis of Family Budgets*. Cambridge, England: Cambridge University Press, 1955.

LIBBY T. RITTENBERG

JACOBY, NEIL

(b. September 19, 1909, d. May 31, 1979), CEA September 15, 1953-February 9, 1955

The role of members of the Council of Economic Advisers is not simply that of economist, rather it is that of *political economist*. This distinction, harking back as it does to the original designation of the field we now call economics, is ideally demonstrated by the career of Neil Herman Jacoby. Jacoby was interested in the policy or political ramifications of economic actions; he was less concerned with the theoretical science of economics.

Jacoby served on the CEA from 1953 to 1955. His tenure coincided with what was arguably the most important stage in the development of the CEA. The disrepute into which the agency had fallen late in the Truman administration meant that the role of the Council would be redefined by its members at the start of the Eisenhower administration.

A curious political dance in Congress accentuated the difficulties of the CEA in 1952–53 and forced the incoming members to engage immediately in political maneuvering simply to continue the existence of the agency. In 1952, during a lightly attended session of the House of Representatives, conservative opponents of the CEA had succeeded in reducing its funding by 25 percent for the July 1952-June 1953 fiscal year. A subsequent compromise allowed the CEA to spend its allocation by March 31, 1953, but that left the incoming Council with no budget from March 31 to June 30, 1953. After much political haggling, the Council was able to obtain sufficient funding for its continuation.

While Jacoby was not part of this initial conflict, his appointment to the Council in the late summer of 1953 meant that his role on it was largely determined, from an institutional perspective, by political factors. The subsidiary funding for the period from March 31 to June 30, 1953, had been approved with the understanding that the money would be used to make Arthur F. Burns*, new chairman of the Council, more of an individual adviser to the president. The other two members were expected to have much less authority than had been the case under Truman. Some members of Eisenhower's inner circle even hoped that this would lead to an eventual dismantling of the Council and its replacement by a presidential economic adviser.

The original setting for Jacoby's entrance to the Council was one of political turmoil, and his appointment was reviewed from a political perspective rather than an economic one. Jacoby's brief and cordial acceptance by the Senate was the result of Senator William F. Knowland's certification of Jacoby's republican views.

One gets a slightly different impression from Jacoby's description of his first interview with Eisenhower. The president sought reassurances that the general ideas of Jacoby were in consonance with his own. Yet it was not Jacoby who presented his views to the president, rather it was the other way around. Ike told him that "my people have checked your professional competence" and that he merely wished to have Jacoby know where he, Ike, stood on general economic issues. Again, one has the primacy of politics—Ike's need to know that Jacoby was politically safe—but in this case, one at least has the assurance that the president did have Jacoby's professional competence checked.

Jacoby's career made him ideally suited for the political aspect of his new role in Washington. While still a graduate student at the University of Chicago (Ph.D., economics, 1938), Jacoby was the chairman of the Saskatchewan Taxation Commission (1936). He had already worked for three years in the province's Department of Finance as the supervisor of the legal and research division. Thus, Jacoby's introduction to economics was precisely in the area of political economics rather than in an academic career.

His first academic post was at the University of Chicago, where he rose from assistant professor of finance (1938), to associate professor (1940), and to full professor (1942). After 1948 he spent his academic career at the University of California, Los Angeles (UCLA), where he was first dean of the Graduate School of Business Administration (1948–68) and then Armand Hammer Professor of Business, Economics, and Policy (1968–79).

Throughout his academic career, Jacoby was involved in the economics of public policy. His publications were not weighty theoretical tomes, rather they were often policy-related volumes aimed at a broader audience. Works such as *Can Prosperity Be Sustained?* (1956), *European Economics: East and West* (1967), and *Corporate Power and Social Responsibility* (1973) placed Jacoby squarely in the field of political economy. He maintained a strong interest in the impact of government policy on economies, and, as a political economist, he felt that it was his responsibility to advise the government as to what its role should be.

This aspect of Jacoby's work, as we have seen, goes back to his original position in Saskatchewan. The political implications of taxation in his native province (Jacoby was born in Dundurn, Saskatchewan) during the 1930s are fairly clear. Throughout his long career of public policy economics, Jacoby was a strong advocate of flexible tax policies. It would seem that his experience as a policy maker in the depth of the Depression convinced him that rigid adherence to hidebound taxation theories was economically disastrous.

One can see this consistency of approach in Jacoby's major policy statements in the 1950s, 1960s, and 1970s. During his tenure on the CEA, Jacoby supported Arthur Burns' call for decreased taxation and limited government spending increases as a response to the recession of 1953–54. Burns and Jacoby were opposed by Secretary of the Treasury George Humphrey. Secretary Humphrey opposed the tax reductions at a time of federal budget deficit.

Jacoby and Burns finally won out. Unable to persuade Humphrey, Jacoby and

Burns were more successful with President Eisenhower. The tax cuts strengthened the response of the economic revival. Things were more complicated than the Burns-Humphrey debate implies. The tax proposals originated in the Treasury Department; Burns and Jacoby merely took up the cudgels against the recalcitrant secretary.

Despite the somewhat conflicting claims of credit, it is clear that Jacoby and Burns supported the Treasury proposals. The nature of the tax cuts, largely relief for corporations, relief in the form of accelerated depreciation and changes in dividend exclusions and credit provisions of the tax code, was in accord with views held by Burns and Jacoby. The government spending advocated by the Council, largely support for the interstate highway system, was also in line with this action on behalf of investment in the corporate sector.

Jacoby consistently argued on behalf of tax reform and adjustment as the major stabilization tool in the hands of the government. He believed tax management was more effective than expenditure management. Jacoby reached this conclusion as a direct result of his government experience, as he saw first-hand that government spending programs have a limited immediate effect. In this respect, the emphasis on taxation rather than spending, Jacoby might be said to represent the ideal moderate Republican political economist.

He had a very clear government program of action in mind, and maintained his attitude toward the economic role of the government throughout his career. Jacoby did not confine himself to analysis of the American economy. He has argued that developing economies, too, needed monetary and fiscal discipline and policies favorable to private enterprise. Jacoby, in his analysis of U.S. aid, concluded that America was wise to utilize market forces in guiding investment decisions, as this increased the average productivity of investment. He further argued that expansion of savings and investment were a consequence, not a cause, of development.

Many of his attitudes were what might be described as main-stream Republican political economy. One finds, in the 1970 *Report of the Presidential Commission on the Future of the American Economy*, a commission of which Jacoby was chairman, a variety of positions that collectively site him in the center of the party. He argues, for instance, in favor of a two-step minimum wage, a position often taken up by party leaders later on. Jacoby argued, as is traditionally the case, that this would lead to higher employment of the unskilled, particularly the young. The 1970 report contains a more mature statement of Jacoby's ideas than his earlier *Can Prosperity Be Sustained?*, but the main thrust of the arguments is the same. As befits someone with his interests in multinationals and the efficacy of foreign aid, there is a considerable emphasis on foreign trade. One finds a similar emphasis in the 1956 work. There he argued that the four pillars of our foreign trade were (1) to provide an example of strong economic growth, (2) to reduce trade barriers, (3) to promote investment abroad, and (4) to give aid to underdeveloped countries. The 1970 report had an entire section on "Expanding Foreign Trade and Investment."

Jacoby, as *U.S. Aid to Taiwan* makes clear, was a strong believer in the benefits of the free market. While he did not openly dismiss interventionism, his 1956 description of it was colored by strong anti-Communism. For Jacoby, interventionism meant constructive tax policy, monetary restraint, and limited regulation. As part of his dislike of interventionism, Jacoby also opposed central planning of development in his recommendations on Taiwan. He argued (in 1956) against overly specific forecasts of GNP or other indicators, on the grounds that government would seek to achieve such goals artificially. One looks in vain for any systematic governmental approach to future economic growth in the 1970 report, although Jacoby saw some use for limited planning.

This is entirely consistent with Jacoby's free market approach. One of the most interesting elements of his thought is its combination of the principles of classical political economy (Adam Smith, David Ricardo) with the pragmatism of government service. While Jacoby was not a Keynesian, nonetheless, he was willing to accept certain of Keynes' recommendations. The Burns-Jacoby advice to Eisenhower in 1954, tax relief in a period of budget deficit, is half of a Keynesian solution to the recession of 1954. On the other hand, Burns and Jacoby were essentially opposed to increased government spending as a stimulus to the economy. They felt that government manipulation of stabilizers, in this case, corporate taxation, would allow the private sector to rectify the supply-demand disequilibrium. Indeed, Jacoby would subsequently argue that government had little role in rectifying such problems, that it should use its stabilizers to correct minor economic dislocations.

He offered several interesting reforms as a method of modernizing what he saw as the actual governmental role in the economy. Citing the example of the Federal Reserve Board's control of the money supply, a control of one stabilizer, he argued that the flexibility possessed by the Federal Reserve should extend to the president. He has argued that more authority be given to the executive to act quickly to offset any changes in business conditions.

Jacoby's writings contain few suggestions for structural reforms. His basic principle remains one of limited intervention, with government deficit spending (in reality deficit taxing) a key weapon against recession. In one report he opposed wage-price controls and urged that they be phased out; he also urged the abolition of non–cost-effective subsidies. This second recommendation might be classified as a structural one, given the extensive use of such subsidies in the American economy. A second structural reform suggested by the report was the simplification and consolidation of government economic regulation.

Several of Jacoby's basic recommendations while on the CEA were equity in the tax system, greater government spending on research and development, and greater government concentration on training and education for workers. The other suggestions were primarily for increased efficiency in the various sectors of governmental involvement in the economy.

Jacoby argued in both the 1950s and the 1970s that taxes on the higher brackets should be reduced to create incentives and on the lower ones to increase equity.

He felt that the middle brackets should pay more. Jacoby also argued, on behalf of investment priorities, that taxes should be paid on state and local bonds; he felt that the tax-exempt status of such bonds reduced the capital available for more effective private investment. Such income, tax free as it was, also contributed to the inequity of the system.

As a moderate Republican, Jacoby accepted the general precepts of classical economics—the primacy of free market forces (low tariffs, market determination of investment, limited government intervention)—yet he adapted his views to the realities of modern times. He accepted the Keynesian interventionist precepts, although primarily in terms of stabilizer adjustments (here, he argued primarily in terms of taxation and money supply). His original abhorrence of central planning, ideologically tainted in the 1950s by its association with command planning (Soviet-style planning), was tempered by the 1970s with the understanding that planning is necessary for complex, interdependent, modern economies.

He argued that the social function of economics is best handled by the free market. This is not the trickle-down approach, with benefits aimed at the rich; rather it is a more subtle method, one of targeting benefits to those sectors most likely to provide investment for future growth. This targeting of investment for growth is central to Jacoby's thinking. The government's role in this is primarily passive (tax and monetary policy), but is active in the training and education field. Despite Jacoby's disclaimer to the effect that American economic goals were shifting in the early 1970s to the original concept of the founding fathers, improvement of quality of life, rather than to simple GNP growth, one finds few social elements in his economic philosophy. In this sense, too, he was the political economist, not the social one.

Given Jacoby's first-hand experience with the recession following the Korean War, one would expect him to have been aware of the complexities posed by the Vietnam War. Perhaps the relative ease (and success) of the recovery program of 1954 lulled him to sleep in 1969–71. Other gaps in his work during this period can easily be cited, but one must be careful not to overwork the advantages of hindsight. The stagflation of the 1970s is not something that fits easily into Jacoby's models, nor did he seem to have anticipated any significant shift in the nature of the American economy, despite considerable statistical evidence of such a change.

The shift to a call for "indicative" planning shows that he understood that something was amiss, but one does not see solutions to rather obvious structural problems. His strong support of American export of capital, for example, does not seem to take into account the social (and economic) consequences of such action. Similarly, his praise of our taxation system as a highly flexible one missed the point of the system's inflexibility (in terms of heavy dependence on one type of taxation). Given the type of income tax (personal and corporate) reform he advocated, one is hard put to understand how he would have solved issues such as Social Security reform.

Other structural changes, such as oil price fluctuations and the consequent reassessment of our energy mix and the definition of cost effectiveness, could not reasonably be foreseen in 1969, or rather, one cannot criticize too heavily those who did not see them. Nonetheless, it seems fair to say that Jacoby and the other political economists of the 1950s do not appear to have understood fully the unique advantages enjoyed by the American economy of 1940–64. Assumptions based on the performance of those years were bound to be off, given the changes that would have to occur in the world economy in the 1960s and 1970s. To a certain extent, one shortcoming of the stabilizer approach advocated by Jacoby is that it treated some of the changes as susceptible to alterations in stabilizer mix (that is, it treated them as changes in independent variables—to use Jacoby's phrase). These changes were structural, and required structural change. Jacoby's advocacy of a planning commission, and his support of multinationals (the free market's answer to the structural changes in the world economy), show that he was moving in the direction of structural reform. While his work was consistent in its ideology and focus, the pragmatic political element in his thinking nonetheless allowed Jacoby to make some movement in new directions.

A picture of Eisenhower and Jacoby figured prominently on the wall of his office at UCLA. Such a portrait is fair to the man and the economist. He was a political economist, and one true to the principles he espoused when in power. His arguments in the 1960s and 1970s were based on the practical experience of the early 1950s and on a consistent analysis of the American economy. Jacoby modified somewhat his positions on the economy, as indeed all observers must in light of changing conditions, but he remained strongly committed to the central principles of Eisenhower's economic policies. He helped draft those policies and continued in his subsequent career to argue on behalf of the underlying analysis he relied upon while a member of the CEA.

BIBLIOGRAPHY

Jacoby, Neil. *Bribery and Extortion in World Business*. New York: Macmillan, 1977.
———. *Multinational Oil*. New York: Macmillan, 1974.
———. *The Polluters*. London: Institute of Economic Affairs, 1972.
———. *The Progress of Peoples*. Santa Barbara: Center for the Study of Democratic Institutions, 1969.

JAMES B. COLLINS

JORDAN, JERRY L.
(b. December 1, 1941), CEA July 14, 1981-July 31, 1982

Jerry L. Jordan's career is characterized by diversity and success. Upon receiving his Ph.D. in economics from the University of California, he briefly held the position of assistant professor at California State University. Then, from 1967 to 1975, Jordan was employed by the Federal Reserve Bank of St. Louis, where he rose to the position of Senior Vice President and Director of Research. Jordan's career at the St. Louis Federal Reserve Bank was interrupted from December 1971 to May 1972, at which time he served as a consultant to the West German central bank.

In October 1975, Jordan became senior vice president and economist at the Pittsburgh National Bank. He held this position until June 1980. While in Pittsburgh Jordan served as president of the Economic Club of Pittsburgh (for three years) and also as a member of the Economic Advisory Committee of the American Bankers Association.

Jordan returned to academia in July 1980, accepting the position of dean of the Anderson Schools of Management at the University of New Mexico. Then, on July 14, 1981, Jordan's career took another turn as he became a member of President Reagan's Council of Economic Advisers. He served in this capacity until July 31, 1982, at which time he returned to the University of New Mexico as full professor and director of the School of Banking. Jordan's career has, in sense, come full circle. After a brief start in academia, he has once again returned to the university, where perhaps he is most happy.

In addition to the above activities, Jordan has served as a member of the Governing Council of the National Association of Business Economists, and also as a member of the U.S. Chamber of Commerce, Council of Trends and Perspectives.

It should also be noted that from 1975 to 1981, Jerry Jordan was a member of the Shadow Open Market Committee, a group of economists that monitors the monetary policy actions of the Federal Reserve System. Upon leaving the Council of Economic Advisers in 1982, Jordan again became a member of this committee.

Regarding his experience as a member of the CEA, Jordan reflects that his experience at the Council was a substitute for military duty. As is so often the case, Jordan served his government and the president of the United States out of a sense of duty. Making his stay in Washington particularly difficult was the fact that his family, including three children, stayed in Albuquerque, New Mexico.

Jordan's views regarding money, interest rates, and stabilization policy were nurtured and sharpened during his early years as an economist with the Federal Reserve Bank of St. Louis. It was at this time that Jordan gained his reputation as a tireless "Fed watcher" and an effective spokesman for monetarism.

In the first of many articles to be published in the *Federal Reserve Bank of St. Louis Review*, Jordan advocates two key principles which together form the basis of modern monetarism: (1) The supply of money is an exogenously controlled policy instrument, and (2) regulating the growth of the money stock is an effective means of controlling aggregate economic activity.

Regarding the issue of how best to control the growth of the money stock, Jordan views the monetary base as the key variable for money control. Noting that the quantity of money in circulation is a function of both the monetary base and the "money multiplier," he argues that the monetary base will dominate the money supply process in the long run. Jordan's views regarding the importance of the monetary base are noted in a 1969 article in the *Federal Reserve Bank of St. Louis Review*. He argues that the primary tool of the Fed—open market operations, changes in reserve requirements, and administration of the discount window—are summarized by the monetary base. Any change in the base reflects the decisions of central policy with respect to money supply growth.

In a 1973 article also appearing in the St. Louis *Review*, Jordan reiterates his belief in the importance of the base as an instrument of monetary control. He argues that demand deposit growth is dependent on reserve growth within the commercial banking system and this, in turn, is a function of the monetary base growth as well as the public's desire to hold currency.

A subject of central importance in macroeconomics in recent years is the relative effectiveness of monetary versus fiscal policies as a stabilization tool. In a widely debated earlier article Jordan presents empirical evidence bearing on this issue. Specifically, he regresses the quarterly changes in GNP (for the period 1952–58) against measures of both monetary and fiscal actions. Monetary actions are measured by changes in the money supply or the monetary base, and fiscal actions are represented by changes in the federal budget deficit and related variables.

In general, the monetary variables possess the anticipated signs and are highly significant, whereas the fiscal variables have low statistical significance and lack the correct signs in some cases. Carefully evaluating the empirical evidence, Jordan draws three conclusions:

1. The hypothesis that fiscal actions have a larger impact on GNP than do monetary actions is not confirmed;
2. The hypothesis that the effect on GNP of fiscal actions is more "predictable" than the effect of monetary actions is not confirmed; and
3. The hypothesis that the effect of fiscal actions on GNP occurs "faster" than the effect of monetary actions is not supported.

Based on these tests, Jordan advises that greater reliance be placed on monetary policy compared to fiscal policy.

A related issue which lies at the heart of the debate over stabilization policy is the relationship between the growth rate in the money supply and the level of interest rates. In this regard Jordan has been a consistent critic of the traditional view that an increased (decreased) rate of growth in the money supply necessarily results in a reduction (increase) in interest rates.

Jordan notes that an increase in the money supply which leads to an increased demand for financial assets will, *ceteris paribus*, lower interest rates. But it is unlikely that all other factors will remain unchanged. Specifically, an increase in the money supply will ultimately raise the level of economic activity and possibly the rate of inflation. In the event of increased inflation, interest rates might actually rise in the long run since lenders will demand higher nominal rates in order to protect their real return.

Essentially, Jordan is arguing that changes in the growth of the money supply have opposite short- and long-run effects. The immediate impact of an increase in the growth of the money stock is to lower interest rates, as the traditional view supposes. But, farther into the future, the level of interest rates will rise (according to Jordan) due to the inclusion of a higher inflation premium.

This view of interest rate determination implies a conflict of interpretation between interest rate targets and monetary aggregate targets. Jordan has argued that monetary variables often offer conflicting signs. He argues, for example, a market consensus of future inflation may push up interest rates, that some observers, however, may interpret the interest rate increase as a money tightening. Paradoxically, he maintains, the money stock may be simultaneously rising, offering a monetary easing to others.

Jordan furthermore argues that it is dangerous to use the level of interest rates as an indicator of monetary ease or tightness. As an example, he notes that during an economic recovery interest rates typically rise due to an increase in the demand for credit. If the Fed perceives this as indicative of too restrictive a monetary policy and reacts by increasing the growth rate in the money supply, this may be counterproductive since an increase in the money supply will further raise the level of economic activity and the inflation rate, both of which will drive interest rates higher.

As an alternative to the use of the interest rate as the target of monetary policy, Jordan suggests that policy makers should put greater reliance on the actual money supply change and rely less on money market conditions.

Regarding the use of monetary policy as a stabilization tool, Jordan advises that the objectives of full employment, stable prices, and economic growth are best served by adherence to a ''monetary rule''—that is, by letting the money supply grow at a moderate and stable rate over time.

Jordan's series of articles appearing in the *Federal Reserve Bank of St. Louis Review* did not, apparently, fall on deaf ears. At the January 1970 meeting of the Federal Open Market Committee (FOMC), it was decided to place greater importance on realizing growth of specific monetary aggregates.

However, in spite of this apparent victory for the "monetary" approach to stabilization policy, the FOMC paid closer attention to money market interest rates in 1970 than to the growth of the monetary aggregates.

In the spring of 1975, Congress passed a resolution requiring that the Fed set and announce actual targets for money supply growth. This second victory for monetarism also was more apparent than real, as it proved ineffective in stabilizing the growth of money. In fact, Jordan later noted that money supply growth was frequently above the target ranges causing observers to disregard target announcements.

In addition to being an influential proponent of the monetary approach to stabilization policy, Jerry Jordan has in recent years carefully considered the technical issues surrounding both the formulation and the implementation of monetary policy.

In an article originally presented in 1980 at the University of Rochester, Jordan presents an agenda of issues relating to the practical application of monetary policy. First, he notes that if several monetary aggregates are targeted there arises the possibility that the various targets may prove inconsistent, which would place the manager of the Fed's Trading Desk in the position of having to choose which target(s) to achieve. In order to avoid this problem, Jordan suggests targeting just *one* monetary aggregate or *one* reserve aggregate. In this way, the directive to the manager of the Trading Desk will be unambiguous and a major source of confusion will be eliminated.

Jordan also feels that it is important for the Fed to set long-run growth paths for the money supply. Although the Fed has formally announced one-year growth targets since 1975, Jordan notes that since these targets were "reset" every quarter, they no longer had effective meaning.

The successful implementation of monetary policy also requires improved money supply data. Specifically, Jordan has argued for a new statistic encompassing currency and all transaction-type balances at any financial institution.

In addition to the above issues Jordan stresses that perhaps the most important aspect of successfully implementing monetary policy is knowing the linkages and relationships between the policy instruments the Federal Open Market Committee can control, the target variable (that is, the monetary or reserve aggregate target), and the ultimate macroeconomic variables, such as prices and output, which the Fed wishes to influence.

These relationships are exceedingly complex, yet the success or failure of monetary policy depends critically on understanding them. As Jordan explains, the Federal Reserve System can affect the reserve and monetary aggregates in several ways, including the use of open market operations, changes in the reserve requirement, and changes in the discount rate. But the control of the monetary or reserve aggregate target is complicated by the fact that other variables which are essentially beyond the control of the Fed (for example, float) also affect the reserve and monetary aggregates. Successful implementation of monetary policy requires that these other variables be carefully considered.

Furthermore, if the Fed chooses a reserve aggregate such as the monetary base (rather than a monetary aggregate such as M1 or M2) as the operating target, there is a further complication since the ''multiplier'' linking the monetary base and the monetary aggregates is changeable. The factors bearing on this relationship must be known and accurately predicted in order to forecast movements in the money multiplier.

Finally, the successful implementation of monetary policy requires that the linkages between the monetary aggregates and the ultimate macroeconomic variables the Fed desires to influence be fully understood.

In a speech delivered in Paris in September 1981, Jordan noted that economic theory has significantly changed in the previous two decades. The impetus for these changes was derived from our experience with inflation. One particularly important development in economic theory has been the analysis of the inflationary effects of ''supply shocks'' and the appropriateness of employing traditional demand management policies to deal with such inflation.

In this context Jordan considers the OPEC oil embargo of 1974–75 and the subsequent increase in the real price of oil. He notes that this autonomous increase in the price of oil in effect reduced the ''economic capacity'' of the consuming nations since their capital stocks were designed to be most effective at significantly lower oil prices. This implied that there would be less output, and, given the same aggregate demand, an increase in the average level of prices to restore equilibrium.

This oil supply ''shock'' and the resulting inflation have important policy implications for the 1980s:

1. The real effects of the oil embargo and similar supply shocks are not caused by nor are they amenable to traditional demand management policies. Jordan explains that the loss of wealth was imposed by political forces, and it is not possible to use monetary policy to prevent the reduction in output. Money won't create energy. Furthermore, Jordan explains that it would have been possible to eliminate the general inflation caused by the oil embargo, but only at the cost of further reductions in output.

2. The usefulness of the concept of the ''GNP gap'' (that is, the shortfall between actual output and potential output) and the belief that ''idle'' resources indicated by a gap can always be reemployed through general stimulative measures are called into question. Due to the effects of supply shocks on output, we do not, in Jordan's view, know how to measure economic capacity for policymaking purposes. If capacity utilization is low due solely to previously restrictive *demand management* policies, stimulative measures might successfully be employed to increase output and employment. But, alternatively, if excess physical capacity results from real (that is, supply) shocks, demand stimulation will not put additional resources to work, since there is no gap between actual GNP and potential GNP.

Jordan left his position as dean of the Anderson Schools of Management at the University of New Mexico to serve as a member of the Council of Economic Advisers, beginning July 14, 1981. At that time, the Council consisted of Murray L. Weidenbaum* (chairman), on leave from Washington University in St. Louis, and William A. Niskanen*, who was on leave from the University of California at Los Angeles. While on the Council, Jordan had primary responsibility for domestic and international macroeconomic analysis, economic projections, and monetary and financial issues. In addition, he served on President Reagan's Gold Commission.

Jordan came to Washington at what seemed a critical moment in history. Reagan had just been elected president on a platform calling for new economic policies to deal with the legacy of stagflation inherited from the 1970s. Reagan's challenge—and the challenge of his Council—was nothing less than a transformation of the economic landscape from one of low growth and high inflation to one of high growth accompanied by a low and stable inflation rate. As President Reagan's chief adviser on monetary policy developments, Jordan would play an important role in the unfolding drama.

Jordan was well prepared for this role, having spent virtually all of his professional career considering the causes and effects of inflation. In talks to various groups, Jordan was critical of past administrations' attempts to deal effectively with the stagflation phenomenon, arguing that the stop-and-go strategy of alternatively fighting unemployment and then inflation could only make matters worse.

Jordan reiterates this theme in the 1982 *Economic Report of the President*. He argued that stimulative monetary and fiscal policy left a residue of higher prices and this, in turn, generated inflationary expectations, which, in their turn, forced episodes of restraint forcing recessions which were then followed by stimulus. Policy and performance were stop and go. The result of this was an inflationary trend, he argued.

While inveighing against attempts to ''fine tune'' the economy, Jordan notes that the stop-and-go cycle played out repeatedly over the previous two decades stems from a failure to correctly weigh the long-run benefits of ending inflation against the short-run costs of doing so. This failure was in part due to a widely held but fallacious view that a once-for-all increase in the inflation rate would lead to a permanent reduction in the unemployment rate.

In signalling a clear change of policy regime, Jordan asserted that the policies to end inflation will be sustained. Short-run costs will be borne for the long-term benefits.

It is Jordan's view, and apparently the view of the Reagan administration, that the key to eliminating the steady upward drift of both the inflation and unemployment rates is to resist the attempt to gain a short-term advantage by pursuing discretionary monetary and/or fiscal policies. In particular, Jordan argues for a moderate and stable money supply growth rate.

With a view toward minimizing the short-term costs of an anti-inflation policy,

Jordan believes that it is extremely important to have a consistent and convincing policy. He would argue that perceptions of policy reversals would only cause price and wage increases and any lack of credibility would simply extend the duration of short-term costs.

A low and stable rate of inflation will, in Jordan's view, provide the appropriate environment for businesses to confidently expand their productive capacity and hire additional labor, leading to a low and stable unemployment rate. Perhaps most revealing about Jordan's philosophy is his assertion that central economic policy must provide a stable environment for confident private decision making.

When Jordan left the CEA on July 31, 1982, to return to the University of New Mexico, the anti-inflationary policy that he had advocated was in place, resulting in a significantly reduced rate of inflation. However, the U.S. economy was simultaneously suffering its deepest post–World War II recession. In the spring of 1983 the recession ended, with many economists predicting a sustained period of robust growth accompanied by a low and stable rate of inflation.

Jordan has been a consistent and effective advocate of the monetary approach to stabilization policy, stressing the importance of a moderate and stable rate of growth in the money supply and the significance of the monetary base as a key policy variable in this regard. In addition, Jordan has made an important contribution to our understanding of the many technical issues surrounding both the formulation and implementation of monetary policy—a subject which has received insufficient attention in the past, even by those whose responsibility it is to regulate the nation's money supply.

Although Jordan's views regarding the appropriate use of money as a stabilization tool are not unique, he must be given a share of credit for the string of successes that monetarism has recently experienced, including the increased emphasis on the use monetary policy, the acceptance by the Federal Reserve System of a "monetary rule" and the formalization of monetary targets, and the redefinition of the monetary aggregates to include all transactions deposits regardless of the type of financial institution.

Still, in spite of these victories and others, Jordan is concerned that the changes may prove to be more apparent than real. He notes that the money supply has recently been "as variable as ever." Only time will tell if there has been a true change in policy regime or if it will be "business as usual" in the future.

BIBLIOGRAPHY

Jordan, Jerry L. "Elements of Money Stock Determination." *Federal Reserve Bank of St. Louis Review* (October 1969).

———. "Federal Open Market Committee Decisions in 1968—A Year of Watchful Waiting." *Federal Reserve Bank of St. Louis Review* (May 1969).

———. "Money in a Quantity Theory Framework." *Federal Reserve Bank of St. Louis Review* (December 1967).

———, and Anderson, Leonard. "The Monetary Base—Explanation and Analytical Use." *Federal Reserve Bank of St. Louis Review* (August 1968).

ROBERT C. WINDER

KEYSERLING, LEON
(b. January 22, 1908), CEA August 9, 1946-January 20, 1953

Leon Keyserling has spent almost all of his professional career working in the area of political economy, and for some portions of that career he occupied prominent positions, positions from which he was able to influence, or provide direction to, public policy. At some time during his career he was even highly esteemed by the profession as an adroit and clever practitioner of the art of economic policy formulation. However, the route he followed to that position in the profession was rather different from the norm. How was this possible? Perhaps the profession was less regimented fifty years ago; perhaps Keyserling's own personality was the unique element in his career; perhaps the economic and social conditions of the Depression provided unusual opportunities. Whatever the reason, Keyserling's career did not follow today's standard pattern.

What were some of the differences? Keyserling never earned a doctorate. Although he had entered a Ph.D. program at Columbia University after receiving an LL.B. from Harvard, he did not complete his degree. Furthermore, Keyserling did not have an affiliation with an academic institution or, at least, an initial home base. He did teach at Columbia as a part of his doctoral program but, upon having entered public life in a professional capacity, he was not tenured at a university or college. Nor was an affiliation with a research institution or foundation a substitute for a university in his professional background. Finally, his professional reputation was not based upon research and publication in the recognized journals of economics. The limited number of his publications is the result of rather than the basis for his public position. Even those are not of the purely theoretical type; rather, they are explanations in support of a particular economic policy, or set of policies, applicable to a specific situation, hence not universal in nature. Nevertheless, Keyserling was one of the significant economic policy role players from approximately 1935 to 1955. Because both his route to prominence and his frequently different exercise of economics are unique, he warrants attention.

Keyserling was born in Charleston, South Carolina, in 1908, to parents who were moderately well off. He entered Columbia University in 1924 and pursued a major in economics, with much distinction, being elected to Phi Beta Kappa. One of his professors was Rexford Tugwell (later prominent as one of Roosevelt's brain trust and a major contributor to the New Deal philosophy and policy), who seems to have exercised considerable influence over Keyserling's intellectual development. Upon graduation from Columbia in 1928, Keyserling entered Harvard Law School and received his LL.B. in 1931, shortly thereafter being admitted to the bar of New York State.

Whether Tugwell radicalized Keyserling or not, Keyserling's interests or professional goals had changed by the time he graduated from law school. Although admitted to the bar, he did not try to open an office for the practice of law. He instead accepted a position as assistant professor of economics at Columbia University and became a graduate student in economics working toward a Ph.D. Given the kind of policy recommendations which Keyserling was to make later in his public professional life vis-à-vis the overriding role of the government, one should seek sources of influence for this centralistic philosophy. Some of these could well have predated his college years. What is known, however, is that during Keyserling's years at Columbia—both undergraduate as well as graduate—there were several professors who espoused institutionalism. These included Wesley Mitchell, John Maurice Clark, and, most prominently, Tugwell. While their interests and approaches were somewhat different, they shared a common concern for preventing depressions and a common belief that this could be achieved via some form of social control. It seems reasonable to argue that Keyserling's persistent adherence to the efficiency of public sector action to direct and control private sector activity was shaped considerably by the intellectual environment at Columbia, and particularly by its institutionalists. Moreover, Keyserling also believed in the use of government legislation for redistributive purposes both for humanitarian reasons and because it was a way of stimulating aggregate demand. Furthermore, institutionalists at Columbia, like Wesley Mitchell, believed in a public policy role for economists, an attitude shared by Keyserling but not necessarily attributable to Mitchell.

Tugwell certainly seems to have been instrumental in introducing Keyserling to techniques of policy formulation. Keyserling was a contributor to Tugwell's 1934 publication, *Redirecting Education*. By this time, Keyserling, through the efforts of Tugwell, had left Columbia and his Ph.D. program to accept a position as an attorney for the Agricultural Adjustment Administration, a position that began and ended in 1933 when he became secretary and legislative assistant to Senator Robert F. Wagner, New Deal Democrat from the state of New York. This association provided Keyserling with the opportunity to make several contributions to New Deal legislation, legislation harmonious with his institutionalist beliefs in the efficiency of social controls and redistribution: the National Industrial Recovery Act, National Housing Act, Railroad Retirement Act, Social Security Act, and National Labor Relations Act.

From this position, he moved to that of assistant to Wagner's Senate Banking and Currency Committee, 1935–37, and from there to general counsel of the United States Housing Authority, an agency established in 1937 by legislation Keyserling helped to draft. It can be argued that the objective of this legislation reflects Keyserling's redistributive interests as well as the belief in social control.

By the end of World War II, interest in aggregate demand/full employment was once more coming into prominence. In addition to the General Housing Act of 1945 and 1946 there was the full Employment Act of 1946, a piece of legislation to which Keyserling had contributed. This act created the Council of

Economic Advisers. Now all three of Keyserling's concerns could be meshed: stimulus for full employment, redistribution, and social control. Nevertheless, there were already a number of economists in important positions within the administration, for example, the Secretary of the Treasury, causing ambiguities in the role and the importance of the CEA. It is possible that this ambiguity was only in the minds of the outside beholders, so to speak, and not to an inside prime mover, such as Keyserling. President Truman filled the three Council positions only after three months. Furthermore, his choices were not all professional economists whose careers had followed traditional paths. The Council's first chairman, Edwin Nourse*, had followed a traditional path, having been a past president of the American Economic Association and associated with the Brookings Institution. John Clark*, a second member, had not followed a traditional path. Although he had a Ph.D. in economics and had taught, he was appointed to the Council for his political contacts in Washington rather than for his research reputation. His position was probably enhanced by his wealth and his former employment as a lawyer for Standard Oil of Indiana. Keyserling, the third member, had neither a fortune nor the reputation of an esteemed member of academia, although he had good political ties.

The Council did not begin as a smoothly working entity. There seems to have been considerable friction between its members, possibly caused by the differences in their backgrounds. Furthermore, Keyserling was nearly half the age of the other two members. Moreover, he was a dedicated New Dealer, which the other two members were not. Even more important, Keyserling, with his institutionalism, believed in central planning as a logical part of social control, while Nourse and Clark did not.

By the beginning of 1947, the Council was ready to present its first report. The economy had gone through the transition from producing arms to producing consumer goods in order to satisfy a substantial portion of the nation's wartime accumulated demand for such items. Some felt that further expansion of output was in jeopardy and that recession was incipient. Consequently, the Council's first report considered the probability of recession and the policies that could be followed to avoid it or to minimize its impact. Part of the concern about recession was unemployment, particularly because it was, via the Full Employment Act of 1946, now a national priority to maintain full employment. While the recommendations were peculiarly non-Keynesian, they were also redistributive to some extent. For example, a non-Keynesian recommendation was the suggestion that a governmental surplus be produced. With respect to redistribution, the government was to seek voluntary price reductions in combination with moderate upward wage adjustments. While these two policies could result in an increase in aggregate demand, hence providing the stimulus sought, they would also result in a redistribution of the income shares by increasing that going to labor and reducing that going to capital. Carrying redistribution further were recommendations to expand both minimum wage and Social Security coverage as well as the continuation of rent controls while expanding government financed housing.

During the first year of the Council's operations, inflation was always present but considered secondary to the threat of recession. By the end of 1947, inflation as a national policy problem had become considerably more prominent, and was a central concern of the Council's report at the end of 1947. The Council urged restraint on governmental policies which were likely to be inflationary. The efficiency of balancing the budget or producing a surplus was not, therefore, questioned. At the same time, one can discern Keyserling's redistributive concerns from recommendations for eliminating imbalances in the structure of wages and for imposing both wage and price controls.

The anticipated recession was in place by the beginning of 1949. Although Nourse continued his non-Keynesian position in favor of the balanced budget, Keyserling urged policies to stimulate the economy, such as public works, as well as those which had a redistributive element, for example, higher minimum wages and higher Social Security payouts. Since Nourse and Keyserling had made their divergent positions public, it was now a matter of record that a severe policy difference, if not a philosophical one, existed between chairman Nourse and member Keyserling. A schism of such magnitude would make the Council ineffective, and as a result the president would be unable to use his Council for the purpose for which it was established. This crisis was resolved by the resignation of Nourse and the appointment of Keyserling, first as acting chairman, and subsequently as chairman of the Council. Recovery was evident by the last quarter of 1949. There was a decline in the unemployment rate and an increase in output accompanied by only moderate price level increases.

However, in June 1950, when North Korea attacked South Korea, the repercussions for the United States were not merely political, but economic as well. A number of controls and interventions became necessary, including a tax increase and wage and price controls. Moreover, to resolve resource and material allocation problems, the Office of Defense Mobilization was established. By 1951 pressures on the price level had mounted, thereby creating a justification for even stronger application of wage and price controls. During the Korean War, and throughout his tenure as chairman, Keyserling did not give up his concern for expanding output and growth. It can be argued, however, that over the years his ideas became refined. Herbert Stein* points out that Keyserling had become an advocate of the Committee on Economic Development's recommendation for the use of the federal budget to stabilize economic activity "around an adequately rising trend," this being held as essential for maintaining a high level of employment.

The fashion for academic economists on the Council continued through the one-term presidency of Democratic president Jimmy Carter. Even Carter's successor, Republican Ronald Reagan, has followed it. Reagan's Council chairman in 1983 was Martin Feldstein*. Nevertheless, as of this writing, Keyserling continues his practice of law in Washington, D.C., and his criticism of those public policies he deems prejudicial to economic progress with social justice. His 1982 attack on Reagan in *Social Policy* is an example of this kind of criticism since it focuses on both the reduction in aggregate demand and the decline in real income of large segments of the consumer population.

BIBLIOGRAPHY

Gruchy, Allan. *Contemporary Economic Thought: The Contribution of Noninstitutional Economics*. Clifton, N.J.: Augustus Kelley, 1972.

Keyserling, Leon. "The Council of Economic Advisors Since 1946: Its Contributions and Failures." *Atlantic Economic Journal* (March 1978).

———. "International Implications of U.S. Economic Performance and National Policies." *Atlantic Economic Journal* (December 1981).

———. "The Keynesian Revolution and Its Pioneers." *American Economic Review* 62, no. 2 (May 1972).

———. "Reaganomics Makes No Sense." *Social Policy* 12, no. 3 (1982).

Sobel, Robert. *The Worldly Economists*. New York: Free Press, 1980.

Stein, Herbert. *The Fiscal Revolution in America*. Chicago: University of Chicago Press, 1969.

ALVIN COHEN

LEWIS, JOHN PRIOR
(b. March 18, 1921), CEA May 17, 1963-August 31, 1964

John Prior Lewis, who has served with the Council of Economic Advisers both as a staff economist and as a member, has had an extensive career with intellectual interests ranging from inventory models, Soviet telephones, and radioactive waste disposal to full employment policy and economic development in the Third World. His array of publications over thirty years is quite prolific, and he has served in various academic, public, and private positions in the United States and abroad. Most of all, he is a compassionate liberal concerned by the underdevelopment of the Third World and unemployment at home.

Lewis was born in Albany, New York, the son of Leon Ray and Grace (Prior) Lewis. After studying from 1939 to 1940 at Saint Andrew's University, Scotland, he completed the A.B. at Union College, Schenectady, in 1941, and went on to Harvard to receive a master's degree in public administration in 1943. Lewis then spent the next three years in the U.S. Naval Reserve, left as a lieutenant, and married June Estelle on July 12, 1946. They have three children, Betsy Prior, Sally Eastman, and Amanda Barnum. For the next four years Lewis was an instructor and assistant professor in economics and government at Union College.

Meanwhile, he was completing his doctorate at Harvard, where he submitted his dissertation in 1949. Entitled "Toward an Administrable Price Policy for Full Employment," it contains many ideas typical of Lewis' later beliefs. In brief they are: Prices may eventually be forced upwards as socially irresponsible producers pass on costs. Although direct and permanent price controls are not necessarily the best solution, some form of governmental price consulting seems workable. The dogma of the perpetually balanced budget is dismissed in favor of compensating fiscal policies in light of the outlook for employment. While such ideas were to be anathema to the business community in the Kennedy era, they were not quite as radical as some were to claim when Lewis was nominated to the CEA.

In 1950 Lewis left Union College to serve in his first government post as staff member and assistant to the chairman of the CEA, Leon Keyserling*. The Council under Keyserling was dynamic. Not only was it instrumental in formulating Truman's economic policy—particularly in wage and price matters—but it also strengthened its purpose and refined its role in a political environment not always sympathetic to the recently established Council.

Lewis has remarked in several places on his experiences as a staffer and how the CEA operated from 1950 to 1953. In an article written a year after leaving the staff, Lewis points out that the Council was originally conceived as a group of specialists ready to do battle, but equipped with only a weakened full Employment Bill. Yet the CEA did become a collection of generalists advising on all aspects of economic policy and interacted frequently with Congress and various governmental agencies. Without becoming an "Economic Supreme Court," the Council did take part in the formulation of broad economic policy. Moreover, the use of a three-man team instead of having just one economic warlord was sometimes inefficient, and not all decisions were arrived at smoothly. Agreement among the members was difficult. The disputes endangered the meeting of deadlines and worse, overcautiousness prevailed. Nonetheless, the structure did allow for a more useful division of labor, and the informal and unbureaucratic assistance of a small yet dedicated staff was helpful. The conclusion is that the Council will survive and not "retreat into the half world of professional isolation."

Some of the exchanges between members and staffers were lively. There was no holding back of opinions, and arguments were the order of the day. Although the staff was not directly responsible for policy recommendations, Keyserling did allow them to contribute. The Council was viewed more as consultants than a coherent group.

The final product of the CEA and the staff was its economic reports, dubbed by Lewis "indespensable engines of consent." However, that consent was frequently the result of intensive discussion on all levels.

One of the great concerns of Keyserling's Council was the pressure exerted on prices in late 1950 as the Korean War escalated. The buildup in defense spending threatened to turn inflation from a temporary phenomenon into a permanent condition. Even though the Council recommended in a memo on December 7 to the president that certain prices be stabilized, Keyserling could not ideologically accept such a step as readily as Lewis would. The warnings on inflation were repeated in the January 1951 report to the president.

The Korean question was significant in Lewis' life, for it solidified his views on pricing and gave him his first chance to formulate his activist ideas on economic development, another subject which would loom large in his career. After leaving his staff position on the Council in 1953, Lewis went to spend five months in the Republic of Korea as an economic consultant to the United Nations Korean Reconstruction Agency (UNKRA) in Pusan. For Korean development, he endorsed a bold plan to achieve rapid economic growth via technology and capital injections from the United States and more effort and coordination from the several levels of the local government. Growth must not be slow. Lewis felt a sense of crisis and was passionate in his belief that Korea must expand its output. Many of his ideas and much of the tone were to reemerge in Lewis' work on India and other countries of the Third World.

During the 1950s Lewis advanced his academic career. In 1953 he went to the University of Indiana, where he was an associate professor until 1956; he thereupon became a full professor of business economics and public policy.

While his list of publications continued to lengthen, he still kept an eye on the CEA. In an essay printed in 1955 entitled "Recent Developments in Economic Forecasting," he criticizes the statistical disaggregation used in the January 1954 *Economic Report of the President*. As Lewis argued, the CEA did not make full use of the advances made in the technology of forecasting.

In the late 1950s, Lewis also served in several capacities to various private and public institutions. Abroad, he was senior staff member in India for the Brookings Institution from 1959 to 1960, and in October 1961 he spent two weeks in Liberia as a member of the Agency for International Development (AID) mission. For years afterwards, Lewis was fascinated by the Indian subcontinent. At home in Indiana, he was adviser to the Governor's Revenue Forecast Committee and did consultancy work for some business firms, notably the Cummins Engine Company in Columbus, Ohio, as it was contemplating a joint venture in India.

Meanwhile, further critical references to the CEA appeared occasionally in his written work. "Short Term General Business Conditions Forecasting" (October 1962) dismisses the use of contrived or "ulterior motive" forecasts which figured in the apparent inability of the Council to detect the beginning of the 1960–61 recession late in the Eisenhower administration.

Lewis clearly favors giving the president more power to stabilize the economy without relying so much on Congress and would like to see the federal budget divided into current and capital expenditures (as in Europe) to ease the constraints imposed by those who adhere to the balance-budget fetish. Lewis also found room to poke fun at monetarists who use money supply variables as the sole criteria to forecast GNP.

On May 21, 1962, Lewis was in Washington to present a paper to the White House Conference on National Economic Issues. It is vintage Lewis and was to be quoted by skeptical critics in Congress and the conservative press after Lewis was proposed for Council nomination. The problem by 1962 was twofold: inflation was no longer merely creeping, yet at the same time there was more slack in the economy than ever. Lewis places the blame both on management and unions who act with little regard to inflationary implications. He held out little hope for monetary and fiscal constraint as the answer to inflation. He also believed that wage controls would be unworkable. Clearly, Lewis was not intellectually willing to support very strong government measures to control inflation, yet he still hankered after some selective stabilization of prices of imported raw materials and credit controls. Kennedy's current policy of national guidelines did not seem very effective, yet Lewis offered nothing more substantive than a call for (1) all corporations to be federally chartered and thus held more socially accountable for their pricing decisions, and (2) an Office of Industry Economics which would closely monitor the activities of corporations and, eventually, serve as the final arbiter in wage renegotiations.

When Kermit Gordon* left the Council later in 1962, Lewis was nominated to take his place. The business community's reaction to this news was hostile, as they were already untrusting of Kennedy after the steel problem, and the appointment of any non–laissez-faire economist was suspect. *U.S. News and World Report* noted that Lewis and Gardner Ackley* favored stronger moves by the government to influence the economy in general and wage-price decisions in particular, and both the *Wall Street Journal* and *Business Week* were suspect with respect to Lewis' appointment.

Lewis was certainly on his guard as he was questioned by the Senate Committee on Banking and Currency. He denied that he favored peacetime controls on prices and stated clearly that the CEA was an advisory group, not one that actually set policies. When asked if he favored inflation, as did his mentor at Harvard, Dr. Sumner Schlicter, Lewis quickly pointed out how "conservative" he had become on that issue, especially in view of the imbalance of international payments, and that inflation was to be curbed. When asked if he advocated government intervention in the economy, Lewis hedged his position by saying that the economy is already a mixture of private and public interest. In particular, he was questioned on his statements at the White House Conference, and for criticizing Kennedy for being fearful of budget deficits at a time of economic softness.

Lewis' appointment was approved May 11, 1963, and confirmed four days later. On May 17 he officially took office. The Council of Economic Advisers under Walter Heller* was energetic and full of a sense of purpose instilled by its chairman. As Lewis put it, "I thought Keyserling worked hard until I saw Heller." Lewis himself came well recommended and the CEA viewed him as a strong addition given his economic reasoning, experience, and communication skills. Lewis was busy as well, as his record during his brief tenure testifies. He served on the Interagency Committee on Transportation Mergers, and in tandem with the Organization for Economic Cooperation and Development (OECD) was chairman of the U.S. delegation to the Committee's Working Party Subcommittee on Costs of Production and Prices. On July 25, 1963, he appeared before the Senate Commerce Committee to discuss the economic effects of a possible railway strike. That day, he also appeared before the House Committee on Banking and Currency. On October 28, the entire Council testified before the Senate's Subcommittee on Employment and Man Power. Perhaps the most important testimony was before the Senate Committee on Finance on November 12 to support Kennedy's tax bill.

The tax cut was a departure from the *Economic Report* of 1962, which assumed an optimistic year without any government action. By the time the 1963 report was published, it was felt that the economy would need some fiscal stimulus to increase *real* output; or, to quote Lewis, "There is a big switch in the 1963 report." The $11 billion tax cut proposed by Kennedy and the Council was dear to Lewis' heart and was hailed as being crucial to solving many problems at once. Since he had specialized earlier in forecasting and the effects of business cycles, Lewis was influential in preparing the 1963 report and promoting the tax cut.

Since Kennedy took a great interest in economic problems, the CEA met more frequently than ever with the president, the Treasury, and the Federal Reserve Board. Although the Council under Heller was not allowed enough time to implement its programs, it left a coherent strategy for the incoming Johnson administration.

Meanwhile, Lewis was turning his attention back to the international sphere. On May 19, 1964, the White House announced that Lewis was leaving the Council to succeed C. Tyler Wood as chief of the United States Foreign Aid Mission in India. The Third World in general and India in particular had fascinated Lewis for some time. In 1962 he had published two works in this field; *Notes on the Nature of Country Planning* and *Quiet Crisis in India*, in which he argued strongly for accelerated economic growth provided by locally devised programs, not just a ready-made plan devised by a consultant imported from abroad.

For the next five years Lewis was to put his theories to an empirical test in India. What emerged in 1969 was another book on that country which dealt with more local problems and what specific progress had been made. The rhetoric is sharper than ever, and he is highly critical of the United States. In *Wanted in India: A Relevant Radicalism* (1976), Lewis as the seasoned observer argued that it would be idiocy to slow growth because it generated contrast and conflict. Indeed, his liberal belief in progress seems tempered by pessimism at this stage. Musing whether his outlined goals for India are obtainable, he answers his own question with a no.

Since his return from India, Lewis has been active as an adviser, administrator, and author of myriad articles. From 1969 to 1979 he was professor of economics and international affairs at Princeton and also served as dean of the Woodrow Wilson School of Public Affairs from 1969 to 1974. He has been a member of the U.N. Committee on Development Planning since 1970 and chairman of the Development Assistance Committee of the OECD in Paris since 1979.

BIBLIOGRAPHY

Lewis, John P. "The Lull That Came to Stay." *Journal of Political Economy* 63 (February 1955): 24–65.

———. "Recent Developments in Economic Forecasting." *Business Information Bulletin*, Bloomington: Indiana University, 1955.

———. "Short Term General Business Conditions Forecasting: Some Comments on Method." *Journal of Business* 35 (October 1962): 330–50.

———. *Wanted in India: A Relevant Radicalism*. Princeton: Princeton University Press, 1976.

———, and Gross, B. M. "The President's Economic Staff During the Truman Administration." *American Political Science Review* 48 (March 1954): 110–23.

MASON J. KLINCK

MACAVOY, PAUL
(b. April 21, 1934), CEA July 13, 1975-November 15, 1976

Paul MacAvoy was born in Haverhill, Massachusetts. He graduated Phi Beta Kappa with an A.B. from Bates College in 1955 and was awarded the M.A. and Ph.D. degrees from Yale University in 1956 and 1960, respectively. Married in 1955, he has two children.

MacAvoy has held a number of academic and professional positions. After serving as assistant professor of economics in the Graduate School of Business at the University of Chicago from 1960 to 1963, he accepted a faculty position at Massachusetts Institute of Technology in 1963. MacAvoy served as a senior staff economist at the Council of Economics during 1965–66 and as a member of the Ford administration Council of Economic Advisers during 1975 and 1976. Subsequently, he joined the faculty at Yale University in 1976. In 1983 MacAvoy left his position as Frederick William Beinecke Professor of Economics at Yale to become dean of the Graduate School of Management at the University of Rochester.

MacAvoy's appointments and memberships are numerous. He was a Brookings Institution senior fellow (1970–71); he also was a member of the Presidential Task Force on Revision of the Antitrust Laws (known as the Neal Task Force) during 1967–68. Of particular significance to economists is his appointment as the first editor of the *Bell Journal of Economics and Management Science*. MacAvoy held this position from 1970 to 1975. Subject material of the *Bell Journal of Economics* is devoted to the regulated sector of the economy. Under MacAvoy's editorial leadership, the journal has become a continuing source of significant contributions to both the theoretical and empirical literature on the economics of regulation.

During recent years, MacAvoy has presented his views to a wide audience through contributions to the *New York Times* "Forum" on economic affairs. Through this medium, he has argued for allowing the Federal Trade Commission to monitor the activities of professional licensing boards and medical associations where these groups use licensing to establish cartels for their members. This column has also been an outlet for his economic views on the underground economy, oil forecasting errors by the Ford Foundation and Harvard Business School, OPEC, and many other topics. A reliance upon market forces to solve many allocation and pricing problems is pervasive in his writings.

Much of MacAvoy's significant academic work has been in the area of econometric modeling of energy markets and evaluating the effects of federal regulation. He is one of the foremost academic authorities on government policies in natural gas pricing and production.

MacAvoy's work is policy motivated and empirically driven. In a 1971 article he employs an econometric model of natural gas demand and supply to illustrate that the major problems of tight gas price control at the wellhead result from the larger number of sources of gas reserve supplies, rather than from output restriction by a few dominant firms as has been commonly argued. Further elaboration upon this theme followed in a 1973 article. MacAvoy and his co-author, Robert S. Pindyck, argue that ceiling prices have led to production shortages and if allowed to continue conditions will worsen. Using econometric analysis, MacAvoy and Pindyck found that the shortage could be relieved by phased deregulation of wellhead gas prices if price deregulation would follow the proposal in President Nixon's April 1973 energy message.

MacAvoy long has been a critic of the performance of regulatory commissions. In 1970 he raised serious questions concerning the work of the Federal Power Commission (FPC). Arguing that the FPC provides services with measurable economic benefits and costs for regulated firms and final consumers of gas and electricity, he did not find the estimated benefits and costs of gas field price regulation encouraging.

With a well-established reputation for expertise in natural gas pricing and production analysis, MacAvoy testified before the Senate Subcommittee on Finance concerning the consequences of relaxing price controls over natural gas. Using the predictions of the MIT Econometric Gas Pricing Model, MacAvoy testified that price ceilings created natural gas shortages during 1972–73 of approximately 10 percent of demand. He and Robert Pindyck argued that the shortage could be alleviated by allowing gas prices to rise. With this kind of testimony before Congress, MacAvoy's economic views were known within political circles prior to his appointment to the CEA. This interest in economic reform eventually drew MacAvoy to the Council in the mid–1970s.

MacAvoy was selected as a member of the Council by President Gerald Ford and Chairman Alan Greenspan* primarily for his expertise in the area of energy deregulation. MacAvoy accepted the position with a hope that he could influence policy. With an eye toward the deregulation movement, he expressed his desire to join the CEA. Viewing himself as a micro-industrial applied economist he hoped to have political impact. His appointment was approved by the Senate Banking Committee on June 3, 1975.

Although MacAvoy was easily confirmed as a CEA member, his economic views were not unanimously well received. Senator William Proxmire evaluated MacAvoy as brilliant and charming. He disagreed with MacAvoy on deregulation. MacAvoy looked forward to conversations with Proxmire to convince him otherwise. From all subsequent evidence exhibited in MacAvoy's work at the Council it is clear that both MacAvoy and Senator Proxmire were unsuccessful in their endeavors.

During the Ford administration, the CEA operated much as usual by having Council members take rough and ready responsibility for specific topic areas but having all members involved in all activities at one stage or another. With Allan

Greenspan as chairman and Burton Malkiel* as the other member, the natural division of responsibility was achieved by each member concentrating on his respective areas of expertise. MacAvoy took care of most microeconomic issues, including regulatory reform, energy, natural resources, transportation, food and agriculture, the real trade side of international policy (commodity policies and such arcane items as the new international economic order or law of the sea). The CEA chairman was actively involved in debates about energy issues, but given the complexity and scope of the problems in that area, both MacAvoy and Greenspan spent considerable time on those issues (particularly the Energy Policy and Conservation Act, natural gas policy, and environmental-energy policy interactions). However, the Council did not in any way slight the main areas of CEA concern—monetary and fiscal policy, and forecasting the economy for the president, although Greenspan maintained the dominant position in these areas, with all Council members participating at all levels.

This overlapping pattern of activities and responsibilities is clear in the *Economic Report of the President.* In both the 1976 and 1977 reports, MacAvoy had responsibility for signing off all except the last draft of the microeconomic chapters, including those relating to social programs and income transfer policies as well as regulation and energy. These necessarily overlapped tax and macroeconomic issues, and it is impossible to tell where one Council member's activity area began and the others' ended.

During the MacAvoy years at CEA, the Ford administration demonstrated an interest in seeing legislative reforms leading to more price flexibility, antitrust enforcements, and freedom of entry into regulated industries. The administration pushed for reduced but improved regulation. Although it is difficult to evaluate the precise impact of the CEA's activities during the MacAvoy era, they clearly contributed to changes in public policy toward the promotion of more competition in regulated industries.

Not surprisingly, part of the thrust of MacAvoy's work during his tenure on the CEA was directly toward the regulatory reform program. During 1977 and 1978 a series of eight volumes comprising the Ford Administration Papers on Regulatory Reform appeared with MacAvoy as editor or co-editor. The volumes covered safety regulation by the Occupational Safety and Health Administration; petroleum regulation by the Federal Energy Administration; regulation of air transportation, trucking, and railroads; cable television regulation; and regulation of milk and other goods. MacAvoy's views on airline and energy regulation are consistent with the general thrust of subsequent economic policy changes (that is, reduced regulation) in those two sectors of the economy.

In the *Economic Report of the President 1977* MacAvoy argued for increased reliance upon competitive forces in the airline market. Like many economists, he believed that the Civil Aeronautics Board's (CAB) restrictions on entry and exit, as well as its pricing policies, had been too flexible, thereby resulting in higher fares and a promulgation of nonprice competition, which lowered profits due to the emphasis upon advertising and service competition. Due to delays in the regulatory process, to the focus upon historical rather than future costs, and to the tendency for regulation to protect industries from change that may be injurious to some industry members, MacAvoy argued that reform could not be achieved by improvements in CAB management. Regulatory change would have to be manifested through more competition. Accordingly, MacAvoy argued that these competitive pressures would be forthcoming in the Aviation Act of 1975 submitted by the Ford administration to Congress. The act would provide for more flexibility in pricing as well as entry and exit from routes as circumstances warranted. During the Carter administration passage of the Deregulation Act of 1978 reduced CAB controls over airline passenger fares and services with an eventual goal of eliminating all controls by 1983.

MacAvoy's policy views on natural gas regulation are outlined in the *Economic Report of the President 1977*. Federal Power Commission (FPC) regulation of the wellhead price of gas destined for interstate commerce created a shortage in those states that produced little or no natural gas. Substitution of more expensive forms of energy, as well as work stoppages and unemployment in industrial sectors heavily dependent upon natural gas as a fuel, were some of the results of these shortages. Although the report acknowledged attempts by the FPC to raise natural gas price ceilings to alleviate the shortage, it argued for legislative action to eliminate price controls, which was consistent with MacAvoy's policy position. In subsequent years there was a move toward deregulation. Although it is impossible to ascertain the magnitude of MacAvoy's policy contributions, he certainly has been a leading proponent of deregulation.

MacAvoy, as chairman of the Food Deputies Group, was also extensively involved in the administration's handling of the 1975 U.S.-Soviet grain export issues. He was responsible for forecasting U.S. and Soviet crops as well as the impact of sales upon price. President Ford's Economic Policy Board Executive Committee depended upon MacAvoy's forecasts and data analysis in its policy deliberations with the president. Subsequently, MacAvoy was called to testify before the Permanent Subcommittee on Investigations concerning the impact of grain sales to the Soviet Union. When pressed by Senator Henry Jackson for a professional recommendation concerning the efficacy of sales to the Soviets, MacAvoy urged caution in the matter.

MacAvoy was somewhat uncomfortable working in the agricultural area. He believed he was not an agricultural economist. While his previous experiences were helpful he felt inadequate to the task. Regardless of MacAvoy's self-evaluation of his performance in agriculture, the work of the CEA and the Food Deputies Group in agricultural policy was highly regarded by the Ford administration's Economic Policy Board.

MacAvoy is a staunch proponent of positive economic analysis. During 1973 testimony before the Senate Committee on Commerce, he exhibited his strong inclination in this direction; interpersonal comparisons of utility gained and lost through policy are tenaciously avoided. Throughout his testimony he was adamant about not making equity comparisons. This position gives some insight into the nature of the economist as an adviser in a political setting such as at the CEA; MacAvoy has the academic tendencies that one would expect from an accomplished researcher.

MacAvoy believes that economists should not be "political economists" at the CEA. His published advice to Reagan upon the latter's election was to recruit an economic policy team exhibiting good technical qualifications and who stubbornly refuse to adjust their forecasts to meet policy. Professor MacAvoy feels that there is little to be gained by economists providing embellished forecasts which are designed to be self-serving but not particularly accurate.

The effectiveness of the CEA during MacAvoy's tenure is very difficult to assess; it is virtually impossible to establish his personal contributions. However, although the regulatory reform program of the Ford administration was an interdepartmental "task force," the economic component was probably important. Little statutory reform was achieved in the Ford administration, but the groundwork had been laid for policy changes in a full Ford 1977–81 term. Undoubtedly, educational efforts undertaken in 1975 and 1976 must have had some impact on the ability of the Carter reform group to achieve improvements in both transportation and health and safety regulation. The CEA was marginally effective in other microeconomic areas such as transportation and agriculture. In particular, the mediation role played by the CEA in dealing with departmental special interests with respect to grain sales to the Soviet Union was important. But the CEA had little impact on energy policy against the political interests both of the various groups in Congress and of the Federal Energy Administration in the White House itself, and this was the area of potentially greatest microeconomic impact.

MacAvoy himself emphasizes that the CEA's major contribution was in its overall impact rather than in practical victories in microeconomics. Although one could speculate over the role of the CEA during MacAvoy's era in promoting a trend toward regulatory reform, the most tangible, significant accomplishment probably was to bring some additional measure of credibility to the CEA. This was achieved through a heavy reliance upon positive economic analysis and a willingness to make policy makers aware of the limitations of empirical studies.

MacAvoy's major contribution to economic policy has been his careful analysis of the impact of federal regulatory policies upon the availability of natural gas supplies. This type of analysis has possibly had a broader intellectual effect by contributing to the academic literature which evaluates the impact of regulation upon industry performance. Along with such eminent economists as George Stigler at the University of Chicago, Paul MacAvoy has created a stir in the academic community by challenging many economists' conventional wisdoms in the regulatory policy area. A veritable explosion of theoretical and empirical articles has followed; these articles either evaluate theories of regulation, or investigate the impact of regulation upon performance. MacAvoy has played an important role in fueling the interest of other academic economists to pursue this line of study, no small contribution to economic analysis.

MacAvoy's work in the area of natural gas price regulation is well known and well respected in political circles. Given the high esteem in which his work is held, MacAvoy certainly has some policy impact in the deregulation trends of the late 1970s and early 1980s.

BIBLIOGRAPHY

MacAvoy, Paul. *The Economic Effects of Regulation: The Trunkline Railroad Cartels and the Interstate Commerce Commission Before 1900*. Cambridge, Mass.: MIT Press, 1965.

———. *Energy Policy: An Economic Analysis*. New York: Norton, 1983.

———. *Price Formation in the Natural Gas Fields: A Study of Competition, Monopsony and Regulation*. New Haven: Yale University Press, 1962.

———, ed. *Deregulation of Cable Television*. Washington, D.C.: American Enterprise Institute, 1977.

———, ed. *Federal Energy Administration Regulation: Report of the Presidential Task Force*. Washington, D.C.: American Enterprise Institute, 1977.

———, and Carron, Andrew. *The Decline of Service in the Regulated Industries*. Washington, D.C.: American Enterprise Institute, 1980.

DANIEL R. HOLLAS

MCCRACKEN, PAUL WINSTON

(b. December 29, 1915), CEA December 3, 1956-January 31, 1959; February 4, 1969-December 31, 1971

Paul McCracken has a unique position among the members of the Council of Economic Advisers. In the space of ten years he was appointed twice and served under two presidents, first as an associate member and then later as chairman of the Council. McCracken's first appointment was under the Eisenhower presidency, where he served from December 3, 1956, to January 31, 1959.

Under Eisenhower the Council was accorded a relatively minor role, as the Eisenhower philosophy was to provide little central guidance to the direction of the economy. Eisenhower even considered the abolishment of the Council in the early part of his administration. McCracken's recollection of Eisenhower is more positive. He recalls that the president's first words were to give him the hard facts without any softening embellishments, sentiments that McCracken would have liked repeated years later under a different president.

Despite his call for openness, Eisenhower tended to set aside the Council's advice, and the economy meandered between prosperity and recession during McCracken's early years on the Council. A 1957 boom was followed by a softening of the economy. At that time McCracken argued vigorously for an antirecession tax cut in an effort to head off further income declines. His arguments went unheeded, and the 1957 boom fell into a major recession by the following year.

McCracken left the Council in 1959 with some frustration, as he believed that the administration's obdurateness to the tax cut recommendation cost the economy a recession, and the Republican party the 1960 election. McCracken's second attempt at influencing the direction of the economy was under the Nixon presidency. In Nixon's Council McCracken was chairman, and his role was more direct and felt with greater impact; however, his tenure at the Council again ended on a discordant note.

Paul W. McCracken was born to Sumner and Mary (Coffin) McCracken in 1915. Raised on his father's farm in Richland, Iowa, McCracken has never lost his allegiance to the Republican party nor his honest and even-handed pragmatic approach to economic realities. McCracken's early years were representative of his wide-ranging ability. In primary school he took first place in a gum-chewing contest, and later he claimed possession of right guard on the Richland High School football team, no mean achievement for an eventual Council chairman of slight frame and only five feet, four inches in stature.

Influenced by both his father and his uncle, an economics teacher, McCracken earned his B.A. in 1937 from William Penn College in Oskaloosa, Iowa, the college both his parents attended. His first position after leaving college was as a teacher at the Foundation School of Berea College, Kentucky. He stayed there for three years and then enrolled at Harvard University. After completing his M.A. in economics in 1942, McCracken joined the Department of Commerce in Washington, D.C., establishing the pattern he was to follow his entire professional life—teaching, government service, teaching.

After one year in Washington McCracken moved to the Federal Reserve Bank of Minneapolis, where he initially served as financial economist, and in 1945 became the director of research and statistics. Leaving the bank, McCracken enrolled in the Ph.D. program at Harvard.

McCracken has stated that his years at Harvard left an inheritance of intellectual excellence and of the relationship of economics to public policy through the influence of such distinguished economists as Edward H. Chamberlin, Gottfried Haberler, and Alvin Hansen. McCracken wrote his dissertation, "Cyclical Implications of Wartime Liquid Asset Accumulation," under the late Professor Joseph Schumpater. Upon earning his doctoral degree in 1948, McCracken returned to teaching at the invitation of Dean Stevenson of the University of Michigan.

McCracken's first appointment at Michigan was as an associate professor in 1948. He was promoted to full professor in 1950, and in 1966 he was appointed Edmund Ezra Day University Professor of Business Administration. At Michigan he is known for his booming lecture voice and his understatement.

McCracken's devotion to teaching and his desire to find diversity in both experience and philosophy, as well as perspective, brought him to campuses around the world. He lectured in Japan during the summers of 1959 and 1965. In December 1963 he was in India, and in January 1967 he lectured in the Netherlands. The same year saw McCracken teaching at three southern Negro colleges. In April and May 1968 he lectured and toured Europe under the auspices of the U.S. State Department. The understanding of different needs and perspectives gained by McCracken by his diverse exposures was a reason why his appointment by Nixon to the Council was so well and broadly received. Whereas McCracken's academic perspectives enhanced his acceptance, it was complemented by his business contacts, which were both personal and wide-ranging.

After leaving the Eisenhower Council in 1959, McCracken increased his business and public exposure. Lecturing before a spectrum of industries, he gathered about him a number of industrialists and newspaper friends who met and dined on a regular basis. Through frequent appearances and lectures at meetings of the American Bankers Association and the National Industrial Conference Board, McCracken's views on money and fiscal matters were widely disseminated. His work as a consultant to the Bank of New York, the Commercial Credit Company of Baltimore, and the New York Stock Exchange not only broadened his audiences but also his expertise. Moreover, he was frequently approached by both the Kennedy and Johnson administrations for counsel.

With Nixon's election, and after heading some nineteen task forces for the

Republicans prior to Nixon's taking office, Paul McCracken was mentioned as a likely candidate to become chairman of the CEA. In response to these early speculations he answered wryly that anyone who would accept it would not be intelligent enough for it. After being offered and accepting the position, he remarked that you can't say no to a job like that. (Joining McCracken at the Council was Hendrik Houthakker*, who left in July 1971, and Herbert Stein*, who succeeded McCracken as chairman in 1972.)

The appointment of McCracken as chairman was hailed by both liberals and conservatives. He was viewed as a centrist, a calm pragmatist with no overwhelming ideological tie to position. To most he represented the liberal Republican. While philosophically aligned to the Chicago School of laissez-faire, as a centrist he believed that national economic policy had the duty to change the direction of the economy if markets were pushing it off course. As a pragmatist he was willing to accept necessary tradeoffs, for example, higher rates of unemployment in exchange for lowered rates of price increases. Before the National Industrial Conference Board in Septemer 1968 he argued, "We must learn to live with the uneasy compromise between inflation and unemployment."

Before taking his position as chairman he did exhibit his Chicago School leanings by berating fiscal policy and its strong adherents as they attempted to fine tune the economy by changing tax rates. He argued that fiscal policy options available cannot influence business activity in the short term. At the same time he also criticized interventionist monetary policy. Before the American Statistical Association in December 1967, McCracken argued that the Federal Reserve had overreacted to the short-run shifts by supplying too much credit in 1965 and 1967 and too little in 1966.

What McCracken represented was an attempt at finding some comfortable middle or centrist ground. While never rejecting Keynesian theory nor fully embracing the Friedman view of monetary policy, he was to bring to his position, and advice, a policy of "gradualism." He sought greater control of money and credit, and of the budget, to restrain the psychology of inflation and inflation itself. He argued before the Congressional Joint Economic Committee on February 17, 1969, that government expenditures and taxation would have been stabilizing over the recent past if it showed greater consistency. With respect to monetary policy he argued along the same lines of his remarks about fiscal policy. What was needed was a steadier rate of growth enhancing economic stability.

McCracken's first concern as he took office was inflation and the economy's strong inflationary psychology. During his entire term of office inflation remained the key to McCracken's policies. In his attack on rising prices he predicted, and later found, that curbing inflation was not easy. In conjunction with this McCracken asserted his strong feeling against any form of "incomes policy." He believed that the benefits of such a program were illusory, particularly in the longer run. He was against the general use of wage-price guideposts and, in particular, against the Johnson administration's attempts at "jawboning" both management and labor to restrain prices.

Another specific aspect of McCracken's first report to Congress was his strong belief that the growing level of aggregate demand was the main cause of the inflation—a classic demand-pull phenomenon. McCracken's initial policy prescription was to counter this with monetary and fiscal restraint. Both of McCracken's early beliefs, that of the inefficiency of controls (either formal or informal) and of the demand-pull cause of inflation, were initially questioned by his critics. While his beliefs were never recanted, they were to give way in practice by the end of his tenure on the Council.

McCracken's initial Council forecast for the economy in 1969 was less than energetic. In setting his battle against inflation he positioned his recommendations to attain a growth rate of well under the 5 percent realized in 1968. This in turn, he believed, would register a slight increase of unemployment from 3.3 percent to 4 percent. In order to meet these objectives McCracken retained the income tax surcharge imposed by Johnson, and he recommended a $3.5 billion cut in federal expenditures, which Nixon did order in July.

By the end of the year, while McCracken argued that his anti-inflation policies showed some evidence of success, the Consumer Price Index edged up over the previous year's level. The unemployment rate did stay within the forecast. McCracken's critics, however, argued for a stronger inflationary fight and urged a return to wage-price guideposts, but McCracken was adamant.

The *Economic Report of the President* for 1970 reaffirmed three points: that inflation was indeed a recalcitrant animal, that the economy was weakening, and that McCracken's policy of gradualism would stay in place. McCracken was not sanguine for the year 1970. He spoke of output increases lagging behind historic growth rates. He witnessed little progress against inflation and a worsening unemployment problem. The voices against gradualism rose, and some in the administration began to demand some form of wage-price action. Conflicts arose among the economic policy arms of the government.

With the economy softening, McCracken sought an easing of the monetary aggregate to reset its growth path. Against his position were the Federal Reserve chairman, Arthur Burns*, and Treasury Secretary David Kennedy. Both wished to hold the money supply in check. Outside the administration both Gardner Ackley* (chairman of the Council under Johnson) and Paul Samuelson called for a more stimulative spending policy. As Congress was opting for the spending alternative, McCracken faced a loss in his battle for fiscal restraint.

In his continuing fight against price increases McCracken inaugurated an "inflation alert" in August 1970. This new barometer, he argued, would bring to the public a greater understanding of the complexity in the price-cost area. It was an attempt to counter the inflation-mindedness that seemed to pervade the economy. Moreover, it emphasized his position that monetary and fiscal policies were inflation's root causes. These "alerts" were again sounded in December

1970 and April 1971. The reactions to this attention-getting phrase were essentially negative.

One group argued that this was an administration ploy that enabled it to appear to be combatting inflation while remaining inactive. Another group argued that the alert was but jawboning in disguise, for, even as McCracken explained in the 1971 *Economic Report of the President*, the alert was to call attention to specific cases of inflationary wage and price behavior. More important, this new sounding appeared to be a retreat from McCracken's policy of gradualism, as well as away from laissez-faire. It was clearly a government intrusion into the price and wage arena. By the year's end inflation had just slightly slowed, but unemployment was approaching the 6 percent level.

The year 1971 was a difficult one for the chairman of the Council. In January McCracken moved further away from his centrist position and into informal controls when he convinced the steel industry to moderate its announced price increases. McCracken also became a target for White House advisers who sought optimistic economic reports from the Council. McCracken's unwillingness to disguise realities and speak overoptimistically culminated in the introduction of a new spokesman for the administration. The newly appointed Secretary of the Treasury, John B. Connally, assumed a very public role of championing the Nixon programs. Moreover, the White House came in conflict with the Council on the economic forecast for the economy. The administration forecast for 1971 was a 9 percent rise in GNP (in part this was due to the president's assumption of a full employment budget, giving rise to the Democratic applause of Nixon embracing Keynesian doctrines). McCracken's Council, however, predicted that under the most favorable conditions GNP would increase by only 7 to 7.5 percent.

The conflict later prompted Paul Samuelson to reflect that McCracken was surrounded by extremists in the administration and never master in his own house.

By July McCracken softened the year's growth target. With inflation still running at 4 percent and unemployment at the 6 percent level, the 7 percent growth target for the year became untenable. The stimulative actions necessary to reach the initial target were necessarily toned so as not to aggravate further inflation. Dramatic changes were yet to come.

On August 15, 1971, President Nixon announced what was heralded as the "most comprehensive new economic policy to be undertaken in this nation in four decades." The president's bold and unexpected plan included a ninety-day freeze on prices, the end of the dollar convertibility, a 10 percent surcharge on imports, a decrease in federal expenditures, a repeal of both the 7 percent auto excise tax and a $50 increase in personal tax exemptions. McCracken was designated vice chairman of the Cost of Living Council under Connally. Labor railed under the cost freeze, and the stock market rallied.

McCracken's advisory role for this new far-reaching policy must be interpreted as supportive. In the weekend prior to the Monday announcement, Nixon assembled his advisers at Camp David. According to the *New York Times* of August

15, George Schultz, Director of Management and Budget, was known to oppose the freeze. Both McCracken's and Burns' supportive counsel to the president for the freeze won the day. Despite his initial role, McCracken remained in the background while these new policies were explained, defended, and implemented.

On November 24 McCracken announced his resignation effective January 1, 1972. Admitting that his policy of gradualism lost to the psychological pressures of inflation, McCracken was characteristically open in his views in his final interview on December 31. He predicted a continuation of controls beyond the initial ninety-day period and observed that without controls inflation would increase at an unacceptable rate. In retrospect, he remarked that he was less "Friedmanesque" than he had been, that money by itself would not produce an expansion of the economy. On the fiscal side he noted that expenditures used for a stimulus when needed were difficult to rescind from the budget when no longer required, a problem often cited by Council chairmen. Last, he admitted to an earlier tactical error, his underestimation of the lags involved in moving from a restrictive to an expansionary policy during the 1970 recession. Upon his resignation, McCracken returned to Ann Arbor and resumed his teaching duties at the University of Michigan.

During his tenure as chairman, McCracken had been called "the most compromised economist of his day." Others have said that he was the victim of political hatchet men who wished for a more malleable interpretation of the disappointing economic numbers. McCracken's successor, Herbert Stein,* stated that his association with McCracken witnessed some of his best days, and the nation was richer as a result of McCracken's service.

After leaving the Council McCracken served as a senior consultant to the Treasury Department under Ford and is currently considered to be an influential adviser to the Reagan administration. Additionally, McCracken has joined the *Wall Street Journal*'s board of contributors and has also joined with the former Secretary of the Treasury, Henry H. Fowler, under the auspices of the International Management and Development Institute, to help shape a national consensus on U.S. industrial revitalization strategy. He has been a member of the President's Economic Policy Advisory Board since 1980 and was a member of the Gold Commission in 1980–81. He was a special consultant to the president in 1974 and a special consultant to the Secretary of the Treasury during 1974–75.

During his academic life McCracken has always been an industrious writer. He has been a consistent contributor to academic journals such as the *American Economic Review*, the *Journal of Finance*, and the *Review of Economics and Statistics*. His range of expertise is exemplified by the subjects of his writings: energy, the balance of payments, inflation, taxes, and wage-price guideposts, among others. Among his many awards have been the William F. Butler Award from the New York Association of Business Economists in 1978, and the Tax Foundation Annual Award in 1971. He also has been honored by the National

Economists Club for his outstanding service as a member of the board of governors. Colleges and universities that have granted him awards include the University of Michigan, Miami University, Albion College, Berea College, Huron College, Iowa Wesleyan College, Central Michigan University, Northern Michigan University, St. Anselm's College, and William Penn College.

BIBLIOGRAPHY

McCracken, Paul. "The End of American Hegemony." *Michigan Quarterly Review* (Spring 1981): 1–19.

———. "Inflation, Profits, and the American Economy." *Proceedings of the Conference on Financial Reporting and Changing Prices*. New York, May 31, 1979.

———. "Is Economic Progress Obsolete?" *International Monetary Conference*. Vancouver, May 25, 1982.

———. "On the Proposal for an Industrial Policy." *Michigan Quarterly Review* (Winter 1984): 71–83.

———. "Prospects for Economic Revitalization." *Economic Impact* 37 (1982): 10–14.

———. "Reflections of an Economic Policy Maker: A Review Article." *Journal of Economic Literature* 18 (June 1980): 579–85.

BERNARD S. KATZ

MALKIEL, BURTON G.
(b. August 28, 1932), CEA July 22, 1975-January 20, 1977

For research economists fortunate enough to be called to serve on the Council of Economic Advisers, appointment usually means instant fame. Even though appointees may have achieved notoriety within the economics profession long before serving on the CEA, their limited fame in academe has seldom been enough to make their names household words. For most new members of the CEA, appointment usually marks the beginning of the public's awareness of their contribution to economics. This was not the case for Burton G. Malkiel. By virtue of his work *A Random Walk Down Wall Street*, one of the most widely read books ever written about the stock market, Malkiel already had a level of name recognition seldom realized by even the most brilliant of research economists. For Malkiel, appointment to the CEA did not begin the public phase of his career but merely enhanced the limelight in which he was already basking.

Born in the midst of depression in 1932 in Boston, Malkiel managed to acquire an impressive record in the field of financial economics at an early age. He graduated from Harvard University in 1953 with a B.A. degree, and in 1955, one year after marrying his wife, Judith Ann, he received the M.B.A. from the same university. He immediately put his academic knowledge to work, serving for two years as a first lieutenant in the Finance Corps of the U.S. Army. In 1958 he joined the Wall Street investment banking firm of Smith Barney and Company as a security analyst. Two years later he left that position in order to attend Princeton University in pursuit of a Ph.D. degree in economics.

In 1962 Malkiel's professional experience in the financial market and his academic background in financial economics paid off in the form of a paper on one of the most controversial subjects of the time, the term structure of interest rates. "Expectations, Bond Prices, and the Term Structure of Interest Rates" was published in the *Quarterly Journal of Economics* in May 1962, a time when considerable uncertainty prevailed in academic literature concerning the factors most responsible for the shape of a given yield curve. The disappointment with previous works stemmed from the fact that they did not offer a comprehensive model of the term structure of interest rates that interpreted the reality of the world of professional money managers. Malkiel's work was based on the expectation theory of the term structure of interest rates developed by Friedrick Lutz. However, Malkiel's approach was general enough not only to incorporate the arguments of "liquidity preference," "institutional rigidities," and "transaction costs" debated by various people, but also to explain the shape of yield curves when no explicit expectations had been formed about the future rates.

Two years after the publication of his first academic paper, Malkiel was awarded a Ph.D. in economics from Princeton University, where he at once became employed as an assistant professor in the department of economics. By 1964 he had already established himself as a prolific and original writer in the area of financial markets and institutions. For example, he appeared twice in the *American Economic Review*, with papers entitled "Equity Yields, Growth, and the Structure of Share Prices" (December 1963) and "The Term Structure of Interest Rates" (May 1964), and once in the *Journal of Finance*, with "The Rejection of the Triffin Plan and the Alternative Accepted" (September 1963).

In 1966 Malkiel was promoted to the rank of associate professor and in 1968 to the rank of full professor at Princeton. One year later he was given an endowed chair and the prestigious title of Gordon S. Rentschler Memorial Professor of Economics. Between 1966 and 1970 Malkiel diligently continued his research on financial markets and institutions. He published numerous papers in professional journals, either single-handedly or with colleagues such as William Baumol and Richard Quandt. His favorite subject at this time was another problematic issue in the area of financial markets—options.

For a number of years it was possible to buy and sell options in the over-the-counter market via individual investment firms. But the volume of transactions was limited, and there was no formal secondary market in which to sell an option before its maturity. Above all, the investment community was unsure about the investment strategies in a world with options because the amount of research, at both the theoretical and empirical level, was scanty. Malkiel, being aware of the issues, set out to remedy the situation. The result was a series of highly technical and enlightening papers. He first published, with Richard Quandt and William Baumol, "Valuation of Convertible Securities" (*Quarterly Journal of Economics*, February 1966). Two more articles co-authored by Malkiel appeared in 1970, "An Organized Option Market and the Public Interest," and "Option Trading, Stock-Price Movements and Investment Strategies." However, Malkiel's most important contribution was *Strategies and Rational Decision in the Securities Option Market* (1969), written with Richard Quandt.

In one sentence, this book brought intellectualism to the fuzzy world of options trading along with a series of recommendations to improve the efficiency of the system. The authors incorporated the theoretical constructs of utility functions and decision-making strategies under uncertainty into a detailed analysis of the securities options market. Their conclusion, given transaction costs, taxes, and other market constraints, was that almost all investors should find dealings in options a part of their overall portfolio strategy if they are to optimize their risk-return tradeoff. The book was very technical, so much so that one book reviewer wrote that this unusual book offered diminishing returns to the reader if read over its entire length. However, almost four years after its publication, the Chicago Board Options Exchange, the first organized options market ever, was established according to the policies for improving options trading recommended in the book. Among those recommendations adopted by the exchange were the creation of a central marketplace with price dissemination capabilities, the standardization of expiration dates, and the creation of a secondary market for unexpired options.

When one examines the nature of the successive articles and papers by Malkiel, one finds a close correlation between what he was doing as a businessman or administrator and his publications. His works on the term structure of interest rates and the options market were the result of his frustration with the market as seen through the eyes of an analyst of debt securities for Smith Barney and Company, and later as director of several mutual funds investment companies. In the same manner, in 1971, two years after he prepared the "Malkiel Report" on Princeton University's investments in the racist countries of South Africa, he published "Social Issues in Investing Endowments." The Malkiel Report was actually the report of an ad hoc committee he chaired which was established by the president of Princeton in late 1968 to consider a student proposal that Princeton sell and refuse to accept further gifts of securities of companies which had subsidiaries or affiliates operating in the South African countries associated with apartheid. At its January 1969 meeting, the faculty of Princeton adopted the recommendations of the ad hoc committee, that is, that Princeton not hold any securities in companies whose primary economic activity takes place in South Africa.

It is safe to say that Malkiel's concern with the morality of investment was also the underlying issue which led him to write his best seller, *A Random Walk Down Wall Street*. Bascially, this book was a beginner's guide on how to invest in the stock market. However, Malkiel manages, in a subtle fashion, to demonstrate the fact that for the majority of investors the stock market is indeed no more than a game in which the players pay to play. The payment is made in two forms: (1) opportunity costs of foregoing investments in a more conservative medium, and (2) brokerage costs. In other words, the real winners of this game are a highly informed minority who operate in an inefficient section of the market and also the brokers. The average stock market investor, on the other hand, can only hope to earn a rate of return equal to the market average commensurate with the financial risk taken.

In this book Malkiel's recommended investment strategy for the average investor during the rest of the 1970s was to put money into mutual funds. Given the extraordinarily volatile performance of the stock market during that period, it now turns out that he gave investors good advice. He actually went further and suggested that a mutual fund comprised of hundreds of stocks that did not trade to catch winners should be made available to the public. What he was outlining was simply the idea of "index funds" which came into existence shortly after the publication of his book.

In 1974 Malkiel became the chairman of the department of economics at Princeton University, a job that he had to leave temporarily one year later to join the Council of Economic Advisers under President Gerald Ford. Malkiel became a member on July 22, 1975, filling a vacancy created on February 25 by the departure of William Fellner*. Alan Greenspan*, the chairman of the

Council, had actually been looking for two people since May 1975. He filled the other vacancy earlier in the year when Paul MacAvoy* replaced departing member Gary Seevers*.

During the mid 1970s two economic issues headed the priority list of any concerned policy maker. One was the energy problem, which was brought to attention primarily as a result of the Arab oil embargo and the subsequent price increase of imported crude oil. The second problem was the growth rate of the economy, which had been sluggish since the early seventies primarily because of the low level of capital spending.

Of course, there were other chronic concerns such as inflation, unemployment, the federal deficit, and high interest rates, but the problems of energy and productivity were thought by many to be the primary causes of these other problems. In 1975 this thinking was clearly reflected in the Ford administration's selection of the two new members of the Council. Paul MacAvoy was one of the top experts on energy, and Burton Malkiel was a recognized wizard in financial market and investment analysis.

Malkiel's views on how to return health to a depressed economy were publicized through an interview in the *New York Times* on July 22, 1975, a few days after his nomination as a Council member was confirmed by the Senate Committee on Banking, Housing and Urban Affairs. In answer to a question on unemployment, Malkiel clearly showed that he did not believe demand management could help pull the economy out of its "long-run problem ditch."

Malkiel assumed responsibility as a Council member mid-way through 1975. Nevertheless, that year's *Economic Report of the President* echoed Malkiel's early remarks in the *New York Times*: the need for a cutback on government expenditure and the inducement of private capital spending. This was a clear indication that both Greenspan, chairman of the Council, and Malkiel subscribed to the same economic ideology.

The year 1976 began with some macroeconomic variables in a more favorable position. The rate of inflation, briefly in the double-digit range, was down to 6 percent, mainly due to the tight rein that Arthur Burns*, the chairman of the Federal Reserve Board, put on the monetary aggregates in the face of an inflationary recession. Long-term interest rates were also lower than before. However, capital expenditures were still at an alarmingly low growth rate of 2 percent, and the unemployment rate was still hovering over the unacceptable 8 percent range.

This situation, especially the combination of inflation and high unemployment, had been prevailing for quite some time, and it appeared that traditional fiscal and monetary policy had become ineffective tools for stabilizing the economy. As a result, a loss of confidence in active fiscal and monetary policy started to catch on quickly in academe and in government policy circles as well, although not as fast. The new school of thought that emerged had policy implications quite contrary to those that had been in use during the previous decade. This theory came to be known as monetarism and was spearheaded by Milton Friedman. According to his theory, there is a ''natural rate of unemployment'' at any given time that neither fiscal policy nor monetary policy can directly decrease. Any demand-oriented policy is apt to be an agent of inflation and instability rather than an agent of full employment above the natural rate. The only hope to decrease the natural rate of unemployment, therefore, rests on the supply side.

Because of his background in financial economics, Malkiel was sympathetic to the ideas of monetarism. In a Congressional hearing on the economic outlook of the country held a few days after Malkiel's confirmation as a Council member, Malkiel noted that capacity bottlenecks would arise before acceptable levels of unemployment were achieved. He followed this by urging programs that would encourage capital formation.

Later, in February 1976, Malkiel submitted a detailed report on the country's capital problem, outlining what the Council thought to be the main reasons behind the shortage of business capital expenditure. According to the report, capital expenditure's share of the GNP had to average an annual rate of 12 percent for the next four years if a full employment level of 4 percent was to be achieved. This was a startling discovery considering the fact that the previous level of capital spending was about 8 percent of the GNP. The report mentioned three problems that needed attention before any perceptible change could occur in the rate of capital spending. First, the rate of return which business required to undertake new investments had increased relative to the actual rate of return, mainly due to an increase in the risk premium as a result of increased uncertainty produced by the government's economic policies. Certainly, when the going rate of return on investment is lower than what the business community considers sufficient, not much new capital can be expected to be formed by the private sector. Second, fiscal policies had become biased against private investment, either through tax policies favoring consumption or through government expenditures competing for funds. Finally, the long-term savings incentives of individuals had been reduced through government policies favoring consumption, such as transfer programs and social insurance benefits. Given the fact that private savings are an important source of loanable funds, a decline in the savings rate produces a grave problem for capital formation.

These problems were not going to be resolved easily. Full cooperation between Congress and the administration would be necesesary. Many tax laws would need to be changed. Certain industries would have to be deregulated. Government spending would have to be brought within manageable limits. These and other issues were not resolved in the year and a half that Malkiel was to serve on the Council. However, when Ford lost the presidency to Carter it was not because of economic problems. By the end of 1976 the country was en route to full recovery with an inflation rate that was low according to the standards of that time. With the change of administration in March 1977, Malkiel returned to Princeton, but before leaving he put before Congress an agenda aimed at returning health and energy to the U.S. economy—an agenda to be picked up by the nation just four years later.

In his last appearance before the Joint Economic Committee of Congress in February 1977, Malkiel argued that low investment was associated with lagging productivity growth, which held down increases in the standard of living. He then proceeded to defend before the cynical committee an economic package which he believed would revitalize the U.S. economy. Among other things, the package recommended more room for free market and private enterprise in the economy with a minimum of government intervention. At one point he proposed to either abolish the minimum wage laws or increase "the natural full employment rate" from 4 percent to 4.9 percent. This brought a heated lecture from Senator Hubert Humphrey of Minnesota who insisted that 4.9 percent unemployment could hardly be considered full employment.

Malkiel's engagement as a Council member did not allow much time for writing. He managed to publish one book, *Managing Risk in an Uncertain Era: An Analysis for Endowed Institutions*, with Paul Firstenberg, and a few articles. However, after leaving the Council he again published prolifically, especially on the topic of capital formation; for example he wrote "The Government and Capital Formation: A Survey of Recent Issues" (1977), with George von Furstenberg, followed by "The Capital Formation Problem in the United States" (1979).

With the onset of the 1980s, Malkiel was sought by magazines and newspapers for his opinion on the economy and the stock market. His essays periodically appeared in the *New York Times*, *Money*, and *Forbes Magazine* as well as in several popular business magazines. His vast academic knowledge and successful hands-on experience, along with his ability to explain difficult and technical concepts in simple language, made him a much sought after authority on financial matters. In 1981 Malkiel left Princeton for yet another challenging position at Yale University, as dean of the School of Organization and Management.

The same year he went to Yale, Malkiel published the third edition of *A Random Walk Down Wall Street*. The new edition, like the previous ones, was a success among laymen, but this time the author had a hard time defending the efficiency of the stock market. The problem was that the market had been continuing on a horizontal trend over the past two decades of inflation and hyperinflation, which implied, contrary to public belief, that stocks were not a good hedge against inflation. In other words, the stock market was not efficient enough to deliver constant real purchasing power. In fact, Franco Modigliani and Richard Cohn pointed out in *Financial Analyst's Journal* in 1979 that the market had irrationally undervalued itself by half. In reply Malkiel wrote that while he did not believe the market is always rational, if forced to choose between the stock market and the economics profession, he would put his money on the stock market every time. He suspected that stock investors were not irrational—they were just frightened. Scared or not, the question still remained: Why didn't this volatile market follow an upward trend along with other prices?

Knowing that the stock market had undervalued itself for years and believing that sooner or later this efficient market would correct past mistakes, Malkiel published another best seller, *Winning Investment Strategies* (1982), in which he continued to recommend investment in stocks for the remainder of the eighties, although this time he was more optimistic than he was in the earlier editions of *Random Walk*, when he advocated investments in the mutual funds.

In recent years, Malkiel has been hard at work analyzing the odds at the race track. He has published several papers on this subject, including "Race Track Betting and Informed Behavior" (*Journal of Financial Economics*, 1982) and "Market Efficiency in Race Track Betting" (*Journal of Business*, 1984), both with Peter Asch and Richard Quandt. Knowing the correlation that exists between what Malkiel does and what he writes, one is forced to draw the conclusion that this multifaceted financial wizard is presently enjoying himself at the track.

BILBIOGRAPHY

Malkiel, Burton. *A Random Walk Down Wall Street*. New York: Norton, 1973.

———. *Winning Investment Strategies*. New York: Norton, 1982.

———, and Firstenberg, Paul. *Managing Risk in an Uncertain Era: An Analysis for Endowed Institutions*. Princeton: Princeton University Press, 1976.

———, and Quandt, Richard. "Option Trading, Stock-Price Movements and Investment Strategies." *Research Memorandum No. 6*. Princeton: Princeton University Press, 1970.

———. *Strategies and Rational Decisions in the Securities Option Market*. Cambridge, Mass.: Harvard University Press, 1969.

MOJTABA SEYEDIAN

MOORE, THOMAS GALE
(b. November 6, 1930), CEA, July 1, 1985-

Thomas Gale Moore was designated the microeconomist of the three-member Council of Economic Advisers when named to the post in 1985. He describes himself as a "free market" economist and has specialized in regulation issues.

Moore was born on November 6, 1930. He received his academic credentials from George Washington University and the University of Chicago. After studying two and one-half years at MIT, he returned to his hometown of Washington, D.C., to complete his undergraduate studies. Having majored in economics, with a minor in international relations, he obtained his B.A. in 1957. He earned his M.A. and Ph.D degrees in economics from the University of Chicago. He finished his studies there in June 1961 and married his wife, Cassandra, in the same year.

Moore has held several academic positions and is presently on leave from Stanford University. He spent four years as assistant professor at the Carnegie Institute of Technology and then taught at Michigan State from 1965 to 1974, where he was promoted to full professor in 1969. In 1974 he accepted the position of Director and Senior Fellow at the Stanford University Hoover Institution's Domestic Studies Program. Moore has also been an Honorary Research Fellow at University College in London (1973–74) and a lecturer both in the Economic Department at UCLA (1975–76) and in Stanford's Graduate School of Business (1978–79). He has taught at the graduate and undergraduate levels in the areas of industrial organization, regulated industries, price theory, macroeconomics, and welfare economics.

Moore was not new to government, nor even to the work of the Council, when he joined the Council of Economic Advisers in July 1985. Over the years, along with teaching and engagement in other professional academic activities, Moore has acted as government consultant, has provided Congressional testimony, and has made a number of state-level government appearances. He has been consultant to the National Industrial Pollution Control Council of the Department of Commerce (1971–72), to the Office of Telecommunications Policy in the Executive Office of the President (1971–73), and to the Department of Transportation (1973–74, 1981–83), as well as a participant on the Task Force on Congressional and Regulatory Reform for the U.S. House of Representatives Republican Research Committee (1982). He has given Congressional testimony since 1971 to numerous committees and subcommittees, including the Subcommittee on Antitrust and Monopoly, the Subcommittee on Fossil and Synthetic Fuels, and the Insider Trading Subcommittee on Securities (June 1, 1987). Presentations on the state level have included three to the California Public

Utilities Commission. Futhermore, Moore served as senior staff economist to the Council of Economic Advisers from 1968 to 1970.

In the business world, he held a position as foreign economic analyst for the Chase Manhattan Bank during his last year of graduate school. Moore also served on the Board of Directors at Stanford Savings and Loan from 1979 to 1982. He was chairman of the board there during 1982.

Moore's publications encompass a broad range of issues. Though he has been most prolific on questions of government regulation, he has also written on the stock market, inflation, urban life, income policy, market concentration, the future of capitalism, freedom, teenage unemployment, health policies, and population issues. He has authored six books, including *Trucking Regulation: Lessons from Europe* (1976) and *The Essence of Stigler* (1986), co-edited with Kurt R. Leube, as well as numerous occasional papers.

Moore's early publications centered on the American theatre. Between 1962 and 1968 he published six pieces on the theatre. In 1968, his first book was released, *The Economics of the American Theater*. Centered primarily on professional theatre, which coincides with the jurisdiction of the Actors' Equity Association, Moore's analysis examines costs on Broadway, as well as subsidies, taxes, and other public policies affecting the performing arts.

Though the majority of Moore's early published articles focused on American theatre, his interest in the effects of government regulation nonetheless began early in his career. His first journal article, appearing in print in 1961, was on licensing. He presented a paper to the Econometric Society in 1966 on electric utility regulation and later published an article on the same topic.

His second book, released in 1972, portended the work for which he has become best known in the area of transportation industry regulation. This book, *Freight Transportation Regulation*, was published by the American Enterprise Institute, an organization for which Moore has continued to write and affiliate himself. Moore has been honored as an Adjunct Scholar by the American Enterprise Institute since 1972.

A self-proclaimed free market economist, Moore advocates deregulation. While deregulation hurts some, he maintains it promotes greater competition resulting in benefits to consumers and to the economy in general. In other words, the advantages outweigh the disadvantages.

According to free market theory, producers compete with one another for consumer dollars. Thoses who are able to produce quality goods for the least cost survive and face possibilities for expansion. Competition assures efficiency, then, as firms must make the best possible use of inputs in order to keep prices down and quality high. Regulation, by imposing additional costs on the producer, may result in higher prices to consumers, and less efficiency since firms have less flexibility.

Moore has investigated the pros and cons of deregulation in trucking, railroads, and airlines, in each case concluding that deregulation fosters a healthier economy. According to Moore, the benefits of partial deregulation of railroads and trucking, effected by the Staggers Act and the Motor Carrier Act, both of 1980, have been useful new services in rail and declining rates in trucking. Shippers, consumers, and the railroad industry have benefitted. On the other hand, the Teamsters union, trucking companies, and some railroad workers have suffered. Overall, however, the positive outcomes are greater than the negative outcomes. More benefit would result if all controls were lifted, Moore argues.

Moore makes a similar case regarding the deregulation of the airline industry. On the negative side, fares have increased for short trips and employees have lost jobs. Such difficulties, however, are compensated for as consumers have good substitutes for air travel over short distances, such as the automobile. In addition, overall employment in the airline industry has grown. On the benefit side, fares are lower on average, consumers face more quality/price options, and stock values have appreciated. According to Moore, deregulation has brought greater efficiency to the industry as, "more passengers [are moved] a greater distance with more full planes and with fewer staff" ("U.S. Airline Deregulation," 1986, 28).

Although critics have claimed that deregulation in transportation has reduced safety, Moore maintains that their evidence is merely "anecdotal." On the contrary, Moore notes that safety has improved steadily in trucking, rail travel, and air flight. He does not, however, attribute this improvement to deregulation.

Moore has been critical of U.S. energy policies, once again calling for greater deregulation. In 1980, Moore claimed that administrations, going as far back as Nixon's, have been communicating a series of energy-related mixed messages. While three administrations advocated greater U.S. independence in energy, policies further entrenched dependence on OPEC. For example, the Energy Policy and Conservation Act of 1975 essentially taxed domestic producers of crude oil. Similarly, greater domestic production of coal was encouraged, but policies discouraged mining. Moore's prescriptions have included deregulation of crude oil and natural gas prices, as well as the facilitation of electric power plant licensing. A maintained trend toward deregulation of energy, he argued, would assure ample domestic supply of traditional fossil fuels, though at higher prices into the next century.

Moore finds fault with some aspects of the Reagan administration's deregulatory program and praises others. While he clearly supports Reagan administration pro-deregulation philosophy, he claims that policies have sometimes favored big business at the expense of greater competition throughout the economy. He does not object to a big business bias, asserting that this serves to balance the antibusiness orientation of the previous administration. He does, however, believe that greater competition is a worthy goal and should be the focus of deregulation policies.

Consistent with his free market beliefs, he applauds Federal Trade Commission dismissal of three long-standing antitrust cases against cereal manufacturers, since he has argued that antitrust laws are regulatory statutes. He further commends the Reagan administration for decontrolling oil prices and lifting auto passive restraint regulations.

While he supports an executive order requiring major regulatory action of administration agencies to be subjected to cost-benefit analysis prior to enactment, he has highlighted the difficulties that may arise in fulfilling this demand. Cost-benefit analysis can be used to justify as well as block a regulation, since wide discrepancies can result among different estimates. He concludes that the outcome of cost-benefit analysis often depends on the analyst's ideological leanings.

Moore believes that further deregulation is needed throughout the economy to promote greater competition. Such action should center, in part, on transportation, environment, and natural gas.

Along with his responsibilities as a member of the Council of Economic Advisers and as frequent government consultant, Moore referees for a number of academic journals, including the *American Economic Review*, the *Journal of Political Economy*, the *Journal of Law and Economics*, the *Review of Economics and Statistics*, and the *RAND Journal of Economics*. He is a member of President Reagan's National Critical Materials Council and the Economic Planning Council of the International Management and Development Institute. He continues his research on regulation, focusing presently on energy regulation and the costs and benefits of environmental regulation. His personal interests include skiing and photography.

Thomas and Cassandra Moore have two children, Charles and Antonia. The Moores' permanent home is in Palo Alto, California.

BIBLIOGRAPHY

Moore, Thomas Gale. *The Economics of American Theater*. Durham, N.C.: Duke University Press, 1968.

———. "The Effectiveness of Electric Utility Prices." *Southern Economic Review* (April 1970).

———. *Freight Transportation Regulation*. Washington, D.C.: American Enterprise Institute, 1972.

———. "The Purpose of Licensing." *Journal of Law and Economics* 4 (1961): 93–117.

———. *Trucking Regulation: Lessons from Europe*. Washington, D.C.: American Enterprise Institute, Hoover Policy Study 18, 1976.

———. "U.S. Airline Deregulation: It Effects on Passengers, Capital, and Labor." *Journal of Law and Economics* 29 (1986): 1–28.

———, and Leube, Kurt R., eds. *The Essence of Stigler*. Stanford: Hoover Press, 1986.

Ott, James. "Safety Experts Cite Need for Increased Monitoring." *Aviation Week and Space Technology* 77 (1987): 50.

MARY P. BECKMAN

MUSSA, MICHAEL
(b. April 15, 1944), CEA, August 18, 1985-

Michael Mussa was born in 1944 in Los Angeles, California. He received an A.B. in mathematics and economics with honors in June 1966 from the University of California at Los Angeles. The University of Chicago awarded him a M.A. in economics in 1970 and a Ph.D. in economics in 1972.

Michael Mussa was invited by the Reagan administration to serve on the president's Council of Economic Advisers in July 1985. During the confirmation process, he worked as a consultant to the Council. His appointment became official in August 1986.

Mussa was appointed to serve on the Council as a macroeconomist, specializing in international business, monetary policy, and macroeconomic issues. His appointment is the culmination of many years of economic research and service to the United States.

Mussa's expertise in such subjects as financial institutions, taxation of municipal bonds, international trade, and monetary policy has led to invitations to appear before the U.S. House of Representatives, the Senate, the American Bar Association, and the Treasury and Civil Service Committee on International Monetary Arrangements of the House of Commons (U.K.). He worked as a consultant to the World Bank from 1983 to 1985. He has been a research associated at the National Bureau of Economic Research since 1981.

Mussa's academic appointments include the William H. Abbott Professor of International Business at the Graduate School of Business, University of Chicago, which he has held since September 1981. He has twice been invited as a research fellow to the Graduate Institute of International Studies in Geneva. He was a research fellow at the London School of Economics from July 1975 to October 1976. He was a visiting professor at the International Monetary Fund in 1980.

Mussa's research interests cover a wide range of subjects. The range of Mussa's research is manifest in the variety of topics he has presented in his published work. He has contributed to such areas as balance of payments analysis, tariff policy, income distribution, investment decisions by firms, the welfare cost of inflation, exchange rate dynamics, market organization, product quality, and the tax treatment of municipal bonds.

An early paper by Mussa, "A Monetary Approach to Balance-of-Payment Analysis," examines balance of payments and trade behavior within the context of the monetary approach to the balance of payments. In this paper Mussa argues that the monetary approach is the appropriate framework for analysis of the balance of payments. He also observes that the money demand function and the money supply process are critical to the analysis.

In "Tariffs and the Distribution of Income: The Importance of Factor Specificity, Substitutability, and Intensity in the Short and Long Run," he analyzes the effects of tariffs on the distribution of income. Utilizing a two-good model, Mussa considers two possible cases with regard to capital specificity: capital is a specific factor and capital is a quasi-fixed factor. He uses the model to examine the effects of relative commodity price changes on the distribution of income among factors of production. In the short run, Mussa concludes, both cases yield the same result, viz. the magnitude of the income changes is a function of factor substitutability. In the long run, however, the second case—where capital is a quasi-fixed factor—results in factor income changes in both direction and magnitude that depend on relative factor intensities.

Mussa's interest in income distribution as it pertains to factors of production has continued in his recent work. A paper published in the *Journal of International Economics* (1982a) addresses the consequences of imperfect factor mobility. Mussa shows that labor has an interest in policies that protect the industry in which it is employed if it is imperfectly mobile. The magnitude of the interest in such policies is inversely related to the mobility of labor.

Mussa has also addressed issues relevant to the conduct of monetary policy. A paper published in the *Journal of Money, Credit and Banking* (1977) discusses the implications of the use of money as a unit of account. The paper shows that inflation affects welfare more than the usual analysis of consumer surplus would indicate because money is used as a unit of account. The additional cost to society due to inflation depends on the cost of changing prices, losses arising from disequilibrium prices, and the distribution of adjustments to relative prices. The analysis of inflation demonstrates that the optimal rate of inflation is zero. However, the analysis also shows that the optimal rate of inflation is positive if the costs of downward wage adjustments are large.

Mussa has also made an important contribution to tax policy. In *The Taxation of Municipal Bonds: An Economic Appraisal* (1980), a book Mussa co-authored with Roger C. Kormendi, Mussa examines criticism of the indirect subsidy to state and local governments through the tax exemption on interest payments on the debt issues of cities and states. Critics of the tax exemption argue that it is both inefficient and inequitable. They argue that it is inefficient because the tax avoided by holders of tax exempt municipal bonds is larger than the subsidy. They argue that it is inequitable because many holders of tax exempt municipal bonds are wealthy.

Mussa and Kormendi conclude that the use of the tax exemption on interest payments on municipal bonds as an indirect subsidy is neither inefficient nor inequitable. Mussa and Kormendi support their argument by considering the investors in municipal bonds. They observe that usually banks, casualty insurance companies, and individuals invest in municipal bonds. With regard to banks and insurance companies, the benefits of the tax exemption would pass to the customers. In this way, the tax exemption is not inequitable, since many low-income people benefit as customers of banks and casualty insurers. Mussa and Kormendi also observe that the true marginal tax rates of many wealthy investors may fall below their official tax rates because of various tax shelters. There is no inefficiency if the taxes paid by wealthy bond holders do not exceed the indirect subsidy to state and local governments.

Mussa's research interests even extend into issues pertaining to market structure. In the paper he co-authored with Sherwin Rosen, ''Monopoly and Product Quality,'' Mussa compares monopoly with a competitive market organization. The paper considers a monopolist that sells differentiated products to consumers with various preferences. Mussa and Rosen demonstrate that a monopolist will not only charge higher prices than a firm in a competitive market but will also offer goods of lower quality than the firm in a competitive market.

Michael Mussa maintains residences in both Washington, D.C., and Chicago. He has never married. He enjoys entertaining friends and associates and considers wine collecting a serious vocation.

BIBLIOGRAPHY

Mussa, Michael. ''Imperfect Factor Mobility and the Distribution Income.'' *Journal of International Economics* 12 (February 1982): 125–41.

———. ''A Model of Exchange Rate Dynamics.'' *Journal of Political Economy* 90 (February 1982).

———. ''A Monetary Approach to Balance-of-Payment Analysis.'' *Journal of Money, Credit and Banking* 6 (August 1974): 333–51.

———. ''Tariffs and the Distribution of Income: The Importance of Factor Specificity, Substitutability, and Intensity in the Short and Long Run.'' *Journal of Political Economy* 82 (November 1974): 1191–1203.

———. ''The Welfare Cost of Inflation and the Role of Money as a Unit of Account.'' *Journal of Money, Credit and Banking* 2 (May 1977): 276–86.

———, and Kormendi, Roger C. *The Taxation of Municipal Bonds: An Economic Appraisal*. Washington, D.C.: American Enterprise Institute for Public Policy Research, 1980.

———, and Rosen, Sherwin. ''Monopoly and Product Quality.'' *Journal of Economic Theory* 18 (August 1978): 301–17.

MARK D. JOHNSON

NISKANEN, WILLIAM A.
(b. March 13, 1933), CEA June 12, 1981–March 30, 1985

William A. Niskanen was a member of the Council of Economic Advisers from June 1981 to March 1985 with primary responsibility for the budget, regulation, and trade issues. Prior to his arrival, Niskanen was professor at the Graduate School of the University of California in Los Angeles, 1980–81, director of economics at the Ford Motor Company, 1975–80, and professor at the Graduate School of Public Policy at the Berkeley campus of the University of California, 1972–75. Before then, he held various positions in the private and public sector which included, in reverse order, association with the Office of Management and Budget, the Institute for Defense Analyses, the Office of the Secretary of Defense, and the Rand Corporation. During his employment at the Rand Corporation, he worked toward completion of requirements for the doctoral degree. In 1962 Niskanen received his Ph.D. in economics from the University of Chicago.

William Niskanen was born in Bend, Oregon, during the early years of the Depression. He is married to Ann Pardee, and they have three children, Lia, Pamela, and Jaime. Though he has been away from university life for several years, he still retains the appearance of an individual involved in academic pursuits. His pipe-smoking habit tends to further this impression.

At the beginning of Niskanen's career he believed in the simple model of the technocrat, having faith that efficiency could be achieved simply by placing intelligent, hard-working people in the right places. He revised his opinion during the late 1960s when he realized that defense decisions were made on the basis of many criteria which had no relationship to either effectiveness or efficiency.

Nevertheless, it was during part of the period when he was associated with the Institute for Defense Analyses, 1965–69, that he developed the ideas for his most outstanding work to date, *Bureaucracy and Representative Government*, which was published in 1971. His position as a research manager at the institute and his stimulating discussions with Gordon Tullock helped him to formulate his views, first presented in a paper at the 1967 annual meeting of the American Economic Association in Washington and published in the *American Economic Review* as ''Nonmarket Decision Making: The Peculiar Economics of Bureaucracy.'' In the summer of 1969, the Institute of Defense Analyses relieved Niskanen of his research manager duties and he was able to write *Bureaucracy and Representative Government*.

The subject of the book (as well as several articles and a second book, *Bureaucracy: Servant or Master? Lessons from America*, which he wrote for the Institute of Economic Affairs in London in 1973), was the development of a theory of the behavior of bureaus. With this as a starting point, Niskanen suggested how existing bureaucracies and political institutions can be improved. The impetus for the first book was his dissatisfaction with other works on bureaucracy by Ludwig Von Mises, Max Weber, Gordon Tullock, and Anthony Downs. According to Niskanen, though the works of these men may exhibit critical insight, most of them are incomplete and/or lacking in economic insight.

Perhaps the main failing of these other works in Niskanen's eye was the lack of a positive theory of supply by bureaus. To him, such a theory was vital. Niskanen dealt with a similar problem in analyzing the relationship between deficits and inflation several years later. Having found no developed theory on the money supply, he constructed his own version in "Deficits, Government Spending and Inflation," which appeared in *Journal of Monetary Economics* (1978). Thus, it is not surprising that Niskanen's later views on the emptiness of the relationship between deficits and inflation reflected the views of many supply siders.

Bureaucracy and Representative Government and *Bureaucracy: Servant or Master?* differ from each other in two major ways. The first represents a mathematical approach along with other approaches because Niskanen believed the former to be the most effective way to analyze and express maximization problems. The second used a verbal approach but analyzed bureaucracy in the manner by which economists analyze the firm. The book's title is suggestive of Hegel's dialectic philosophy. In fact, Niskanen used the same example, "master" and "servant," to illustrate that one concept could not be defined without its negation or contradiction. Niskanen, however, did not develop the complexities of this method but rather proceeded analytically to study how the size of the bureaucracy is determined, how its efficiency is measured, and related topics.

The second difference between the two works concerned setting, and hence the relevant institutions covered. Though each book was specifically based on United States institutions, the audiences were different and they reacted differently. *Bureaucracy and Representative Government* was published in the United States and attracted a readership of economists, sociologists, political scientists and administrators in this country. As *Bureaucracy: Servant or Master?* was published in the United Kingdom, its audience, though composed of similar groups, was concerned particularly with its applicability to the British environment. Four commentaries on this topic by two former British civil servants and two former ministers appeared in the British publication; two commentators approved of the analyses for the United Kingdom and the other two insisted that the domestic framework is so different that the theory in its present form would not be suitable.

For Niskanen, the essential elements in a positive theory of the supply of bureaus consist of (1) the quantity that bureaus try to maximize, (2) the nature of the relation between bureaus and their surroundings, and (3) the distinguishing characteristics of bureaus.

In the case of bureaus, bureaucrats serve as their directors. Therefore, the important information is contained in the bureaucrat's personal utility function. Niskanen replaced this function with a single proxy, budget maximization. He argued that the substitution is valid because all variables contained in the bureaucrat's utility function are positively and continuously associated with the level of the budget.

The relation of the bureau with its surroundings would be another way to distinguish bureaus from other organizations. The bureau has a sponsor, and the relationship between the bureau and its sponsor is that of a bilateral monopoly.

Bureaus furnish their sponsors with expected outputs generated by an agreed upon set of activities in exchange for a budget. A private organization exchanges units of output for a price. While the private organization is concerned with demand for its services, the bureau is concerned, rather, with its possible influence on the behavior of the sponsor. According to Niskanen, the distinguishing characteristic of bureaus is that they are nonprofit organizations that receive at least part of their funds from a periodic appropriation or grant.

Bureaucracy and Representative Government contains detailed mathematical formulations of production and output behavior of the bureau in a static framework. Other topics include a revised model which treats the effects of changes in demand and cost conditions; variations of the basic model dealing with nonprofit organizations; the mixed bureau (partly financed by grants, partly by sales); the multi-service bureau; and effects of changes in time-distribution of expenditures.

The central motivational assumption of both books is that bureaucrats maximize the total budget of their bureaus, subject to the rule that the budget must be equal to or larger than the minimum total cost of supplying the output expected by the sponsor.

Both books also come to the conclusion that bureaucracies are too large. Three ways of correcting this problem are discussed: (1) through political reorganization; (2) through development of market alternatives to bureaus; and (3) by improving efficiency through internal competition and use of profit-like incentives to bureaucrats. Political reorganization deals with restructuring legislative review committees to reduce their monopoly power. Development of market alternatives to bureaus involves the encouragement of competition among bureaus while allowing new bureaus to form and old ones to expire.

Niskanen claims that improving efficiency appears to rest primarily on stimulating bureaucrats to perform in such a way as to maximize the difference between the obtainable budget and the minimum total costs of the service. This may be achieved by (1) letting bureaucrats keep some proportion of the difference between the total budget and total cost; (2) making a deferred payment to a bureaucrat some years after leaving office; (3) letting the bureaucrat spend some proportion of the difference between the budget and cost of programs on a particular set of activities.

Niskanen offers these recommendations after observing that competition in the market does not increase because of more or better analysis. The difference in the performance of this model versus others would be due to structure and to incentives given to managers. Economists in the Soviet Union must have recognized these relationships as clearly as Niskanen when they introduced, in the late 1960s, the Liberman reforms, which included profit-like incentives for plant managers.

In the case of government bureaus, Niskanen argued that evidence revealed that, for any given output, costs can be reduced by reducing the size of bureaus, by contracting with private firms, and by increasing competition among bureaus. After eight years spent in the Pentagon, Niskanen recommended a way to discipline the growth of defense spending. Noting that there are usually two, if not three, services performing similar military missions, he suggested that they be encouraged to compete with one another, possibly via a monetary incentive.

When *Bureaucracy and Representative Government* was published in 1971, Niskanen was assistant director of evaluation at the Office of Management and Budget under George Shultz. During the next year, Niskanen returned to teaching as professor of economics at the Graduate School of Public Policy at Berkeley. During his three-year stay at the university, Niskanen's writings reflected a deep-rooted interest in budgeting processes and problems.

An article in the *Public Administration Review*, "Why New Methods of Budgetary Choices? Administration Aspects" (1972), was highly critical of the then existing budgetary process. It would be two years before the adoption of the new process contained in the Congressional Budget and Impoundment Control Act of 1974 and another three before the process would be in operation. Even the new process did not correct all the problems Niskanen identified. The article included an enumeration of the main problems of planning-programming-budgeting systems (PPBS), which had recently been abandoned as a budgetary tool. Niskanen drew attention to two analytic models in use that were not suitable for many of the problems studied. The "defense" model, for example, would be useful only for a problem of maximization, for example, finding the minimum cost of a given defense output. Many domestic programs, however, require some knowledge of social and institutional behavior and a normative theory of government in a federal system.

The second type of model, the "national income" model, focused exclusively on allocation conditions. It assumes that individuals are subservient to the state itself or to a form of accounting construct such as national income. Frequently, the model completely ignored the distributional preferences expressed by the political system.

One last complaint concerning the budgetary process was made with reference to aggregate demand. Niskanen argued that the presumed fiscal effect on aggregate demand of a particular measure becomes more doubtful and the effect, if any, is delayed a year or more. Thus, the public expenditure decision should be separated from any consideration of a possible impact on aggregate demand. At this point, Niskanen recommended several changes: alternative structures of government; an analytic data system which permits the presentation of different formats by objective of government activities; a new policy review procedure which uses the zero base budgeting approach (which was adopted officially under President Carter for fiscal year 1979); and a new method of program analysis which identifies national problems and which accounts for the distributional consequences of governmental activities.

Niskanen's next book, *Structural Reform of the Federal Budget Process* (1973), addressed four major flaws of the budget process. The first flaw had been noted by other economists as well: the lack of relation between federal spending and tax rates. The Congressional Budget Act of 1974 eliminated this flaw by requiring Congress to pass resolutions on budget totals for outlays and receipts before considering specific items. Later on, Congress would reconsider budget totals to establish consistency with the specific programs.

William Niskanen would have taken the process one step further to satisfy both allocation and stabilization goals. He recommended a "marginally balanced budget policy" which would be operable over a specified outlay target. A dollar-for-dollar relation between marginal federal spending and expected tax revenues would become effective at this point. Thus, both the allocative and stabilization function of fiscal policy would be better served. Unfortunately, the imprecision of macroeconomic forecasting would make it difficult to satisfy the stabilization goal, in its usual sense, using this technique. This is particularly the case since the adoption of the new budgetary process in which budget totals are decided so far in advance of the fiscal year.

The other three flaws were not corrected by the act. For example, Niskanen claimed that the federal government has used a huge amount of resources whose value is not included in the budget. These resources include, but are not limited to, land and structures, underfunded civilian pensions, and nuclear materials. Next, he noted that most federal decisions do not consider the future costs of present decisions. An appropriate balance of future and present costs should be achieved. In a sense, the act has dealt with this item in its provision for multiyear projections of various programs. But Niskanen would prefer a multiyear budget process where outlay ceilings were established within the executive branch in terms of the discounted total of outlays for the initial planning year and four additional years ahead. As Niskanen has mentioned, the British government has used (and is using) a similar technique without any visible signs of better budget decisions. Recently, the United Kingdom has dropped one year from the multiyear budget and has returned to the employment of current dollars after having planned in volume terms for more than a decade. Niskanen would opt, also, for use of some general index of prices but with reference to the private sector, whereas it has been recommended in the United Kingdom that plans proceeed with a sort of GNP deflator.

Though multiyear planning by the executive branch may contribute to improved performance and greater efficiency, it is not clear how Congress would achieve an appropriate balance of present and future costs in its own deliberation.

The fourth flaw was internal to the executive branch. In Niskanen's view, there has not been sufficient policy guidance from the Executive Office to the Office of Management and Budget.

Though many budget specialists around the world have been convinced that the principle of a ''comprehensive'' budget is of the utmost importance in achieving meaningful budget totals, Niskanen suggested in this book that adopting such a principle in a less than perfect world may backfire. He referred to the movement to the consolidated cash budget in the 1960s in the interest of comprehensiveness. The new budget contained the trust funds which the old had not. Niskanen commented that the budget director was encouraged to hold back trust fund spending and to support increases in trust fund revenues in order to use the trust fund surplus to finance other programs. Finally, the switch to the unified budget in fiscal year 1969, which was only slightly different from the consolidated cash budget but unlike the national income accounts budget with its accrual basis, encouraged further manipulations of payments between years.

Instead of observing the principle of comprehensiveness, Niskanen indicated that it should be replaced by a study of outcomes of the budget process. Like Aaron Wildavsky, the political scientist, Niskanen arrived at the conclusion that if satisfactory budget outcomes are not achieved through politically feasible changes in the budget process, then the political system should be changed.

In sum, Niskanen found four main failings in the federal budget: it was too large; its rate of growth was too fast; it included too many programs that yield benefits only to small sectors of the economy; and it used too much of certain types of resources.

Niskanen was convinced, also, of the evils of federal deficits. An increase in the deficit is financed by borrowing from the public or via money creation. As either of these methods hides the cost of government spending, total government output and aggregate demand will be higher than if tax rates had been used to balance the budget. Thus, as far as Niskanen was concerned, federal deficits were linked to the growth in federal spending. In ''Deficits, Government Spending and Inflation,'' which appeared in the *Journal of Monetary Economics* in 1978, Niskanen reported that after performing two empirical tests, he found that federal deficits did increase the level of federal expenditures but did not appear to contribute to the rate of inflation.

As an outcome of the idea that federal deficits and the growth of federal spending were linked, Niskanen observed that lowering taxes would not be the way to restrain spending. Just the opposite would be in order: taxes should be raised to reduce excess demand for federal expenditures. But economic considerations and other concerns were different in 1978 from what they were in 1981, when Niskanen presented a paper, ''The Growth of Government and the Growth of the Economy,'' in Tokyo before the International Institute of Public Finance. As a member of the Council of Economic Advisers at the time, Niskanen stated his firm conviction that the president's plan to reduce personal and business tax rates along with reducing regulation and monetary growth would be consistent with the reduction of the real growth of federal spending.

However, back in Washington barely four months later, he shocked the administration, Congress, and fellow Council members at the American Enterprise Institute's Public Policy Week during December. He repeated what he had said three years before, that federal deficits were not inflationary; that neither deficits and inflation nor deficits and monetary growth had any necessary relationships. The implication of these remarks is that the relationships may depend on the particular interests of the viewer and the assumptions made. Most of these factors hinge on how one expects the deficit to be financed. In addition, Niskanen denied the "crowding out" hypothesis: that deficits crowd out private borrowers. Niskanen's stance was particularly troublesome at this time because Ronald Reagan had been associated with balanced budgets for years and the Council chairman, Murray Weidenbaum*, had been arguing that deficit spending is the basic source of inflation. After the meeting, Weidenbaum denied any support for Niskanen's statements and affirmed that, as chairman, all authority for the Council rested with him.

The event led to responses by the White House, the Treasury, and some Republican senators. But, as Niskanen had already pointed out, the Reagan economic program was inconsistent at that time, and tolerating deficits might be preferable to increasing the money supply or raising taxes.

Other remarks by Niskanen in the paper delivered in Tokyo included an expression of admiration for an important contribution to public finance made by Geoffrey Brennan and James Buchanan in their book *The Power to Tax*. According to Niskanen's summary of the book, government spending tends to be an increasing function of the size of the tax base, the types of taxes, money creation, deficit financing, and the central government's share of revenues.

The central concern of Niskanen's Tokyo paper was an analysis of two major fiscal issues: (1) the reason for the relative growth of government, and (2) the reason for the decline in the growth of real gross national product. Niskanen reported that the annual rate of real growth in total U.S. government spending during the period 1965–79 was 4.4 percent; for the federal government alone, it was 4.6 percent.

Niskanen listed the factors contributing to growth. These included (1) a rise in the real unit cost of government services, (2) a rise in real per capita gross national product; and (3) a rise in the U.S. population. Together, these factors accounted for 70 percent of total growth. The balance was accounted for mainly by federal grants and higher state and local spending.

Nevertheless, after mentioning certain political conditions which may have contributed to budget growth, Niskanen concluded the paper with a discussion of a series of studies which provide estimates of the effects of taxes and transfers. It was Niskanen's contention that tax policy may not significantly influence the size of total savings but that it may increase business investment. On the other hand, tax policy may contribute to the relative increase in government spending. The rapid rise in Social Security tax collections, for example, may have been the catalyst for increased government spending.

It has been many years since anyone has evinced an interest in the overall tax structure other than from a purely distributional point of view. Even the *Budget of the U.S. Government for Fiscal Year 1983*, like others before it, contains only 20 pages on the subject out of a total of 552. Perhaps the long overdue resurgence of interest in supply factors so evident in Niskanen's work may lead to a new synthesis which acknowledges a longer time frame and the necessity of considering supply as well as demand in macroeconomic analysis.

BIBLIOGRAPHY

Niskanen, William A. *Bureaucracy and Representative Government*. Atherton, N.Y.: Aldine Publishing, 1971.

———. "Nonmarket Decision Making: The Peculiar Economics of Bureaucracy." *American Economic Review* 58, no. 2 (May 1968): 293–305. Papers and Proceedings of the 80th Meeting in Washington, D.C., 1967.

———. *Structural Reform of the Federal Budget Process*. Washington, D.C.: American Institute for Public Policy Research, 1973.

———. "Why New Methods of Budgetary Choices? Administrative Aspects." *Public Administration Review* 32, no. 2 (March/April 1972): 155–61.

ANNETTE E. MEYER

NORDHAUS, WILLIAM DAWBNEY
(b. May 31, 1941), CEA March 18, 1977-February 4, 1979

William Dawbney Nordhaus was born in 1941 in Albuquerque, New Mexico. He attended the Institute d'Etudes Politiques in Paris, where he obtained a *certificat* in 1962; Yale University, where he earned a B.A. in 1963; and Massachusetts Institute of Technology, which granted him a Ph.D. in economics in 1967. His numerous academic honors include membership in Phi Beta Kappa; graduating magna cum laude, with distinction in economics, from Yale University; a Ford Foundation Fellowship; National Science Foundation graduation and postdoctoral fellowships; and an honorary M.A. from Yale University.

Since 1967 Nordhaus has taught at Yale, where he reached the rank of professor of economics in 1973; currently he is the John Musser Professor of Economics. He is also on the editorial board of *Emergy Economics*, *Journal of Policy Modeling*, and *Journal of Conflict Resolution*; he served on the editorial board of the *American Economic Review* between 1975 and 1978. Earlier affiliations include staff member of National Bureau of Economic Research, 1967–68; staff member of Cowles Foundation for Research, 1967–82; member and senior adviser of Brookings Panel on Economic Activity, 1972–82; member Social Science Research Council Committee of Stability and Growth, 1979–82; and board member and co-chairman, Economic Policy Study Group, Center for National Policy, 1981–82. The respect accorded Nordhaus by his colleagues for his contributions to the discipline is evidenced by the many honors he has received as well as by his recent election to the Executive Committee of the American Economic Association.

The economics profession knows Nordhaus best for his work in the areas of inflation, energy, and productivity. Throughout his work, however, he has demonstrated certain characteristics. First, he often has been concerned with long-term trends in such areas as pollution, corporate profits, and labor productivity. Second, although Nordhaus has written some theoretical articles, his analysis has usually incorporated a wide variety of empirical tests. Third, he consistently demonstrates considerable interest and insights into current economic issues.

In January 1977 President James E. Carter nominated Nordhaus as a member of his Council of Economic Advisers. (At that time, Professor Nordhaus had been teaching at Yale University for ten years; he was married with three children. He left the Council to return to Yale in February 1979.) His tenure in the government stimulated his interest in regulatory reform. In addition, for several years he contributed regularly to the *New York Times*.

As a member of the Council of Economic Advisers, Nordhaus' responsibilities included helping to prepare the Council's annual report. He had primary responsibility for microeconomic analysis in areas such as energy, agriculture, labor markets, and regulated markets, and for the international economic analysis. Although he was the microeconomist on the CEA, he participated in the debates about macroeconomic policy, which has always formed the core of the Council's work. Prior to joining the CEA, he had summarized his views on the inflation process in a speech delivered at the 1975 American Economic Association meetings; his position, articulated in that paper, is consistent with the CEA's policy recommendations during 1977 and 1978.

At that time, he criticized conventional inflation theory for its analysis of the effect of changes in aggregate demand on prices. His simplified model divides the economy into two sectors: auction markets, where prices are flexible, and administered markets, where use of market power limits price movements. Because these administered markets include much of the government, labor, manufacturing, and utility sectors, their importance has increased over time. In administered markets, prices are determined by costs normalized by the business cycle with at most a slight effect of the *actual* level of demand and costs on actual prices. In part, his belief results from an extensive empirical study in postwar U.K. manufacturing which Nordhaus, Wynne Godley, and Kenneth Coutts had completed before his appointment to the Council.

In Nordhaus' administered wage model, current wages are dominated by past wages with a much smaller effect resulting from unemployment changes. Nordhaus recognizes the important role of demand in those auction markets—the clearest examples are those for raw materials such as copper, zinc, manganese, and new fibers. While exogenous changes in auction prices affect current inflation, Nordhaus, citing a George L. Perry study, contends that only about 15 percent of this exogenous price inflation would be passed through into wages.

Economists are well aware of the policy conclusions which arise from neo-Keynesian synthesis. Neo-Keynesians contend that using slow growth of aggregate demand to reduce inflation is too costly in terms of lost output and increased unemployment; instead, they believe that only the use of some form of income policy can substantially reduce inflation with a deep and lengthy recession. Nordhaus in 1976 admitted that the weakest aspect of past price-wage policies has been that they confused inflation policy with income redistribution. He scolded economists for not demonstrating enough inventiveness in devising antidotes to inflation other than recessions, and he thought it worthwhile to consider seriously an inflation tax to penalize firms or workers deviating from a national norm because these tax-based income policies would rely on market forces to adjust relative prices.

The apparent low level of utilization of economic resources continued throughout 1977, thereby allowing the CEA to postpone development of a specific incomes policy; moreover, the Council did not foresee an acceleration of inflation in 1978. Indeed, in January 1978, President Carter asked for a $19 billion cut in individual income taxes and a $6 billion reduction in corporate profit taxes to sustain a high level of demand throughout the year. By May, however, the expansion was so strong that President Carter recommended to Congress that it reduce by $5 billion and delay by three months the proposed tax cut. Throughout 1978, inflation accelerated to about 8 percent and the dollar continued to decline on foreign exchange markets. These events forced the government to adopt anti-inflationary actions, including Carter's announcement on October 24, 1978, of a new voluntary restraint program and the Federal Reserve's announcement on November 1, 1978, of a tighter monetary policy.

Although it is not possible from the public record to determine the impact of Nordhaus, the policies adopted by the Carter administration were consistent with his neo-Keynesian views. The administration rejected exclusive reliance on monetary and fiscal restraint as being too costly to society. The Council of Economic Advisers estimated in 1978 that an unemployment rate of approximately 6 1/2 percent would reduce inflation by no more than one-half of a percent a year. Thus, it would take at least six years of economic sluggishness to reduce the inflation rate from 6 to 3 percent. To achieve the same results in less time would require even higher unemployment rates.

The Carter administration, therefore, decided to intervene directly in the wage-and-price-setting process. The results of the 1971–74 controls episode had convinced most economists and policy makers that mandatory price and wage controls were ineffective in reducing inflation. Carter's CEA, therefore, focused attention on some form of tax-based incomes policies as Nordhaus had been suggesting for several years. In January 1978, the Council admitted that all these proposals contained problems of administration, effectiveness, and equity, and that to propose implementing them without a much more complete evaluation would be imprudent.

As it turned out, the momentum of inflation was greater than the Council had anticipated and demanded some form of immediate action. Although the major thrust of Carter's program was "voluntary," his program included a provision for "real-wage insurance." The president in January 1979 asked Congress to enact tax legislation which would give taxpayers who abided by the wage guidelines a tax rebate if inflation exceeded the (7 percent) guidelines, in hopes that this would reassure people that they would not suffer if they complied with the guidelines. Congress, of course, did not adopt the real-wage insurance program.

Several months after returning to Yale University, Nordhaus expounded on his views about real-wage insurance at a conference held at Middlebury College. He contended that in the United States the social contract is not important for the success of income policies; instead, a successful income policy must change economic incentives of workers and firms. Moreover, because of administrative difficulties that result in multiple exceptions and exemptions in any price tax incentive program (TIP), Nordhaus argued that a TIP should only apply to wages. This fact, in turn, produces a rationale for using subsidies rather than taxes because if a 'stick' TIP were to be used, it would be 'fair' to workers only if applied also to firms.

Elsewhere Nordhaus discussed problems such as inclusions, exclusions, and treatment of union versus nonunion workers, his comments on the budgetary consequences provide extremely informative insights into the policy-making process. He writes that the insurance approach (rather than using tax credits) was decided upon because it was thought that it would be cheaper than paying a bribe. The cost of an insurance approach depends on the rate of inflation and the number of qualified workers. For example, under the Carter program if about one-half of workers qualified, every point of inflation over 7 percent would have resulted in $4.5 billion of after-tax cost; the Carter administration decided to limit cost by providing insurance only up to a 10 percent rate of inflation. Nordhaus contends that the $10 billion price tag of this new and "gimmicky" plan contributed significantly to its congressional defeat.

Since leaving the Council, Nordhaus has continued to articulate forcefully his neo-Keynesian views. He criticizes the rational expectations or new classical macroeconomics for the ambiguous nature of the basic flexible price assumption, which results in policy views (especially the view that deceleration of inflation can be easy and costless) that are sophisticated but irrelevant. He strongly agreed with Arthur Okun's* dismissal of supply-side economists, saying that their stance simply could not be taken seriously. His vigorous and articulate support of the neo-Keynesian synthesis has drawn mixed reviews.

In his defense of the neo-Keynesian synthesis, Nordhaus did not answer several themes of the new classical economists. First, his models assume a substantial amount of price stickiness, but the source of this price stickiness does not possess a convincing theoretical basis. Indeed, the second theme of new classical economics is that policy changes can affect the structure of the economy; certain dramatic policy changes might reduce price stickiness rapidly. Robert Solow states, "The world may have its reasons for being non-Walrasian"; but the lack of convincing justification for those reasons weakens Nordhaus' defense of the neo-Keynesian synthesis.

He is skeptical about increasing the growth rate of productivity (see below), and he realizes the difficulty of enacting direct cost-reducing measures—such as freezing minimum wages and agricultural supports and new regulations—as faced with well-entrenched constituencies. Therefore, he advocates the use of incomes policies as efficient strategy for the reduction of chronic inflation.

A second crucial economic issue with which the Carter administration wrestled involved difficulties in the energy sector. Nordhaus had published extensively in this area prior to joining the CEA. His original interest, however, involved the intertemporal allocation of energy resources, and he especially was concerned with the view that a finite amount of exhaustible resources limited economic growth. In addition, he had edited and contributed to a volume of studies on the international demand for energy.

Nordhaus believes that the basic problem in the efficient use of energy resources is that resources that require little labor and capital are severely limited in supply, and resources that are abundant require substantial research and development for recovery and use and carry higher capital costs than fuels they would replace. To derive efficiency prices, he constructs complex demand and supply models. He relates the demand for net energy inputs to parameters of the production and preference functions and to prices and incomes. His empirical work covers Western European countries as well as the United States and incorporates some disaggregation into various sectors.

In his modeling of the supply side of energy markets, he utilizes both a competitive and a pure monopoly model. The key to both models is his concept of the "backstop technology," the time horizon for the planning process; the "backstop technology" is one capable of producing energy at relatively high cost but on a "virtually infinite resource base." Nordhaus found that the efficiency price of oil is relatively low because the cost of the alternate resource is relatively low, and the time at which replacement occurs is distant. He notes, however, that in the latter half of the 1970s actual prices were above the competitive efficiency prices because of OPEC's actions. He concluded in 1979 that the wealth-maximizing price of OPEC oil was in the lower end of the $10.00 to $20.00 per barrel range in 1975 prices and that the evidence indicated that any further advance in the price of oil would take prices well above the long-run monopoly price. In late 1978 and throughout 1979, oil prices rose substantially above that range. Nordhaus explained that for many OPEC countries, production targets were decided upon using noneconomic criteria. In his view, price and output may not follow either a competitive or a monopolistic course because the backstop technology will only restrain OPEC pricing in the long run.

He was, therefore, well versed in both the theory of exhaustible resources and the empirical studies of the world's energy markets when he joined the Council in 1977. He believed that economic analysis can provide significant aid in determining efficient prices for energy resources and that because of uncertainties markets may need effective governmental intervention to achieve the efficient price. Although he was the point man for the Council's effort in developing a coherent energy policy, the newly created Department of Energy under James Schlesinger possessed primary responsibility for formulation of Carter's program. Nordhaus, however, testified extensively in favor of Carter's energy program. In his testimony, he emphasized four benefits of the Carter energy program. It would reduce U.S. dependence on imported oil, allow the United States to improve the efficiency of its use of current energy resources, provide incentives to shift from oil and gas to other energy resources, and obtain an equitable policy.

Nordhaus, in his published work and in his testimony to Congress, emphasizes the need to reduce energy consumption by allowing prices of energy to rise toward their replacement cost. He contends that, although short-run elasticities of demand for gasoline and heating oil are low, the longer-run elasticities are much higher. He worried, however, about disruption during the transition period, and continually stressed that the economy adjusts to higher real energy prices only gradually because of the relatively long life of the existing capital stock. He agrees that industrial users and utilities should face higher energy prices first because, compared with households, they have the greatest potential for low-cost conversion.

His extensive model simulations lead him to advocate a policy of high oil taxation to reduce oil consumption when his formal analysis concerns Organization for Economic Cooperation and Development (OECD) nations acting together and when the energy taxes are used for useful purposes because the gain from high energy taxes came about because the revenues were domestic income rather than foreign. Discussants of this study disagreed with many parts of his analysis but thought a tax based energy policy appropriate as well as important.

As mentioned above, the slowdown in productivity growth after 1973 intensified pressures and caused Carter's CEA to revise estimates of potential output. Nordhaus had already demonstrated expertise in this area. In 1972, he studied the slowdown in labor productivity through use of the normal output concept, which is "the level that GNP would attain if the unemployment rate were at its normal level, defined as its postwar average of 4.7 percent." He concluded that cyclical factors were not crucial in slowing down the growth of productivity. Instead, he identified a change in the composition of demand toward those industries with low levels of productivity (not productivity growth) as the major cause. Nordhaus saw this trend continuing but not worsening throughout the 1970s.

Because the record of measured productivity growth continued to be dismal in the 1970s, interest in this topic has increased. In a recent article, Nordhaus places his analysis within the "growth accounting" literature. Before examination of his provocative analysis of the "residual," it is instructive to look at the suspects which he clears as causes of the declining productivity growth. Because the productivity slowdown occurred in most industrial countries, Nordhaus argues that analysts should seek common explanations. These common explanations include energy, slow economic growth, slow growth of capital, inflation, and increased business regulation. Many economists see energy as a prime causal factor because in the 1970s energy industries experienced dramatic declines in productivity growth and because higher energy prices reduce the productivity of other factors of production. Nordhaus contends that the capital-complementarity controversy has obscured the real issue—the embodied nature of energy use. Because the long-run substitution of more energy-efficient capital takes place over several decades, higher energy prices will affect productivity over many years, but the impact in any one year will be smaller than some analysts have claimed.

Nordhaus also clears a lack of investment as a major contributing cause, as "in no country is the estimated contribution of capital more than one-fifth of the size of the productivity slowdown." He obtains this result in part by assuming that productivity changes due to lower utilization rates of capital are associated with cyclical factors and not increased obsolescence of existing capital. Moreover, he does not discuss problems associated with the composition of capital;

in the United States housing became a larger share of net investment during the 1970s.

He attributes about 20 percent of the productivity slowdown to "self-inflicted wounds." Poor stabilization policy, he thought, resulted in slower economic growth and therefore fewer opportunities to exploit economies of scale, which he finds to be more significant than do most economists. Inefficient regulation harmed productivity. He blames depletion for about 65 percent of the productivity slowdown. Along with a general lack of investment opportunities, he sees exhaustion of economies of scale, an ending of the productivity gain in shifting from agriculture to industry, and fewer great inventions as qualitative evidence of current depletion of sources for significant improvements in productivity. Although he does not resort to the concept of the Krondratieff cycle, his review of the historical evidence indicates that the recent productivity slowdown had precedents in the 1912 to 1979 period. His major question concerning the depletion hypothesis is "the implausibility of coincident timing."

Nordhaus has repeatedly written that one method to reduce inflation involves regulatory reform that provides cost-effective regulation and removes regulation's adverse effects on productivity. In general, he advocates removal of most economic regulation of prices and entry within a single industry and closer scrutiny of "social" (energy, environmental, health and safety) regulations. In his view, economic regulation, while benefitting certain firms, has reduced the economy's efficiency by reducing competition and, in many cases, by providing perverse incentives to market participants. Negative externalities associated with events such as air and water pollution provide the need for governmental intervention into the social regulation arena. Nordhaus, however, cautions that the nation must evaluate the tradeoff between regulatory and economic objectives and that it should attempt to achieve its regulatory goals at the lowest cost.

Although the CEA supported deregulation of the airline industry, it did not play a major role in this important economic initiative of the Carter administration. The CEA was substantially more involved with Carter's creation in January 1978 of the interagency Regulatory Analysis Review Group (RARG), which furnished Nordhaus with an excellent opportunity to translate his general principles into actual operation. As the CEA representative to RARG, he chaired this committee, whose responsibility was to examine alternative approaches to proposed regulations. In 1978 the committee asked whether the proposed regulation was cost-effective, whether the agency could justify analytically the standard's stringency, and whether the agency had examined varying implementation schedules. During 1978 and early 1979, RARG reviewed six regulations.

Nordhaus considers the examination of alternative approaches to be an improvement over the content of the previous economic impact statements. He contends that the most important innovation of the Carter administration was the integration of this analysis into the normal process of decision making rather than using it as an "ex post facto justification." He admits that this procedure dealt unsatisfactorily with reforming or removing old regulations ("the barnacles on the ships") but argues that the government would have to learn how to analyze rationally new regulations before it could deal with the more difficult problem of old regulations.

Nordhaus is highly regarded by his peers for several reasons. First, he has demonstrated expertise with the tool kit of the economics profession. His work with intertemporal optimization models clearly reflects this facet of his career. Second, he consistently incorporates empirical analysis into his work. Third, and probably most important, other economists believe that he tends to ask the right questions.

His impact on the profession presents a more difficult problem because, in large part, of his vigorous advocacy of the currently unfashionable neo-Keynesian synthesis. Of course, Nordhaus has not subscribed to the 1950s version of the impotent monetary policy and lack of concern about inflation which continues to tarnish the "Keynesian" tradition. However, Nordhaus has not yet provided a convincing microeconomic foundation for his inertial inflation, although his work on international comparisons is probably a step in the correct direction.

His work in energy and productivity has been important but clearly has not dominated these areas, which remain a tangle of empirical studies, each of which utilizes a different methodology and data base. His long-run contributions may center around his attempts to study the intrinsic value of exhaustible resources. The need to devise feasible methods to price resources optimally over time is clearly one of the most important topics in economics.

BIBLIOGRAPHY

Nordhaus, William. *The Econometrics of Price Determination*. Washington, D.C.: Federal Reserve Board, 1972.

———. "How Fast Shall We Graze the Global Commons?" *American Economic Review* 72 (May 1982): 242–46.

———. *Industrial Pricing in the United Kingdom*. Cambridge, England: Cambridge University Press, 1978.

———. "The Political Business Cycle." *Review of Economic Studies* (April 1975): 169–90.

———. "The Recent Productivity Slowdown." *Brookings Papers on Economic Activity, 1972*. Washington, D.C.: The Brookings Institution, 1972.

———. "The Worldwide Wage Explosion." *Brookings Papers on Economic Activity, 1972*. Washington, D.C.: The Brookings Institution, 1972.

ROBERT S. HERREN

NOURSE, EDWIN GRISWOLD

(b. May 20, 1883, d. March 7, 1974), CEA August 9, 1946-November 1, 1949

Edwin Griswold Nourse was born in Lockport, New York, in 1883. As the first chairman of the newly created Council of Economic Advisers, he played a major role in the initial structure and functioning of this important addition to the Executive Office. The novelty of this new position was further complicated by the other two appointments to the Council—Leon Keyserling* and John D. Clark*. The dissimilarities and conflicts among this diverse trio and the inexperience of President Truman and his limited interest in economics created a less than effective tenure for Nourse.

In his *Memoirs*, Harry S. Truman described his signing and acceptance of the Employment Act of 1946. In just two pages he described the background of the law, its objectives, the appointment of his Council of Economic Advisers and their backgrounds, and his few actions during his seven-year administration. It was not lack of approval for the law and its objectives but the pressures of international affairs that occupied his efforts in those turbulent times.

Presumably Nourse's agricultural economics expertise and research background were the reasons for his selection. Nourse had had a distinguished but not spectacular academic career. Raised in upstate New York, he earned an A.A. degree at Lewis Institute in 1904 and graduated from Cornell in 1906. After a year as instructor in finance at Pennsylvania's Wharton School, he served as head of economics and sociology at the University of South Dakota in 1910–12. He married Rae Marie Tyler, a Wellesley graduate, in 1910, and they had a son, John Tyler. He taught for the next few years and completed his Ph.D. at the University of Chicago in 1915. Nourse was professor and head of economics at the University of Arkansas for three years and professor of agricultural economics at Iowa State, where he also was chief economist at the Experimental Station until 1923. He then moved to Washington as chief of the Agricultural Division at the Brookings Institution, becoming a director in 1929 and vice president in 1942. In 1924 he was elected president of the American Farm Economic Association and became president of the American Economic Association in 1942. He also served as chairman of the Social Science Research Council from 1942 to 1945. Nourse participated in international meetings of the League of Nations and other organizations between the wars. His numerous publications during this period were on agriculture, marketing, and cooperatives, and he later analyzed agriculture legislation and industrial price policies. The press generally characterized him as politically independent.

The Employment Act of 1946 committed the United States to maintain "maximum employment, production and purchasing power''; a Council of Economic Advisers had been created, and the president designated Nourse as chairman. CEA members were to assist and advise, gather, analyze and interpret, appraise and recommend on economic matters and make an annual report to the president. Although a Joint Economic Committee of Congress was also established, Nourse believed that he and the CEA were in the Executive Office. This attitude would cause problems with the Congress.

Six years after becoming chairman, while in retirement, Nourse analyzed the law, the conditions of its creation, and his role in its implementation in his *Economics in the Public Service*. It is a careful and comprehensive treatment, despite his participation in the events. External sources, particularly Stephen K. Bailey's *Congress Makes a Law*, and the press are quoted extensively to give a balanced analysis of his own recollections, which were supplemented by his ''personal record'' or diary.

According to Nourse, Charles Ross, Truman's press secretary, called on July 24, 1946, and asked him to talk with the president about appointment to the Council. Keyserling and John D. Clark had already accepted. Oscar Chapman had refused the post in June, and the nomination of Winfield W. Riefler had been withdrawn because of political opposition. Nourse accepted reluctantly five days later; he was personally uncertain but professionally challenged by the position. After the Council was sworn in on August 9, President Truman gave his ''sailing orders.'' The press viewed the three appointees as a conservative former businessman (Clark), a liberal bureaucrat (Keyserling), and a ''middle of the road researcher'' (Nourse).

Nourse recognized the need to establish his chairmanship and the Council on a sound and independent base if it was to succeed. His Washington experience led him to avoid association with previous activities. Chairman Nourse rejected the old National Resources Planning Board (NRPB) quarters proposed to house the new CEA. The NRPB had been abolished by a disgruntled Congress in 1944. It was necessary to have a fresh start to implement the Employment Act of 1946, established by a reluctant Congress. The president too needed education in economics, something not really achieved until the time of President Kennedy and CEA chairman Walter Heller*.

The search for quarters and staff was time-consuming and cautious, but formal labors began on October 14 in the old State Department Building. The staff consisted of four full-time men, four part-time and an executive officer, Bertram Gross.

The new chairman, after conferring with President Truman on September 18, began preparation of its first annual economic report. Additional conferences were held monthly on outlines and drafts, and by December 4 the Council's report was submitted to President Truman. After some minor changes, it was released at a press conference but without comment by the president. It was a cautious and careful document, reflecting the divergent views of its authors and the ground-breaking nature of the program.

All three members of the Council met with President Truman during December to discuss various aspects of the economic report to be presented to Congress. Clark Clifford, legal counsel, John Steelman, Director of the Office of War Mobilization and Reconstruction (OWMR), and James E. Webb, the Budget Director, coordinated the state of the union and budget messages with Chairman Nourse's economic report. The first version was substantially shortened by Steelman's staff, but then revised by the Council with a satisfactory restoration of the omitted material. On January 8, 1947, President Truman called Chairman Nourse to tell him that he had just finished reading the Economic Report prior to sending it to Congress. The press reaction was generally favorable, and the analysis and proposals were viewed as middle of the road and as comprising a workable program.

This first and ground-breaking *Economic Report of the President* is an interesting document. Unlike later reports, the fifty pages of text and ten pages of tables are presented and signed by the president, who said that it was prepared with the advice and assistance of the CEA, cabinet members, and the heads of independent agencies. After an optimistic appraisal of economic conditions, the first part summarizes employment, wages, and prices. The nation's economic budget is then reviewed and unfavorable factors and trends are summarized. Recommendations for short- and long-range programs to strengthen the economy are made. They are generally cautious and limited to resisting economic fluctuations.

The CEA suggested to the president in April 1947 that midyear report would be useful and appropriate because of rapidly changing conditions. President Truman agreed and in July another economic report was submitted to Congress. This document was almost twice as long as the earlier report and had more statistical material and current analysis. The primary focus was on postwar adjustment without a depression. The Council began submitting quarterly memoranda as the problem became the rising inflation. As their efforts and output increased, additional staff and resources were added by the Council, but a divided Congress reduced the budget to $350,000 (from $400,000) in 1948. This prevented further expansion of staff and forced tighter organization, greater division of responsibilities, and restriction of activities.

It was necessary to establish relations with farm, business, and labor groups for cooperation and support of the new program. Invitations were extended to the Farmers Union, National Grange, Chamber of Commerce, Committee for Economic Development, AFL, CIO, and other representative bodies. The consumer was represented by twenty-two organizations which had indicated interest in participating. Meetings were held, information sought, criticisms solicited, and roundtables established to facilitate the work of the CEA. Its members made numerous public addresses and met with professional groups. Most important was cooperation with other government agencies for information and research as well as other resources. For example, *Economic Indicators* was initiated by the Bureau of the Budget, expanded by the Council, and then continued by the Joint Economic Committee of the Congress as its major publication.

The proposal of the Marshall Plan in 1947 gave the Council the responsibility for setting up a special committee to assemble necesary data. Chairman Nourse and his staff also provided liaison with other departments during this great program's successful implementation. The first three years of the CEA were very active and productive, especially in establishing and developing a new organization.

Relations with President Truman after the initial report were less satisfactory. Although Nourse was given appointments whenever he requested, he did not feel that he was making an impression on Harry Truman. Moreover, Nourse felt that he was rarely consulted on impending issues and problems. The president did not object to CEA advice and recommendations but did not seem to respond to them. His assistants and cabinet officers provided most of the reaction and follow-up. The second annual report of the Council (December 1947) elicited only a brief note of thanks and no discussions with the president.

Relations with Congress were also a problem. The Joint Economic Committee established its own staff, and its director, Charles O. Hardy, sought to sit in on Council deliberations. The CEA members felt that cooperation rather than participation would be more appropriate. Moreover, Congress was now Republican controlled with a presidential election looming in the fall. Minority and majority reports on the economy were emerging from the Joint Committee, and cooperation became difficult. Nourse felt—and President Truman agreed—that the CEA was an executive agency and reported to the president. Consultations with Senators Robert Taft and Ralph Flanders explaining his view enabled Nourse to avoid appearing before their committees for testimony regarding the CEA's reports.

Council members Keyserling and Clark disagreed with Chairman Nourse's desire to avoid political and policy-making roles, but he insisted that that was his understanding of his role on the Council and that would be the way he would perform. This led to continuing controversy and disagreement within the CEA which was further aggravated by politics in a presidential election year.

In May 1948 Secretary of Commerce Sawyer sent a memorandum to the Council with a formal recommendation for a change. Now the Council of Economic Advisers' report would be "a purely factual report, with no statements of policy." The President's Economic Report to the Congress would present policy recommendations, and the Council would "assist in its preparation." Nourse was concerned that this separation would show the difference between the Council and the president, but his colleagues were eager to perform in this fashion. This difference in their attitudes would necessitate majority rule for presenting the Council's views. In the politically charged presidential election year of 1948, President Truman wanted to avoid political issues in his economic reports. Moreover, he wanted those CEA members who did not object to testify before Congress. Nourse continued to ask to be excused from appearing and testifying.

Inflation, labor strife, and other postwar adjustment problems were plaguing the economy, and Nourse provided studies and recommendations about them.

However, the president and his advisers were less accessible and responsive than they had been. The divided Council was less and less able to agree upon issues, and dissents were increasing. The economic report of the Council in 1949 "kept pretty well to the factual level" despite its greater length, but Nourse (and Clark) felt that it relied too heavily on projections and judgment. Future Council memoranda had to abandon the unanimous approach.

After the reelection of President Truman, Nourse composed several letters of resignation which would permit the president to select a new chairman for his second administration. Those he sent were not acknowledged. At an acrimonious Council meeting, he announced his desire to leave to his colleagues, saying that "they would be relieved of his incubus." Nourse continued to be engrossed in his work on Council studies but limited his public appearances to avoid public disagreements with his colleagues. Additional letters regarding his proposed resignation were sent after the midyear economic report since he wanted to leave on the third anniversary of his swearing in. Memoranda of the CEA became separate documents, with Nourse disagreeing with his colleagues and the administration on major issues. Still President Truman did not respond to Nourse's resignation requests. Presidential adviser Steelman informed Nourse that they wanted to announce his replacement at the same time his resignation was announced but that they were having trouble finding a successor of "considerable prominence." He asked for suggestions, and Nourse added several names to their list. It was felt that promoting an outstanding staff member would be impractical, while few outside economists seemed to want the position.

Nourse left the Council on November 1. He was sixty-six years old when he retired and had served over three years in that demanding position. The disagreements and controversies had been taxing, and he was disappointed with conditions and outcomes, especially in the final year. As an economist and proponent of the Employment Act, he was concerned for its future. No replacement was named, and Keyserling, the Council's vice chairman, became acting chairman. It would be a different Council and approach, especially in the chairman's role.

Commenting on the Council in 1950, Nourse concluded that after the initial welcome and acceptance, the actual position of the Council underwent progressive attrition or debasement, so that its influence soon became negligible. He felt that Truman had used the Council as a dignified mask for his policies, although he had tried to make good appointments. Particularly disappointing to Nourse was his inability to establish an effective working relationship with Truman and the professional staff of experts.

In his writing and speeches, Nourse continued to criticize Truman's utilization of the Employment Act and the Council.

It is interesting that Arthur Burns*, chairman under President Eisenhower, played his role in the Nourse tradition and felt that Nourse had made it possible for him to do his job.

Nourse remained in Washington as a consulting economist after leaving the

Council. He continued his research, writing, and participation in professional societies and was a senior Guggenheim fellow in 1950–52. In 1959 he served as a visiting distinguished professor at Pennsylvania State University. He died in 1974 at the age of ninety.

BIBLIOGRAPHY

Nourse, Edwin. ''Early Flowering of the Employment Act.'' *Virginia Quarterly Review* (Spring 1967): 78–90.

———. *Economics in the Public Service*. New York: Harcourt Brace, 1953.

Stein, Herbert. *The Fiscal Revolution in America*. Chicago: University of Chicago Press, 1969.

ALFRED E. PIERCE

OKUN, ARTHUR MELVIN

(b. November 28, 1928, d. March 23, 1980), CEA November 16, 1964-January 20, 1969

The economic community suffered a great loss when Arthur Melvin Okun died suddenly from a heart attack at age fifty-one on March 23, 1980. His colleague Joseph A. Pechman, director of economic studies at the Brookings Institution, lamented the loss of a man he considered a brilliant economist, a gifted writer, a patient teacher, and above all, a superb human being.

Okun was born in 1928 in Jersey City, New Jersey. He was the son of Louis Okun, a candy and tobacco wholesaler, and Rose Cantor. His fame began in 1949 when *Life* magazine selected him for its list of college graduates "most likely to succeed." He had received a B.A. in economics that year from Columbia College of Columbia University and also had won the Albert Asher Green Prize for having the highest scholastic average in his class. He continued his studies in economics at Columbia under Arthur Burns* and earned a doctorate seven years later with a dissertation entitled "The Effect of Open Inflation on Aggregate Consumer Demand."

In 1952 Okun was hired as an instructor by Yale, where he advanced through the academic ranks and became director of graduate studies in 1963 with the rank of full professor. In 1961 James Tobin*, a Yale colleague, was invited to become a member of the Council of Economic Advisers, and he asked Okun to go with him as a staff economist. Okun was persuaded and took a leave of absence from Yale to serve as a senior staff economist in 1961 and 1962. He specialized in projecting growth in the gross national product and soon became famous for formulating what was to be called Okun's law: the coefficient of the rate of change between real GNP and unemployment is approximately one-third. Economists have continued to be interested in Okun's findings, and there have been attempts to refigure the coefficient and make it more accurate for the performance of the economy in recent years.

Okun was in the fortuitous situation of being in the right place at the right time. Under the Kennedy administration the Council was to grow in importance. Kennedy was interested in the Keynesian school of economics with its belief that government fiscal and monetary policies could be used to stabilize the economy; and Walter Heller* was the first member of that school to chair the Council. Heller succeeded in winning Kennedy's confidence, and the White House began to rely more and more on the Council for economic advice.

Okun's reputation grew during the short period that he was a staff member. Heller believed that Keynesian economics could be used to bring the economy out of the slump it was in, and Okun was the person who could do the calculations required to argue the case with the administration and the Congress.

After his year's leave, Okun resumed his teaching career at Yale, but his return to academia was very brief. In November 1964 Gardner Ackley* replaced Heller as chairman of the Council. Ackley recommended Okun for membership on the Council, and President Johnson agreed. Thus in November 1964, at age thirty-six, Okun became the youngest person to ever serve on the Council.

The tax cut Heller had supported had been enacted and was successful in stimulating the economy. However, during Ackley's tenure the Vietnam involvement drew dramatically, and concern shifted from full employment to the possibility of inflation. Okun, with his brilliance in forecasting, was to be the author of many of the memoranda from the Council to President Johnson. The Johnson administration initially attempted to deal with inflation through the use of wage and price guidelines, but soon capitulated on that approach.

By the beginning of 1967 Okun and the other two members of the Council saw the need for a tax increase. It soon became Okun's task to lead the battle for the increase, as in January 1968 Ackley resigned from the Council to become ambassador to Italy, and Okun became the chairman. He put a tax increase at the top of his agenda.

At that time Johnson's Great Society programs were under attack by the conservatives in Congress, and the president was unwilling to sacrifice his domestic programs as a *quid pro quo* for a tax increase. Eventually, however, the administration accepted the need for the increase, and in June 1968 taxes were raised.

Okun was able to maintain the clout of the Council during the Johnson administration because he was very aware of political realities. He believed that the ability of officials in the White House depended on their relationship with the president. Having no agenda of their own, the Council, thought Okun, could be interesting and effective only to the extent that it won the president's confidence. Okun thought that Council members should choose the president's position rather than that of the consensus of economists in all public statements. He felt that the opinions of the profession might best be conveyed by setting up another, separate institution outside the administration consisting of economic experts ready to speak up on policy matters involving technical results or widespread professional agreement. (In December 1984 an excellent example of the situation Okun feared occurred; the news media carried reports that the administration was considering abolishing the Council as a cost-cutting move on the grounds that other economists in the government could perform its duties. The administration was obviously reacting to the public statements contrary to Reagan administration policies made by Martin Feldstein* when he chaired the Council.)

Okun noted that during the tax surcharge fight he found it as important to state conclusions simply as to work forecasts and technical analysis. He clearly realized that an economist who wished to see theory turned into policy must have the ability to explain economics in terminology that lay people could understand and would remember. Fortunately, Okun was clever with words and had a keen sense of humor, which served him in good stead during his tenure on the Council.

In addition to having a talent for developing clever analogies, he was quite a skillful phrase-maker. For example, he created the "discomfort index," which is the sum of unemployment and inflation. Likewise he coined the term "invisible handshake" to indicate that in both resource and labor markets there are implied contracts regarding fair treatment that companies must observe in dealing with both their customers and their employees.

In 1970 Okun often was mentioned as a likely sucessor to Arthur Burns, and he responded to the speculation by saying, "Just because my name is Arthur, I smoke a pipe, graduated from Columbia, and am Jewish, some members of the press are convinced that I should be the next chairman of the Federal Reserve Board. Not me."

Considering the Council's role in retrospect, Okun had believed that the changed activist approach would result in economic growth rather than just attempts to ameliorate the effects of business cycles. At the same time, he was sobered by the failure to control inflation in the late 1960s, blaming much of this on the expenses incurred by the Vietnam War. He also acknowledged that the tax surcharge did not bring about the results Keynesians had predicted. Okun speculated that factors such as the delay in the tax increase and its temporary nature might have weakened its effect on aggregate demand and inflation. However, he felt that the appropriate response was to continue to perform research and not to slip back into a sterile negativism.

Okun watched inflation ravage the economy in the 1970s, and much of the rest of his professional life was devoted to a search for ways to rein in inflation without causing a severe recession. Okun's major fear was that the government might decide to induce an economic slowdown for that purpose. While much of his work had been in the area of forecasting, it was forecasting with a purpose. Okun's law had been concerned with the heavy cost of low economic output on employment, and, given all of his compassion, he was basically concerned about the misery that a government-induced recession would cause for those who would be thrown out of work. His hope was to keep the economy growing and the unemployment rate low through maintaining adequate aggregate demand in the Keynesian tradition and using an incomes policy to handle the inflation problem.

Okun's fear was realized when the government responded to the double-digit inflation of 1973–74 with restrictive monetary and fiscal policies that brought what was, at that time, the worst recession since the 1930s. In a 1977 speech Okun explained why he believed that even a relatively severe recession would not serve to halt inflation. He argued, in a *Challange* magazine article in 1977, that for many sectors of the economy, prices no longer responded quickly to changes in demand and supply:

> the nature of price- and wage-making has been transformed in the modern era . . . .The pricing policies designed to treat customers reasonably and maintain their loyalty in good

times and bad times rely heavily on marking up some standard measure of costs . . . .For most products, prices do not rise faster than standard costs during booms nor do they rise less rapidly than costs during slumps.

They (employers) know that if they curbed wages stringently in a slump, they would pay heavily for that strategy with swollen quit rates in the next period of prosperity.

Since he concluded that government attempts to deliberately hold down aggregate demand would have only a modest effect on wages and prices and cause intolerable unemployment, Okun sought innovative, alternative ways to hold down inflation. He wanted government to be sure that it avoided policies that would contribute to rising costs, and he wanted Congress to provide grant-in-aid programs for state and local governments that would be willing to lower their sales taxes as well as give tax breaks for workers and companies that accepted price-wage constraints.

Okun's compassion for the poor permeated his book, *Equality and Efficiency*, which argued that the traditional economic concerns with efficient allocation and use of resources must be tempered with concerns as to the outcomes. The debate over tax reform in the Reagan administration that suggested less redistribution of income in order to create more efficiency was anticipated in the book. While the Reagan administration argued in terms of less taxes on the wealthy for more efficiency, Okun proposed more redistribution of income from the rich to the poor. He used the analogy of a ''leaky bucket'' to raise the issue of how much ''water'' (tax revenue) should be taken from the rich and given to the poor when some of the benefit was to leak out in terms of less incentives for economic productivity and hence less total income for society. Okun's contribution was to remind people that the issue was indeed one of tradeoff and the need was to reach some decision as to how much efficiency should be sacrificed for a more equitable distribution of income. He felt that both concerns were legitimate and that society should choose some reasonable compromise between the two. He was emphatic that society should avoid the extreme position of sacrificing unreasonable amounts of one to attempt to obtain more of the other.

In characteristic fashion, Okun did not beg the issue. He arrived at concrete policy recommendations. He favored suggestions by Pechman that capital gains exclusions be reduced or eliminated and that transfers of capital by bequest or gift also be taxed. These revenue sources would help ''fill the bucket.'' He favored a poverty program that would guarantee $5,000 to families with no earnings and cut the subsidy by fifty cents for every dollar earned. Five thousand dollars was the proverty line for nonfarm families of four in 1974. He also hit hard at the policy of providing aid to fatherless families (AFDC, aid to families with dependent children), but denying benefits to husband-wife familes. He also favored subsidized medical care and food stamps for the poor and suggested that the working poor might be helped by federal subsidy for low minimum wages.

His final work, *Prices and Quantities: A Macroeconomic Analysis* (1981), was devoted to stagflation and rounded out the ideas that he had presented in his 1977 speech to the Economic Club of Chicago. He remained convinced that wages and prices were so insensitive to aggregate demand changes that any attempt to decrease demand to lower inflation would have to result in an intolerably great recession. On the last page he wrote:

> I expect the era of chronic inflation to end in the eighties. I am not particularly optimistic, however, that the era will be terminated by a coordinated program that combines a deceleration of nominal income growth with the cost-reducing elements and incentives to wage and price restraint . . . I believe that it is more probable that the era of chronic inflation will end with a deep and prolonged recession or with a protracted period of rigid mandatory wage and price control. I am not resigned to that conclusion, and I hope economists will work hard to prevent it.

Okun was not around to continue the call for an income approach to inflation, and the recession he dreaded did happen. While the recession was not as prolonged as many feared, the cost in terms of unemployment was probably much higher than this brilliant but compassionate man would have wanted to pay.

In 1972 Okun and George Perry founded and co-edited a journal called *Brookings Papers on Economic Activity*, a technical journal on macroeconomics that was very successful. By the time of Okun's death it had reached fourth place in terms of circulation of economic journals. The journal attempted to bring economic theory to bear on contemporary policy issues and was noted for being willing to publish the writings of recently graduated economists who had not yet become well known. Okun put a great amount of energy into the journal, and he demanded that the articles not only be technically correct but also that the writer's results be very carefully explained.

Although Okun was a rather prolific writer, he also engaged in other professional activities. He was frequently an adviser to politicians and had been advising both President Carter and Senator Edward Kennedy at the time of his death. He also served as a consultant to banks and brokerage houses. His clients included Donaldson, Lufkin & Jenrette and the American Security and Trust Company.

As might be expected of such a warm individual, he found time for his family. He had married Susan Grossman on July 1, 1961, and they had three sons, Lewis Edward, Matthew James, and Steven John. In addition to giving his sons medicine, he indulged them in games of chess, stamp collecting, and trips to baseball games.

Okun was a member of organizations that included Phi Beta Kappa, the American Academy of Arts and Sciences, the Econometric Society, the American Statistical Association, and the American Economic Association (vice president in 1972).

He received Columbia University's Medal of Excellence in 1968 and received a book award from the McKinsey Foundation in 1970 for *The Political Economy of Prosperity*.

Probably the tribute Okun would most value would be that by fellow economists at Brookings who referred to him as the nation's most inventive and effective policy economist. Okun had written in his book, *The Political Economy of Prosperity*, that a political economist must have special characteristics.

To convey the professional view effectively requires the talents of a missionary, an outstanding pedagogue, and a supersalesman: it also takes skillful and sympathetic understanding of opposition views and, especially, of noneconomic considerations in policy choices . . . .Political economy has to be a separate and distinct activity of the profession. It is not science, but it is a source of potential benefit to the nation.

Okun, always modest, did not claim to have these characteristics, but he had them all and in great abundance. He could develop and analyze theory as well as anyone in the profession, but he found it important to be "the missionary" and apply economics to current problems in a way that politicians and voters could appreciate. He left a mark on both Washington and the economics profession that will be remembered for years to come.

BIBLIOGRAPHY

Okun, Arthur. *Equality and Efficiency*. Washington, D.C.: Brookings Institution, 1975.

———. "The Great Stagflation Swamp." *Challenge* (November-December 1977): 7–15.

———. *The Political Economy of Prosperity*. Washington, D.C.: Brookings Institution, 1970.

———. *Prices and Quantities: A Macroeconomic Analysis*. Washington, D.C.: Brookings Institution, 1981.

MANLY E. "TOM" STALEY

PECK, MERTON JOSEPH
(b. December 17, 1925), CEA February 15, 1968-January 20, 1969

On February 15, 1968, Merton Joseph Peck of Yale University joined the President's Council of Economic Advisers, replacing Gardner Ackley* in the Council's twenty-second year of operation. If Arthur Okun*, so well known within the economics profession, and chairman of the Council during Peck's tenure, was not well known to the general public, Merton Peck was almost invisible, partly because 1968 was one of those years during which the CEA's policies had a disappointingly small effect in stabilizing the economy, and also because Peck served the Council for less than a year. His separation date of January 20, 1969, gave him the shortest tenure in the history of the Council.

At the time of his nomination by President Johnson, January 3, 1968, Peck was the chairman of the department of economics at Yale University and considered by his associates as a mainstream "new economist." His ideological leanings were not considered by most observers to change the complexion of the three-member presidential Council. He was, however, considered to be an articulate administrator and a specialist in transportation economics and market organization. In short, Peck brought with him a background that appears at first to be no different from that of most successful economists.

Peck was born in Cleveland, Ohio, in 1925. His early childhood and formative years were influenced mostly by his two affectionate aunts, Mrs. A. R. Lyon and Olive S. Peck, who raised him after the death of his parents. Peck received his elementary and high school education in the public school system. He started school at Shaker Heights, a suburb of Cleveland, but after a few years there transferred first to Medina, Ohio, and thereafter to Evanston, Illinois, where he eventually received his high school diploma. He served in the United States Army from 1944 to 1946 as a technician at the rank of sergeant in Texas and later in Okinawa, Japan. He recalls his army experience, in retrospect, as the foundation for his disciplined outlook on life in general and his reputation among colleagues as an efficient administrator. He developed an interest in the Japanese love for excellence and their desire for technological advancement during this period. After the war, Merton was admitted to Oberlin College as a history major in 1946. With the advice and direction of Dr. Benjamin Luis, Merton graduated in 1949 in economics. He proceeded to undertake his graduate training under Carl Kaysen and Edward Mason at Harvard University, where he earned both a master's degree and a Ph.D. in 1954.

Peck began his successful academic career as a teaching fellow and instructor of economics at Harvard in 1951 but, for a brief period in 1955, accepted an appointment as an assistant professor of economics at the University of Michigan. He returned to the Harvard School of Business in 1956; after a series of publications on industrial organization he gained the recognition of his peers and was awarded tenure and promoted to associate professor in 1960. Merton's early accomplishments did not go unnoticed outside of academia. Soon after his promotion, during the early years of the Kennedy administration, he participated in the reorganization of the Department of Defense as a member of a group of young professionals dubbed by the press "McNamara's Whiz Kids." As an assistant deputy controller, his work at the Pentagon helped Peck to further sharpen the policy implications of his work, including antitrust, transportation, and defense economics. He returned to Yale University as a full professor in 1962, and at the prime age of forty-two was named by President Johnson in 1968 as a member of the CEA. Upon his return to Yale, Peck was appointed chairman of the department of economics from 1969 to 1974, and again from 1978 to 1984. In recognition of his distinguished service to the department, Peck was further honored in 1981 by his appointment as the Thomas DeWitt Cuyler Professor of Economics and Transportation.

Peck's first publication after his graduate work at Harvard focused on the long neglected but logical interrelations which he believed should obtain between location theory and trade theories. His treatise "Locational Theory and International Interregional Trade Theory," published in the *Quarterly Journal of Economics* and co-authored with Walter Isard, examined the hypothesis put forward by H. Ohlin in 1933 that "international trade is only a part of a general localization theory." Peck and Isard's major contribution to this area of economic theory was the explicit demonstration that the concept of distance inputs, transportation orientation, and cost—redefined as the opportunity cost doctrine—can be fused to yield a superior set of analytical tools, thus paving the way for location theory as well as trade theory to take over many of the sound doctrines of the other. Peck soon followed this accomplishment in 1957 with a joint publication entitled "Avoidable Costs of Passenger Train Service," and his first book, *The Maintenance of Way Employment on U.S. Railroads*, jointly authored with William Haber, John Carroll, and Mark Khan in 1957.

Perhaps the most significant accomplishment during this early stage of Peck's career was his completion and publication of his third book, *Competition in the Aluminum Industry, 1945–1958*. Merton has been quick to acknowledge the overwhelming influence and guidance he received from Edward S. Mason, his mentor and doctoral thesis adviser during his days as a student at Harvard. Peck's work examining the nature of competition in the postwar aluminum industry helped explain the economic results of the impact of market control and changes in the structure of the aluminum industry brought about by formal antitrust litigation and administrative action. He also made available a case study on inventory output behavior in the aluminum industry, utilizing marginal analysis to explain business behavior under uncertainty. The decade of the 1950s in Merton Peck's scholarly career came to a close with the publication of "The

History of Transportation,'' his contribution to *Essays in American Economic History*, edited by Seymour Harris.

Merton became an assistant deputy controller during the reorganization of the Department of Defense in the early years of the Kennedy administration. The transition from the academic environment at Harvard University to the bureaucratic diplomacy in Washington did not create any serious adjustment problems for Peck, who found the Washington experience valuable to his professional development. It led to a new direction in his research and provided the first-hand experience necessary for his subsequent works in the area of decision making within public institutions. Toward the end of 1962 Peck published *Weapons Acquisition: An Economic Analysis*, with F. M. Scherer. In the period following his Department of Defense appointment, Peck's contributions to formulating public policy continued through lectures, scholarly discussions, and published contributions in books that sharply focused on his strong belief in competitive markets and the economics of deregulation.

Peck's perspective on the extent to which the transportation industry should be subjected to direct regulation leaves no doubt in the minds of his audience or readers of his belief that competition should be the dominant public policy. Writing in 1965, Peck found the extensive direct regulation of interstate rail, water, and motor carriers by the Interstate Commerce Commission (ICC) to be a failure and therefore an area of central importance to competitive policy. He concluded that the allocation of transportation resources under the auspices of the ICC was grossly inefficient. He found the economic cost of regulation inadequate to meet the transportation needs of the economy with a minimum total expenditure of resources. Peck maintained that competition allowed traffic to shift from high-cost to low-cost carriers where rates were flexible. But with regulation, there were enough shifts from the low-cost to the high-cost mode of transportation, as measured in the sum of shipper and carrier cost, to produce the misallocation of transportation resources under the ICC's rate policy.

Peck believed that a rate structure based on such simple and objective phenomena as distance, special costs of handling a particular commodity, and so on, would still allow some forms of price discrimination in transportation rates, but would also automatically reduce the unevenness of competition by forcing transportation companies to make price reductions to many broad classes of products without the need for devising more regulation to meet every specific competitive situation.

Peck showed the same tenacity in analysis of national communications policy when he was appointed a member of President Johnson's Task Force on Communications Policy in 1967. The executive charge "to investigate whether the present division of ownership in our international communication facilities best serves our needs" contained in the president's global communications system message to the 80th Congress of the United States challenged the clear-thinking Peck, named by the president as head of the task force. The final report of the task force, despite Peck's reputation as an astute advocate of deregulation, called for the establishment of a single entity to operate the long-distance portion of international telecommunications, a radical change.

In a discussion on the economics of science policy held at the American Economic Association's annual convention in December 1965, Peck's willingness to apply economics to sectors that in his graduate school days were considered noneconomic, being in the proper realm of the political scientist and sociologist, illustrated his maturity as an economist and his ambition to actively blend economics with education, defense, and welfare. At the time of Peck's nomination hearing before the Senate Committee on Banking and Currency, Abe Ribicoff, who introduced him in absentia by way of a letter addressed to the chairman, Senator John Sparkman, was also careful to announce the publication of Peck's latest book, *Technological Change, Economic Growth, and Public Policy*. Senator Ribicoff strongly urged the committee to recommend Peck for the wide experience that he would bring to the CEA.

To the general public, the decade of the 1960s is viewed as the most recent period of sustained prosperity in American history. There was an unprecedented influx of economists into policy-level positions during that decade, and Merton Peck was one of the brotherhood of economists whose involvement in Washington made the economic prosperity and social reforms of this era possible. However, to the members of the CEA, a number of difficult economic decisions and philosophical questions about the virtues and popular acceptance of Keynesian macroeconomic policies conflicted with the established forms of unregulated capitalism. The predominant cause for disagreement was over the potential blunders of overregulation. The successful revival of the economy after President Johnson's enactment of the 1964 tax cut made it easier to accept Keynesian fiscal and monetary policy tools in government policy making. It also enabled economists like Peck to use the tools of quantitative analysis to provide specific estimates of benefits and costs to ensure the impact of a policy on some desired outcome.

It was clear at the beginning of Peck's tenure on the CEA that neither higher taxes nor mandatory controls on prices and wages were considered acceptable antidotes to the inflationary pressures that existed within the economy in 1967. The tone of the Council's February 1968 report was one of resounding disdain for any suggestions that would even remotely distort resource allocation, require reliance on clumsy and arbitrary rules by government officials that, apart from the temptations for evasion, would require a vast administrative apparatus.

The urgency of the need for economic restraint began to dawn on the politicians and the business community when the CEA's forecast of an acceleration in overall economic activity beginning in 1967 continued through 1968. The CEA's recommendation was an immediate tax increase to restrain the boom, but the wisdom of this course of action was less obvious to Congressional skeptics. According to Peck, that inaction contributed to the continuation of the upsurge in spending during the first half of 1968. Gross national product in current prices rose at an annual rate of 8.5 percent, 4.8 percent of which reflected a rapid increase in prices unrelated to growth in real output.

The tax surcharge of 1968 centered on Congressional skepticism and public opposition to the tax increase. The Congressional stalemate was due to the more difficult question of finding the right combination of budget cutbacks and tax increases to placate constituents in an election year. The opposition to higher taxes was overcome when President Johnson agreed to a ceiling on federal spending instead of cutbacks in some very sensitive programs. On June 28, the Revenue and Expenditure Control Act was signed into law, leaving the Council free to devote its energies to monitoring other areas of fiscal policy. Working very closely with the Treasury Department, the Bureau of the Budget, and a newly established Cabinet Committee on Price Stability, Peck recalls enlisting the services of a large number of task forces to analyze and evaluate a variety of proposals designed to improve price performance as well as ways to monitor the effects of the tax surcharge on the domestic economy and international financial markets.

The Revenue and Expenditure Control Act provided a 10 percent surcharge on individual and corporate incomes, retroactive to January 1 for corporations and April 1 for individuals. Further restraint on government expenditure was achieved in the form of a $6 billion cutback in the 1969 federal budget proposal. This policy brought to a virtual halt increases in federal government expenditures on goods and services as well as the rise in consumer spending, although the latter did not peak until the fourth quarter of 1968. Furthermore, the CEA's prescription for expenditure moderation could be credited with the slowdown in real output growth from almost 7 percent in the first quarter of 1968 to less than 3 percent by the beginning of 1969. In other sectors of the economy, however, the expansion continued. According to Peck, the members of the CEA did not feel that they had misled the president and Congress as to the contradictory effects of the tax surcharge on the economy. In fact, most of the signals provided by the available data remain unexplained even today, but it became obvious by early autumn that although the forecasts were correct, the monetary policy prescriptions required to bolster the effects of the tax surcharge came a little too late to have any effect on aggregate expenditure in 1968. There was a 2.5 percent drop in the growth of real GNP by the end of the year, but a more remarkable change was needed to curb the unexpected resilience in consumer demand.

During the next six months, Peck relied heavily on his quantitative skills and sharp analytical capabilities in forecasting long-term inflationary tendencies on business and households. These efforts were centered on manpower training and development; industrial markets; wages; various social insurance and income maintenance programs designed to address the challenge of reducing poverty; collective bargaining; and a smooth economic transition to peace after the end of the Vietnam War.

By the end of the CEA's reporting period for activities in 1968, the outgoing

Peck and his colleagues concluded that the economy had had an exceptionally big year, perhaps too big. The economy and economic policy had followed a complicated and difficult course throughout the year: gross national product increased by $71 billion, an inflation-adjusted gain of 5 percent; unemployment fell by 160,000; and an estimated 4 million Americans escaped from poverty. The nation's balance of payments surplus was the highest in eleven years, and after-tax average real income increased by 3 percent. However, by the time the year's principal fiscal policy tools became effective, the forces of expansion and inflation had gathered enough momentum to render them impotent. A wage and price spiral had already been set in motion, causing nearly fifty cents out of every extra dollar spent during the year to be added to prices rather than to production.

What went wrong? Peck agrees with Arthur Okun and other economists that the failure to take decisive action in early 1968 was exacerbated by the temporary nature of the tax surcharge. Theoretical explanations based on rational expectations and the permanent income hypothesis argue that both consumers and investors looked past the tax surcharge, originally intended to last only a year, to long-term income expectations. Business firms geared their investment and employment plans to an optimistic future as rising unit labor costs and inflation encouraged the substitution of capital for labor. Consumers, on the other hand, sustained spending throughout the second half of 1968 by sharply reducing their savings rate after the surcharge went into effect.

With the election of President Nixon in November 1968, Peck knew he would be stepping down from the CEA to resume his career in academia. He recalls thinking much more frequently about his family, the peace and serenity of the Yale University campus in the summer, and the honest excitement of teaching and conducting research with students eager to learn.

The experiences of 1968 gave Peck and other economists an invaluable education in managing the economy via discretionary public policy. Arthur Okun, who took the brunt of public criticism of the CEA's policy prescriptions during Peck's tenure on the Council, thought that, apart from how much economists have to learn, they also remind us that changes in attitudes in the private economy can at times overcome decisions of public policy. They argue for humility in forecasts and for flexibility in the making of policy. But they offer no excuse for inaction. Reflecting on his role as a member of the CEA, Peck found the most gratifying part of his membership to be the processing and forwarding of economic intelligence for the president, frequently presented in the form of direct verbal discussions and short memos as well as lengthy reports. The difficult part of the job, according to Peck, was not providing the economic rationale underlying forecasts of future economy activity, but more often furnishing explanations for a proposed policy and choosing language easily understood by noneconomic audiences and by the president.

In the area of defense economics, Peck's comments on defense contracts, incentives, and performance, and his own studies of major weapons projects incorporate his first-hand knowledge of the centralization and decentralization of resource allocation decisions in the defense sector. Having served as comptroller and director of systems analysis in the office of Charles J. Hitch, the Assistant Secretary of Defense during 1961 and 1962, Peck noted that a coalition exists and enables defense contractors to frustrate some objectives of the Office of the Secretary of Defense (OSD). Their principal device is the use of Cost-Plus-Fixed-Fee (CPFF) contracts which encourage frequent understatement of cost, thereby enhancing the chances of project approval by the OSD. Peck pointed out that such contracts allow the understatement of costs without making the contractor absorb the understated cost. Instead, the government pays all of the actual cost overrun, which of course goes to the service contractors.

Peck's interest in reforming government regulation has not changed since he began his career in the 1950s. In fact, since 1968 his experience of leading the president's Task Force on national communications policy has increased his conviction that although regulation can serve useful purposes, changes in technology and the national economy have aroused increasing concern that regulation is imposing excessive burdens on individuals and business. Peck has consistently advocated competitive markets and decentralized market decisions as an efficient way to allocating goods and services. In sum, and in characteristic style, Peck continues to submerge himself in contributing to policy formulation and deregulation reform in ways that seem to affect the life of every American.

BIBLIOGRAPHY

Peck, Merton. *Competition in the Aluminum Industry, 1945–1958*. Cambridge, Mass.: Harvard University Press, 1961.

———. *Marginal Analysis and the Explanation of Business Behavior in the Aluminum Industry*. Washington, D.C.: Social Science Research Council, 1958.

———; Haber, William; Carroll, John; and Kahn, Mark. *The Maintenance of Way Employment on U.S. Railroads*. Detroit: Wayne State University Press, 1957.

———. Meyer, John; Stenason, John; and Zwick, Charles. *Economics of Competition in the Transportation Industry*. Cambridge, Mass.: Harvard University Press, 1959.

———; Noll, Roger; and McGowan, John. *Economic Aspects of Television Regulation*. Washington, D.C.: Brookings Institution, 1973.

REXFORD A. AHENE

POOLE, WILLIAM
(b. June 19, 1937), CEA December 10, 1982-January 20, 1985

William Poole is a man of no meager talents. Moving back and forth between academia and government—including a longstanding and distinguished tenure with the Federal Reserve and a professorship at Brown University—he has shown himself to be a competent administrator, a level-headed and sympathetic counselor, an amiable colleague, an honest critic, and above all, a superb economist. To those familiar with the man, his writings, or his career, Poole's nomination to the Council came as no surprise.

Poole's reputation in Washington and in the academic community to which he has since returned remains unsullied. That it remained so while he was at the Council was no mean feat. This was a time when the Council's head, Martin Feldstein*, was openly sparring with other high-ranking presidential advisers, occasionally with the president himself, and when the notion of dissolving the Council was under serious consideration. While Murray Weidenbaum* was head of the Council, the Reagan White House began to pay less attention to the forecasts developed at the Council, increasingly relying on those constructed at the Treasury or the Office of Management and Budget—two places more sympathetic to supply-side economics.

Poole's term at the Council coincided with great upheaval in the economics profession as well. Participants in the financial markets were awakening angrily to economists' inability to precisely predict scores of economic variables which the market had come to rely upon as signals of both economic growth and future interest rate movements. Of course, economists had always warned of the risks associated with any particular forecast. But the market hardly listened to the caveats until it was, in many cases, too late. This did not stop the economics profession as a whole from catching the brunt of their frustration, however.

The economics profession itself was in the midst of a shakeout, with eclecticism replacing hard-line monetarist or Keynesian ideologies. Most practicing economists in the eighties, it seems, do not consider themselves of one particular school or another, which has been in and of itself a revolution in the profession. It is a credit to the man and a sign of his integrity that Poole survived those times with his reputation intact.

Poole was educated at Swarthmore College, where he earned his B.A. degree with high honors and was elected Phi Beta Kappa, and at the University of Chicago, from which he received his M.B.A. and Ph.D. in finance. His dissertation, which remains unpublished, dealt with the Canadian experience with flexible exchange rates between 1950 and 1962.

When he left Chicago, Poole became an assistant professor at Johns Hopkins

University in Baltimore, a position he held until 1969. His initiation into the Fed took place while he was a faculty member at Johns Hopkins—he worked during the summer of 1966 as an economist at the Board of Governors in Washington. Poole returned to the board full-time as an economist in 1969 and was promoted to senior economist the next year. He stayed at the Fed until 1974, although he was officially on leave during the academic year of 1973–74. During his time there he specialized in monetary policy, becoming head of the Fed's prestigious Special Studies section, in which much of the more rigorous theoretical research is undertaken. He also taught at the American University, Georgetown University, and George Washington University in the evening during these years.

In the fall of 1973, while on leave from the Fed, Poole lectured at Harvard University. He went on the next spring to lecture at the Massachusetts Institute of Technology. He became a professor of economics at Brown University at the start of the next academic year, and he has remained at Brown since then, taking time out, of course, to ferry back to government. Poole served first as an adviser and then as a consultant to the Federal Reserve Bank of Boston while teaching in Cambridge and Providence. In the summer of 1977 he became a visiting scholar at the Federal Reserve Bank of San Francisco. And during the academic year 1980–81, Poole was a visiting economist at the Reserve Bank of Australia.

Poole was officially on leave from Brown University while at the Council of Economic Advisers. His role as a consultant from August to December 1982 ended with his official appointment as member on December 10, 1982. Poole left the Council to return to Brown on January 20, 1985. At the Council in 1983, Poole chaired the interagency subcabinet forecasting group, consisting of representatives from the Department of the Treasury and the Office of Management and Budget, with participation by the Department of Commerce. The development of economic assumptions and the monitoring of current economic developments were major areas of interest for Poole, who took charge of the macroeconomic aspects of the Council's duties.

Poole takes an activist approach to research. Indeed, while many economists work for the entirety of their professional lives in an academic setting, often dealing with theories and equations that bear little direct consequence to the world we live in, Poole belongs to a different group of economists, those who strive to improve in one way or another the quality of life. This is noticeable in the topics he chooses to study: wage-price controls, flexible versus fixed exchange rates, inflation, and, of course, monetary policy. But it is also noticeable in his approach to the subject matter, for what distinguishes Poole's career perhaps most visibly is the rigor with which he approaches these topics of national political and economic importance. On any subject on which he speaks with authority, there are hours, days, and perhaps years of critical attention and study behind each conclusion and suggestion. Matters of importance are not taken lightly.

Poole is most widely known as a monetarist. His book, *Money and the Economy: A Monetarist View*, is quite clear about what he believes. For purposes of explaining Poole's beliefs on the subject, one can do no better than to quote from the text eight propositions that, in his mind, contain the elements of monetarism:

1. Inflation is a monetary phenomenon.
2. In the short run, while the price adjustment process is working itself out, a change in the rate of growth of money, especially if it is unanticipated, will affect the level of national output.
3. The long run trend rate of growth of a nation's output is completely independent, or almost so, of the level and rate of growth of the nation's money stock.
4. The level of nominal interest rates depends importantly on the rate of inflation and, therefore, on the rate of growth of the money stock.
5. The high correlations that exist between the money stock and a number of other variables reflect a line of causation running from the money stock to the other variables and not the other way around.
6. It is technically feasible to control the money stock and, therefore, the government should be held responsible for the consequences of monetary instability.
7. The attempt to use deliberate changes in the money stock to offset disturbances originating in the private sector has been a failure; the monetary authorities ought simply to maintain a constant rate of growth of the money stock.
8. In analyzing why the world works as it does, it is best to accept the premise that households and firms are rational utility- and profit-maximizers.

In the book, which is meant to be a primer on monetarism, Poole goes on to explain these eight propositions, providing along the way some theoretical and expository evidence to back up his arguments.

Poole's collected works provide some excellent examples of his economic and political insights.

Monetary Growth and the Economy. Being a monetarist, Poole believes that swings in economic growth—the business cycle—are primarily caused by destabilizing policy. This much is clear from the second of his eight propositions. But while this result is now quite widely accepted by the financial and economic community on the basis of recent economic history, Poole's ideology stems from more than casual empiricism or a reading of economists' works. Proof in point is his *Journal of Finance* article published in 1975 entitled "The Relationship of Monetary Decelerations to Business Cycle Peaks." The question asked is a narrow one: Is it true that a decline in money growth is a necessary and sufficient condition for a business cycle peak? After defining a monetary deceleration in four different ways—all comparing the growth rate of money to past trends—and comparing it with business cycle peaks as defined by the National Bureau of Economic Research, Poole concluded that "the evidence for the necessity of a decline in money growth for a business cycle peak is evident. For every peak there is decline in the rate of growth of the money stock. That result is a standard of monetarism, first declared by Milton Friedman and Anna Schwartz in their pathbreaking article "Money and Business Cycles." Poole found their method of dating turning points in the rate of growth of the money stock "subjective," however, and sought further substantiation.

Money Growth and Inflation. Probably the most widely understood tenet of monetarist thought is that inflation is a monetary phenomenon. This widely accepted notion of the cause of inflation was not quite so popular, however, when Poole began his career at the Fed. He soon became known as a monetarist for his prescriptions for stable money growth to restrain inflation and to dampen business cycle fluctuations.

If the links between money growth and economic growth and inflation over the long run are well known, it is nevertheless true that the relationship between the variables in the short run has always been less clear-cut. Poole took on the challenge in the mid–1970s with his paper "Benefits and Costs of Stable Money Growth." He had two specific tasks in mind: first, to investigate the relationship between short-run fluctuations in money growth and, second, to explore the effects on GNP of short-run fluctuations in money growth.

Poole's conclusions set him apart from other monetary economists. On the first subject, he broke with established wisdom, namely, that at the cost of greater fluctuations in money growth, short-term interest rates could be smoothed. Instead, Poole concluded, setting aside the merits of the goal of reducing interest rate fluctuations, it seems that fluctuations in money growth do not in fact smooth interest rates. At a time, then, when many economists shrank from following a "monetarist" money growth rule for fear of destabilizing interest rates, Poole found that "the claimed benefit from fluctuating money growth" was hollow and, additionally, that the policy of interest rate smoothing has become increasingly counterproductive as participants in the financial markets anticipate the Federal Reserve's reaction.

Poole's work in the second section was hampered by data problems. He reported, "It is an unfortunate fact of life that for postwar U.S. data, the seasonal effects on GNP are so much larger than the monetary effects that there is no way of being confident" of econometric tests.

Despite the problems in the second part, Poole's work for the "Benefits and Costs" paper was important. It paved the way for his somewhat radical stance on monetary policy in the seventies. Not only did he believe—along with many—that long-run cycles in money growth would produce long-run cycles in economic growth and inflation, but he also felt that there were no beneficial effects to be had from *not* controlling money growth closely. Consequently, Poole became an outspoken critic of Fed policy in the seventies and an advocate of stable money growth policies.

Some of the most important contributions Poole has made to the economics profession come from his work on the mechanism of monetary policy. He has written extensively on the implementation methods of the Federal Reserve—to interpret their methods for outside economists and laymen and to suggest alter native ways of conducting day-to-day operations. It is not surprising that Poole has a particular interest in this work—it stems from his conviction that money matters so much. Those who advocate stable monetary policy have a lot hanging on the ability to control money growth. Excerpts from a few articles authored by Poole help describe his viewpoints on the technical matters of policy making.

In 1975 "The Making of Monetary Policy: Descriptions and Analysis" was published in the *New England Economic Review* (a publication of the Federal Bank of Boston). Poole's purpose was twofold: "to present a simple description of current policy procedures in the hope of improving the ongoing debate over monetary policy" and "to analyze the effectiveness of current procedures in order to identify major problem areas." To be sure, Poole accomplished his second task. Writing about the inappropriateness of the Federal Funds rate as an implementation tool for monetary policy, the feasibility of targeting reserves, and the changes that could be made to carry-over provisions on reserve requirements, he displayed his thorough "soup to nuts" understanding of the monetary policy system. And once again, he offered corrective measures.

In Poole's 1976 article "Interpreting the Fed's Monetary Targets," published in the Brookings' Papers on Economic Activity, a primary purpose, it is clear, was to inform. Written after the passage of the House Concurrent Resolution 133 (passed in March 1975), which instituted procedures for the Fed to report to Congress on its planned money and credit growth targets for the next year, Poole's paper explained the Fed's method of selecting target growth paths for the monetary aggregates. Poole generally lauded the Fed's decision to target money growth over the course of months and quarters.

In fact, Poole's major argument in the paper has not been heard frequently (the second is far more popular). His point is that although there may be times that monetary policy should stray temporarily from its long-run growth target, policy makers should not incorporate these deviations into the long-run targets. It was and still is a suggestion well worth taking. In most years since the institution of targets, some amount of base drift (where next year's target is not an extension of this year's targeted path but rather a target derived from the actual growth path) has been allowed.

In the ten years since these two papers were published, the public's focus on the Fed has gotten finer. Although Poole has lost his near-monopoly on monetary policy, he continues to bring to the subject his own combination of description, analysis, and suggestion, as well as fundamental beliefs that are all his own.

His 1982 *Journal of Money, Credit, and Banking* article is a case in point. After the adoption of "reserve" targeting procedures in 1979, most critics honed in on the lagged method of determining revenues which was thought to affect most of the benefits of the switch to reserve targeting. In his 1982 article, Poole examined theoretically the difference between contemporaneous reserve accounting (the preferred system) and lagged reserve accounting (then the current method), but decided that the real issue lay elsewhere—namely, in the destabilizing effects of expectations. He came to a conclusion reached by others that a return to the 1920s policy of controlling the borrowing at the discount window is inadequate—but he got there in his own way, using his own method, and in so doing elevated the professional discussion a notch or two.

Perhaps disenchanted by Fed policy year after year, Poole was among those economists who, years ago, called for a less activist policy at the Fed. Poole wrote as early as 1974, that in studying possible reasons for the postwar experience, he was unable to convince himself that an activist policy would be superior to a ''steady-as-she-goes'' policy. His point is made further on in the article: Because the private sector bases its decision on forecasts of future policy actors and that the structure of the economy is ''dependent on the nature of the policies followed,'' Poole concludes, ''there is a further reason to doubt that the current body of knowledge is adequate to the demands of countercyclical stabilization policy.''

In 1972 Poole co-authored with Charles Lieberman a paper that publicized his suggestions for improving Fed operating procedures. Before that time, while at the Fed, Poole is known to have been an ardent critic of policies designed to smooth interest rates and target moderate economic growth. The 1972 paper, entitled ''Improving Monetary Control,'' was about the technical feasibility of controlling the money stock, assuming its desirability. The authors developed what they called a ''reform shopping list'':

1. Eliminate reserve requirements against Treasury deposits in commercial banks.
2. Require all nonmember banks to adhere to the Federal Reserve reserve requirements specified for member banks.
3. If M1 is accepted without qualification as the definition of money for policy purposes, eliminate reserve requirements on time and savings deposits.
4. Abandon lagged reserve requirements in favor of contemporaneous reserve requirements.
5. Amend regulations and invest in additional data processing equipment to reduce Federal Reserve float to the greatest extent possible.
6. Change the treatment of vault cash in the reserve requirements so that only a percentage, equaling the marginal reserve requirement on demand deposits for each bank, is allowed as reserves.
7. Set the discount rate so that it is always above money market rates of interest, and end administrative control over member bank borrowing.
8. Until item (2) is implemented, require all nonmember banks to furnish deposit and vault cash data to the Federal Reserve more frequently.
9. Determine seasonal factors for the money stock as an expression of the seasonal aspects of monetary policy rather than by standard seasonal adjustment techniques. Since these seasonal factors would define seasonal monetary policy they would not be subject to later revision.

Their ''laundry list'' was obviously not geared to the layman—their audience was economists and policy makers. Suffice it to say that all of the above-mentioned suggestions (some of which have been adopted) would have strengthened the Fed's day-to-day control over the nation's money stock.

Economics aside, Poole's papers offer another lesson, one he discussed in 1974, saying that if policy is to be viable in the long run, it must be not only economically sound but also understandable to the citizenry. In a successful democracy, good decisions are made when the government and the public are well informed on the issues.

Poole's career as an economist has been varied; in subject matter he has laped from the Canadian fixed exchange rate system to contemporaneous reserve accounting rules. And while focusing on monetary policy, he has worked within the Fed system, from the outside, and at the Council, or on par with the Fed's major players. Nevertheless, some aspects of his career have not changed at all—the scrutiny to which he submits all work, his honesty, his ability to see multiple facets of an issue, including many overlooked by others, and his driving concern that it all be conveyed to decision makers and the public.

BIBLIOGRAPHY

Poole, William. "Burnsian Monetary Policy: Eight Years of Progress?" *Journal of Finance* 34 (May 1979): 473, 484.

———. "Housing Finance under Inflationary Conditions." In *Federal Reserve Staff Study: Ways to Moderate Fluctuations in Housing Construction*. Washington, D.C.: Board of Governors of the Federal Reserve System, 1972, pp. 355–76.

———. "Indexing and the Capital Markets." *American Economic Review* 66 (May 1976): 200–204.

———. "The Making of Monetary Policy: Description and Analysis." *New England Economic Review* (March/April 1975): 21–30.

———. *Money and the Economy: A Monetarist View*. New York: Addison-Wesley, 1978.

———. "The 1975 CEA Report: Long on Analysis, Short on Policy." *American Economic Review* 65 (September 1975): 539–47.

———. "The Relationship of Monetary Decelerations to Business Cycle Peaks: Another Look at the Evidence." *Journal of Finance* 30 (June 1975): 697–712.

———. "Rules of Thumb for Guiding Monetary Policy." In *Open Market Policies and Operating Procedures—Staff Studies*. Washington, D.C.: Board of Governors of the Federal Reserve System, 1971, pp. 135–89.

———. "Speculative Prices as Random Walks: An Analysis of Ten Time Series of Flexible Exchange Rates." *Southern Economic Journal* 33 (April 1967): 468–78.

———, and Liberman, Charles. "Improving Monetary Control," in *Brookings Papers on Economic Activity, 2: 1972*, ed. A. Okun and G. Perry. Washington, D.C.: Brookings Institution, 1972, pp. 293–335.

NANCY KIMELMAN

SAULNIER, RAYMOND JOSEPH

(b. September 20, 1908), CEA April 4, 1955-January 20, 1961

When Raymond Joseph Saulnier (pronounced son-ya) was appointed chair of the Council of Economic Advisers in 1956, he became an instant object of media interest. This represented a complete turnabout for a professional research economist who had heretofore been practically unknown to the general public and press. Even the news stories about his initial appointment to the CEA in 1955 contained more information about his immediate predecessor than himself. When he assumed the position of chair, however, all that changed.

The *New York Times* (November 14, 1956) greeted Saulnier's nomination as chair with a lengthy profile in which he was described as an affable thinking machine. *Newsweek* (November 26, 1956) featured him in the column "This Week's Newsmaker." The portrait in *Newsweek* contrasted Saulnier's style with that of the outgoing chair, Arthur F. Burns*. Saulnier was a neat, banker-like, lifelong Republican, while Burns was a shaggy-haired academic who was a Democrat-for-Eisenhower. Despite their obvious physical and political differences, *Newsweek* was quick to observe that the two men thought alike when it came to economic theory and policy.

The journalistic interest in the new head of the CEA was certainly justified, for in his capacity as chair, Saulnier became this country's most prominent economist. He held the position of chair from 1956 to 1961, and during that time he was the government's most authoritative economic spokesman and a principal architect of economic policy during President Dwight D. Eisenhower's second term.

Born in Hamilton, Massachusetts, in 1908, Saulnier was one of four children. He grew up in a family of modest means, his father being a skilled factory mechanic. While in high school, Saulnier, nicknamed "Steve," worked at part-time jobs in the local movie house and telegraph office.

After graduating from high school in 1925, Saulnier continued his education at Middlebury College in Vermont as a scholarship student. In 1929 he received the B.S. degree in economics and went on to graduate school at Tufts University, earning the M.A. degree in 1931. He then entered Columbia University as a George W. Ellis Fellow and in 1938 was granted a Ph.D. in economics. In 1934 he married Estelle Sydney; the couple had two children, Mark and Alice.

Saulnier began his teaching career in 1934 as an instructor at Columbia University. He held that post until 1938, when he became an assistant professor at Barnard College. He was promoted to associate professor in 1945 and to full professor three years later. Saulnier was named chair of the department of economics in 1950. He is still associated with the college to this day, maintaining an office in Lehman Hall on the Barnard campus.

While at Columbia, first as a graduate student and then as an instructor, Saulnier developed what turned out to be a lifelong interest in monetary theory, policy, and institutions. His doctoral dissertation, *Contemporary Monetary Theory: Studies of Some Recent Theories of Money, Prices, and Production* (1938), was a comparative discussion of the views of John Maynard Keynes, R. G. Hawtrey, D. H. Robertson, and F. A. von Hayek. A reviewer in the June 17, 1939, issue of *The Economist* characterized Saulnier's analysis as a sharp critique of the theories of the four men and called Saulnier a realist who insists on "the necessity for theory to justify itself as a guide to practice and on the relevance of monetary theory to trade cycle programs."

The bulk of Saulnier's published works stems from his association with the National Bureau of Economic Research (NBER) in the 1940s and 1950s. Working alongside such economists as Neil H. Jacoby* and Arthur F. Burns, he produced a number of volumes on banking, mortgages, and insurance companies for the NBER. In 1946 Saulnier was appointed director of the National Bureau's Financial Research Division.

As a research economist, Saulnier clearly comes from the Arthur Burns–Wesley Clair Mitchell mold. His major works—*Industrial Banking Companies and Their Credit Practices* (1940), *Cost and Returns on Farm Mortgage Lending by Life Insurance Companies, 1945–1947* (1949), and *Urban Mortgage Lending by Life Insurance Companies* (1956)—are detailed empirical investigations of specific financial institutions or arrangments. Saulnier's approach to research shows a clear disdain for deductive economics in which a theoretical hypothesis or model is formulated and then analyzed to see what logically consistent conclusions it yields. Rather, his work is distinctively inductive in nature—a sifting through mountains of empirical observations to see what underlying patterns consistent with or predicted by conventional monetary economic theory emerge.

Principally because of his recognized expertise in credit and financial matters, Saulnier became a consultant to the Board of Governors of the Federal Reserve System in 1950 and 1951. In that capacity he helped write the system's "Regulation X," a measure designed to curb mortgage credit during the Korean War. He also assisted in the administration of "Regulation W," aimed at control of retail time credit. In addition to his consulting at the Federal Reserve, Saulnier also served on a special advisory committee of the Farm Credit Administration in 1951 and 1952. In 1951 he was elected president of the American Finance Association.

Working for the National Bureau of Economic Research did more than provide Saulnier with an environment in which he could develop the expertise to become a prominent government economist; it also gave him the most important professional friendship of his career, with Arthur F. Burns. Burns had been associated with the NBER since 1930, becoming director of research in 1945. When, in 1953, Burns was appointed chair of the CEA, one of his first official acts was to name Saulnier as a consultant to the Council. In April 1955 Saulnier became a member of the Council by presidential appointment, replacing Neil H. Jacoby, another former colleague from the NBER.

Saulnier's selection reflected Burns' desire to staff the CEA with fiercely professional economists and thus continue the depolitization of the Council which Burns had begun in 1953. At least that's the way the *New York Times* saw the appointment when, in an editorial on March 26, 1955, it characterized Saulnier as an excellent economist as scientifically minded as any physicist or chemist. When Burns resigned as chair of the CEA in 1956, Saulnier was chosen as his successor.

As chair, Saulnier had regular access to the highest levels of power in the U.S. government. He saw President Eisenhower once every two weeks, if not more. Their personal meetings were of two types: discussions involving a specific problem such as a pending housing bill, and general sessions in which the state of the economy was considered. Saulnier was usually alloted fifteen minutes to half an hour of the president's time when discussing specific issues and a half hour or more for the general reviews. In addition to his many face-to-face opportunities with the president, Saulnier had unlimited access to key presidential advisers such as chiefs-of-staff Sherman Adams and Jerry Persons, and special presidential assistant George Hauge.

Saulnier's direct responsibility was to the president, but he also had many ancillary duties that carried considerable influence. He attended every cabinet meeting and every meeting of important legislative leaders. He had numerous contacts with William McChesney Martin, chief of the Board of Governors of the Federal Reserve, and met frequently with the Director of the Budget and the secretaries of Commerce, Treasury, and Labor. Saulnier chaired the President's Advisory Board of Economic Growth and Stability and, in 1960, a Cabinet Committee on Governmental Actions Affecting Costs and Prices. Occasionally, he even attended meetings of the National Security Council and the Office of Defense Mobilization to discuss the economic implications of national defense policy such as the stockpiling of strategic materials.

Saulnier viewed his job as chair of the CEA as having two basic responsibilities: (1) to advise the president on economic matters, and (2) to behave in a professional rather than a political manner. This was precisely what the president wanted, and he said so in his very first meeting with Saulnier. Although Saulnier was appointed for his recognized expertise as an economist, Eisenhower had the luxury of knowing that the professional judgments and pronouncements of his principal economic adviser would always reflect the distinctively conservative bent both men shared.

Eisenhower firmly believed in the virtues of a balanced budget. In three of the eight years he was in office, the federal government had budgetary surpluses, and in four other years government deficits were comparatively small. To Eisenhower, economics was a simple and moral issue: you paid your debts and lived within your means. This puritan approach had worked for his family while he was growing up in Abilene, Kansas, and, Eisenhower believed, it would work for the federal government as well.

Saulnier was not nearly as dogmatic about government deficits as Eisenhower. He believed in the necessity of preserving options rather than adhering to hard and fast rules. Thus, while wishing to avoid deficits whenever possible, Saulnier would personally opt for a fiscal program to balance the budget over the business cycle and not each and every year. Still, he was anti-Keynesian and remains so today. His aversion to liberal economics, however, did not cause Saulnier to embrace monetarism, although his sympathies clearly lie in that direction.

In retrospect, many economists today agree that the economic policies Eisenhower and Saulnier devised were overly cautious for the times. When Saulnier became chair of the CEA in 1956, the economy was in a period of robust expansion that had begun with the automobile boom of 1955. When he left government service in 1961, the economy was in the midst of the second recession in five years. In the interim, the nation had lived through the recession of 1958, which, up to that time, was the severest economic downturn the United States had experienced since 1941, the last year of the Great Depression.

While not personally responsible for this economic transformation, Saulnier was instrumental in helping establish a fiscal strategy that ultimately turned the 1950s into a decade of slow growth and unrealized economic potential. He himself sees exogenous events such as the 116-day steel strike of 1959 as contributing to the sluggish economic conditions of the times. In the case of the steel walkout, stockpiles accumulated in anticipation of the strike minimized its general impact until all but the last few days. The lackluster performance of the U.S. economy in the late 1950s was more a consequence of philosophy than of any single event or program.

Saulnier advocated a restrained fiscal and monetary policy on the premise that if the federal government did otherwise it would fuel the fires of inflation. The fear of inflation was almost an obsession with Saulnier. One of his first pronouncements as the new chair of the CEA was on its dangers; he called inflation an immediate hazard and saw it as the country's number one economic problem for the coming years. The fact is that during Eisenhower's eight years as president, the rate of inflation, as measured by the Consumer Price Index, increased at an average annual rate of 1.4 percent, with a maximum of 3.4 percent and a minimum close to zero percent. Nevertheless, Saulnier took up the battle against inflation as soon as he became chair of the CEA in 1956 and continued the fight right through Richard Nixon's loss to John F. Kennedy in the 1960 presidential election.

Given Eisenhower's distaste for deficits and Saulnier's concern with inflation, fiscal policy invariably became distinctly passive. The desire to eliminate deficits, adhere to a balanced budget regardless of the economic consequences, and rely almost exclusively on the initiative of the private sector to promote growth and stability ran counter to the fiscal activism espoused by the emerging mainstream Keynesian paradigm. Liberal economists frequently criticized Saulnier's go-slow approach, noting that real GNP had grown at an annual rate of 4.7 percent during the Truman years compared to the 2.8 percent rate of the Eisenhower years. Saulnier responded to this by saying that while the rate of growth of the real GNP was lower under Eisenhower, civilian consumption grew faster. This earned Saulnier the label "high priest of gadgets" from liberals who characterized the economy as "lopsided," with too much of the nation's income being spent on private indulgence and not enough on defense, education, and other common welfare projects.

Saulnier's critics, especially Leon Keyserling*, the chair of the CEA under President Harry Truman, were particularly vocal during the recession year of 1958. Keyserling and other liberal economists thought Saulnier's overriding concern with inflation was wholly inappropriate at a time when the annual unemployment rate was approaching 9 percent. Some even went so far as to charge that the government had induced the 1958 recession to stop inflation, a charge Saulnier vehemently denies. He believes, however, that the primary source of the government's contribution to the downturn was inappropriate monetary policy and not inappropriate fiscal policy.

Regardless of the reasons, the five years of Saulnier's tenure as chair of the CEA were not among the most prosperous in the nation's history. Assessing the state of the economy in 1961, the *New York Times* (February 5, 1961) saw it as not wholly depressed but rather full of paradoxes. It was against this backdrop of unevenness that the Kennedy administration took office and pursued an active fiscalism that turned the 1960s into the economic antithesis of the 1950s.

After leaving the CEA in 1961, Saulnier returned to teaching at Barnard College. He remained on the faculty until his retirement in 1973. Since 1961 Saulnier has served on several presidential commissions, been a member of the board of the Federal National Mortgage Association, and was elected president of the Catholic Commission on Cultural and Intellectual Affairs. For twelve years he was a public governor of the American Stock Exchange. He has also been a member of the board or consultant to a number of leading American companies and financial institutions. Currently he is writing a book on the Eisenhower Economy from 1952 to 1960, which may bear the subtitle "Recollections of Better Times."

In looking back over Saulnier's association with the CEA, especially in the role of chair, it is evident that he has helped make that position what it is today: basically a nonpolitical presidential adviser. Of course, no chair, including Saulnier, is apolitical. Yet, given the many temptations to become an economic demagogue, Saulnier clearly resisted most.

BIBLIOGRAPHY

Saulnier, Raymond. *Financing Equipment for Commercial and Industrial Enterprise*. New York: National Bureau of Economic Research, 1940.

———. "A Monetary and Fiscal Strategy for the 1970s." In M. R. Laird, ed., *Republican Papers*. New York: Praeger, 1968.
———. "Policies That Ended Inflation in 1956–61." In C. Lowell Harriss, ed., *Inflation: Long-Term Problems*. Proceeding of the Academy of Policy Science 31, no. 4. New York, 1975.
———. *The Strategy of Economic Policy*. New York: Fordham University Press, 1962.
———; Halcrow, H. G.; and Jacoby, N. H. *Federal Lending: Its Growth and Impact*. New York: National Bureau of Economic Research, Occasional Paper 58, 1957.

JULIANNE CICARELLI AND JAMES CICARELLI

SCHULTZE, CHARLES LOUIS
(b. February 19, 1924), CEA January 22, 1977-January 20, 1981

The Godkin Lectures on the Essentials of Free Government and the Duties of the Citizen, established at Harvard University in 1903, are given annually under the auspices of the Harvard Graduate School of Public Administration. As advertisements appeared on the Harvard campus in November 1976 announcing the location and times at which Charles Schultze would deliver that year's lectures, more than one student was heard to ask, "Why is the author of 'Peanuts' giving lectures on political economy?" The story is not apocryphal, though even if it were it would serve to make the same point. The point is not that the names Charles M. Schulz and Charles L. Schultze are easily confused, but that although virtually the entire membership of the economics profession then, and now, knew of Schultze and his work, he was then, and is now, largely unknown to the general public.

Current Biography profiled Schultze in January 1970 and noted that "from June 1965 through January 1968, Schultze was one of the most powerful—though little publicized—men in Washington, controlling the purse strings of the federal government's massive operations." That comment recalls Keynes' remark that practical men of affairs are, unbeknownst to themselves, frequently in thrall to the theories of past economists. Even vital economists such as Schultze frequently labor in obscurity, exerting effects of great magnitude on a world which remains largely ignorant of their existence. Yet Schultze was far better known than were most persons ever appointed to the Council of Economic Advisers when he joined it as chairman on January 22, 1977. He continued until January 20, 1981, a length of service as chairman exceeded only by Raymond Saulnier* in the Eisenhower administration.

At the time of the 1976 Godkin Lectures Schultze already had been selected by the incoming Carter administration for appointment to a high-level post. Most frequently mentioned were Secretary of the Treasury and chairman of the CEA. Intimates were quoted as saying that the position he most wanted was Secretary of Energy, assuming that the new president was able to carry out his campaign promise to establish that department. One position that he apparently did not want was the one with which he was most familiar, Director of the Office of Management and Budget. As the Budget Director during the Johnson years, Schultze had come to have a greater knowledge of the intricacies of the federal government than probably could be claimed by anyone else in the administration that prepared to take office in January 1977.

Schultze's familiarity with Washington was lifelong. Born across the Potomac in Alexandria in 1924, he had grown up in that city and graduated from Gonzaga High. He then enrolled in Fordham University in New York City, but left after one year to join the United States Army, in which he served from 1943 to 1946. He was separated from the army as a private first class who had been awarded the Bronze Star and the Purple Heart.

It was to Georgetown University in Washington that he returned to complete his college education, graduating in 1948. His year at Fordham, however, had been invaluable, for while there he met Rita Irene Hertzog, whom he wed on September 6, 1947.

For two years Schultze was an instructor in economics at the College of St. Thomas in St. Paul, Minnesota, but the magnet of Washington drew him back, first as an economist in the Office of Price Stabilization, and then, from 1952 to 1959, as a staff economist for the Council of Economic Advisers. During these years of government service he studied economics part-time and received the Master of Arts degree in 1950 from Georgetown and the Doctor of Philosophy degree in 1960 from the University of Maryland. An indication of the respect in which he was already held was the publication, in 1959, of his doctoral dissertation, *Recent Inflation in the United States*, by the Joint Economic Committee of the United States Congress.

The next year the Committee for Economic Development published Schultze's *Prices, Costs, and Output in the Postwar Period*. Analyzing inflationary trends in the years from 1947 to 1957, Schultze concluded that the root of the postwar inflation was to be found in the sharply increased demand for the products of a small number of industries, and that inflation in those industries had triggered inflation in the rest of the economy.

Schultze's last extended absence from Washington was during 1959 to 1961, when he was an associate professor at Indiana University. But his activities there soon brought him back to the capital, for it was while at Indiana that he developed the concept that the impact of the federal budget on the economy might best be measured by the surplus or deficit that would be generated if the economy were operating with an unemployment rate of 4 percent. This figure was widely regarded among economists at that time as representing full employment.

The actual deficits or surpluses occurring in the budget had proved to be unreliable indicators of the impact of the government's budgetary impact on the economy. The full employment surplus (or deficit) is a hypothetical figure, actually an estimate, of the difference between revenues and expenditures which current tax and expenditure programs would generate if the economy were operating at full employment, that is, at 4 percent unemployment as in 1960. (Of course, the 4 percent figure was itself an estimate of the minimum level to which unemployment normally could be reduced.) This hypothetical surplus (or deficit) could then be used as a benchmark against which to measure the macroeconomic effects of changes in government tax or spending policies. Any policy change that reduced the full employment surplus could be considered contractionary, while any policy change that increased the full employment surplus could be considered a stimulus.

Schultze presented his concept to the Joint Economic Committee in 1960, and it was quickly adopted by economists in the Kennedy administration. In 1961 Schultze became a professor of economics at his former graduate school, the University of Maryland, only to take a leave of absence a year later when David Bell, Director of the Bureau of the Budget and one of those who had implemented the full employment surplus concept in government practice, invited Schultze to become one of his assistant directors.

Schultze left the Bureau of the Budget very briefly in 1965, resigning in February of that year to return to teaching at Maryland. Within a few weeks, however, he was invited back to the bureau, this time as Director, replacing Kermit Gordon*, who had accepted appointment as vice president of the Brookings Institution. Schultze finished his semester at Maryland and became, in June 1965, the youngest person ever to head the Bureau of the Budget.

Within the next few months Schultze completed the preparation of the fiscal year 1967 budget. Since this task had been well under way before he became Director, his impact was limited; but for fiscal year 1968 he recast the budget and put his stamp upon it. Fiscal year 1968 was the first year in which the planning-programming-budgeting system (PPBS) was used for all departments of the federal government. Until PPBS was adopted the massive federal budget was cast in line-item form, with each expenditure spelled out in detail. The budget was complex and incomprehensible. Schultze had developed expertise in PPBS during his time as assistant director by studying the budgetary reforms that Robert McNamara had been implementing in the Department of Defense.

The purpose of the PPB system of budgeting is to rationalize the budget-making process by centering attention upon the *purpose* of expenditures and by encouraging the consideration of alternative means of achieving these objectives. The PPB system, if fully implemented, should increase the efficiency of the public sector. Why this should happen was the subject of a brief article which Schultze wrote in the *Monthly Labor Review* the year after leaving the Bureau of the Budget.

That article was a concise description of how the absence of private sector type incentives leads to a failure to equate the marginal benefit and marginal cost of any government expenditure. In the private sector any program or expenditure has a visible opportunity cost; buying A means giving up B. In the federal government the opportunity cost of an expenditure is not made apparent to the individual responsible for making the decision to spend. Since there is no recognition of a need to make tradeoffs among programs, the federal budget grows inexorably. PPBS is, among other things, the introduction of incentives into the governmental budgeting system.

Schultze's suggestions were radical, given the nature of the federal government, for he proposed a decentralization of decision making, a movement of authority away from Congress into the field and down to the local level. And he was suggesting this during a period when the authority of the federal government was being extended into even more areas of the society.

During his tenure as Director of the Bureau of the Budget, Schultze had been responsible for the preparation of three federal budgets, for fiscal years 1967, 1968, and 1969. The PPBS reforms were introduced in the fiscal year 1968 budget. When the 1969 budget preparation was completed, he resigned in January 1968, something he had wanted to do since the previous summer. The workload of the Budget Director was all-demanding, and Schultze was getting tired of it.

Schultze returned to the University of Maryland as a professor of economics and also joined the Brookings Institution as a senior fellow. He was to hold both of these positions until President Carter recruited him to be chairman of the Council of Economic Advisers. While at Brookings he produced a series of analyses of most of the federal departments, and it was during these years that he, along with other fellows, originated a series of annual studies, *Setting National Priorities*.

During the Republican administrations of presidents Nixon and Ford, Schultze had been part of the "shadow government." His service to the Democratic opposition included membership on Hubert Humphrey's economic task force during the 1968 presidential campaign. His return to appointive office under the Democratic President Carter was heralded in the economics profession and in the news magazines.

By education and experience, Schultze was extremely well qualified for the post to which the new president appointed him. But philosophically and personally as well, he was an ideal choice. To read Schultze's Godkin Lectures, published in 1969 under the title *The Public Use of Private Interest*, is to discover a well-articulated philosophy of public policy with which the major campaign positions of President Carter were quite compatible. Throughout his campaign, Carter had spoken of the dissatisfaction of the American people with a large, overreaching, and inefficient government. He had promised to reduce the size of government and to simplify and rationalize its structure and programs. For the previous fifteen years, Schultze had been defining policies to accomplish this.

His view of the relationship between the private and public sectors was, in an important way, opposite to that usually taught in undergraduate economics courses. There, attention is concentrated upon the need for the public sector to correct the failures of the private sector. The failure of the market to provide public goods, or to provide the efficient quantity of goods, requires the corrective intervention of government. But Schultze argued cogently that what is more often necessary is that the market intervene in government.

While recognizing the situations in which a pure market system could not achieve an efficient allocation of resources, Schultze saw as well that a collective system which completely abandoned market mechanisms could claim to be efficient only if it also claimed that bureaucrats were all-knowing and all-wise. Whatever kinds of creatures were recruited by such a government, apparently they were not *homines economici*.

At the beginning of his tenure as CEA chairman, Schultze shared with the president an apparent agreement on the principles which ought to govern the public sector. Personally as well, the two men seemed unusually compatible. Like Carter, Schultze was a man comfortable with informality, a man with a style of his own. A photograph of Schultze that appeared in a national news magazine over the story of his appointment to head the CEA shows him in his office at the Brookings, feet up on the desk, wearing loud checked pants, a polka dot shirt, and a large-patterned tie. The reader was spared a view of the jacket which completed this ensemble.

It might be stretching the comparison to say that residents of Georgia would consider Schultze to be "a good old boy," but his rapport with the new president was exceptional. The two men took to each other instantly and completely. Economist Joseph Pechman, also a senior fellow at the Brookings, said early in the administration, "There is this chemistry. The President listens more intently when Charlie talks and seems to understand immediately." Like the president, the new chairman had a love of outdoor sports; he and his wife, Rita, had a great fondness for backpacking in the Blue Ridge Mountains.

Although six other men have served longer terms on the Council than did Schultze, only one ever served longer in the position of chairman. For all of Jimmy Carter's time in the White House Charles Schultze was, officially, his chief economic adviser.

As 1977 began it seemed clear enough what the major immediate challenge was—to pep up the sluggish economy. Advice to the president on how to achieve this was not a scarce commodity, and that advice reduced itself to a debate on whether to raise spending or cut taxes. Whichever advice Schultze might give the president, it seemed that political considerations might well intrude into the choice of economic policy.

Carter's own advisers, including Schultze, were arguing for a tax cut. That Schultze would argue for a tax cut rather than for a public expenditure program is consistent with the recognition of government's limitations that recurs in his writings and speeches.

In both the micro and macro policy areas Schultze saw the temptations to which the economist in government would be subject. Even in the micro area the "advocate of efficiency" should remind himself that there is no objective way to compare large losses concentrated among the few with small losses dispersed among the many, that markets do fail, and that there are real political opportunity costs to reforming programs. In the macro area the economic adviser should be conscientious to disclose the costs of a proposed macroeconomic policy, and equally conscientious to avoid the temptation to manipulate expectations by means other than solid policy.

The following jest circulated in Washington in the winter of 1977: "When the economy turned sour Lyndon Johnson could blame the Vietnam War and Gerald Ford could blame the Arab oil embargo, but Jimmy Carter will be able to blame Charles Schultze.''

The economy did turn sour during Carter's administration, with a timing that could not have been more disastrous for his reelection bid. The Consumer Price Index increased during every year of the Carter presidency. Although the civilian unemployment rate fell during each of the first three years of his administration, it increased quite significantly, from 5.8 percent to 7.1 percent, in the election year of 1980, as the number of unemployed increased by 1.5 million persons. Even as the unemployment rate was falling during the first three years of the administration, the ''distress index,'' the percentage increase in the Consumer Price Index added to the civilian unemployment rate, was inching upwards, from 13.5 in 1976 to 13.6 in 1977 to 13.8 in 1978, and then exploding to 17.1 in 1979 and to 20.6 in the election year. Real gross national product had been growing at a healthy enough rate in 1977 (5.5 percent) and 1978 (5 percent). The growth rate slipped to 2.8 percent in 1979, having actually decreased in the second quarter of that year. Again, in the election year, the news was the worst of all, as real GNP decreased for the year, and the economy was in a recession.

There may be many reasons why the voters declined to return President Carter to the White House in 1980. Major failures of his administration included the inability to bring about the release of the American hostages in Iran. Nevertheless, domestic economic discomfort and the perception that the president's stewardship of the economy had failed were certainly major factors in making him a one-term president.

Jimmy Carter had run his campaign on an ''anti-Washington,'' ''anti-big government'' posture. Yet in macroeconomic policy he seemed to adopt the ''We are all Keynesians'' attitude of one of his predecessors. It is ironic that by 1980, the successful challenger for the White House was also able to run an ''anti'' policy, in this case ''anti-Keynesian,'' ''anti-conventional economic wisdom,'' and to raise the slogan of supply-side economics as a banner around which those dissatisfied with Carter's policies could and did rally.

The macroeconomic policies of presidents and of presidential candidates are very much alike. They are each for growth, against unemployment, and against inflation. The great departure of President Reagan's policy was simply a change in the label. The basic economic policies of the Reagan administration—reduction in the size of the federal government and simplification of the tax system—were the same policies espoused by candidate Carter in 1976.

BIBLIOGRAPHY

Schultze, Charles. *National Income Analysis*. New York: Prentice-Hall, 1960.

———. *The Politics and Economics of Public Spending*. Washington, D.C.: The Brookings Institution, 1969.

———, with Kneese, Allen V. *Pollution, Prices, and Public Policy*. Washington, D.C.: The Brookings Institution, 1975.

JEROME F. HEAVEY

SEEVERS, GARY LEONARD
(b. May 24, 1937), CEA July 23, 1973-April 15, 1975

At the time of his nomination to the Council of Economic Advisers in June 1973, Gary Seevers was a senior CEA staff economist. Joining the council staff in 1970, Seevers had been serving, as of August 1972, as special assistant to the chairman, Herbert Stein*. The youngest appointee at thirty-six, he is the only economist up to the present to move directly to the Council from a staff position.

Food prices were escalating rapidly in the spring of 1973 as a result of declining world food production and the unprecedented low levels of U.S. food stocks. Since incipient food shortages as well as inflated food prices were causing public consternation, the farm background of the newly appointed economist was given favorable attention in the press. Presiding at the confirmation hearings on June 10, Senator William Proxmire expressed his approval of Seevers' strong background in agricultural economics, as an indication that the Nixon administration would be giving attention to an area which he felt had been neglected by past administrations.

Gary Leonard Seevers was born on the family farm near Jonesville, Michigan, in 1937. An only child, he raised purebred livestock to help finance his college education in addition to assisting his parents with other farm chores. Majoring in animal husbandry at Michigan State University, Seevers received the College of Agriculture's Outstanding Senior Award upon graduation in 1959. He remained at Michigan State to earn a Master of Science degree (1966) and a Ph.D. in agricultural economics in 1968. During this period he was employed by the Michigan State University Cooperative Extension Service as county extension agent. He also served as associate director of a 4-H study project of the National 4-H Club Foundation.

After receiving his degree in 1968, Seevers accepted an appointment as an assistant professor of economics at Oregon State University at Corvallis. In the spring of 1970, he received a call from Hendrik Houthakker*, a Council member, asking if he would accept, if offered, a CEA staff position. Agreeably surprised, as he had had no prior contact with the government agency, he was pleased to accept the offer. Seevers learned later that his major adviser at Michigan State, Dale Hathaway, a respected agricultural economist in academic and government circles and Under Secretary of Agriculture in the Carter administration, had given Houthakker his name when asked to recommend an able young agricultural economist. Since he was a registered Democrat and had voted for Hubert Humphrey, Seevers cites his appointment in the Nixon administration as an example of the bipartisan recruitment which is characteristic of the Council.

Although the appointment was for one year, Seevers was asked to remain; he became a special assistant to Herbert Stein in his third year. Then, when the Council experienced some difficulty in filling the vacancy created by the resignation of Ezra Solomon* during the Watergate hearings, Seevers accepted an offer of membership and joined Stein and Marina von Neumann Whitman*.

Food aid to developing countries, the subject of Seevers' doctoral dissertation, is one of several areas of food policy on which he has written. A 1968 journal article, "An evaluation of the Disincentive Effects Caused by PL 480 Shipments," has been cited in a number of subsequent studies. Title I under this law permits governments in recipient countries to purchase foodgrains on concessional terms. The increase in food supplies, however, by depressing food prices may displace domestic production, or if supply is inelastic, redistribute income away from a poor agricultural sector. Extending a model developed by Franklin Fisher, Seevers determined the magnitude of the price and output effects for varying values of demand and supply elasticities. Using parameter estimates for India from previous studies, Seevers showed that a 20 percent average increase in PL 480 shipments would decrease foodgrain prices by 1.58 percent and reduce food production by .4 percent. Conversely, in the absence of food shipments, prices and output would have been 6.7 and 1.7 percent higher, respectively (Seevers, "Evaluation," p. 638). These conclusions argued against views held by a number of economists on the magnitude of the disincentive effect. It was found in a later comprehensive study that the net loss in domestic production was only 3 percent of the amount of food aid, confirming Seevers' results, although differing views of the efficacy of reliance on cheap food imports remain.

Assuming unitary elasticity of demand for food cereals, the government would be able, Seevers maintains, to compensate producers from the revenue from food sales; if the additional income were allocated to government investment programs, the increase in real income would increase food demand, providing an additional important benefit from food aid. In this case, however, the increase in nonfood prices would redistribute income away from food producers. "Returning to the example with estimates for India if, initially shipments provided 5 of 100 units, an increase to 6 units would decrease producers' money incomes by 1.8%. This, coupled with even lower real incomes and the probability of larger shifts in PL 480 shipments, could impose real hardships on the welfare of a relatively poor rural sector" (Seevers, "Evaluation," p. 640). But, Seevers concludes, the benefits to the country as a whole, through the release of resources and improved production possibilities, should receive primary consideration.

Seevers estimated the additional cost of food aid to recipient countries as a result, primarily, of the shift from foreign currency sales (recipient country currency) to credit sales mandated under the Food for Peace Act of 1966. An estimate of the present value of the flow of dollar repayment for the stipulated credit terms depends on the discount rate. For a 10 percent discount rate, Seevers estimated the cost to be 50.6 percent of the loan's nominal value—approximately twice the cost of past foreign currency sales. Although, as Seevers points out, food aid through credit sales is still less expensive than commercial purchases, the effects of the change in policy should be evaluated from the perspective of the objectives of U.S. policy for development assistance. Seevers questioned the policy change. By adding to long-term indebtedness, debt servicing, already a growth constraint for developing countries, would be substantially increased.

Early PL 480 food shipments were surplus farm commodities. As a result of altered conditions in world food markets, however, the PL 480 budget allocation for fiscal year 1975 was a politically sensitive issue for the Ford administration. Drought conditions in the United States had caused a 5 percent decline from the previous year in world grain production in 1974–75; food prices in the United States increased at a 13.4 (annualized) rate between June and December 1974. Seevers chaired the Food Deputies Group under the President's Committee on Food, organized in June 1974. They worked through the summer and fall to resolve the conflicting interests of consumer, farm, humanitarian, and foreign policy groups. "PL 480 and domestic food assistance programs focus attention on the trade-offs that exist in policy between satisfying needs of low-income domestic consumers, low-income foreign consumers, and domestic consumers ineligible for food assistance" (Mayer and Seevers, "Food Policy Issues," p. 362). It was feared that even the announcement of increased food aid, which Secretary of State Henry Kissinger pressed for as evidence of U.S. concern for world food need, would result in further increases in food prices. Congressional debate over allotments for specific countries further delayed the final appropriation. Although many, including Lester Brown, a spokesman for Worldwatch Institute, attributed hundreds of thousands of deaths from starvation to the delay in food shipments, the $1.2 billion in food shipped in FY 1975 was the largest dollar amount since FY 1968.

In a paper written after these events, Seevers points out that the appropriations continue to increase modestly, and that although the tendency of administrations is to use food for political purposes, Congressional directives have channeled aid to achieve humanitarian objectives (Seevers, "Food Policy: Implications," pp. 273, 274).

While awaiting confirmation to the Council, Seevers joined Stein and Whitman for an impromptu press conference on June 26, 1973, to discuss alternative plans of action to ameliorate the critical food situation. Although price controls had been lifted in January 1973 (Phase II), President Nixon had ordered a sixty-day freeze on all prices except for farm products on June 13. The Consumer Price Index and, more specifically, the food index had increased dramatically in the interim period: from November 1972 to May 1973 the index increased from 150.0 to 159.7. Since the ceilings imposed at later stages of production placed a limit on the prices processors could pay for food, it had become unprofitable to raise eggs, chickens, or meat. That dairy, poultry, and livestock producers would be forced out of business, reducing supplies and further increasing food prices, was a possibility that had to be considered. Either ceilings had to be raised on food, or export controls on feed, particularly soybeans, had to be imposed.

An interagency group chaired by Seevers had been studying the possible impact of export controls. Although the group concluded that controlling exports would reduce feed prices, they were generally opposed to their imposition: a system of export monitoring was recommended. Analyses of the effects of the embargo were hampered by poor data on agricultural exports. The repercussions were both immediate and long-term. When the record 1973 soybean crop was harvested in September, the embargo was lifted. Before the embargo, 80 percent of the world exports of soybeans was supplied by the United States; the share at present is 35 percent.

Although this experience might have been expected to deter policy makers from using export controls as a policy tool, Seevers states that controls on wheat exports were considered in the winter of 1974. "In a twelve month span, the government intervened to restrain exports, acted to discontinue all restraints, and then intervened again" (Seevers, "Food Policy: Implications," p. 273). A number of programs had been developed under conditions of farm surpluses including direct subsidies, differential pricing, and extension of low-cost credit. Seevers writes about the limitations of these policies:

> Periodic interventions to restrict imports . . . have had very disruptive market effects. The limitations of using this approach to achieve domestic objectives are many. Such steps are often contrary to a liberal trade policy; actions tend to be disruptive not only to domestic markets but also markets abroad. Even if only domestic objectives are considered, the lags between problem recognition, making a decision to act, and the impact of the action are sufficiently long that the effect on domestic markets is often untimely. As the problems with ad hoc actions to influence trade flows are recognized, the propensity to use trade measures for short-term domestic purposes has diminished. (Seevers, "Food Policy: Implications," p. 274)

In the same paper Seevers argues that a movement toward multilateral trade liberalization would be the most effective method of providing stability to commodity markets; he was particularly critical of the 1976 U.S. bilateral grain agreements with Poland and the USSR. Not only was the most favored nation principle violated, but in addition "a new rigidity into trade flows" was introduced by committing purchases to a narrow range of tons per year.

Consistent with these views, in an analysis of the distributive effects, and the costs and benefits, both to the agricultural sector and to the country of Nixon's New Economic Policy (NEP), his approval of the flexible exchange rate system inaugurated by the Smithsonian Agreement was predicated on its trade liberalizing effects. Since agricultural prices, as Seevers points out, are determined by domestic programs, exchange rate flexibility would not affect agricultural markets. The NEP, however, also included a commitment to promote trade nego tiations (Tokyo Round), presenting an opportunity to liberalize trade in agriculture.

In reviewing the changes in agricultural markets from 1972 to 1975, Seevers contrasts this period, in which domestic instability and the interaction between government policy and market fluctuations were the major sources of market instability, with the period before 1972, when export markets provided the main source of market instability. The rapidity of the changes and the uncertainties produced by policy makers unfamiliar with altered market conditions compounded the problem of restoring stability. Added to these factors were the competing concerns of interest groups, for example, consumers, that had not been particularly concerned with food policy prior to 1972. Although Seevers believes that the unusual circumstances underlying the events of this period are unlikely to be repeated, among the consequences are an appreciation of the importance of more accurate data and improved data gathering techniques. Since he chaired the Committee on Economic Statistics, which was organized to review existing procedures and to develop methods of improvement in the collection and organization of economic data, Seevers had first-hand knowledge of the dimensions of this problem. Janet Norwood and Julius Shiskin, statisticians at the U.S. Bureau of Labor Statistics, and Edgar Fiedler, Assistant Secretary, U.S. Department of the Treasury, served on the committee. The eminent statistician Karl A. Fox was a consultant.

Another consequence of the volatility of commodity price changes in this period was an increasing reliance on the futures markets as a method of hedging. A grain reserves policy and grain price supports remain unresolved issues, Seevers asserted. When he spoke before the New York Association of Business Economists, Seevers advocated cooperative efforts by the United States to institute an international reserve system.

The supply shocks of 1973–74, which resulted in increases not only in food prices but also in prices of materials like zinc and copper, had a concomitant effect on the commodity futures market. Speculative activity increased considerably as new investors were attracted to commodity markets. The requirements for hedging by producers in volatile markets, especially in grain futures, contributed to record trading volumes. Congress, concerned about regulation in these markets, passed the Commodity Futures Trading Commission Act of 1974, which established the Commodity Future Trading Commission (CFTC) and transferred regulatory control from the Commodity Exchange Authority in the Department of Agriculture. Gary Seevers was one of the five commissioners appointed for a four-year term to the new agency, which came into existence on April 31, 1975; he resigned his position on the Council.

Because he is convinced of the importance of economic analysis in regulatory work, and noting the influence of government regulation in the operation of the economy, Seevers urges economists to give more attention to regulatory research, pointing out that the analysis of both regulation and deregulation was a major activity of the CEA when he was a member. Most regulatory agencies employ a legalistic approach, that is, enforcement, which is a short-term perspective. Economists, in contrast, provide the framework for determining the costs and benefits of regulation. There is a larger proportion of economists in the CFTC than in any other regulatory agency. In "A Regulator's Perspective of Regulatory Research," Seevers offers a list of some of the questions that would be posed in an economic approach to regulation:

(a) Is regulation really necessary, or will competition provide satisfactory performance?

(b) If a regulation is justified, would it be better done by industry self regulation?

(c) How much burden will the regulation impose on those being regulated?

(d) Is the regulation enforceable and at what cost?

(e) Does it provide economic incentives to achieve the desired objective?

(f) Does it provide useful information to the buyer or beneficiary of the regulation?

(g) Will it actually contribute to the objective being sought, or does it only give the appearance of contributing?

(h) How will it affect industry structure and competitive incentives among firms? (p. 788)

Because results are not immediate, the economic approach is often perceived to be more expensive than the legalistic approach. Actually, administering and enforcing regulations are more costly.

Seevers is concerned that commodity futures and the role of futures in producing, processing, and distributing commodities are not understood outside the financial community. Markets in futures contracts provide information inexpensively, promote competition, and permit the transfer of risk from producer to speculator. Speculative activity, in his opinion, is also poorly understood. Seevers discusses the role of futures in the international grain market. Since there are no significant grain futures markets outside of the United States, the conduct and regulation of markets here are the major determinants of the production and distribution of world grain.

Seevers was appointed acting chairman of the CFTC following the resignation of William Bagley in November 1978. The *New York Times* headline on March 21, 1979, "A Vacationing Seevers Leads Battle Over Wheat," referred to his efforts to stop the last three days of trading in March futures on the Chicago Board of Trade. When reached by telephone, Seevers said that the case would be appealed because the commission regarded it as a critical issue.

When Seevers resigned his position on the commission effective June 1, 1979, the articles in major newspapers were unanimous in their assessment of his effectiveness.

At the time of his resignation he was being considered for renomination to another four-year term. There was also considerable support in Congress for his appointment to chair the commission. He had, however, been appointed in a Republican administration, although he considers himself a political independent. James Stone, a former Massachusetts insurance commissioner, was given the post. An editorial in a recent issue of the *Journal of Commerce* lauded the work of the CFTC and pointed to its increasing prestige.

Seevers joined Goldman, Sachs & Company in June 1979 as a vice president in the commodities department, a position he holds presently. The department serves institutional and corporate customers that use futures markets for trading, hedging, and investment purposes.

BIBLIOGRAPHY

Mayer, Leo V., and Seevers, Gary. "Food Policy Issues in the United States." *American Journal of Agricultural Economics* 56 (May 1974): 359–63.

Seevers, Gary. "The Cost of Food Aid to Recipient Countries." *American Journal of Agricultural Economics* 51 (December 1969): 1588–92.

———. "An Evaluation of the Disincentive Effects Caused by PL 480 Shipments." *American Journal of Agricultural Economics* 50 (August 1968): 630–42.

———. "Food Policy: Implications for the Food Industry." *American Journal of Agricultural Economics* 58 (May 1976): 270–76.

———. "A Regulator's Perspective of Regulatory Research." *American Journal of Agricultural Economics* 59 (November 1979): 787–90.

HARRIET MORRIS HINCK

SMITH, WARREN LOUNSBURY

(b. March 23, 1914, d. April 23, 1972), CEA July 1, 1968-January 20, 1969

Warren L. Smith served as a member of the Council of Economic Advisers under President Lyndon B. Johnson from July 1, 1968, to January 20, 1969. As an academic economist whose career spanned two decades, he became a well-known international authority on monetary theory, economic stabilization policies, and banking. His research focused on the macroeconomic structure, primarily from the point of view of the public sector at the federal level.

Smith was born in Watertown, New York, in 1914, to Burt W. and Fannie Sylvia (Allen) Smith. After receiving his high school diploma, he was employed in the accounting office of the General Electric Company in Schenectady, New York, until 1940, when he matriculated at the University of Michigan. His studies there were interrupted by the outbreak of World War II; he entered the Army Air Corps in 1942, serving as a weather observer in the European theater. Upon his release from the service in 1945, Smith returned to the University of Michigan, earning a B.A. in 1947, an M.A. in 1949, and a Ph.D. in 1952.

Smith's academic career began and ended at the University of Michigan, Ann Arbor. He was instructor of economics there from 1952 to 1953. He later accepted a position as assistant professor at the University of Virginia (1953–56), and moved to Ohio State as associate professor (1956–57). He returned to the University of Michigan as full professor of economics in 1957, a position he occupied until his death in 1972. He was a visiting lecturer at Harvard, 1958–59, and served as chairman of the economics department at Michigan from 1963 to 1968 and in 1970–71. He was a member of the board of editors of the *American Economic Review* (1968–70). Smith's professional memberships included the American Economic Association, the Econometric Society, and the Finance Association.

On numerous occasions Smith acted as a consultant to agencies of the federal government, among them the Federal Reserve Bank of Richmond, Virginia (1953–56); the Joint Economic Committee of Congress (1959–60); the Commission on Money and Credit (1960–61); the Anti-Trust Division of the U.S. Department of Justice (1961–63); and the U.S. Department of the Treasury (1961–68).

When James S. Duesenberry* returned to Harvard after two and one-half years on the CEA, President Johnson named Smith as his replacement. He had previously served as a consultant to several federal monetary agencies, and also as a senior staff member of the CEA (1962–63). Smith, upon Congressional approval of Johnson's nomination, became a member of the CEA during a period when that agency began to play a more active role than previously in the direction of national economic affairs, especially in the area of price-wage relationships. The CEA was also considerably more aggressive in pursuing economic equality and an end to poverty during Smith's tenure than it was to be later.

In the decade before his service on the CEA, Smith had consistently recommended a more diversified and flexible approach to economic stabilization. In March 1959, for example, in an address given before the American Assembly at Duke University, he argued that fiscal policy could more efficiently achieve a desirable balance of economic growth and structural stability than could monetary policy operating through Federal Reserve controls. By the 1960s, Smith was increasingly concerned with the problem of maintaining economic growth in a full employment economy without exacerbating the burden of inflation. He continued to argue that monetary policy was the weakest tool in the economist's arsenal, but in testimony before the Joint Economic Committee of Congress in February 1960 he expressed misgivings about the efficacy of recent fiscal policies as well. Smith remained critical of Congressional fiscal policy until the time of his appointment to the CEA.

By early 1969, the mandate of the CEA, established by the Employment Act of 1946 "to promote maximum employment, production, and purchasing power," seemed within reach in the areas of productivity and employment—GNP had risen by $71 billion between 1968 and 1969, and unemployment, at 3.6 percent, was at a fifteen-year low. The economy, however, was the victim of an overenthusiastic buoyancy of consumption. The inflationary pressures of excessive consumer demand and rising wages had pushed the Consumer Price Index (CPI) up by what was considered an unacceptable 4 percent, and interest rates had also increased sharply—the prime rate stood at about 7.25 percent and conventional mortgage rates were about 7 percent in 1969 as compared to 5 percent and 6.25 percent, respectively, in 1960.

While the general erosion of purchasing power was a persistent problem in the late sixties, it was more of an annoyance than a hardship for the majority of Americans. The same cannot be said, however, for the approximately 11 percent of the population (22 million people) that was poor. While it was true that there had been a sizable reduction in the sheer numbers of the poor since the end of World War II (figures for 1948 indicate that 30 percent, or about 42 million, were below the poverty line in that year), Democratic economic presuppositions held that there were still too many poor Americans. The main problem for national economic policy in 1968–69, then, was how to restrain inflationary tendencies without reducing economic growth in the context of a massive, ongoing antipoverty program.

The recommendation of the CEA for 1969 was liberal-Keynesian—"fine tune" the economy by decelerating the growth of demand to a rate less than the capacity for growth of the economy as a whole while still providing enough demand impetus to maintain expansion. The evaluation of economic performance in 1968 led the CEA to propose a policy for stabilization that moved in the direction of a more flexible monetary policy that Smith had suggested in the early sixties. Also in line with Smith's policy recommendations of the early sixties was the CEA proposal for a more vigorous executive initiative in employing federal taxation as a stabilization tool. Simple adjustment of government nondefense expenditure (only about 10 percent of the GNP) could hardly be expected to be an effective method of achieving ideal allocation of resources between public and private sectors; stabilization required a more potent means of affecting economic decisions in the private sector. That means, the CEA believed, was taxation.

In fact, the CEA had advised President Johnson to raise taxes in 1966 to counter a sharp rise in the annual rate of increase of the CPI of 1.2 percent (a fluctuation of the rate of increase of 71 percent since 1965). Johnson, fearing a conservative counteroffensive that would seek reduction of expenditures for his Great Society programs, was reluctant to reverse the fiscal policy initiated by President Kennedy's proposed tax cut in 1963. Nevertheless, Johnson had moved, however reluctantly, in the direction of a tighter fiscal policy in the latter half of 1966. He proposed the weak and ineffectual Tax Adjustment Act (passed by Congress), and in November a temporary suspension of the investment tax credit was instituted. Twice in 1967 Johnson proposed an income tax surcharge—first 6 percent (in January) and than 10 percent (in August). Congress did not pass the surcharge until June 1968 and insisted on a concurrent $6 billion reduction in governmental expenditures, the bulk of which came out of the budgets of Great Society programs.

The dilemma, even for a more efficient and integrated monetary-fiscal policy in the late sixties, thus was clear. The difficulty arose out of the reciprocal relationship between prices and unemployment. Smith and his liberal Keynesian colleagues on the CEA, however, did not believe that price stability could only be achieved through a decline in productivity and a rise in unemployment. In their view, inflation was fueled by a tendency for wage increases to exceed productivity gains and for prices to rise proportionally to offset rising labor costs. A traditional solution to this dilemma was the institution of mandatory wage and price controls, but these were considered unattractive as "incompatible with a free enterprise economy . . . a last resort appropriate only in an extreme emergency such as all-out war." The best approach, it was believed, was to reinstitute the voluntary wage-price guideposts established by the CEA in 1962, but on a more integrated, cooperative basis. Instead of the guideposts being determined by governmental initiative, as had been the case between 1962 and 1965, labor and business would play a more direct role in the process of economic self-regulation, chiefly through the Labor-Management Advisory Committee.

This groping, tentative domestic economic policy, which was essentially ineffective in combatting the rise of inflation—the CPI increased by 1.5 percent between 1969 and 1970—was further complicated by external economic difficulties. The main problem with international economic organization was that the Bretton Woods system, developed in 1944 to provide the machinery for international monetary stability, had become increasingly dysfunctional by the late 1960s. The postwar economy had been predicated upon a number of assumptions about world and American economic growth that had proven to be inaccurate. It had been assumed that full employment would be a primary goal of all national economic policies, and that this end could be achieved largely through domestic fiscal and monetary policies. It was further assumed that full employment and economic growth could be achieved without drastic price increases, and that, for the most part, chronic deflation or inflation could be avoided. The heart of the system was the U.S. dollar. It was both the principal reserve currency and the standard of value for other world currencies. The technical term for this arrangement was the "gold exchange standard." It was imperative to the smooth functioning of the system that the dollar hold a constant relationship to gold—a parity of $35 per ounce—so that other nations would feel secure holding dollar reserves in place of gold.

But the Bretton Woods system had been effectually undermined by two unforeseen developments. The first was the continual rise in the American balance of payments deficit from the early 1950s to the late 1960s, a function of the international economic situation, while the second was the result of domestic failures in the struggle to curb inflation both in the United States and abroad. In this area, too, the CEA proposals were moderate and grew out of an optimistic belief that the system was basically sound and with a little judicious tinkering might be set right. Their proposals for international economic adjustment essentially followed the same laissez-faire, free-trade direction as their domestic policy recommendations. Specifically, they recommended reducing overseas defense expenditures by giving preference to domestic manufactures and linking foreign aid to increased purchases by recipients in the United States. In the face of mounting pressures to opt for a "floating" exchange rate system to replace the pegged exchange rate based on the U.S. dollar as a standard, the CEA chose stability over flexibility, and only very tentatively moved toward a sliding parity or "crawling peg" system that would allow the par value in terms of the dollar of a given nondollar currency to respond to the international balance of payments situation in small increments on a periodic basis. Smith's influence on the direction of the CEA's thinking on the problem of the international monetary system, and his own uncertainty about the potentially best long-term policy to pursue in this area, are quite clear here.

In the context of an essentially healthy economy, even one that was engaged in an expensive war in Southeast Asia, the CEA shared Smith's optimism that minor adjustments would cure any petty ailments, and that the economy was strong enough to continue along essentially Keynesian lines. The CEA, therefore, went beyond mere passive consent to the crusade against poverty that was the cornerstone of Johnson's Great Society programs and recommended the use of economic tools to effectively eliminate poverty. This revolutionary proposal to use economic policy to achieve social change was embedded in a four-part strategy. The first element of the proposed program, its prime necessity, was sustained high employment coupled with economic growth. In fact, this was more of an assumed precondition of any program to reduce poverty than an integral element in such a program. It was the sine qua non of an attack on poverty, and the difficulties that inflation had increasingly posed to its continued realization threatened to undermine any antipoverty strategy from the outset. The essential optimism of Smith and his colleagues on the CEA, however, convinced them that inflationary pressures could be substantially reduced and the process of social reform via economic policy could go on apace. Consequently, the second point in their proposed program against poverty was to provide greater access for the poor to education, training, medical care, and better-paying, more stable jobs. Third, they proposed to promote public and private investment in poverty areas and to provide relocation assistance to those who found work elsewhere. Finally, in an effort to strike at the roots of hard-core poverty, the CEA recommended income redistribution and an income maintenance program for those who, because of age, disability, family responsibilities, and so on, could not earn enough on their own to pull themselves out of poverty. But the emphasis was less on a specific program than on continued commitment.

In the course of his scholarly career, Warren Smith wrote several volumes, but the most important were his revision of the orthodox economic theory of Earl Rolph in his seminal study of debt management for the Joint Economic Committee of Congress (1960), and his introductory text in macroeconomics (1970). The basic argument Smith set forth in *Debt Management in the United States* is that techniques for the reduction and stabilization of the publicly held debt (held by households, business firms, commercial banks, and other financial institutions) are auxiliary tools that can be used to complement traditional fiscal and monetary policies. It might be more accurate to say, however, that debt management, as defined by Smith, really consists of a combination of fiscal and monetary policy directed toward the regulation of outstanding federal securities of a specific kind. For debt management comprises all Treasury decisions on what new securities shall be issued and how maturing securities should be refunded as well as Federal Reserve decisions concerning the types of securities it will purchase or sell in open market operations. Clearly, debt management can serve as a complementary tool to the Federal Reserve's setting of discount rates and federal taxation of expenditure as a means of influencing interest rates and achieving economic stability.

Smith suggests that if the federal government wields the club of debt management more vigorously, it will be more effective in achieving economic growth and stability. In effect, what he proposes is that the federal government cease to play the role of a nun in a bordello, maintaining standards for those whose profits depend on the existence of transcendent criteria of behavior that limit competition and raise the value of their wares. Instead, the Treasury and Federal Reserve should themselves imitate business practices, should become more businesslike in their debt management policies. This would require a reversal of traditional methods of operation. The Treasury, for example, instead of relying on "market professionals" (including life insurance companies and savings and loan institutions) in deciding on the nature and extent of securities to be offered, should make an independent and extensive survey to determine where investment money is and how it might best be attracted. Less reliance on the opinions of potential investors would make Treasury debt management policy more flexible and more responsive to overall market conditions.

Flexibility is the key to Smith's proposals for debt management and is the element in his system that provides the basis for its wider applicability in achieving sustained economic growth and stability. Smith's theory of debt management not only provides a means to influence the interest, rate structure and the allocation of credit, but allows for a more selective use of economic controls. Thus, during inflationary periods, controls might be initiated (by repealing the interest rate ceiling, for example) against the most inflationary sectors of the economy—for Smith these include consumer credit, housing, and bank lending—without affecting other economic sectors. Smith's economic philosophy is quite clear here. In contrast to those who hold that the role of the federal government should be that of a neutral, honest broker—a minimalist position, or "minimum intervention—Smith favors expanding the role of government intervention in the economic process by increasing the area of discretion open to federal economic decision makers through dependence on the most flexible tool for manipulating the economic structure—debt management. In this neo-Keynesian vision, the role of government includes not simply the general power to control the total supply of money and credit, but, more important, the ability, through "intelligent selectivity," to fine tune the economy by changing policies applicable to certain areas of the economy while leaving others alone. Smith's theory stands as a refinement of federal technique that promised to make policy more responsive to economic stability through its ability to independently influence discrete sectors of the economy. But the notion of selective credit controls has not found widespread acceptance in practice, probably because it runs counter to the liberal ideology of the free operation of the open marketplace.

Smith's other major work, *Macroeconomics*, also takes an inductive approach to economic analysis. It focuses on the central sectors of the economy—household, business, government, and so on—developing an explanation for each and then combining these sector models to explain the behavior of the economy as a whole. Again, Smith's primary goals for the American economy remain growth, stability, and full employment, which can best be judged, he feels, in terms of the "progressive improvement of living standards." Ideally, he believes this would be achieved with a level of 4 percent unemployment and 2 percent inflation. Smith's primary concerns here remain those of an economic liberal, and his broad approach to economic problems is neo-Keynesian. His critique of the Keynesian system, however, emphasizes his belief that the role of government in the economy should be both more positive and more businesslike. The basic shortcoming of Keynesian analysis, from Smith's point of view, is that it fails to consider the impact of investment on productive capacity. Keynes' system, therefore, provides an inadequate model for analyzing economic growth. Smith's reworking of Keynesian thought emphasizes the role of public policy decisions in economic growth.

Smith's economic liberalism, which sought to achieve basic humanitarian social goals through positive but flexible governmental planning, and which emphasized the role of public direction of the private sector on the supply side of the economy, stands as the culmination of neo-Keynesian thinking in America. When Smith died in 1972, the gradual withdrawal of the federal government from an active economic role was already under way; the wave of New Deal social and economic reform had broken during Johnson's administration on the shoals of the Vietnam War and spiralling inflation, and a movement toward reduced governmental involvement in the economy began under President Nixon. That movement would culminate in the so-called supply-side economics or minimalism of the Reagan administration, which is the direct antithesis of Smith's neo-Keynesian model. Had Smith and his liberal colleagues been able to formulate a program to effectively bring inflation under control, it might have been possible for them to realize their visions of an equitable society in the context of economic growth and stability. Liberal failure to control the juggernaut of inflation, however, insured the decline of their influence, disenchantment with their ideals, and the triumph of more conservative social and economic visions.

BIBLIOGRAPHY

Calleo, David. *The Imperious Economy*. Cambridge, Mass.: Harvard University Press, 1982.

Smith, Warren L. *Debt Management in the United States*. Washington, D.C.: Government Printing Office, 1960.

———. *Macroeconomics*. Homewood, Ill.: Irwin, 1970.

LOUIS J. KERN

SOLOMON, EZRA
(b. March 20, 1920), CEA September 9, 1971-March 26, 1973

Ezra Solomon was a member of the Council of Economic Advisers during the administration of President Richard M. Nixon from September 9, 1971, to March 26, 1973. He is a noted international authority on finance, corporate management, and macroeconomic theory whose academic career has spanned nearly four decades. His research has primarily focused on domestic monetary and financial theory, the mechanics of interest rates, and the institutional dimensions of investment.

Solomon was born a British citizen in Rangoon, Burma, in 1920, son of Ezra and Emily (Rose) Solomon. He received his early education in Rangoon schools, where he became fluent in Burmese. In 1940 he took his B.A. degree with honors from the University of Rangoon. When Burma was overrun by the Japanese in December 1942, Solomon fled with his family to India, where he joined the Royal Navy Volunteer Reserve, Burma Division. He saw four years of active service as commander of a gunboat and attained the rank of lieutenant. After the war, he remained in the inactive Naval Reserve for another two years. In 1947 he was awarded a graduate fellowship for overseas study as a Burma State Scholar and chose to do his advanced work at the University of Chicago, from which he received his Ph.D. in 1950.

Solomon began his academic career as an instructor of economics at the University of Chicago between 1948 and 1951. He progressed through the academic ranks at Chicago, becoming an assistant professor of finance in 1951 and an associate professor in 1955, and serving as full professor there from 1957 to 1961. In the latter year, he was invited to come to Stanford University as the founding director for a new International Center for the Advancement of Management Education, a position which he held until 1964. He held a concurrent full-time teaching appointment as Dean Witter Professor of Finance in the Graduate Business School.

During a distinguished career, Solomon has also held visiting professorships in twelve foreign countries and has acted as an economic consultant to governmental agencies and private industries both in the United States and abroad. In the private sector, his more important clients included Wertheim and Company, Inc.; the United Finance Corporation; Kaiser Aluminum and Chemical Corporation; S-G Securities, Inc.; the Encyclopaedia Britannica; and the New York brokerage firm, Shearson, Hammill and Company. Prior to his nomination to the CEA, Solomon had served as a member of the Presidential Commission on Financial Structure and Regulation, chaired by Reed O. Hunt, chairman of the Crown Zellerbach Corporation. Solomon has also been active over two decades as an academic editor. His editorial credits include a term as editor of the *Journal of Business* (1953–57) and service as a member of the board of editors of the *Journal of Finance* (1965–66; 1969–72) and the *Journal of Quantitative and Financial Analysis* (1969–71).

A naturalized American citizen (1951), Solomon is an urbane man with a keen sense of humor. He has been a consistent supporter of a free market approach to economic adjustment both domestically and internationally, and has been reluctant to have government interfere in price and wage decisions, which he feels are best left to the private sector. In his politics, he tends to be moderate to moderate-conservative. He married Janet Lorraine Cameron in 1949, and they have three daughters, Catherine Shan, Janet Ming, and Lorna Cameron. Solomon, a member of the American Economic Association and the American Finance Association, remains Dean Witter Professor of Finance at Stanford and maintains a residence on campus.

On July 15, 1971, when Hendrik S. Houthakker* resigned from the CEA, President Nixon nominated Solomon as his replacement. His appointment was confirmed on July 17. Solomon's tenure in office (September 1971-March 1973) corresponded to a period of some crisis for the CEA. As an arm of the executive branch, the CEA came under increasing fire from academic economists for not maintaining professional integrity and independence, and for excessive politicization. While it is certainly true that the CEA (a body of professional advisers that is an integral part of the president's administration but that has no connection to any cabinet department) has always played a dual role—part advisement, part explanation of administrative policy decisions—its political activities became less restrained in 1972–73. This may help to explain why, apart from the natural dynamism of his personality, Solomon was more publicly visible than some of the previous members of the CEA. And yet, while Solomon played an important role in the political presence of the CEA in these years, the preeminent force behind its increased politicization seems to have been its chairman, Herbert Stein*. It was Stein who provided a new, more aggressive role for the Council by instituting a policy of providing a monthly commentary, at full-scale press conferences, on price and employment statistics as they were made public. He also set an example of political involvement for the other members of the Council by openly campaigning for Richard Nixon against George McGovern in the 1972 electoral contest.

Solomon's service on the CEA also came at a time of increasing economic difficulty for the United States. By the middle 1960s the United States was pursuing economic policies whose goals were contradictory—domestic economic expansion and international financial integration. The cumulative effect of these policies was a rising net outflow of dollars to the international market—an American balance of payments deficit; economic overextension. Numerous ingenious and largely ineffectual measures were employed to curb the growth of dollar holdings abroad. "Operation Twist," one such measure, sought to equate U.S. short-term interest rates with world rates while depressing U.S. long-term interest rates. It was hoped that such a policy would prevent the outward flow of dollars while promoting domestic investment in housing and industry. In the long run, despite such measures, the U.S. situation grew worse, and it became more and more apparent that American economic power was no longer sufficient to allow it to run the world alone. Consequently, the Bretton Woods system, which had been the keystone of the international economy since the end of World War II, was progressively weakened until it collapsed under accumulated structural stress in 1971. The U.S. officially suspended indefinitely the right of foreign central banks to convert their holdings of dollars to gold on demand, and the era of American international economic hegemony came to an end. Actually, as Solomon made clear in his retrospective consideration of economic developments in the decade 1963–73, the Bretton Woods system did not die a sudden, violent death, but expired gradually from a lingering illness. He denied that the United States was passing through a crisis and preferred to see the post–Bretton Woods era as a major date in American economic history, as important as that marked by the end of the war.

In the course of Solomon's CEA confirmation hearings before the Senate Banking and Currency Committee on June 16, 1971, he stated that he felt the dollar to be overvalued, and suggested that the United States, while still maintaining the gold standard, should allow the value of the dollar to float relative to other world currencies. He also expressed himself in favor of avoiding formal wage and price controls if possible. Solomon thus indicated his concurrence with the broad outlines of what has come to be called the ''New Economic Policy'' or the ''Nixon Revolution.'' The New Economic Policy, initiated on August 15, 1971, involved devaluation and flotation of the dollar; a temporary 10 percent surcharge on imports; a ninety-day freeze on domestic wages, rents, and prices; and a concurrent federal expenditure and tax cut.

During his first six months on the CEA, Solomon's major responsibilities were concentrated in the areas of international trade and finance, foreign aid, price behavior, technology, energy, housing, and urban problems. Solomon's policy responsibilities thus overlapped with the most urgent economic problems of the decade—inflation, unemployment, and the American balance of payments deficit. As Solomon and his CEA colleagues saw the health of the American economy in 1971, U.S. economic planners were faced with a dilemma. They could opt either to accelerate the pace of American economic growth, thus raising employment, or they could undertake measures to achieve price stability that might bring inflation under control, and in the long term reduce the balance of payments deficit. On the whole, Solomon chose the latter course. In domestic matters, he became a supporter of the wage-price freeze as a means of economic stabilization. When it became apparent in November 1971 that the temporary freeze had not permanently arrested the inflationary trend, Solomon advocated the President's Phase II policy, which established a system of self-administered, mandatory price-wage guidelines that allowed the maximum operation of the free market economy.

Solomon's philosophical preference for free market operations, however, led him to predict an early end to mandatory controls. Indeed, in the area of energy policy, he felt that price regulation in the natural gas industry was detrimental both to total available supplies and to the maintenance of efficient pollution standards. Since a price ceiling on one kind of fuel only led to increased demand for other varieties and a consequent rise in their prices, the net effect of regulated gas prices was to increase the consumer's energy bill. Solomon therefore recommended deregulation of gas prices. In the area of pollution, he proposed a sliding scale of effluent fees or pollution emission charges rather than a uniform standard because it would maximize free market operations in that area. Each source of pollution would be able to rationally assess the utility of compliance with federal standards. For those sources where the abatement costs were low, there would be a maximum of pollution control, which might well exceed a uniformly established standard. In essence, a cost-benefit analysis would be undertaken to determine the degree of compliance—pollution abatement would be undertaken only up to a cost equal to the charge for noncompliance.

In accordance with his preconfirmation pronouncements, Solomon firmly supported President Nixon's New Economic Policy in its international aspects. Suspension of convertibility and floating the dollar seemed ideal ways to achieve the traditional economic liberalism in international trade for which Solomon stood. In the 1970s such policies would clearly contribute to promoting a worldwide economic ''Open Door Policy'' based on free exchange; they embodied Solomon's desire to spread the benefits of the American system—the free operation of a market economy—to the rest of the world. As it was expressed in the *1972 Annual Report* of the CEA, the long-term goal of U.S. international economic policy was ''an open world economy in which trade and investment flows among countries are not distorted by national barriers to free exchange.'' Such a policy would help to solve domestic as well as international economic difficulties, for ''international exchange permits mutually beneficial specialization in production among countries; it provides healthy competition to ensure efficiency in domestic industries; it expands the variety of goods available to U.S. consumers and purchasers; and in times of inflation it provides a wholesome brake on price increases,'' (pp. 164–165).

Although Solomon remained committed to and continued to work for the broad goals of the New Economic Policy throughout the remainder of his CEA service, the Council's division of labor for 1972 shifted his responsibilities from a primarily international to a domestic concentration. His main work for the CEA during 1972 focused on national growth policy, domestic fiscal and monetary policy, taxation, defense, and manpower programs. Given the relatively pessimistic tone of the Council's 1972 *Report*, its 1973 edition was remarkably sanguine. Gone were the nagging doubts about the possibility of achieving concurrent economic growth and stability. The greater optimism in 1973 arose out of the belief that the wage-price controls and Phase II had effectively brought the rate of inflation under control and restored the economic faith of the nation.

Therefore, consumer spending could be confidently expected to rise, and with increased demand creating a pull on manufactures, healthy economic growth, characterized by an absence of debilitating inflation, could go on apace. "The principal question on the economic outlook for 1973," it was asserted, "is not whether, but how fast, output and employment will expand." Policy recommendations for 1973, therefore, sought to "eliminate the vestiges of the post–1965 inflation and to place the economy squarely on a sustainable path of subsequent non-inflationary growth.

But such a rosy forecast was purchased at the expense of ignoring some of the more glaring American socioeconomic problems of the decade. The Council's 1973 *Annual Report* and, indeed, the work of its members both individually and collectively during the preceding year, came under withering public attack by other professional economists. The first salvo was fired by Carl F. Christ of Johns Hopkins University in the *American Economic Review*. Critics pointed out the disingenuousness of the CEA and again questioned the professional integrity of its members in the light of the partisan tone of the economic analysis in the 1973 *Annual Report*. The consensus among economists in the fall of 1973 held the Nixon administration responsible for continuing inflation, and faulted the administration's advisers on the CEA for having failed to accurately predict the effects of its major international and domestic economic decisions. The prediction that devaluation of the dollar would lead to parity and stability in the international economy had clearly been inept in light of the fact that a second devaluation had been required in 1973. The effectiveness of the price control policy was certainly not as permanent as the CEA *Report* claimed either, since shortly after the controls were removed or relaxed another price explosion ensued. Indeed, under the wage-price control structure, the annual percentage increase in the CPI had been reduced by one point between 1971 and 1972. When controls were lifted in 1973, the CPI rose by 4.2 points to reach the highest inflationary level of the decade 1964–73: an 8.2 percent annual increase. In sharp contrast to the CEA, many professional economists concluded that the price control system had acted merely as a passing phase affecting short-run inflationary expectations. The sharpest criticism of the CEA and its *Report*, however, focused on the Council's willful oversights that made its perceptions of the American economy fabulous, rather like those of the blind men of the elephant. The *Report*, it was maintained, omitted any sustained consideration of unemployment, poverty, and the special economic problems facing black Americans. Other harassing problems that received short shrift in 1972 included welfare programs, tax reform, environmental protection, energy development, and health care.

In part, such criticisms reflected the frustration of disillusioned liberals who saw the ravages of decade-long inflation consuming the social gains of the New Deal welfare state structure. But there was substance to this critique as well. Solomon and his CEA colleagues were saying that economic priorities would have to be shifted; in the jargon of the day, there would have to be a tradeoff—a higher rate of unemployment would have to be accepted in return for greater price stability and higher production. In this context, Solomon was attacked by the liberal Senator William Proxmire (D-Wis.), chairman of the Joint Economic Committee, as a propagandist for the Nixon administration. Proxmire disputed Solomon's putative claim that it would be a mistake in 1972 to try to get unemployment down to 4 percent. In his reply, Solomon pointed out that he had actually said that the use of expansive monetary and fiscal policies to get unemployment down to 4 percent "could be a mistake in today's context." He would later suggest, in fact, in the 1973 CEA *Report* that a 4.5 percent unemployment rate would not be an unreasonable goal (the rate remained 5.6 percent for 1972, but dipped to 4.9 percent in 1973).

The key to Solomon's approach to domestic economic policy was cost-effectiveness. His discussion of such matters as social services programs and employment in terms of economic utility made him seem inhumane to some of his critics. Concurring with administration policy, for instance, Solomon recommended a policy of reducing federal expenditures rather than raising taxes as a means to achieve a balanced budget and a modified full employment economy by 1974. Since the largest increases in governmental expenditures between 1955 and 1971 had been for health, education, and welfare programs, it was precisely here that the axe must fall. Cutbacks would prevail until economic recovery led to an expansion in federal revenue. His point was merely that Americans would have to choose; the prosperity and world economic dominance that had allowed the United States to do everything in the decade 1954–63 no longer prevailed. Changed economic realities necessitated some hard choices. One might well disagree with the direction in which Solomon thought American policy should proceed, or with the priorities he established, but to fail to recognize the necessity for curtailment of some economic goals if others were to be achieved was to cavil at the inevitable.

In the course of an extensive and distinguished scholarly career, Solomon has written numerous articles and books on financial management and banking as well as a few works for the more casual reader. Of his technical treatises, *The Theory of Financial Management* (1963) is probably the most widely known. It was an experimental work produced at the request of the Ford Foundation as part of a program to provide new directions in business education and has had a major impact on the management field both in the United States and abroad. The burden of the work, which has been employed as a text in many business programs, is to provide a normative management theory. In essence, Solomon argues that the traditional concentration solely on profit maximization is a distortion of the managerial function. The professional manager is a kind of middleman whose task is to balance the interests of society as a whole and those that exclusively pertain to the owners. The manager serves as a trustee for all parties associated with the enterprise—owners, creditors, customers, government, the general public, and management itself. The key to the modern managerial function is not profit maximization, although that is its precondition, but a much broader sphere of interrelated decisions about what to do with the value accrued through initial investment and financial decisions directed toward profit maximization.

Solomon's management theories remained consistent from the late 1950s to the late 1970s. They were grounded in his faith in a classical economic liberalism—the laissez-faire, free competition, open marketplace economy of Adam Smith. What was good for the few (corporate owners) in the short run would, in the long run, be socially and economically beneficial to the many (society as a whole). The function of the professional manager within the corporate structure, then, is first to ensure owners' profits, and secondarily to serve society as a whole through "value maximization," a decision-making criterion based on cash-flow analysis and compound interest principles. Value maximization achieves a beatific marriage of individual and social value, according to Solomon.

While Solomon's management theories had a salutary effect on business behavior, providing a theoretical basis for a corporate conscience (albeit of secondary importance to the profit motive), the same cannot be said, unfortunately, for the more extensive adoption of his new financial management techniques. For, when value maximization was applied, as Solomon suggested it might be, to nonprofit organizations—churches, hospitals, educational institutions, and federal, state, and local governments—his system was frequently distorted. Contrary to explicit caveats against allowing value maximization to become an end in itself rather than an auxiliary decision-making tool ("decision criterion"), nonprofit organizations forged ahead with cost-effectiveness, cost-benefit, and cash-flow analyses that led to cutting back many programs deemed financially irrational, ignoring Solomon's warning that social benefits are frequently difficult if not impossible to quantify. The result was ironic; while value maximization management techniques redeemed the corporate soul, it led many nonprofit organizations down the broad road to damnation. Despite Solomon's realization of the importance of qualitative criteria in the decision-making process of nonprofit organizations, his own attitude toward social service and public welfare projects during his term on the CEA was frequently conditioned by quantitative, cost-effectiveness considerations. In that sense, his managerial precepts, conscientiously and accurately followed, would have provided nonprofit organizations a more humane standard of social service than did his managerial practice as adviser to the president.

In his less technical writings, Solomon's preoccupation with the necessity for choice and the rational weighing of alternatives, an approach that might be called an existentialist economics, was equally prominent. His earliest general work was the fruit of a three-year research project sponsored by the Chicago Association of Commerce and Industry, a survey of industrialization in the greater Chicago area (including the Indiana steel mill region) that was published in 1960. This study, which focused on the period 1940–56, was prescient in its warning that the economy of the area was particularly vulnerable due to a high concentration of metal industries. The inherent instability of a one-product economy, he predicted, was only likely to worsen in the future, producing high levels of unemployment during periods of recession, a prophecy that has been vindicated by events in the 1980s. But in a prepublication interview, Solomon's faith in the rationality of a free market economy led him to affirm that this might be necessary in order to sustain our rate of growth and high levels of output and income.

Solomon's latest general work, *The Anxious Economy* (1975), is concerned with the epochal economic changes in the period 1955–75 that he feels constitute a "major watershed" in both the domestic and the international economies. Solomon believes that the economic problems associated with that watershed have produced an international economic angst and in many quarters an intellectual paralysis and pessimism that have been major stumbling blocks to reaching creative solutions. The major problems of these two decades are all interrelated and pivot around the central economic problem of the second half of the twentieth century—inflation. Worldwide recession, the irrationality and threat of breakdown in the international monetary system, rising interest rates, and shortages and consequent huge price increases for raw materials constitute the galaxy of problems that revolve about inflation. The bulk of the work, which is written in a very down-to-earth, straightforward style, provides a historical discussion of how these problems arose. But it is more than that. It is also a clarion call to Americans to recognize the interdependency of the world economy and to establish a rational set of economic priorities.

Solomon's predictions for the future of the American economy were right on target. He emphasized the irrevocable necessity of bringing governmental budget deficits under control as a precondition to ending inflation. He predicted that traditional Keynesian pump-priming activities designed to boost aggregate demand and stimulate productivity would be replaced by programs directed toward the supply side of the economy (especially in the areas of food and energy production). Encouragement of the supply side, he felt, would proceed through both positive and negative inducements to increased productivity. Finally, he predicted that the rapid rise in the percentage of funds flowing to the public or governmental sector at all levels would be halted. All in all, not a bad foreshadowing of the general course of Reaganomics!

Solomon's public career has been a distinguished one. He has consistently been a bellwether in both theoretical and applied economics. His presence and perspicacity while serving on the CEA led then Council chairman Herbert Stein to dub the two-year period of Solomon's tenure the "Phase Solomon." Solomon's personal optimism and belief in the ability of the American economy to recover from sustained and enervating inflation provided a beacon of hope amid despair. Yet he was no fatuous Polyanna; he was forthright about the decline in American economic power in the international economy and about the inability of the United States to do everything it wanted to do. He held up the glass so that those who wished to could see the real appearance of the American economy and would be able to make the hard and painful choices that might lead the economy out of the inflationary abyss. He was unpopular with many, especially doctrinaire liberals and those who could not believe that America was no longer economically omnipotent, but he consistently held his ground. Unfortunately, many who saw the wisdom of Solomon's economic analysis have been unable to employ his insights with flexibility and compassion. It remains to be seen whether Solomon's neoconservative economics can be wedded, as he himself suggested, to a more liberal social conscience to bring a more equitable and humane end to an era of corrosive inflation.

BIBLIOGRAPHY

Economic Report of the President. Washington D.C.: Government Printing Office, 1972.
Economic Report of the President. Washington, D.C.: Government Printing Office, 1973.
Solomon, Ezra, ed. *The Anxious Economy*. San Francisco: Freeman, 1975.
———. *The Management of Corporate Capital*. Glencoe, Ill.: The Free Press, 1959.
———, and Pringle, John. *An Introduction to Financial Management*. Santa Monica: Goodyear, 1977.

LOUIS J. KERN

SPRINKEL, BERYL WAYNE
(b. November 20, 1923), CEA April 21, 1985—

Beryl Wayne Sprinkel was born in 1923 near Richmond, Missouri. His parents, Clarence and Emma (Schooley) Sprinkel, were farmers in northwest Missouri. Sprinkel began his collegiate career at Northwest Missouri State University as a music major in 1941. Shortly thereafter he transferred to the University of Oregon, where, like so many young men of his generation, his college training was interrupted by World War II. From 1943 to 1945 Sprinkel served with the United States 3rd Army as a tank gunner in the 11th Armor Division. His rank upon release from the army was private first class.

After the war, Sprinkel renewed his education at the University of Missouri, where, after taking a course in economics with Pinckney Walker, he developed a taste for monetary theory. In 1947 Sprinkel received his B.S. degree in public administration from Missouri, and then in rapid succession the M.B.A. and Ph.D. in economics and finance from the University of Chicago in 1952. It was at the University of Chicago that Sprinkel developed his lifelong commitment to free market economics and monetarism. Besides his academic degrees, Sprinkel is a chartered financial analyst.

In September 1947 Sprinkel married his first wife, Esther Pollard, with whom he had three children, Dennis Wayne, Gary Lynn, and Kevin Glenn. After the end of his first marriage, in 1970, Sprinkel married Barbara Angus Pipher, with whom he has two stepchildren, Debra Pipher and Pamela Pipher.

Sprinkel's professional career began with instructorships in finance at the University of Missouri (1948–49) and the University of Chicago (1950–52). After obtaining his doctorate, Sprinkel began work as an economist with Harris Trust and Savings Bank in Chicago. His stay with Harris Bank lasted nearly thirty years, terminating with his appointment as Under Secretary of the Treasury for Monetary Affairs in 1981.

Within the Harris Bank Sprinkel was promoted to vice president and economist in 1960, director of research in 1963, and senior vice president and economist in 1968. From 1974 to 1981 he held the title of executive vice president. As executive vice president, Sprinkel was in charge of the Harris Bank's economic research office and served as a member of the bank's management, investment guidance, and trust investment committees.

Besides his research and committee responsibilities at the Harris Bank, Sprinkel and his colleagues also prepared and published *Harris Economics*, an economic and financial forecasting service, which included the "Sound of Business," an audio tape cassette program produced monthly. While at Harris Bank, Sprinkel was also a founding member of the Shadow Open Market Committee, an unofficial body that oversees Federal Reserve Bank monetary policy. Sprinkel left the bank in 1981 to serve as Under Secretary of the Treasury for Monetary Affairs, and on April 21, 1985, began serving as the chairman of the Council of Economic Advisers.

In addition to his various career posts, Sprinkel has also held a multitude of consulting positions with both private and public institutions. From 1955 to 1959 he worked with the Federal Reserve Board in Washington, D.C., and from 1962 to 1970 was a consultant to the Bureau of the Census. He served as a member of the Joint Economic Committee of the U.S. Congress on four separate occasions—1958, 1962, 1967, and 1971. During 1963 he worked with the House of Representatives Banking and Currency Committee. In 1975 he was a consultant for the Senate Banking Committee, and between 1967 and 1968 he was a member of the economic advisory board to the Secretary of Commerce. Sprinkel has also served as a board economist with *Time* magazine, as chairman of the Economic Advisory Committee of the American Bankers Association, and as a member of the board of directors with the U.S. Chamber of Commerce.

Sprinkel's literary output has centered mainly on monetary issues and the popularization of the monetarist view in macroeconomics. Besides contributing numerous articles to professional journals, he has authored *Money and Stock Prices* (1964) and *Money and Markets: A Monetarist View* (1971), and has coauthored with Robert Genetski *Winning with Money: A Guide for Your Future* (1977).

The theme emphasized by Sprinkel throughout these three books is that money matters, at least in terms of relative asset prices. For example, in *Money and Stock Prices* Sprinkel develops through line graphs and tabulations a technique of timing investment purchases and sales by analyzing monetary changes, business cycles, and stock market fluctuations over a forty-five-year period.

In *Money and Markets: A Monetarist View*, besides polarizing the "fiscalist" and "monetarist" macroeconomic perspectives, Sprinkel again attempts to improve the judgment of the investor by demonstrating the relationship between changes in the supply of money and security prices. And in *Winning with Money: A Guide for Your Future*, Sprinkel again argues how monetary policy affects relative changes in the prices of financial assets.

Sprinkel's professional memberships basically reflect his orientation as a business economist. He is a member of the American Financial Association, the American Statistical Association, the American Bankers Association, and the U.S. Chamber of Commerce. In addition, he is a fellow of the National Association of Business Economists and a member of Beta Gamma Sigma.

In recognition of his broad-based career in both the private and public sectors of American life, Sprinkel has been the recipient of many awards and honors. In 1964 he received from the University of Chicago its Alumni Leadership and Service Award; in 1968 he was awarded the Hamilton Bolton Prize by the Financial Analysis Association; and in 1971 he received from the University of Missouri a Merit Citation. Also, upon leaving the Treasury Department Sprinkel was awarded the Alexander Hamilton Award, the department's highest honor. In addition, he has received an honorary Doctor of Humane Letters degree from DePaul University and an honorary Doctor of Laws degree from St. Michael's College.

By the early 1980s, Sprinkel's Republican and monetarist views proved to be the right combination to be invited to join a presidential administration. With the election of Ronald Reagan as president in 1981, Sprinkel left Harris Bank and joined the Reagan administration as part of a troika brought into the Treasury Department by Treasury Secretary designate Donald Regan.

The other members of the Treasury team brought in by Regan were Norman Ture, a Washington economic consultant and supply sider who was to become Under Secretary for Tax Policy, and Paul Craig Roberts, another Washington economist and supply sider who was to become Assistant Secretary for Economic Policy. Before joining Treasury, Roberts was one of the main forces behind convincing Representative Jack Kemp to introduce a bill to cut personal income taxes by 30 percent.

The major thrust of the economic policy put forth by this Treasury team reflected the monetarist and supply-side orientation of its members. The three policies that were advocated for the national economy were lower marginal tax rates, less government, and greater stability in monetary growth. The intermediate goals of these three policies were to increase the rate of savings and investment in the United States, to expand the size of the private economy, and to stabilize the growth of national nominal income, the ultimate goal being to reinvigorate the U.S. economy.

Sprinkel's official title at Treasury was Under Secretary of Monetary Affairs, a position once held by Federal Reserve Chairman Paul Volcker in the early 1970s. As Under Secretary of Monetary Affairs, Sprinkel brought his monetarist and free market beliefs to play in fulfilling his responsibilities "for formulating and implementing U.S. international financial and credit policies; developing U.S. policy toward the international financial institutions; establishing Treasury financial policies; and coordinating the economic policies of the Administration with the monetary policies of the Federal Reserve" (Council of Economic Advisers biography on Sprinkel, May 1985).

Sprinkel's stay with Treasury was at times uproarious. His critics characterized him as blunt, pugnacious, and narrow-minded. Right from the beginning of Sprinkel's appointment as Under Secretary, he marched to a slightly different drummer. In 1981, while Ture, Roberts, and Regan were sounding the supply-side theme that marginal tax rate cuts would lead to a rapid and strong expansion in the macroeconomy, Sprinkel pushed the monetarist doctrine that in the short run a tightening of the money belt—a policy then being pursued by the Federal Reserve—would lead to a temporary contraction of the real economy. Sprinkel was proved correct.

As Under Secretary, Sprinkel emphasized four themes: (1) monetarism, (2) free market economics, (3) European economic policy, and (4) the international debt crisis. One of the more controversial monetary policies advocated by Sprinkel was that of restricting the independence of the Federal Reserve by placing on the Federal Reserve Board a political appointee such as the then Treasury Secretary Donald Regan. This suggestion encountered such fierce opposition from the Federal Reserve and various politicians that it was immediately dropped.

Sprinkel's other recommendations dealing with monetary policy were more typically monetarist in orientation. He argued against the then existing system of lagged reserve accounting, since it diminished the ability of the Federal Reserve to control monetary aggregates. Sprinkel also advocated the idea that the Federal Reserve should pay more attention to stabilizing the growth of the U.S. money supply and less to the level of interest rates and unemployment statistics.

Sprinkel's free market beliefs were expressed in many forms. He argued strenuously against the European desire for the United States to interfere in international currency markets in order to stabilize the value of the dollar. Sprinkel believed that if the Europeans followed the correct monetary policy (read monetarism) that the U.S. dollar would ultimately converge to its correct relative value. At home, he fought against the idea that the Federal Reserve should try to stabilize and lower the level of domestic interest rates. Again he advocated letting the market set interest rates independent of Federal Reserve action. And finally, Sprinkel attempted to get the Japanese to both open up their capital markets to foreign competition and begin allowing the yen to play a more important international role, the purpose behind these positions being to increase the efficiency of the world's financial flows and to remove some of the pressures from the U.S. dollar as the world's most important form of liquidity; this would reduce the relative value of the dollar in order to bolster U.S. exports.

Some of the toughest battles fought by Sprinkel during his Treasury years were with European finance ministers. At one point the situation had become so bad between Sprinkel and his European counterparts that the *London Financial Times*' Samuel Brittain called him "the arch bad guy" of the international scene. The thrust of the Europeans' complaints against the United States was the high U.S. interest rates and what they perceived to be an overvalued U.S. dollar. Sprinkel's response to these complaints was to chide the Europeans for their preoccupation with high U.S. interest rates. He berated the French for pursuing faulty economic policies, and his response to the European complaint of an overvalued dollar was that they should pursue a sounder monetary policy.

Internationally, Sprinkel considered the debt crisis to be the single most important world economic problem. Besides involving the potential bankruptcy of some of the world's leading developing nations—for example, Mexico and Brazil—Sprinkel recognized the great danger this debt crisis held for the solvency of many large and important U.S. banks and in turn the world financial system.

His response to this problem was fourfold. First, he advocated that the International Monetary Fund (IMF) should increase its lending pool to developing nations. Second, he wanted debtor countries to reduce their budgetary deficits and bring their money supplies under control. Third, he suggested that banks keep lending to problem nations. Finally, he believed that if the international debt crisis was to be overcome the developed countries of the world would have to reinvigorate their own economies.

In Sprinkel's case, it is difficult to gauge exactly how successful he was as Under Secretary of Monetary Affairs. His liberal and supply-side critics argued against his policies with an animus rarely directed at a Treasury appointee. Liberals disliked his free market approach to economic problems, while supply siders disliked his emphasis on stabilizing the growth of monetary aggregates over cutting marginal tax rates. Sprinkel's more traditional conservative supporters expressed the same intense passions for his policies. The only sensible conclusion that one could draw from all of this is that, for better or worse, Sprinkel was one of the most influential under secretaries of monetary policy ever appointed to Treasury.

One of the most interesting quirks of the Reagan administration's first term in office was its obvious shift away from considering the Council of Economic Advisers as the main economic counseling authority to the president. The reason for this was twofold: first, the president developed an excellent working relationship with Treasury Secretary Donald Regan; and second, the advice and public stance of the chairman of the Council (first Murray Weidenbaum* and then Martin Feldstein*) seemed at times to be at odds with what the president wanted to present to the nation. In fact, at one time communications between the president and the Council had diminished to the point that there was talk of abolishing the Council altogether. Politically, it became apparent that this could not happen, but the idea was given serious consideration nonetheless.

It was in this atmosphere that Sprinkel, by now a Reagan loyalist, was appointed chairman of the Council of Economic Advisers in April 1985. His prime mission was be to revitalize the Council so that it could once again become a trusted source of economic advice for the president. Even though Sprinkel is considered a ''safe'' chairman, he is still not the administration's point man on economic policy. That job still resides with the Treasury Secretary. Sprinkel's major responsibilities as chairman of the Council of Economic Advisers are to provide the president with general economic advice and to assist him in formulating national economic policies. The major source of policy recommendations, though, will still flow primarily from the Treasury Secretary, James Baker III, and White House chief of staff Howard Baker.

BIBLIOGRAPHY

Sprinkel, Beryl. *Money and Markets: A Monetarist View*. Homewood, Ill.: R. D. Irwin, 1971.

———. *Money and Stock Prices*. Homewood, Ill.: R. D. Irwin, 1964.

MARK A. NADLER

STEIN, HERBERT
(b. August 27, 1916), CEA February 4, 1969-August 31, 1974

Herbert Stein was a member of the President's Council of Economic Advisers from 1969 until 1974, under presidents Nixon and Ford. He was appointed chairman of the Council by President Nixon effective January 1, 1972, upon the resignation of Paul W. McCracken*, and continued as chair in the administration of President Gerald Ford after the resignation of Nixon.

When his resignation from the Council was accepted in 1974 Stein then assumed a previously arranged academic appointment as professor of economics at the University of Virginia. He is currently a senior fellow at the American Enterprise Institute. Most of his professional life has been spent in government or private and industry-related research organizations. A self-styled "conservative's liberal and a liberal's conservative," his professional views reflect a conservative monetarist approach but one that is tempered by the pragmatism of his years in and around government and the Washington economic scene. His major fields of professional expertise are, quite naturally, macroeconomic policy and public finance.

Herbert Stein, the oldest child of David and Jessie (Segal) Stein, was born in 1916 in Detroit, Michigan, where his father was a machinist with the Ford Motor Company. In 1929 the Stein parents along with Herbert and his younger sister Pearl moved, first to New York City and then after a few months to Gloversville, New York, where David Stein ran a dry goods store. Shortly afterwards the family moved again, this time to Schenectady, New York, where during the 1930s the father worked intermittently for the General Electric Company.

In 1931, at the age of fifteen, Stein graduated from Schenectady High School and then matriculated on a scholarship at Williams College. He majored in economics, a decision which he said reflected the serious economic problems of the time. Although he always worked part-time, Stein was able to maintain an outstanding undergraduate academic record, which included being initiated into Phi Beta Kappa and in 1935 graduating magna cum laude. Following graduation he went on to the University of Chicago for graduate study in economics.

As Stein himself has noted, there is a tendency for economists who have been trained at a particular institution to have its characteristic beliefs, and the University of Chicago, as it often does on those who attend, has had an important and lasting influence on Stein. While not a "Chicago economist" in a rigid sense, his thought and writings continue to show its traces. He often refers to his teachers and peers at the University of Chicago. In 1938, after completing the course requirements for the Ph.D. (he submitted his dissertation and received the degree in 1958), he left Chicago for Washington to take a position with the

Federal Deposit Insurance Corporation, where Clark Warburton was the chief economist. It was an important move, and as a result Stein has been in and around Washington most of his professional career.

In 1940, amid growing concern about the spread of the war in Europe, Stein shifted to the National Defense Advisory Commission to work on price stabilization. After the United States entered the war in 1941 he was appointed head of the economic analysis section of the War Production Board. These positions gave him experience in the use and administration of price controls that was to be useful later when in 1971 President Nixon suddenly introduced controls. He was later commissioned in the navy as an ensign, but in 1944 was loaned to the Office of War Mobilization and Reconversion. Also in 1944 he won a $25,000 prize in a contest for the best essay on postwar employment sponsored by the Pabst Brewing Company. In his winning essay he presented a policy program that is well within the spirit and tone of his policy suggestions in the 1980s. He argued for the achievement of stable full employment through the use of tax policy to encourage private investment, strict enforcement of antimonopoly legislation, and limited government spending. His policy position is now more sophisticated and cognizant of the changes in the economy over the past forty years but does show a remarkable consistency with his earlier views.

Following his discharge from the navy in 1945 Stein joined the newly formed Committee for Economic Development (CED). He remained there for the next twenty-two years, as economist (1945–48), associate research director (1948–56), research director (1956–66), and then as vice president and chief economist (1966–67).

At the CED Stein was the principal author of the Committee's influential cyclically balanced budget proposal. This "full employment budget" concept was a remarkable step forward, particularly for a business-related institution. Government expenditures were to be set so that they would yield a budget balance or perhaps a small surplus at the full employment or, as it is now called, the high employment level of national income. If output fell below that level, the fall in tax revenues and increase in transfers would automatically generate a budget deficit; if income rose above the high employment level, the opposite would occur.

In 1967 Stein left the CED to become a senior fellow at the prestigious Brookings Institution in Washington. Then, during the presidential campaign in the summer of 1968, Stein, on the recommendation of the eminent University of Chicago economist Milton Friedman, was asked by candidate Richard Nixon to prepare a study of federal budget problems. This was not his first active participation in political campaigns. As early as 1952 he had worked on the macroeconomic policy program for the Eisenhower campaign.

In November 1968, Stein completed a paper on macroeconomic policy for a Brookings study in which he called for policies to reduce the inflation rate, including a tax surcharge like that passed by Congress in mid–1968. He acknowledged that such policies, to be effective, might require the acceptance of a period of higher unemployment. The views presented in this paper received wide press coverage because of his new role as Nixon's fiscal adviser. On December 17, 1968, President-elect Nixon announced Herbert Stein's appointment to the Council of Economic Advisers. The new chair of the Council was to be Paul McCracken, who had been a member of the Council when Nixon was vice president, and the other new member was Hendrik Houthakker*. That announcement came on the day of Stein's first meeting with President-elect Nixon.

Inflation was the main policy concern of Stein and the other members of the new CEA. The new president was also concerned about inflation but not to the extent that his economists were. By the time the Nixon administration took office in 1969 the Federal Reserve had already begun to slow the growth of the money supply, and Stein and his colleagues endorsed the restraint.

According to Stein, he and the others on the CEA were influenced by Milton Friedman's natural rate theory wherein only an ''unexpected'' high rate of inflation that pushed prices up faster than wages and reduced the real wage rate would allow output to rise and unemployment to fall below the long-run ''natural rate of unemployment.'' An implication of that theory is that a reduction in the rate of inflation requires a period during which unemployment is above the ''natural'' level. But by early 1970 the economy was slowing down more than the administration expected. The 1970 recession was shallow, but inflation proved stubborn and persistent. In 1971 the administration began to be concerned about the approaching 1972 election. They did not want to be caught with an economic policy that was not working.

On August 13–15, 1971, President Nixon met with his economic advisers, including Stein, at Camp David. The result of that meeting was the adoption of mandatory wage and price controls. It is a strange paradox that a free market economist under a conservative Republican president should embark on a policy that gave the country its first peacetime wage and price controls. Stein had consistently argued against an ''incomes policy,'' that is, direct government intervention in wage and price decisions, even though the Nixon administration seemed to be moving ever closer to such a policy. The president and some of his other advisers were more pragmatic and much less opposed ideologically to wage and price controls or any milder form of an incomes policy than were Stein and the other members of the CEA.

In spite of his fundamental opposition to controls, Stein was adaptable and enough of a pragmatist himself to support the controls. In addition, he was himself caught up in the enthusiasm of the Camp David weekend. He later reported that the meeting was one of the most interesting events in the history of economic policy. On the return of the economics ''team'' from Camp David, Stein volunteered to work on the transition to the period following the immediate ninety-day freeze, the period that became known as Phase II. His enthusiasm did not completely obscure his judgment, and he was reported in the press to give the controls only a fighting chance.

The rationalization of the adoption of peacetime price controls under a conservative Republican president and his politically appointed economic advisers has been a matter of obvious interest to Stein since his service on the Council. He maintains that Nixon, like Stein himself, had an aversion to price controls from his unhappy experiences working on them during World War II. But Nixon also longed for dramatic action and was dissatisfied and impatient with the prescriptions of conventional conservative economics (and economists). According to Stein, the decision for the price freeze (and closing the gold window to foreign central banks) was a "one-on-one" decision by Nixon and his new Secretary of the Treasury, John Connally, and was communicated to Budget Director George Shultz and CEA chairman McCracken but to no one else. Stein feels that Connally was the key factor since in him Nixon found another major force in his administration.

During the period of the freeze and through the end of 1971 the controls seemed to be achieving the Nixon administration's desired ends. Unemployment remained at around 6 percent, and there was virtually no inflation. Nixon, upon the advice of his economic advisers, decided to increase government expenditures rapidly during the first part of 1972. At the same time, the Federal Reserve under Board of Governors chairman Arthur Burns* began to increase the growth of the money supply, leading to a rapid increase that continued through the middle of 1973. There was enough slack in the economy so that the resulting real expansion in 1972, an election year, was strong, but by the second quarter of 1973 it began to be clear that the economy was in a strong demand-pull inflation which emasculated the price controls. The administration's hope that the ending of controls would be accompanied by a stabilization of inflation was vain. The controls ended when the authority for general price controls expired in April 1974. At that point all that was left were the controls on domestically produced oil, a legacy of the initial 1973 OPEC price increases.

Stein remained on the Council of Economic Advisers through President Nixon's resignation and the swearing in on August 9, 1974, of the new president, Gerald Ford. By that time he had already announced his resignation and Alan Greenspan* had been appointed as his successor.

In summing up his experiences on the Nixon CEA, Stein has said that he and his colleagues thought themselves conservatives and different from their predecessors of the Kennedy-Johnson regime. In fact, the differences were not that great.

Since his resignation from the Council Stein has continued to speak out publicly on the issues of fiscal policy that interest him. He has written a number of articles for popular magazines and for the American Enterprise Institute, appears regularly on the op-ed page of the *Wall Street Journal*, has given numerous speeches at business and professional meetings, and is, partly as a result of his dry humor, a favorite source for interviews and quotations by journalists on current economic policy. He has also published an important work on economic policy making, *Presidential Economics* (1984), much of which reflects his personal experiences on the Washington scene with the CED and the Council of Economic Advisers.

The issues on which he has recently spoken are the same ones which have been a matter of concern to him for most of his professional career: budget deficits, inflation, the need for an adequate defense policy, and the general subject of economic policy making. Although he has maintained a consistently conservative, mildly monetarist stance and actively supported the candidacy and reelection of Ronald Reagan, he has not been sympathetic to "supply-side economics," a term, incidentally, that he coined.

To Stein supply-side economics is nothing new, but is merely a repackaging of old ideas that sound plausible but are not particularly relevant. He found that it provided a convenient argument for conservative Republicans to use to advocate a tax cut that would have popular appeal and not appear to benefit only the rich.

A major reason for Stein's antipathy toward supply-side economics is the inability of those who espouse it to provide what Stein considers an adequate response to the problem of large federal budget deficits. Stein has not been willing to accept the position that growth itself will adequately take care of the problem of the large budget deficit, and he consequently thinks that the tax cuts of the early Reagan administration were unduly large.

Although Stein has been very explicit in his concern about the federal deficit and the need to reduce expenditures, he has not been willing to cut defense spending to do so, firmly resisting any attempts to use the deficit as an argument for reducing the defense budget.

On the other hand, Stein has not been favorably disposed toward the efforts to enact a constitutional amendment requiring a balanced budget. The talk of such an amendment, given the size of recent and prospective deficits, led Stein to remark, in a characteristic display of wit, that enacting a constitutional amendment for a budget balance after 1988 is like devising a chastity belt for one's widow.

Perhaps the most important of Stein's achievements in the period since his resignation from the Council are his reflections and comments on the role of economists in policy making. Of particular interest have been his comments on the role of the Council of Economic Advisers. He readily admits that economists do not have all the answers to policy problems, and he has pointed out that economists reflect their own personal and professional histories so that there is a great deal of such nonscientific influence in what economists believe. Mistakes in national economic policy, in Stein's view, partly reflect deficiencies in economics, but the main source of the problem is political. Politics leads to a very short-run approach; economists must consider the long view equally.

In discussing the role of the Council of Economic Advisers, Stein has pointed out that its importance lies not only in the guidance it can give the president on national macroeconomic policy but also its "micro" function. That is, the Council can play an important role in formulating policies and programs for specific industries and areas of the economy. When in the winter of 1984 President Reagan publicly questioned the desirability of continuing the Council, Stein quickly came to its defense. He took the position that Reagan especially ought to value the Council of Economic Advisers because the Council is the place from which the strongest support for free market policies comes. Stein argues that to be effective the Council has to be listened to. It will be effective only if it can get the president's attention. If the chairman of the Council is an outside "kibitzer," he may just as well not be there.

Herbert Stein's career has been active and distinguished. He has served the economics profession and his country well. His professional standing and the scope of his scholarly ability are well attested by his two major works, *The Fiscal Revolution in America* (1966) and the more recent *Presidential Economics* (1984) as well by the many other articles and books he has written under the auspices of the CED and the American Enterprise Institute.

BIBLIOGRAPHY

Stein, Herbert. "Bricks Without Straw: Making Economic Policy Out of Economics." *Contemporary Policy Issues* 3, no. 1 (Fall 1984–85): 8–9.

———. *The Fiscal Revolution in America*. Chicago: University of Chicago Press, 1966.

———. *Presidential Economics*. New York: Simon and Schuster, 1984.

R. NEWBY SCHWEITZER

STEWART, WALTER W.
(b. May 24, 1885, d. October 7, 1958), CEA December 2, 1953-April 29, 1955

Walter Winne Stewart was sixty-eight years old and retired when he was appointed to the President's Council of Economic Advisers on November 26, 1953. Why did President Eisenhower and CEA chairman Arthur F. Burns* feel it necessary to call someone out of retirement to serve on the Council? There were two main reasons. One was Burns' view that Stewart, a close friend for many years, was an extraordinary man, and one of the wisest he ever knew. Another reason was the nature of the economic problems of the 1950s; these made Stewart the right man for the job.

In the late 1920s and early 1930s Stewart had helped guide international leaders through the economic problems caused by World War I. It was a sad fact of history that the economic problems of the 1950s mirrored those of the 1920s. Stewart had, in fact, made economic history thirty years before; in 1953 he was again called on to advise a president.

Stewart was born in Manhattan, Kansas, in 1885. His father was a printer and editor of one of the first agricultural papers in the country. When Stewart was in grammar school the family moved to Nesbro, Missouri. They were not well off financially, and Stewart quit high school to work in a local bank. Even as a teenager he displayed what would become lifetime traits: a devotion to work and a fascination with the problems of money and credit.

He left the bank after three years and entered the University of Missouri, earning his way by tending the university president's furnace and later by tutoring his fellow undergraduates in money and banking. His primary interest was his school work, with one exception—the track team. He earned his letter as a quarter- and half-miler. He was elected Phi Beta Kappa and graduated in 1909 with highest honors.

After teaching one year at the University of Missouri, Stewart taught the next year at the University of Michigan. He then returned to the University of Missouri, where he stayed until 1915. In 1916 he became a professor at Amherst College, specializing in banking. During the war years he also served on the Price Section of the War Industries Board.

Colleagues said that one of the most striking things about Stewart was how much his students respected and admired him. And they spoke about Stewart's shyness; it was an inherent part of his personality all his life. He was friendly but very reticent, and tended to devote most of his energy to his work. His way of life and tastes were simple. Although he eventually made a considerable fortune, this never changed his work habits or his lifestyle.

Most of Stewart's publications were written during these early years. His first article, "Social Value and the Theory of Money," appeared in December 1917. Another article, "An Index of Production Numbers," came from his work on the Price Section of the War Industries Board and appeared in *American Economic Review* in March 1921.

Stewart's research was important to the war effort; and his work for the Price Section was an important stepping-stone in his career. His later career path would pretty much follow the same route as that of some of the influential men he met on the board. During the war years, the entire U.S. industrial production was governed by seven men, mostly wealthy business and financial experts, who made up the War Industries Board. They, because of their business expertise, were given the responsibility of deciding what was produced, who produced it, and what prices were paid. They were to guard against war profiteering and at the same time ensure that the needs of a wartime economy were met. Stewart helped their work by designing an indexing system which systematized some of their decisions on prices. A pamphlet written by Stewart, "The Prices of Iron and Steel, and Their Products," was published by the board in 1919.

Stewart continued his teaching duties at Amherst. However, during a controversy between the Amherst College trustees and the president of the college, the president, Dr. Meiklejohn, was asked to resign. Stewart ardently supported Meiklejohn. When Dwight Morrow, a college trustee, urged Stewart to become president in Meiklejohn's place, and retain Alexander Meiklejohn as head of the philosophy department, Stewart refused, choosing instead to resign as a matter of principle in 1922.

Stewart's research capabilities then took him to the Federal Reserve System in Washington, D.C. The Federal Reserve System had been created by Congress only nine years before; its primary purpose was to improve the supervision of banking. The Fed, and the Federal Reserve Board that governs the system, have a much more vital role today. Much of the Fed's present ability to function in the order it does can be traced back to Stewart's work in the 1920s.

He became director of, and in fact organized, the Bureau of Research and Analysis of the Federal Reserve System. This was the first real division of research in central banking and is now recognized as a turning point in central banking history. At the Fed, Stewart continued the work on indexing production that he started during the war.

This research led to the Federal Reserve Board's Index of Industrial Production, still in use today. Stewart is also generally credited with devising the System of Open Market Operations that the Federal Reserve Board still uses to implement national monetary policy and interest rates. And he edited the Federal Reserve Board's monthly newsletter, *The Bulletin*.

It was through his work at the Federal Reserve that Stewart became known as a "research expert in action." His advice was sought by many, and as his reputation grew he was ultimately called in to advise President Calvin Coolidge, as later he would advise Herbert Hoover, Franklin Roosevelt, and finally Dwight Eisenhower.

This practice of giving background consultations to national and international leaders would continue for the rest of Stewart's life. When the occasion warranted it, Stewart would be called in by the current administration for his economic and banking expertise. His advice was given with no public fanfare, and because he cherished his privacy, he never gave any press interviews. While Stewart was not known to the average newspaper reader, his reputation among professionals grew. He came to be regarded as an unusually gifted theorist and, later, as one of the leading authorities on foreign exchange rates and gold. He was an independent in politics and never publicly supported any political views. He limited his advice to economic and banking issues and published little, reportedly because of the high standards he set for himself.

In 1926 Stewart left Washington and the Federal Reserve to help organize Case, Pomeroy and Company, a Wall Street investment securities firm. In 1927 he was appointed as an adviser to the Bank of England. On October 16, 1927, the *New York Times* said that the Bank of England, Britain's central bank, was paying the fourteen-year-old Federal Reserve a compliment by picking Stewart to help it with its own central banking system.

He worked for the Bank of England from 1927 until 1930, helping to establish its first research division. He became familiar with and helped advise financial leaders on the problems of the postwar economy in Europe, particularly those growing out of the reparation payments of Germany. He attended the Conference at Baden-Baden that put together the machinery of the World Bank.

Stewart's stature among the British was evident in 1930 when he was asked to testify before the Macmillan Committee, a British government committee convened to discuss currency devaluation and monetary manipulation in England's depression economy. This meeting would be historic for many reasons, one being the interchanges that took place between Stewart and a member of the committee, John Maynard Keynes. In 1950 the American Enterprise Association published these testimonies in a monograph entitled *Monetary Policy and Economic Prosperity*. In his introduction Donald B. Woodward said that they were remembered as some of the most stimulating analyses of the limitations of central bank policy.

In discussing the government's role in helping ease unemployment—a question still being debated today—Keynes asked Stewart if an administration were to come forward as a borrower for public works, and there was an expansion of credit, would you in those conditions expect to diminish unemployment.

Stewart considered that it would be so. During the course of their exchange on the efficacy of pump priming, Stewart may even have planted in Keynes' mind the idea of the marginal efficiency of investment when he observed that "the conditions necessary to investment seem to me to be only in part the rate of interest. It is the margin between the rates of interest and prospective profit that matters."

While Keynes and Stewart saw eye to eye on a number of issues, they did have some significant disagreements. Stewart saw increased exports through judicious devaluations as virtually the only way England could solve its unemployment problems in the early 1930s. American economists have heard similar recommendations in more recent times, namely from Europeans, especially the French in the late 1960s when Eurodollars began flooding the Continent.

Stewart resigned from the Bank of England in 1930 and returned to the United States to become chairman of the board of Case, Pomeroy and Company. He stayed at Case for the next eight years, during which time he made a considerable private fortune.

In 1931, in a rare public airing of his views, Stewart was asked to testify before the LaFollette Committee of Congress, which was investigating a proposal to establish a National Economic Council. George A. Soule, director of the National Bureau of Economic Research, appeared as an advocate for an increase of wages as a means of preventing depressions. Stewart said that on the basis of his experience at the Federal Reserve Board, he believed economists had made a mistake in endeavoring to force stabilization through control of price levels.

Later in 1931, Stewart left Case and Pomeroy temporarily when he was appointed a member of a special international advising committee of the Bank of International Payments. This committee was convened in Berlin at the request of Germany because it was having problems making its reparation payments. Stewart, who had continued to keep in close touch with the major problems of the European economies, was selected by the Federal Reserve Board to serve because of his experience in London. Before sailing for Berlin, Stewart was asked to go to Washington, D.C., to confer with government officials. The reparations issue had political as well as economic implications.

Stewart was suggested as chairman of the committee, but upon his arrival in Berlin, he declined any support for the chairmanship, saying he lacked the proper experience. However, it was suggested that Stewart declined for two reasons. One was that France, without American leadership of the committee, would have a freer hand in dealing with Germany. The other was economic: by not being the presiding officer of the committee, Stewart could defend American banking interests without being placed in the role of an intermediary between the Europeans. Stewart's only public comment about the committee's work was to express pleasure in the selection of Alberto Beneduce, an Italian, as chairman.

Back at work at Case, Pomeroy and Company, Stewart next received press attention when the chairman of the Federal Reserve Board, Eugene Meyer, resigned. Meyer and Stewart were close friends, having worked together at the War Industries Board. In mentioning Stewart as a possible replacement for Meyer, the *New York Times* cited Stewart's past work at the Federal Reserve Board and called him one of the foremost authorities on economic affairs in the country. Stewart did not get the chairmanship of the Federal Reserve Board, nor did he get any other high administration posts, although he was often mentioned as a possible candidate.

Stewart was an early advocate of the Institute of Advanced Studies at Princeton and served on its board of trustees from 1933 until 1938. In 1938 he switched career paths again and returned to his first love, teaching. He resigned from Case, Pomeroy and Company and joined the institute as a professor in the School of Economics and Political Studies. It must have been a satisfying change. Many years later Arthur F. Burns would remember how Stewart's office at Princeton became a sort of Mecca for both the young and the old seeking Stewart's counsel. But in 1939 the coming war interrupted Stewart's academic work. By September Europe was at war and the United States was attempting to stay neutral.

Stewart was asked by Secretary of the Treasury Henry Morgenthau to be part of a six-person emergency advisory group. Three economists—Stewart and Winfield W. Riefler, both loaned to the administration from the institute, and Jacob Viner from the University of Chicago—joined three bankers to advise the secretary daily.

In April 1940, John D. Rockefeller, Jr., resigned as chairman of the board of the Rockefeller Foundation, and Stewart was elected to take over. In 1942 he also took over as head of the General Education Fund. For the next eight years, until his own retirement at sixty-five, Stewart would continue teaching at the institute as well as directing the vast philanthropic activities of the Rockefeller Funds.

In 1951, in retirement, he was given honorary degrees from both Princeton and Columbia. He was cited by Columbia as a "master of the thinking word and a man of active intelligence who had a great and useful influence on contemporary economic thinking and policy."

In 1953 he was appointed to the President's Council of Economic Advisers. He served for only two years, resigning in 1955 for personal reasons. There is no public record of what he said or did in his two years on the CEA. In 1953 the Eisenhower administration was dealing with a world economy readjusting itself after World War II. Many European countries, including Great Britain, were thinking about currency devaluations as a way to promote exports, thereby stimulating their economies. Stewart was the recognized expert in this area; his function on the CEA was to share that expertise, particularly with Chairman Arthur Burns.

Although Stewart's stay on the Council was too brief to leave much of a mark, he nevertheless occupies a rather unique place in the American economic tradition. In the 1920s he was a leading force in developing research methods to record and analyze economic activity. At the same time he warned economists not to forget their humanistic traditions. He advocated and developed effective statistical methods to help analyze economic problems, but cautioned that economists must be prepared to study the processes of change whenever possible, and to keep the statistical methods from getting lost in meaningless numbers. For thirty years he was a research expert operating in a complex, worldwide, industrial economy, but he never lost sight of human institutions.

BIBLIOGRAPHY

Stewart, Walter. ''Controlling Business Cycles.'' *American Economic Review*. Supplement (March 1922): 33–45.

———. ''An Index of Production Numbers.'' *American Economic Review* (March 1921).

———. ''Prices During the War.'' *Journal of the American Statistical Association* (September 1920): 305–13.

———. ''Prices of Iron and Steel, and their Products.'' War Industries Board pamphlet. Washington, D.C.: Government Printing Office, 1919.

———. ''Social Studies in the Humanistic Tradition.'' *The American Scholar* (October 1947): 468–71.

———. ''Social Value and the Theory of Money.'' *Journal of Political Economy* (December 1917): 984–1002.

JULIANNE CICARELLI AND JAMES CICARELLI

TOBIN, JAMES
(b. March 5, 1918), CEA January 29, 1961-July 31, 1962

"A mandarin-like midshipman named Tobit, with a domed forehead, measured quiet speech, and a mind like a sponge, was ahead of the field by a spacious percentage." So read Herman Wouk's portrait of a character based on Officer Training School classmate James Tobin in *The Caine Mutiny*. Although he says that it was his claim to fame prior to winning the Nobel Prize in Economics, economists of all ideological persuasions know James Tobin's work. Those that know him personally say that it is an apt description of the man who served on the "Camelot" Council of Economic Advisers under President Kennedy.

In awarding the Nobel Prize to Tobin in 1981, the committee stated, "Few economic researchers of today could be said to have gained so many followers or exercised such influence on contemporary research." But James Tobin has always seemed to rise above his peers with his brilliant work, even with his quiet and shy manner. His roots are in Illinois, where his father, Louis Michael Tobin, whom he credits for his intellectual curiosity, was director of publicity for athletics at the University of Illinois at Champaign. Born in 1918, Tobin graduated from University High School and in the fall of 1935 entered Harvard as a freshman under the new National Scholars program.

Coming from the Midwest during the Depression of the 1930s made Tobin receptive to new approaches to societal issues. His enrollment at Harvard coincided with the beginning of the Keynesian revolution in the United States. The publication of Keynes' *The General Theory of Employment, Interest and Money* would influence most of his future contributions to economics. At the time Tobin also came under the tutelage of Alvin Hansen who, although outnumbered by his Harvard faculty colleagues against Keynes, won Tobin over to the Keynesian camp permanently.

After earning his Bachelor of Arts degree in 1939, with highest honors, Tobin stayed at Harvard to continue his study of economics and received his master's degree in 1940. Tobin then went to Washington for his first stint as a government economist with the Office of Price Administration in 1941. He also worked for the Civilian Supply and Production Board. The bombing of Pearl Harbor convinced him to enter the Navy, where he met Wouk and received a gold watch for best officer in his training class. Tobin served as a line officer on the destroyer USS *Kearny* and rose to second in command by the war's end.

In 1946 Tobin married Elizabeth Fay Ringo and returned to Harvard to finish his education. He completed his doctorate in 1947. His dissertation, "A Theoretical and Statistical Analysis of Consumer Behavior," reflected his interest in combining the theoretical aspects of economics with the realities of the world.

This interest remains and is apparent throughout most of his work. He stayed at Harvard as a member of the prestigious Society of Fellows. Usually, promising junior fellows fill the ranks of tenured Harvard faculty, but Yale University made him a better offer, and he was on his way to helping to create an economics department at Yale that is ranked in the top few among American universities.

While at Yale, he and Lloyd Reynolds helped create, as Paul Samuelson put it, "the best Harvard department outside of Cambridge." Important in this development was the attraction of the Cowles Foundation research unit from the University of Chicago to Yale in 1955. The science of econometrics at Yale now entered a period of rich development with the addition of Jacob Marschak and two other future Nobel laureates, Tjalling Koopmans and Gerard Debreu.

The year 1955 brought Tobin two well-deserved recognitions. At Yale he was promoted to the rank of full professor, and the American Economics Association awarded him the prestigious John Bates Clark Medal, given every other year to the best and most promising economist under the age of forty. Tobin claims to be proud to work in the tradition of John Maynard Keynes, but he recognized that the original Keynesian doctrine was not unflawed. Some of his research was an attempt to "fix up" some of the contradictions of Keynesian economics. His early work focused on how to improve the Keynesian model and the study of the government's role of monetary policy on national income. William Brainard, a student and later a colleague of Tobin's at Yale, remarked that for Tobin "the ultimate justification for economics and social science was to benefit people." Tobin's orientation has always been toward theory and public policy.

Tobin's important early contributions to economic analysis were concerned with the demand for money and the relationship between real physical assets and financial markets. Keynes faced the task of explaining the idleness of people's cash holdings during the Depression. Keynes developed, and Tobin described, the "regressive expectations" model as an explanation. Keynes argued that people had some expected rate of return from bonds based on both the yield and its capital gains. This expected return, however, depended not just on current interest rates but on future rates as well, since they determined the capital gains. With a zero return on cash holdings, an asset holder would put his liquid holdings into bonds if he expected the rate to be greater than zero. On the other hand, if the rate were expected to be less than zero the money would be held. In this model, each investor's expected interest rate corresponds to some long-run average rate. When the rate is above the average the investor expects it to fall, and vice versa, hence the term regressive expectations. The problem with the model is that it concludes that an investor holds all cash or all bonds. Tobin recognized this flaw. With the knowledge of economic diminishing marginal utility theory, he realized that a loss to an individual had more effect than a gain. Coupling this with his knowledge of mathematical theory to explain that the expected return on a risky asset would be greater than zero, Tobin developed the portfolio balance approach model.

The model is developed on the assumption that an asset holder has a range of expected gains, with each having an associated probability of occurrence. Tobin then showed that, using this expected gain and the standard deviation of the gain, a measure of the riskiness of the asset can be determined. Each investor then has a tradeoff between risk and expected rate of return, with most investors demanding increasing returns for holding higher-risk assets. Tobin then identified different classes of investors—those that preferred risk, those that averted risk, and those that went with all or no risk—to show the types of investment choices they would make. Empirical evidence showed that most fell into the averters category, and thus they would diversify their holdings between bonds and money.

What this amounted to, as Tobin put it, was "telling people not to put all of their eggs in one basket." Yet this mean variance analysis provided investors with a method to make efficient choices about their portfolio balances given individual preferences. It was also used to develop capital asset pricing models.

Reverting to Keynes again, in his work he argued that in times of depression, with increasing risk and falling returns, people will be more likely to hold cash. Thus the interest rate becomes established as an important influence on the demand for money. It explains why the velocity of money slows during a depression.

Using these findings, Tobin advocated policies of government involvement in the economy that would mean stimulation in times of slowdowns and constraint in times of expansion. It was his thoughtful approach to economics and his belief in active public policy that led to his becoming one of the "Whiz Kids" in the Kennedy administration. In December 1958 he was first asked to be part of the academic advisory committee to the candidate. After the election, when asked by Kennedy to be the first Yale professor to serve on the Council of Economic Advisers, he at first refused on the grounds that he was something of an "ivory tower economist." Supposedly the president responded, "That's okay, I'm an ivory tower president."

The early Kennedy Council faced a national economy in recession. This Council went back to the letter and the spirit of the full Employment Act of 1946. They advised the president and also submitted their own reports to Congress. Under Kennedy they looked at almost all questions of economic policy and viewed the economy as a whole for ultimate and remote consequences. It was the Council's belief that the government was not doing enough to spur recovery. Tobin believed in a mixed economy with public and private enterprise, with the emphasis on the private sector. He felt that government should take a more active role by decreasing personal income tax rates in order to stimulate the economy in the face of, at that time, high unemployment, while labor and management working together should provide guidance and leadership on the issues of wage and price stability.

While on the CEA Tobin supervised a policy of stimulation in times of slowdown and restraint during expansion. He felt that the Federal Reserve Board should put strong brakes on credit if unemployment was low and ease off if unemployment was greater than 5 percent. At the same time, relatively easy money should be available for investment in productive capacity, education, and research, but he advocated a tight fiscal policy on consumers to control inflation.

While on the Council Tobin developed the investment tax credit program as a means to spur private sector formation by providing a decreased tax as incentive. Unfortunately, due to political considerations the program was never instituted.

Looking back on his experiences on the Council, Tobin felt that it was the outpost of academic economists in the federal government and that both sides benefitted. Tobin wrote that the CEA had to understand that economics was not an exact science so that they could not be coldly scientific and apolitical, but to be effective the Council had to be identified with the president and the administration.

After his stint on the Council, and returning to Yale, Tobin published several books which were mostly collections of articles. His most important work following his tenure on the CEA was that on the Q-ratio, which he developed in an effort to present an alternative to the monetarists' account of how the transmission process between monetary policy changes in expenditures for gross national product. The Q-ratio was derived empirically and is a measure of market value of a capital asset in relation to its replacement cost. This ratio is important not only for the government but for the investment community as well because it provides an explanation of business behavior.

In a perfectly competitive economy with constant returns in scale, in equilibrium the normal value of Q will sustain capital replacement and expansion of the economy at its natural rate. In the short run, however, events, policies, and expectations will move the value of Q above and below this natural level and influence the incentives for investment. When the ratio is low the market value of an asset is less than its replacement cost, and so corporations will tend to acquire existing assets rather than pay a higher price for new ones. Monetary policy certainly will influence the value of Q; but, Tobin makes clear, it is only one of many factors that will do so. Interest rates will also influence Q, with high rates tending to make acquisition of existing assets cheaper. This will mean a sluggish growth rate in the economy.

Tobin wrote two books which were collections of essays geared toward the general public, not just economists. *National Economic Policy*, published in 1966, is a well-reasoned series of essays on the opportunities for public policy to effect an improvement in the general well-being of society. The essays cover a broad range of topics, from the role of government in economic planning and taxation, to monetary policy and inflation, to taxation, to the role of business in the economy. There are three main points in Tobin's book: (1) the government should always keep in mind its main object, efficient use of the nation's resources; (2) the government should seek stability and adequate growth in the economy; and (3) economic myths and ideology raise impediments to rational economic policy. In developing his points, Tobin demonstrates his pragmatic approach to economics and public policy. It is clear that Tobin is a strong believer in free market economics, but he also sees the ultimate goal of economics as improving the welfare of the people. This goal requires different policies for different times and market conditions, sometimes requiring tax incentives and at other times fiscal policy.

The second book by Tobin, *The New Economics One Decade Older* (1974), is a collection of lectures given at Princeton discussing Keynesian economics, monetarists, and monetary institutions in the era of the New Economics. In it Tobin responds to the monetarists' arguments against government deficit spending. The monetarists argued that the deficits raised the interest rate by increasing the money supply, which then affected all markets, not just securities and interest rates. Tobin's answer was that many things determine the money supply and that monetarists are not consistent in the treatment of savings deposits. He also wrote that velocity, responding to interest rates, would refute the monetarist propositions and that one must look at the tradeoff of inflation versus employment.

Tobin has served as president of the Econometric Society (1957) and of the American Economic Association (1971), perhaps the two most prestigious posts an economist can fill. He has also served as president of the Eastern Economic Association (1977) and as section chairman of economic sciences for the National Academy of Sciences (1979–82). Tobin has been the recipient of several honorary degrees, including the LL.D. from Syracuse, Illinois, Dartmouth, and Swarthmore.

Tobin's most prestigious honor was the 1981 Nobel Prize in Economics. The Nobel Committee presented him with the prize for his technical contributions to economic science, noting especially his analysis of financial markets and his breakthroughs in analyzing the relationships between financial markets, for example, stocks and bonds, and real markets, goods and services. This has always been a classic problem in economics.

BIBLIOGRAPHY

Tobin, James. *Asset Accumulation and Economic Activity: Reflections on Contemporary Macroeconomic Theory*. Chicago: University of Chicago Press, 1980.

———. *Essays in Economics: Consumption and Econometrics*. New York: North-Holland Publishing Co., 1975.

———. *Essays in Economics: Macroeconomics*. Chicago: Markham Publishing Co., 1971.

———. *Essays in Economics: Theory and Policy*. Cambridge, Mass.: MIT Press, 1982.

———. *Financial Markets and Economic Activity*. New York: Wiley Publishing Co., 1967.

———. *National Economic Policy*. New Haven: Yale University Press, 1966.

———. *The New Economics One Decade Older*. Princeton: Princeton University Press, 1974.

———, Harris, S., et al. *The American Business Creed*. Cambridge, Mass.: Harvard University Press, 1956.

———; Pechman, J.; and Mieszkowski, P. *Is a Negative Income Tax Practical?* Washington, D.C.: Brookings Institution, 1967.

KEITH C. FINAN

TURNER, ROBERT CLEMENS

(b. March 2, 1908, d. December 5, 1978), CEA September 8, 1952-January 20, 1953

Robert Clemens Turner served one of the shortest terms on the President's Council on Economic Advisers, occupying a position from September 1952 until January 1953. Turner had previously held several positions in the Roosevelt and Truman administrations, starting with the War Production Board (1941–45). He began there as an economist but quickly became deputy director (1942) and then director of the foreign division (1943). At the end of the war, he shifted to the Civilian Production Administration (CPA), where his responsibilities centered on the problem of American provision of scarce commodities, such as cotton, to foreign markets.

Turner's precise role within the Truman administration is extremely difficult to pin down. While he was a presidential economic adviser in 1947–48, working for John Steelman, and he seems to have played a part in the internicene warfare between the staff in the East Wing of the White House and the CEA, it is unclear if he had a critical role in any of the major economic decisions of the period.

Unfortunately, none of the memoirs of this period mentions Turner's role in the administration, save for the occasional reference to his service with the CPA. There, he was often a spokesman on the necessity for export quotas in certain vital commodities. In June 1946, for example, he spoke out on the need for export quotas on cotton, noting that U.S. policy in such matters was not based on economic considerations but on political ones. Turner warned that the United States should, from a future economic perspective, seek to maintain and to expand its export markets; however, he pointed out that current needs (particularly from the point of view of goods-starved consumers) necessitated export quotas. Even those exports allowed by the CPA were based on political criteria; Turner noted that the United States should export only to those countries it found to be politically reliable (export for the purpose of helping to satisfy their equally frustrated consumer demand, and thus help to promote domestic stability in such countries).

Turner's career in the late 1940s, and after, reflected his efforts to work both in the government sector and in academia. In 1948, for example, he left the full-time White House staff to become a professor of business administration at Indiana University (Bloomington). Turner maintained a strong midwestern flavor throughout his life. Born in Hiram, Ohio, in 1908, he died in Bloomington in 1978. He received all of his degrees at midwestern institutions: B.A. from Hiram College (1930), M.B.A. from Northwestern (1932), and Ph.D. from Ohio State (1937). His doctoral dissertation was a study of how banks tailor their borrowing policies in response to Federal Reserve policy changes.

Turner maintained his affiliation with Indiana University throughout the remainder of his life. He was a professor of business administration from 1948 to 1961 and a distinguished professor of business, economics and public policy from 1961 to 1978. He served as the chairman of the department of business economics and public policy from 1958 to 1961, and as vice chancellor of the university from 1969 to 1973.

While at Indiana, Turner acted as a consultant both for the United States government and for foreign governments. He went to India in 1962, and spent six months in the Philippines in 1968–69 as an economic adviser to President Ferdinand Marcos. His Indiana activities included monitoring the state's tax revenue forecasts and, somewhat later, oversight of the university's administration and budgetary affairs. Turner also was an ardent botanist, becoming sufficiently expert in the cultivation of orchids to publish articles on them in botany journals. Turner had married in 1932; he and his wife raised two children in Washington and Bloomington.

Turner's activities in the late 1940s and early 1950s are not easy to trace. The positions he held do not reveal the importance he seems to have had in inner government councils. His expertise in export controls and in general matters of mobilization of the economy made him a key White House adviser in 1947 and 1948. The *Economic Report of the President* for 1947, for example, was first drafted by the CEA (at that time composed of Edwin Nourse*, Leon Keyserling*, and John Clark*).

The CEA subsequently met on January 3 with Steelman and his three assistants, as well as with three cabinet members. These subsequently designated other experts—Ewan Clague, C. C. O'Connell, and Philip Hauser—to work with Steelman and his assistants. This group revised the Steelman draft, and they then worked on the new draft with the CEA members.

It is clear from Irvin Grossack's biography that Turner was, in fact, one of those responsible for the *Economic Report of the President* in 1947 and, one suspects, in 1948 as well. As one of the president's chief in-house economic advisers, he must have had considerable input into the discussion of the Taft-Hartley Act in 1947 (if only in his function as Steelman's chief adviser). His greatest role in this period, however, was in the dual responsibility of export controls and wage, price, and commodity control policies.

When he reached the CEA (named in July 1952; confirmed in September), Turner found himself involved with the 1952 *Economic Report of the President*. A dead letter when it was released, the 1952 *Report* reflected the ideas of the outgoing Truman administration rather than the incoming Eisenhower one. The *Report* called for a continuation of wage, price, and supply controls in 1953 and urged Congress to refrain from voting a tax reduction, in fear of creating a substantial budget deficit. Turner wrote the report; Keyserling, then chairman of the CEA, supported it; the third member of the Council, John Clark, opposed it.

Throughout this period, one finds Turner closely associated with all matters related to economic controls. As we have seen, he spoke up strongly in favor of export controls in 1946; most of his experience as a government economist and administrator was precisely in the field of economic controls: War Production Board and OWMR. Indeed, in 1948, when Truman sought to examine the possible needs for further economic controls, he turned to Turner.

Turner's activities in export control in the late 1940s included *Export Control*, published in 1947 during his tenure with the CPA, and, in 1951, a working paper entitled "Problems in Business and Industrial Mobilization: Control of International Trade During War Mobilization." His other publications included *Member Bank Borrowing* (1938); the second edition of *Business Conditions Analysis* (co-authored with J. P. Lewis); and a broad variety of working papers, among the better known of which are "U.S. Economic Growth: Prospects for the Next Twenty-Five Years" (1976) and "An Economic Portrait of Indiana" (1970).

It is hard to find Turner in the forefront in any particular government economic decision. The positions he occupied usually carried with them the responsibility to do the background work for important policy decisions, but Turner did not receive credit for those decisions. Under the Kennedy administration, Turner returned again to Washington as an economic adviser. Kennedy appointed David Bell to be head of the Bureau of the Budget; Bell selected Turner to be his assistant director for fiscal policy.

In the important economic policy discussions of the Kennedy administration, Turner had the prime responsibility for the preparatory work of the meetings of Secretary of the Treasury Douglas Dillon, Bell, and CEA Chairman Walter Heller*. The Kennedy response to the sluggish economy was hashed out at these meetings. Heller, Bell, and Turner argued for a planned deficit to stimulate the economy. While they had a partial success in 1963, they did not get the full tax cut stimulation until 1964. Here again, Turner was cast in a familiar role: background adviser to those with operational responsibility (in this case, Bell). Turner even wrote the speech used by Bell to explain the full employment budget to Congress.

Turner left the Bureau of the Budget in 1962 to return to Indiana. He continued to act as a consultant for the Kennedy and Johnson administrations, not only for the Bureau of the Budget, but for the CEA and the Treasury Department as well. Under the Republicans, he served as an adviser to the Comptroller General (beginning in 1969). This considerable experience with government forecasting of future economic trends carried over into his written work. In 1969, for example, after his stay in the Philippines, he wrote "Macro Forecasting in the Philippines: An Experiment." A year earlier, he had given a discussion paper on a related but more general topic: "Forecasting in Southeast Asian countries."

Closer to home, Turner focused on economic forecasts for the state of Indiana (1970) and for the United States as a whole (1975 and 1976). In these publications on economic forecasting, Turner's consistent concern with eminently practical matters, notably problems of resource supply, is evident. Certainly, his experience during World War II and in its immediate aftermath gave him considerable expertise in such matters, under very strained circumstances. His "U.S. Economic Growth: Prospects for the Next Twenty-Five Years" (1976), a relatively short report for the Bureau of Business Research of Ball State University, devotes fully half of the text to problems of resource supply, and another significant chunk to labor resource issues.

In a similar pamphlet written in 1975, "Economic Growth: The Outlook for Ten and Twenty-Five Years," Turner predicted ten-year trends with mixed results. He suggested the population would reach 228 million (plus or minus 5 million) in 1985; the actual figure is closer to 240 million. Current GNP is closer to 1 trillion 1958 dollars than to Turner's projected $1.2 to 1.3 trillion 1958 dollars. He was too optimistic about unemployment, expecting an average rate of around 5 percent. On the other hand, he estimated inflation for the period 1975–85 to average between 7 and 10 percent and correctly foresaw a decline in the personal savings rate in the late 1970s followed by a rise in the mid–1980s (although that rise would not take it out of his projected range of 5–7 percent for the late 1970s).

Such an assessment of his predictions is a trifle unfair, given the severity of the recent recession; his long-term projections, up to the year 2000, would be a more accurate measure of his success or failure. Indeed, one of Turner's finest qualities was precisely his willingness to put such predictions down on paper, to put his reputation on the line.

Robert Turner, though he served for only a few months on the CEA, played a key role in a long series of presidential economic decisions. Beginning with the Truman administration and continuing with those of Kennedy and Johnson, Turner was one of the key behind-the-scenes players in the governmental economics game. It seems clear that he was the chief author of two *Economic Reports of the President*, in 1947 and 1952; in the former case revising the work of the CEA, in the latter carrying it out himself. It seems likely that he had a role in the 1948 report as well. Turner later played a critical role in the economic policy debates of 1961–64. While he can hardly be claimed as a major economic theorist of his time, he was one of the most important economists in another way—he had to apply that theory to economic reality. While little known to the public, Turner had a significant impact on American governmental economic policy under the Democratic administrations of three decades.

BIBLIOGRAPHY

Grossack, Irvin. *A Biography of Robert C. Turner, Working Economist*. Bloomington: School of Business, Indiana University, 1981.

Nourse, Edwin. *Economics in the Public Service*. New York: Harcourt Brace, 1953.

Turner, Robert. *Member Bank Borrowing*. Columbus: Ohio State University, 1938.

———, and Lewis, J. P. *Business Conditions Analysis*. 2d ed. New York: McGraw-Hill, 1967.

JAMES B. COLLINS

WALLICH, HENRY C.
(b. June 10, 1914), CEA May 7, 1959-January 20, 1961

The career of Henry C. Wallich, who served on the President's Council of Economic Advisers from 1959 until the end of the Eisenhower administration, provides an excellent example of the varied roles of the professional economist in the mid-twentieth century. Wallich has been a businessman, an academician, a public servant, and a prolific writer. He has formulated economic theory in his scholarly writing, has helped implement policy as a presidential adviser and a member of the Board of Governors of the Federal Reserve, and has translated economics for the general public as a commentator in the national media. He has been, in short, an economist for all seasons.

Henry Wallich was born in 1914 in Berlin. He studied ancient languages at the Bismarck Gymnasium there, and later economics at Oriel College, Oxford, and New York University. Between 1933 and 1940 he worked in the business world, with Chemical Bank and the Wall Street firm of Hackney, Hopkins and Sutphen. In 1941 he joined the Foreign Research Division of the Federal Reserve Bank of New York and served as chief of that division from 1946 to 1951.

While working for the Federal Reserve Bank, Wallich continued graduate study in economics at Harvard, where he earned an M.A. in 1941 and a Ph.D. in 1944. In 1951 he accepted a faculty appointment in the economics department at Yale, which for the next twenty-three years became his base. In 1970 he was named the Seymour H. Knox Professor of Economics.

Wallich's years at Yale were not ones of ivory tower intellectualizing, for he soon became involved in government. In 1958 he took a leave from his academic appointment to serve as assistant to the Secretary of the Treasury. After a year in this post, he was appointed to the CEA. Wallich returned to New Haven when the Kennedy administration took office, but with the election of Richard Nixon in 1968 he was again called to Washington. For five years he was a senior consultant to the Secretary of the Treasury and in 1974 was appointed a member of the Board of Governors of the Federal Reserve System.

For nearly three decades, then, Wallich has been one of a handful of economists whose views have consistently been sought out by policy makers. And this was true even during those years when he was not directly involved in policy formulation in Washington. Between 1961 and 1964 he was a guest editorial writer for the *Washington Post* and from 1969 to 1974 a regular contributor on the economic scene in *Newsweek*. Wallich freely admitted that his views did not always coincide with the general editorial positions of these publications, but he obviously enjoyed the opportunity to express them.

Remarkable, too, has been the consistency of Wallich's economic views.

Throughout his career, he has been a steadfast proponent of the conservative, free market position that, at least until 1980, characterized the policy of postwar Republican administrations. He enunciated these views most completely and forcefully in his 1960 volume, *The Cost of Freedom*. Written while Wallich was a member of the CEA, this book sought to explain the intellectual foundations of economic conservatism, which found expression better perhaps in action than in writing.

While probably a bit too demanding for the general audience for which it was intended, *The Cost of Freedom* is a careful, reasoned assessment of the social, political, and philosophical implications of the free market system. As in all of Wallich's writing, its arguments are laboriously constructed and its prose measured. And, like the period of American history in which it was conceived, its message is ultimately optimistic. Throughout, Wallich emphasizes that change is necessary to ensure continuity, but that in the long run forces work on the side of freedom. There is little evidence that Wallich in his other writings and in his government service has ever deviated from this basic philosophical premise.

Henry Wallich's academic writing has covered a wide range of areas within the field of economics. Early in his career, his main focus was on international economic development. His first book, written with John A. Adler, was *Public Finance in a Developing Country* (1951), a detailed study of the economy of El Salvador. In light of recent events in that country, the book seems a reminder of simpler times in Latin America, but its value to the historian remains. Likewise, his encyclopedic 1955 study of postwar West Germany's economic recovery, *Mainsprings of the German Revival*, is still one of the most comprehensive treatments of that subject available.

In the late 1950s and on into the 1960s, Wallich's writings turned more to the macroeconomics of the United States economy, a result, no doubt, of his government experience. His articles in the major economic journals, his contributions to collections of essays, and his writings in popular publications such as the *New York Times Magazine* and the *Harvard Business Review* dealt with the ramifications of monetary and fiscal policy. And throughout the 1970s and in the 1980s, he has continued to be a steady contributor to the economic literature, especially on monetary issues.

Perhaps the most striking characteristic of Wallich's writing is the wide breadth of his interests. Never has he felt constrained to remain within one subdiscipline of his field. He has written on the Japanese economy, contributed to a collection on marketing, and spoken eloquently—from a free market perspective—on the complex issue of corporate social responsibility. He has always stood ready to state his views on current economic conditions and events, from the economics of Eisenhower in 1956 to the international monetary crisis of 1971 to the heavy debts of less developed countries in 1981. Unlike many of his younger colleagues, Henry Wallich has not sought refuge in mathematical models from the often surprising twists and turns of the global economy. He has consciously sought out the public eye, and this is probably the key to understanding the importance of his career.

Important, too, in assessing Wallich's career are the reason and pragmatism that have characterized his views, especially since 1974, when he joined the Federal Reserve Board. At the time of his appointment, observers called him eclectic rather than extremist, and his performance has confirmed this assessment.

The years of Wallich's term as a Federal Reserve Board governor have been tumultuous ones. High inflation, high interest rates, and balance of payments deficits have all created controversy, not only about the nation's economic policy, but about the role of the Fed in its development. Throughout these years, however, Wallich's has consistently been a voice of caution and realism.

This has been especially apparent in his role in the debate over inflation. In the late 1970s, Wallich, like many other economists, commented frequently, and publicly, about the damage that high inflation was doing to the U.S. economy. In typical fashion, he viewed the problem in its largest sense, pointing out that inflation did moral as well as material harm to the nation. High inflation not only devalued the currency of the realm, he suggested, but also the honesty of business decisions, management-labor relations, and public policy.

Yet even with this deep concern, Wallich has not been one to espouse quickly the various—and often faddish—inflation fighting prescriptions advanced during the past five years. His position on tax cuts has been moderate and cautious. He has, at various times, both opposed and supported such cuts. He has never, though, advocated massive tax reductions like those favored by supply-side economists.

In 1981, for example, he pointed out that the supposed supply-side incentives for economic growth that would result from a large tax cut would not solve the problem of rising federal deficits unless expenditures were also addressed. With a sense of history uncommon in Washington, he noted that this idea had originally been propounded by Federal Reserve Board chairman Marriner Eccles in 1940. The idea became known among many economists of the day as "Eccles' error," Wallich observed. The results of the Reagan administration's 1981 tax cuts suggest just how perceptive this observation was.

Neither has Wallich become a kneejerk proponent of other popular ideas, such as a rigid short-term cap on the money supply or a return to the gold standard. His was a voice of skepticism on the 1981 presidential commission that examined the feasibility of returning to the gold standard. He commented, "I am still very doubtful that a gold standard would allow us to maintain stability." Throughout all of these debates, he has stressed that addressing the economic problems of the day is a complex business that demands thoughtful, comprehensive analysis, not quick fixes.

Yet this is not to suggest that Henry Wallich has not come up with his share of specific, and often controversial, ideas. He has advocated a lower capital gains tax, regulatory and tax relief to spur exports, restraints in the increase of corporate dividends, and a tax incentive plan for achieving more moderate increases in wages and salaries. The last of these was a frequently discussed, but never implemented, strategy in the battle against inflation in the late 1970s.

Wallich's personal style reflects his measured and conservative economic views. When he was appointed a Federal Reserve Board governor, the *New York Times* observed that he was "pin-striped to the core," and this appropriately describes him. Scholarly, mild-mannered, and quiet, he has relied upon the cogency of his arguments rather than upon his personal charisma. Yet he does enjoy a good cigar, and his wine tasting parties have been famous for years among his friends in New Haven. His wife Mabel, whom he met during his first tour of duty at the Federal Reserve, shares his professional interests and has frequently been a co-author of articles with him.

BIBLIOGRAPHY

Wallich, Henry. "The American Council of Economic Advisers and the German *Sachverstaendigenrat*: A Study in the Economics of Advice." *Quarterly Journal of Economics* 82 (August 1968): 376–82.

———. *The Cost of Freedom: A New Look at Capitalism*. New York: Macmillan, 1969.

———. *Mainsprings of the German Revival*. New Haven: Yale University Press, 1955.

———, and Adler, John A. *Public Finance in a Developing Country: El Salvador—A Case Study*. Cambridge, Mass.: Harvard University Press, 1951.

JAMES W. SCHMOTTER

WEIDENBAUM, MURRAY LEW
(b. February 2, 1927), CEA February 27, 1981-August 25, 1982

Murray Lew Weidenbaum, after approximately one and one-half years as chairman of the Council of Economic Advisers, submitted his resignation on July 20, 1982. Weidenbaum's views were generally regarded to be more conventional than those of President Reagan and other senior economic advisers. But this had nothing to do with his resignation, according to Larry Speakes, the deputy White House press secretary, as quoted in the *New York Times* on July 23, 1982.

As was widely reported, Weidenbaum was returning to his former academic pursuits at Washington University in St. Louis. He had been a member of the faculty at the school since 1964 and had been designated Edward Mallinckrodt Distinguished University Professor in 1971. In 1975 he also assumed the title of director of the new Center for the Study of American Business. Now, he was coming back once again to the St. Louis community in which he had lived for more than fifteen years with his wife, Phyllis, and their three children, Susan, James, and Laurie.

Weidenbaum was born in the borough of the Bronx in 1927, and graduated at age twenty-one from City College of New York. After completing his studies there, he went on to Columbia University and earned his M.A. degree in 1949. In 1954, during his period of employment at the Bureau of the Budget, he married Phyllis Green. To a large extent, Weidenbaum's business and government career proceeded concurrently with his academic career. Some of his non-academic positions include fiscal economist at the Bureau of the Budget, 1949–57, corporate economist at the Boeing Company, 1958–63, and Assistant Secretary of the Treasury for Economic Policy, 1969–71. Thus, he was a practicing economist for more than eight years before receiving his Ph.D. in economics from Princeton University in 1958.

Other titles held by Murray Weidenbaum include member of the Research Advisory Board of the Committee for Economic Development and member of the Research Council of the Center for Strategic and International Studies at Georgetown University. He has also received recognition on several occasions, including an honorary LL.D. by Baruch College, the Townshend Harris Medal, presented by the City College Alumni Association for distinguished achievement, and the Alexander Hamilton Medal, presented for his distinguished leadership of the Department of the Treasury.

In Weidenbaum's view that there is a close correspondence between economic freedom and personal liberty, he followed closely upon the words of Friedrich von Hayek in *Road to Serfdom* and *Freedom and the Economic System*. In fact, Weidenbaum bolstered his arguments with citations from Hayek.

One of the earliest subjects dealt with by Murray Weidenbaum in book form was federal budgeting. *Federal Budgeting: The Choice of Government Programs* was first published in 1964; one year later, under the overall title *Congress and the Federal Budget*, it was reissued along with a work by John S. Saloma III. Both books were published by the American Enterprise Institute, the Washington-based think tank. In the republished monograph, Weidenbaum claimed that efforts to reduce public expenditure or reform budgetary recommendations fail because of lack of public understanding of the budgetary system, including how government programs are funded and methods of review and control. Another reason cited was the lack of effective budget reviewing tools to determine the amount and allocation of funds among programs.

During the three-year period that Murray Weidenbaum was chairman of the department of economics at Washington University and director of the NASA Economic Research Program, he wrote *Prospects for Reallocating Public Resources* (1967), another work concerned with budgeting. The basic finding of the work was that federal budgets appeared to be heading toward surpluses after the close of the Vietnam War, while state and local budgets appeared to be heading toward continuous deficits. Weidenbaum observed, also, that federal revenues are endogenous to the economic model, while expenditure estimates are, in general, exogenous. Thus, federal revenues are determined primarily by the level of economic activity, while expenditures influence the level of economic activity but are significantly affected by it. Weidenbaum devoted considerable space to an extensive discussion of six alternatives for reallocating funds among the state and local governments: direct federal expenditure, tax sharing, tax credits, federal grants for specific program areas, block grants, and block grants with equalization. This subject was also carefully evaluated in ''Federal Aid to State and Local Governments: The Policy Alternatives,'' prepared for the Joint Economic Committee as part of a two-volume work, *Revenue Sharing and Its Alternatives* (1967).

More observations on the budget by Murray Weidenbaum appeared in the 1970s. *The Federal Budget for 1973: A Review and Analysis* (1972) was written with Dan Larkins; *Matching Needs and Resources: Reforming the Federal Budget* (1973) was written with Larkins and Philip N. Marcus. In the former, Weidenbaum expressed concern with budget spending for research and development. Public and private investment in this activity has been a major source of output growth and productivity, according to Weidenbaum. Nevertheless, research and development spending had been declining since 1964. Though the 1973 budget increased funding for several existing research and development projects, few new research and development programs were adopted. In the latter work, the emphasis was on nine proposals to improve the Congressional budget process:

1. Consolidate and simplify the budget
2. Reorganize the appropriate committees along program lines
3. Revise the Congressional calendar, leaving more time for Congress to study the budget

4. Enhance the role of *Economic Report of the President*; move annual report forward to fall
5. Limit annual authorization; move up to precede hearings on budget and recommend no amounts or limits, these to be left to appropriations committees
6. Submit and enact a bill for appropriation increases to control spending
7. Reduce backdoor financing
8. Use a budget scorecard: up-to-date recording of impact of Congressional action on overall budget aggregates
9. Improve program analysis and evaluation: Congress needs its own professional staff

Only suggestions 3, 8, and 9 were adopted as part of the new budget process of the Congressional Budget and Impoundment Control Act of 1974. Weidenbaum's idea that responsible fiscal policy in the budget means balance in the full employment budget was not adopted either.

Approximately eight years later, when Weidenbaum was chairman of the Council of Economic Advisers, he rejected this interpretation of responsible fiscal policy. In a speech entitled "Recession and Recovery," given in May 1982 in Washington, he stated his new position: "We do not succumb to the Keynesian heresy, and the 1982 Economic Report does not contain any budget estimate proposed on a high employment basis." The second position would be the more appropriate one for a "conservative" economist who sees the supply side as well as the demand side, but it does create a schism within conservatism, nonetheless. It was Milton Friedman who was the first to suggest that we examine fiscal policy in terms of the high employment budget in a paper delivered before the Econometric Society in September 1947. Later, the Council of Economic Advisers adopted the technique when Walter Heller* was chairman.

Closely related to Weidenbaum's concern about the federal budget is his concern about federal credit activities, a subject he has been writing about since 1970. In March 1982, during a talk in Washington entitled "Federal Credit Programs and the Economy," Weidenbaum noted a dramatic increase in off-budget lending, most of it undertaken through the Federal Financing Bank.

Two months later, in a speech entitled "The Case Against Bailouts" before the Pennsylvania Bankers Association, he stated that bailouts make the budget situation worse by increasing federal borrowing and raising interest rates; furthermore, they are inequitable and eliminate private sector worries about risks and costs. In this speech, as in his earlier book, *Government Mandated Price Increases* (1975), Weidenbaum indicated that the size and scope of federal credit programs can contribute to inflationary pressures. They do not foster larger flows of savings or investments, and when they are federal loan guarantees, they disguise different credit risks and thus interfere with the resource allocation function of credit markets. Of course, concern about private credit and its negative effects on the economy can be traced back to many early writers who associated money and credit with the business cycle. Knut Wicksell, the Swedish economist, was one of the earliest in the group of adherents which later included Friedrich von Hayek, Ludwig Von Mises, and Milton Friedman.

Another topic that concerned Weidenbaum early in his career was military expenditures. His first book completely devoted to it was *Economic Impact of the Vietnam War* (1967). At that time, in addition to his position as chairman of the department of economics at Washington University, he was consultant to the Joint Economic Committee. In the book, a clear assessment of the linkage between military expenditure and inflation during the Vietnam War period is established. (1) Virtually all of the rise in the federal share of GNP from 6.2 percent in 1940 to 10.3 percent in 1964 was due to military-security expenditures. (2) A military buildup took place during the period 1963 to 1966 though it was not recognized either privately or publicly. Inflationary pressures were under way but only credit restrictions were imposed, and these were imposed late. (3) Increases in military expenditures from 1964 to 1966 competed for resources with the expanding business environment. (4) A final problem was that military expenditures were not recorded until final delivery, but the rise in tax revenues as a result of the inflationary pressure was recorded immediately. Thus, the budget of fiscal year 1966 did not reflect the full inflationary pressure for that year. Though he offered no detailed solution, Weidenbaum suggested a combination of better communication techniques for the budget items and economic restraints to curb inflationary pressures.

Two years later, Weidenbaum published another book which dealt, in part, with military expenditures, but from a different point of view. In *The Modern Public Sector: New Ways of Doing the Government's Business* (1969), he notes that until a few years following the end of World War II, wage and salary payments to federal employees were the largest category in the budget. After that, the largest item of expenditures was disbursements under contracts with the private sector for goods and services. Smaller amounts were spent on grants in aid to state and local governments and transfer payments to individuals. Weidenbaum asked several policy questions with long-run implications. One of the most compelling of them concerns the nature of the government-industry-business relationship. Is the contract method a way to nationalization or socialization of industry? The question was not answered because Weidenbaum predicted a new organizational development. As a result, it would be necessary to introduce a new definition of nationalization or socialization. Weidenbaum views the future of the mixed economy as containing mixed organizations which combine both public and private characteristics under one roof. Hence, simply asking who owns the means of production, said Weidenbaum, will not give us the answer.

Weidenbaum's motivation for writing *The Economics of Peacetime Defense* (1974) came, in part, from the changing role of the military in American society and the need to review previous conclusions in the light of new factors at work. Some of these include the shift from military contracts as the largest item in the budget of 1965 to the domination of civilian expenditures, including Social

Security pensions and welfare assistance, in the budget of 1974. This book earned its author the Distinguished Writer's Award from the Center for Strategic and International Studies at Georgetown University. The magnitude of U.S. military expenditures is widely attributed, Weidenbaum claimed, to the pattern of interaction between major world powers. Arms spending, therefore, is based upon the result of a mutual challenge and response between the United States and the U.S.S.R. Weidenbaum noted that analysis of spending for the period 1950 to 1962 supported this view. In fact, approximately one-half of each nation's military spending could be explained by the spending of the other.

In conclusion, Weidenbaum remarked that raw military power is no longer an effective instrument of national policy because of the destructiveness of modern weapons. Instead, Weidenbaum sees future disagreements resolved by technological and economic competition and propaganda. Power relationships have been changing and have been affected by availability of energy sources and international economic rivalry as well as ideological concerns. His argument could be important even in the context of the current discussion of quantity versus quality in the provision of military weapons. Nevertheless, in the *Economic Report of the President* for 1982 and in an article, "It's Time for a Hard Look at Defense" in the *New York Times* (October 31, 1982), Weidenbaum spoke of an overriding need for maintaining the level of military expenditures appropriate for national security. Some of the biggest problems in achieving that goal would be the economic impact on prices, the effect on delivery timetables for military goods, and the temporary crowding out of private investment. However, since his return to Washington University, Weidenbaum has argued that he approves of the defense buildup but not at too fast a pace. The huge federal deficits, in Weidenbaum's opinion, must be reduced by cutting outlays on entitlement programs and defense as well as subsidies to agriculture and business.

As a strong believer in the efficiency qualities of a free enterprise system, Weidenbaum, not surprisingly, reacted sharply to the growing network of government regulations. In fact, the keynote is struck in his 1979 book, *The Future of Business Regulation*, in which he declares that government regulation should not interfere with the basic functioning of society. In an earlier book, *Government Mandated Price Increases: A Neglected Aspect of Inflation* (1975), he not only argued that government regulations serve as a disincentive to business but that they encourage inflation. Regulations increase the cost of production, which in turn raises the prices of goods and services to the consumer. The final step occurs when easy monetary policy validates the price rise. (It was for this book and other works on the subject that his publisher, William J. Baroody, president of the American Enterprise Institute (AEI), called Weidenbaum one of the pioneers in putting regulatory reform on the national agenda.

Furthermore, prospects for economic growth and productivity are affected by federal regulations. Real investment may appear to be increasing when, in fact, a larger proportion of investment is devoted to pollution and safety outlays.

In *The Future of Business Regulation: Private Action and Public Demand*

(1979) Weidenbaum enumerated the four groups who suffer from the costs of regulation: the taxpayer for administration of regulation; the consumer for added production costs due to regulation; the economy for loss of small businesses because they cannot afford the burden of regulation; and society because of reduced production of new goods and the slower rise in the standard of living.

It was the approach to regulation that Weidenbaum particularly desired to change. The focus of a regulatory program should be directly on its objective—say, reduction of accidents. According to Weidenbaum, minor events, such as a form filled out incorrectly, should be given little attention. A second concern was finding the right method to achieve the goal. If the object is to reduce the number of fatalities from traffic accidents, it may not be the best choice to introduce more complicated auto safety equipment. Most fatal accidents involve a pedestrian or a driver who has been drinking.

In the book, Weidenbaum included recommendations on what business should do to improve the situation. These included furnishing more complete information on the impacts of government involvement on business and identifying objectives and clarifying its position on public policy issues. Weidenbaum believed that business must take an activist position in public policy matters. He advocated corporations stepping into the political arena to champion candidates and legislation of their choice. One of the main supports for Weidenbaum's argument is the fact that this is exactly what unions do. On the other hand, Weidenbaum notes that business, generally speaking, has lost the esteem of consumers, and in these circumstances political activism by business may not be the wisest move.

Weidenbaum's article, entitled ''The Power of Negative Thinking: Government Regulation and Economic Performance,'' which emphasized the disincentive aspect of government regulations, was published in the *Proceedings* of the 1980 Economic Policy Conference sponsored by the Center for the Study of American Business and the Federal Reserve Bank of St. Louis. In it, he found costs of government regulations to be both direct and induced. The latter include (1) innovative product and process research and development which have been reduced in favor of that work necessary to meet regulatory requirements; (2) reduced investment in plant and equipment because of regulatory requirements and the need to meet new social requirements in safety, health, and environmental areas; (3) reduction of the number of workers hired due to federal regulations; and (4) reduction in the entrepreneurial nature of the private enterprise system.

Another article which appeared in the *Labor Law Journal* in 1979 was devoted entirely to OSHA, the regulatory agency created under the Occupational Safety and Health Act. In ''Four Questions for OSHA,'' Weidenbaum claimed that OSHA had not concentrated on the basic causes of job-related illnesses and accidents, had not investigated alternative ways of reducing them, had not located the most effective way of reducing them, and had not had a significant impact in reducing them. Weidenbaum would like to see a fundamental overhaul of the basic premises of OSHA's functioning. Emphasis should be shifted from standards, inspections, and sanctions on employers alone to performance in terms of desired end results and sanctions on employees, too. The idea of the revision would be to provide maximum incentives to all involved to achieve a healthy and safe environment. Weidenbaum's writings have stressed the importance of benefit-cost and cost-effectiveness analysis for evaluating government projects and regulations. Weidenbaum, who enjoys writing as a hobby as well as a part of his professional endeavors, has written guest columns for newspapers, magazines, and other publications, including the *Washington Report*, the *Wall Street Journal*, and *Business Week*.

Weidenbaum's long exposure to forecasting at the macroeconomic level as chief economist of Boeing (1958–63), as economic adviser to several companies and institutions, and as member of the Conference Board's Economic Forum (one of the most prestigious groups in the field) led him to formulate his opinions on government planning by 1977. "Corporate Planning Versus Government Planning," written with Linda Rockwood, which appeared in the winter issue of *Public Interest*, emphasized the distinction between government and corporate planning in terms of internal versus external direction and in terms of the intellectual dimension of the planning effort. Corporation planning tends to be concentrated within the industry, and executives have no problems reading plans which contain familiar material. Government planning, however, focuses on all sectors and is large and complicated enough that members of Congress would have difficulty understanding it. Furthermore, according to Weidenbaum and Rockwood, government planning would end up setting goals for private industry. As government has not been able to manage itself properly, the authors question its ability to successfully plan the economy. The budgeting process, according to Weidenbaum and Rockwood, is the way to establish priorities and allocate resources. But when these words were written in the first full year of the new budgetary process, the process had not been used to set overall priorities. Since that time, to a limited extent, the two budget concurrent resolutions have caused attention on the matter of priorities. However, there has been continuous pressure in Congress to change the process once again. As an alternative to the budget process, Weidenbaum and Rockwood would look forward to an adaptation of the former Planning-Programming-Budgeting systems; they would like to see a government-wide program planning budget. Within such a budget, an objective would be viewed via alternative ways (departments) of achieving it.

A month before Murray Weidenbaum resigned as chairman of the Council of Economic Advisers, he addressed the Joint Economic Committee on the topic "Is Reaganomics Working?" He made two comments that reveal the state of the economics profession and his own position within that profession at the same time. He remarked that economists have no acceptable account of why interest rates have remained high. But he did believe that interest rates were the key to why the recession persisted. In that view, it is likely that Murray Weidenbaum had a great deal of company. Weidenbaum also admitted that he is not a devoted supply sider and that, for him, the term demand is not obscene.

BIBLIOGRAPHY

Weidenbaum, Murray. *Business, Government and the Public*. 2nd ed. Englewood Cliffs, N.J.: Prentice-Hall, 1981.

———. *Economic Impact of the Vietnam War*. Special Report Series No. 5. Washington, D.C.: The Center for Strategic Studies at Georgetown University, June 1967.

———. *The Economics of Peacetime Defense*. Praeger Special Studies in U.S. Economic, Social and Political Issues. New York: Praeger Publishers, 1974.

———. ''Freedom and Enterprise.'' *Society* 18, no. 6 (September/October 1981): 38–40.

———. *Government Mandated Price Increases: A Neglected Aspect of Inflation*. Washington, D.C.: American Enterprise Institute for Public Policy Research, 1975.

———. ''Is Reaganomics Working?'' Statement before the Joint Economic Committee. Washington, D.C., June 9, 1982.

———. *The Modern Public Sector: New Ways of Doing the Government's Business*. New York: Basic Books, 1969.

———. ''Recession and Recovery.'' Statement prepared for a debate at Georgetown University co-sponsored by the Public Interest Economics Foundation. Washington, D.C., May 27, 1982.

———, and Rockwood, Linda. ''Corporate Planning Versus Government Planning.'' *The Public Interest* 46 (Winter 1977): 59–72.

ANNETTE E. MEYER

WHITMAN, MARINA VON N.
(b. August 10, 1935), CEA March 13, 1972-August 15, 1973

Born in New York City in 1935, Marina Whitman is the daughter of the noted economist John von Neumann. She graduated summa cum laude from Radcliffe College in 1956 and later received both her M.A. and Ph.D. degrees from Columbia University (in 1959 and 1962, respectively).

Whitman's academic career began in 1962 as a lecturer in economics at the University of Pittsburgh, where she became an associate professor in 1966 and professor in 1971. Her association with this institution is long but not continuous. In 1970–71 she served as a senior staff economist on the President's Council of Economic Advisers and in 1971–72 was a member of the National Price Commission. From March 1972 to August 1973 Marina Whitman served as the first female member of the Council of Economic Advisers.

Subsequently she returned to the University of Pittsburgh as Distinguished Public Service Professor of Economics. Then, following a year as a fellow with the Center for Advanced Study in the Behavioral Sciences (Stanford, California), Whitman's career took another turn as she became vice president and chief economist for General Motors Corporation in August 1979.

Throughout her career Marina Whitman has remained highly active. She has been an adjunct scholar with the American Enterprise Institute (1976–79), a member of the Brookings Panel on Economic Activity (1974–75), and a member of the Commission on Critical Choices for Americans (1976–79). Currently, among many other activities, Whitman belongs to the Trilateral Commission, is a senior adviser to the Brookings Panel on Economic Activity, and is on the board of directors of the Atlantic Council. Whitman has also frequently served in an advisory capacity to the U.S. government and is presently active on the Economic Advisory Committee on the Reform of the International Monetary System (U.S. Department of the Treasury).

In 1978 and 1979, branching into a new area, she acted as moderator of the television series "Economically Speaking," which aired on over 200 Public Broadcasting System stations. In addition to all her other activities, Marina Whitman has published extensively. Many of her most important works to date are brought together in her 1979 book, *Reflections of Interdependence: Issues for Economic Theory and U.S. Policy*. Whitman, who is married and has two children, has lived up and down the East Coast (many years were spent on Long Island and in Cambridge, Massachusetts). Since becoming chief economist for General Motors in 1979, she has made Princeton, New Jersey, her home. Regarding her long commute from Princeton to New York City, she has accepted it stoically as a fact of life.

The twin concepts of economic openness and economic integration have always dominated the thoughts and works of Marina Whitman. Her first major study in this area was *International and Interregional Payments Adjustment: A Synthetic View*, published in 1967 by Princeton University. In this study Whitman considers the balance of payments adjustment process between closely integrated economies, with particular emphasis on the role played by capital flows. She argues that the important implications of a high degree of capital mobility (under fixed exchange rates) are that (1) the ability of central banks to control domestic money and credit conditions is diminished, and (2) economic disturbances in one country will "spill over" into other countries.

Regarding traditional balance of payments theory, Whitman notes that both the Keynesian and classical views essentially focus on the trade balance while excluding the capital account from consideration. They are both theories of balance of trade adjustment rather than theories of balance of payments adjustment. Whitman argues for a general equilibrium approach to the adjustment process with the capital account receiving equal billing with the trade balance.

In a 1969 article appearing in the *Journal of Money, Credit and Banking*, Whitman pursues the themes of economic openness and economic integration. Economic integration, she believes, is properly calculated in terms of how clearly a group of economies approximates a single, frictionless market, characterized in the limit by the equalization of all prices. An important conclusion for which Dr. Whitman finds empirical support is that the effectiveness of domestic stabilization policies falls as the degree of economic integration rises.

One is struck by the apparent parallels between Whitman's views and the school of thought now referred to as "global monetarism," which is a variant of the more general "monetary approach" to balance of payments analysis. Both the monetary approach and the global monetarist variant adopt a general equilibrium, Walrasian approach to the international adjustment process, emphasizing the importance of the capital account as well as the trade balance. Global monetarism, in particular, assumes that the world is a highly integrated market in which purchasing power parity prevails across all countries and currencies. An implication of the global monetarist view is that the effects of a nation's monetary policy will be spread out on a worldwide basis.

Given Marina Whitman's views on the openness and interrelatedness of the world economy, her apparent sympathy with some aspects of global monetarism is natural. She describes their general approach as stressing the interactions among economies in an interdependent world and the inability to analyze or manage a national economy in isolation. She notes how starkly this contrasts with the traditional Keynesian view, which treats the national economy as the fundamental unit. However, even though sympathetic with the internationalist thrust of global monetarism, Whitman does not go so far as to endorse it, saying that this school goes too far (that is, its assumptions are too extreme) and hence lacks applicability to current problems.

Marina Whitman is an avid student of the experiment with flexible exchange rates following the breakdown of the Bretton Wood system. In a 1975 article entitled "The Payments Adjustment Process and the Exchange Rate Regime: What We Have Learned," Whitman notes that this period (1971–73) of managed floating was characterized by substantial fluctuations in exchange rates.

Whitman also addresses the related question of whether or not exchange rate flexibility is an effective means of correcting payments imbalances. Although the econometric evidence is weak, she argues that there does seem to be some support for the view that the merchandise trade balance improves following a devaluation.

A 1976 article published by the American Enterprise Institute represents, perhaps, Marina Whitman's most extensive survey of the nature of interdependence among national economies. She notes that although international trade theory has long recognized economic interdependence among nations, traditional macroeconomic theory cannot make such a claim. Both Keynesian theory and traditional monetarism represent economic models that describe basically closed economies. In the former case domestic fiscal policy is the "key macroeconomic variable," whereas in the latter the key variable is domestic monetary policy.

According to Whitman, the events of the 1970s exposed the glaring fallacies of the traditional closed economy models and spawned a maelstrom of interest in new approaches that incorporated international interdependence as a fundamental tenet.

Concerning the United States specifically, Whitman notes that since its share of total world output has steadily declined in recent years, and due to the fact that the world economy is becoming more "open," the United States must, out of necessity, become more aware of the nature and consequences of interdependence.

Whitman spells out an essential paradox of increased interdependence that the United States is just coming to realize: along with the benefits of integration (for example, increased competition, specialization) there are costs, including the attenuated effectiveness of domestic policy instruments in achieving domestic policy goals.

As a result of increased international economic integration, the United States and other countries are simply losing their economic autonomy. According to Whitman, this interdependence "creates an enhanced need for the coordination of national economic policies in order to increase the probability of each nation achieving its own economic goals."

It is commonplace for economists to be criticized for being too abstract and theoretical, and having little, if any, policy orientation. This refrain does not apply to Marina Whitman. Partly as a result of her experience as a member of the Council of Economic Advisers, Whitman has developed a sense of policy awareness that is unusual in the ivory towers of academia.

Although it is difficult to determine exactly where theory ends and policy begins, a few of Whitman's works stand out as being particularly policy-oriented. In her article "Sustaining the International Economic System: Issues for U.S.

Policy,'' Whitman argues that despite the recent loss of world influence, the United States must still stubbornly press for liberalization on a nondiscriminatory basis.

In Whitman's view the principle of nondiscrimination, once taken for granted (and embodied in the General Agreement on Tariffs and Trade [GATT]), faces a serious challenge today for several reasons. First, in the past quarter century the focus of domestic economic policy making has shifted from efficiency and growth to stabilization and equity (that is, income distribution). Second, the general philosophy of the European nations is somewhat more interventionist and planning-oriented than that of the United States, and as the hegemony of the United States wanes the influence of the European Economic Community (EEC) countries is enhanced. And third, the developing countries—who are newcomers to the system—are largely hostile to the laissez-faire, liberal view long held by the United States.

The area of international investment, according to Whitman, requires particular attention. There are two reasons for this: (1) the role of multinational corporations is constantly expanding, and they are the primary vehicle of international investment; and (2) there are currently no world organizations in place that can adequately deal with the issues and problems related to multinationals and international investment. Unfortunately, Whitman feels that liberalization in this area may be particularly vexing since the United States alone is holding that freedom of international capital movements contributes in the same way to the maximization of world income as freedom of international trade.

Regarding the international monetary system, one might expect that given her belief that flexible exchange rates do not (fully) insulate a country from external shocks and that consequently policy coordination across countries is necessary, Whitman might favor returning to a fixed exchange rate system. However, rather than supporting fixed rates, Whitman claims that ''managed exchange rate flexibility with rules for intervention is essential [to provide] a more effective adjustment mechanism'' than the Bretton Woods system. She feels that it will be particularly important to have rules that govern under what circumstances a country may and may not intervene (either by direct central bank intervention or by more subtle means) in order to avoid any attempt by countries to export either unemployment or inflation—the familiar beggar-my-neighbor policies.

In 1969 Richard M. Nixon's original Council of Economic Advisers consisted of Paul McCracken* of the University of Michigan, Herbert Stein* of the University of Chicago, and Hendrik Houthakker* of Harvard University. In July 1971 Houthakker left the CEA and was replaced by Ezra Solomon*. Later in 1971, McCracken resigned as chairman to return to the University of Michigan. Stein became the new chairman, and on March 13, 1972, Marina Whitman filled the slot vacated by Stein.

Marina Whitman had been well groomed for this position, having served as a senior staff economist to the CEA in 1970–71 and also as a member of the National Price Commission from October 1971 to February 1972. Her primary responsibility as a member of the Council was the analysis of international economic developments and policy. Her role as the Council's international economist took on special significance since President Nixon's New Economic Policy (NEP), formally announced on August 15, 1971, included important controls on the international monetary system as well as wage and price controls.

Specifically, Nixon's New Economic Policy suspended the convertibility of the dollar into gold, thus formally marking the end of the Bretton Woods fixed exchange rate system. Temporarily replacing the Bretton Woods system was the Smithsonian Agreement, which attempted to realign exchange rates to relieve the payments imbalances that had been building throughout the late 1960s and early 1970s.

The CEA's recommendations for long-term reform of the international monetary system placed primary emphasis on the need to effectively deal with fundamental payments imbalances for all countries, including the United States.

In addition to allowing for greater exchange rate flexibility, the Council was also clearly concerned with the provision of adequate international liquidity, arguing for a reduced role for gold in any future international monetary arrangement along with a concomitant increase in the importance of Special Drawing Rights (SDRs).

The CEA's proposals fell short of calling for a floating exchange rate system, although the door was left open to this possibility. The Council did state that U.S. suggestions regarding the exchange rate mechanism assume that most countries will usually continue their practice of maintaining established values for their currencies. But, in recognition that some countries had already established (de facto) a policy of nonintervention in the foreign exchange market, the CEA noted that the U.S. proposal would permit either transitional or indefinite periods of floating.

In spite of the domestic and international economic problems that plagued the Nixon administration, it has been argued that his Council of Economic Advisers did not obtain the notoriety or importance that the Council had achieved under some previous administrations. There may be several reasons for this.

First, Richard Nixon apparently possessed little interest in economics, except insofar as it related to international affairs. Second, the White House staff, which included H. R. Haldeman and John Ehrlichman, made it difficult for members of the CEA to get close enough to the president to have any significant impact. Third, and perhaps most important, Nixon sometimes chose to bypass the Council in favor of other economists in his administration. At the very beginning, Nixon relied heavily on Arthur F. Burns*, an economic counselor to the president, for economic direction. Later, in 1970, George Shultz seemed to dominate economic policy making from his position as Director of the Office of Budget and Management. In 1971 the new Treasury Secretary, John Connally, became the principal economic spokesman for the Nixon administration, until he was replaced by Shultz. To some extent, these individuals eclipsed the power and prestige that the Council once had.

In defense of the Council on which she served, Marina Whitman admits that Richard Nixon was ''not terribly accessible,'' but she notes that this is true of almost all presidents. Whitman did meet with Nixon several times, usually as part of a small group, but she had little contact with Nixon's ''Palace Guard,'' including Ehrlichman and Haldeman. In fact, Whitman does not remember ever meeting Haldeman, although he remembers meeting her.

Concerning the issue of whether or not the CEA was underutilized by President Nixon, Marina Whitman actually did not have this impression at the time she served, although it is true that the Council was not involved in the formulation of Nixon's New Economic Policy.

With respect to the allegation that President Nixon was not really interested in economic affairs, this may partly be a reflection of his later preoccupation with containing and then managing the ramifications of the Watergate scandal. Marina Whitman notes that it was just when she left the CEA that Nixon began to get ''really distracted'' and started paying less attention to economic issues.

It should be made clear that Marina Whitman's decision to leave the Council in August 1973 was not directly related to the incipient scandal. Although she saw ''storm clouds'' forming and began to have ''personal doubts,'' she was entirely unaware of the magnitude and gravity of the situation.

Marina Whitman's career is characterized by diversity and success. She has demonstrated talent and effectiveness in academia, in government, and, most recently, in the private sector with General Motors Corporation. The essence of Marina von Neumann Whitman's career is succinctly captured in the title of her 1979 book, *Reflections of Interdependence*. She has dedicated her life to analyzing the implications of the interdependence of nations. The recent realization by economists and policy makers of the importance of economic integration is a tribute to Marina Whitman's efforts.

Whitman has willingly served her country when called. First, as a member of the National Price Commission, Whitman gave her best effort to a controversial program which she did not personally believe would achieve its intended goal. Later, she served as the CEA's international economist at a critical time in the development of the international monetary system. While on the Council, she advocated greater flexibility of exchange rates as a means of eliminating the payments imbalances which had led to the collapse of the Bretton Woods fixed exchange rate system.

When asked if she has any regrets about her service under the Nixon administration, Marina Whitman simply states that her loyalties were always institutional and never personal. This was true when she served on the National Price Commission, and it remained true while serving first as a senior staff economist and then as a member of the President's Council of Economic Advisers.

BIBLIOGRAPHY

Whitman, Marina. *International and Interregional Payments Adjustment: A Synthetic View*. Princeton: Princeton University Press, 1967.

———. *Reflections of Interdependence: Issues for Economic Theory and U.S. Policy.* Pittsburgh: University of Pittsburgh Press, 1979.

———. *Sustaining the International Economic System: Issues for U.S. Policy.* Princeton: Princeton University Press, 1977.

ROBERT C. WINDER

APPENDIX: MEMBERSHIP IN THE CEA BY PRESIDENTIAL ADMINISTRATIONS

HARRY S. TRUMAN, 1945–53

Edwin Nourse	Chairman	August 9, 1946–November 1, 1949
Leon Keyserling	Member	August 9, 1946–May 9, 1949
	Chairman	May 10, 1949–January 20, 1953
John Clark	Member	August 9, 1946–February 11, 1953
Roy Blough	Member	June 29, 1950–August 20, 1952
Robert Turner	Member	September 8, 1952–January 20, 1953

DWIGHT D. EISENHOWER, 1953–61

Arthur Burns	Chairman	March 19, 1953–December 1, 1956
Neil Jacoby	Member	September 15, 1953–February 9, 1955
Walter Stewart	Member	December 2, 1953–April 29, 1955
Raymond Saulnier	Member	April 4, 1955–December 2, 1956
	Chairman	December 3, 1956–January 20, 1961
Joseph Davis	Member	May 2, 1955–October 31, 1958
Paul McCracken	Member	December 3, 1956–January 31, 1959
Karl Brandt	Member	November 1, 1958–January 20, 1961
Henry Wallich	Member	May 7, 1959–January 20, 1961

JOHN F. KENNEDY, 1961–63

Walter Heller	Chairman	January 29, 1961–November 22, 1963
James Tobin	Member	January 29, 1961–July 31, 1962
Kermit Gordon	Member	January 29, 1961–December 27, 1962

Gardner Ackley	Member	August 3, 1962–November 22, 1963
John Lewis	Member	May 17, 1963–November 22, 1963

LYNDON B. JOHNSON, 1963–69

Walter Heller	Chairman	November 22, 1963–November 15, 1964
Gardner Ackley	Member	November 22, 1963–November 15, 1964
	Chairman	November 16, 1964–February 15, 1968
John Lewis	Member	November 22, 1963–August 31, 1964
Otto Eckstein	Member	September 2, 1964–February 1, 1966
Arthur Okun	Member	November 16, 1964–February 14, 1968
	Chairman	February 15, 1968–January 20, 1969
James Duesenberry	Member	February 2, 1966–June 30, 1968
Merton Peck	Member	February 15, 1968–January 20, 1969
Warren Smith	Member	July 1, 1968–January 20, 1969

RICHARD M. NIXON, 1969–73

Paul McCracken	Chairman	February 4, 1969–December 31, 1971
Hendrik Houthakker	Member	February 4, 1969–July 15, 1971
Herbert Stein	Member	February 4, 1969–December 31, 1971
	Chairman	January 1, 1972–August 9, 1973
Ezra Solomon	Member	September 9, 1971–March 26, 1973
Marina Whitman	Member	March 13, 1972–August 9, 1973
Gary Seevers	Member	July 23, 1973–August 9, 1973

GERALD R. FORD, 1973–77

Herbert Stein	Chairman	August 9, 1973–August 31, 1974
Marina Whitman	Member	August 9, 1973–August 15, 1973
Gary Seevers	Member	August 9, 1973–April 15, 1975
William Fellner	Member	October 31, 1973–February 25, 1975
Alan Greenspan	Chairman	September 4, 1974–January 20, 1977

Paul MacAvoy	Member	July 13, 1975–November 15, 1976
Burton Malkiel	Member	July 22, 1975–January 20, 1977

JIMMY CARTER, 1977–81

Charles Schultze	Chairman	January 22, 1977–January 20, 1981
William Nordhaus	Member	March 18, 1977–February 4, 1979
Lyle Gramley	Member	March 18, 1977–May 27, 1980
George Eads	Member	June 6, 1979–January 20, 1981
Stephen Goldfeld	Member	August 20, 1980–January 20, 1981

RONALD W. REAGAN, 1981-

Murray Weidenbaum	Chairman	February 27, 1981–August 25, 1982
William Niskanen	Member	June 12, 1981–March 30, 1985
Jerry Jordan	Member	July 14, 1981–July 31, 1982
Martin Feldstein	Chairman	October 14, 1982–July 10, 1984
William Poole	Member	December 10, 1982–January 20, 1985
Beryl Sprinkel	Chairman	April 21, 1985–
Thomas Moore	Member	July 1, 1985–
Michael Mussa	Member	August 18, 1985–

INDEX

The page numbers set in *italic* indicate location of main entry.

ABOUT THE CONTRIBUTORS

REXFORD A. AHENE, Professor of Economics, Department of Economics and Business, Lafayette College.

SANDRA R. BAUM, Professor of Economics, Department of Economics, Wellesley College.

MARY P. BECKMAN, Department of Economics and Business, Lafayette College.

THOMAS H. BRUGGINK, Professor of Economics, Department of Economics and Business, Lafayette College.

JAMES CICARELLI, Chairman of the Department of Business, State University of New York, Fredonia.

JULIANNE CICARELLI, writer of articles on women's issues.

ALVIN COHEN, Professor of Economics, Department of Economics, Lehigh University.

JAMES B. COLLINS, Professor of History, History Department, Georgetown University.

JOHN P. CULLITY, Professor of Economics, Rutgers—The State University of New Jersey, Newark College of Arts and Sciences.

BRUCE R. DALGAARD, Professor and Director, Center for Economic Education, University of Minnesota.

KEITH C. FINAN, Senior Consultant, Hospital Association, New York State.

EUGENE B. GENDEL, Curator, Mark Taper Hall of Economics and Finance, California Museum of Science and Industry.

JEROME F. HEAVEY, Professor of Economics, Department of Economics and Business, Lafayette College.

ROBERT S. HERREN, Professor of Economics, Department of Economics, University of Mississippi.

HARRIET MORRIS HINCK, Professor of Economics, Department of Economics, Trenton State College.

DANIEL R. HOLLAS, Professor and Chairman, Department of Economics and Finance, University of Mississippi.

JAMES M. HVIDDING, Professor of Economics, Department of Economics and Business, Lafayette College.

MARK D. JOHNSON, lecturer in money and banking and financial markets, Department of Economics and Business, Lafayette College.

LOUIS J. KERN, Professor of History, History Department, Hofstra University.

NANCY KIMELMAN, Economist, Salomon Brothers, Inc.

MASON J. KLINCK, consultant and lecturer on financial markets and foreign exchange.

MARIA M. MCKINNEY, Professor of Economics, Department of Economics, Framingham State College.

JAMES N. MARSHALL, Professor of Economics and Finance, Department of Economics and Finance, Muhlenberg College.

ANNETTE E. MEYER, Professor of Economics, Department of Economics, Trenton State College.

GEOFREY T. MILLS, Assistant Dean, School of Business, University of Northern Iowa.

MARK A. NADLER, Professor of Economics, Department of Economics, State University of New York, College of Fredonia.

ALFRED E. PIERCE, Professor of Economics and Business, Department of Economics and Business, Lafayette College.

DANIEL POPE, Professor of History, Department of History, University of Oregon.

LIBBY T. RITTENBERG, Professor of Economics, Department of Economics and Business, Lafayette College.

GEORGE G. SAUSE, Professor Emeritus of Economics and Business, Department of Economics and Business, Lafayette College.

JAMES W. SCHMOTTER, Assistant Dean, Graduate School of Business and Public Administration, Cornell University.

R. NEWBY SCHWEITZER, Professor of Economics, Department of Economics, San Francisco State University.

MOJTABA SEYEDIAN, Professor of Finance, Department of Business Administration, State University of New York, College of Fredonia.

MANLY E. ''TOM'' STALEY, Professor of Management, Department of Management and Marketing, School of Business, San Francisco State University.

C. DANIEL VENCILL, Professor and Chair, Department of Economics, San Francisco State University.

ANDREW WEINTRAUB, Professor of Economics, Department of Economics, Temple University.

ROBERT C. WINDER, Professor of Economics, Department of Business and Economics, Salisbury State College.

About the Editors

ROBERT SOBEL is Professor of Business History at Hofstra University. He is the author or editor of numerous books including the series Contributions in Economics and Economic History (Greenwood Press) and *The Age of Giant Corporations: A Microeconomic History of the United States* (Greenwood Press, 2nd ed., 1984). He is a financial columnist for *Newsday* and a consultant with the Winthrop Group. His 1975 book, *For Want of a Nail . . . If Burgoyne Had Won at Saratoga,* was a Pulitzer Prize nominee.

BERNARD S. KATZ is Associate Professor of Economics and Business at Lafayette College, where he served as Department Chairman from 1978 to 1982. In recent years he has also been a visiting professor at San Francisco State University. He has worked both as a consultant and a principal in a variety of business ventures. He is the co-author of *Evaluations of 20th Century Economic Classics—Reviews Through Time* and of numerous articles on a variety of topics in economics.